ISC2® CISSP®

Certified Information Systems Security Professional

Official Practice Tests

Fourth Edition

ISC2® CISSP®
Certified Information Systems Security Professional
Official Practice Tests
Fourth Edition

Mike Chapple, CISSP

David Seidl, CISSP

SYBEX®
A Wiley Brand

Acknowledgments

The authors would like to thank the many people who made this book possible. Jim Minatel at Wiley Publishing helped us extend the Sybex CISSP franchise to include this title and has continued to champion the International Information System Security Certification Consortium (ISC2). Carole Jelen, our agent, tackles all the back-end magic for our writing efforts and worked on both the logistical details and the business side of the book with her usual grace and commitment to excellence. Aaron Kraus, Shahla Pirnia, and Emily Vandewater, our technical editors, pointed out many opportunities to improve our work and deliver a high-quality final product. Kelly Talbot served as our project manager and made sure everything fit together. Many other people we'll never meet worked behind the scenes to make this book a success, and we really appreciate their time and talents to make this next edition come together.

About the Authors

Mike Chapple, PhD, CISSP, is an author of the best-selling ISC2 CISSP *Certified Information Systems Security Professional Official Study Guide* (Sybex, 2024), now in its 10th edition. He is an information security professional with more than 25 years of experience in higher education, the private sector, and government.

Mike is currently a teaching professor of IT, analytics, and operations at the University of Notre Dame's Mendoza College of Business. He previously was a senior director for IT service delivery at Notre Dame, where he oversaw the information security, data governance, IT architecture, project management, strategic planning, and product management functions for the university.

Before returning to Notre Dame, Mike served as the executive vice president and chief information officer of the Brand Institute, a Miami-based marketing consultancy. Mike also spent four years in the information security research group at the National Security Agency and served as an active-duty intelligence officer in the U.S. Air Force.

Mike earned both his BS and PhD degrees from Notre Dame in computer science and engineering. He also holds an MS in computer science from the University of Idaho and an MBA from Auburn University. His IT certifications include the CISSP, Security+, CySA+, CISA, PenTest+, CIPP/US, CISM, CCSP, and PMP credentials.

Mike is the author of more than 100 technology books and video courses focused on security and privacy certifications. He provides books, video-based training, and free study groups for a wide variety of IT certifications at his website, `CertMike.com`.

David Seidl, CISSP, is the vice president for information technology and CIO at Miami University where he leads a nationally recognized and award-winning IT organization. During his IT career, he has served in a variety of technical and information security roles including as the senior director for Campus Technology Services at the University of Notre Dame where he co-led Notre Dame's move to the cloud and oversaw cloud operations, ERP, databases, identity management, and a broad range of other technologies and services.

He also served as Notre Dame's director of information security. He has taught information security and networking undergraduate courses as an instructor for Notre Dame's Mendoza College of Business and has written more than 20 books on security certification and cyberwarfare, including coauthoring the previous editions of *CISSP ISC2 Official Practice Tests* (Sybex, 2021) as well as *CompTIA CySA+ Study Guide: Exam CS0-003*, *CompTIA CySA+ Practice Tests: Exam CS0-003*, *CompTIA Security+ Study Guide: Exam SY0-701*, and *CompTIA Security+ Practice Tests: Exam SY0-701* as well as other certification guides and books on information security.

David holds a bachelor's degree in communication technology and a master's degree in information security from Eastern Michigan University, as well as CISSP, CySA+, PenTest+, GPEN, and GCIH certifications.

About the Technical Editors

Aaron Kraus, CISSP, CCSP, began his career as a security auditor and has gone on to work in security and compliance roles across financial services, insurance, consulting, and tech start-ups. He is currently a senior consultant at Latacora and runs his own consulting business, with experience ranging from initial implementation to aligning large, multinational organization's security programs to meet evolving compliance needs, respond to emerging threats, and accommodate new and changing business practices. He has been a course author, instructor, and dean of cybersecurity curriculum at Learning Tree International for more than 15 years and has worked on several publications at Wiley. He is the author of *The Official ISC2 CCSP CBK Reference, 4th Edition,* and coauthor of *The Official ISC2 CISSP CBK Reference, 6th Edition,* as well as the technical editor for the official CISSP and CCSP study guides and practice test books.

Shahla Pirnia is a freelance technical editor and proofreader with a focus on cybersecurity and certification topics. She currently serves as a technical editor for `CertMike.com`. Shahla earned BS degrees in computer and information science and Psychology from UMGC and an AA in information systems from Montgomery College, MD. Shahla's IT certifications include CompTIA Security+, Network+, A+, and ISC2 CC.

Emily Vandewater is a senior principal security consultant at Elteni Cybersecurity Consulting and Advisory, where she focuses on building information security programs and providing strategic guidance to mitigate cyber risks and ensure regulatory compliance. With more than 15 years of progressive experience in the tech and cybersecurity sectors, Emily has distinguished herself through key leadership positions, notably as a former director of information security at an IT managed service provider. Beyond her consulting work, Emily applies her expertise as a freelance technical editor and content developer for leading publishers, including Wiley. Her deep understanding of cybersecurity is backed by an array of IT certifications, including ISC2 CISSP and SSCP, CompTIA CASP+, CySA+, Security+ and Cloud+, Azure, and Microsoft Administrator Expert.

Contents

Introduction

ISC2 CISSP® Certified Information Systems Security Professional Official Practice Tests Fourth Edition is a companion volume to *ISC2 CISSP Certified Information Systems Security Professional Official Study Guide, Tenth edition (Sybex, 2024)*. It includes questions that cover content from the CISSP Detailed Content Outline and exam that became effective on April 15, 2024. If you're looking to test your knowledge before you take the CISSP exam, this book will help you by providing more than 1,300 questions that cover the CISSP Common Body of Knowledge (CBK) and easy-to-understand explanations of both right and wrong answers.

If you're just starting to prepare for the CISSP exam, we highly recommend that you use the *ISC2 CISSP Certified Information Systems Security Professional Official Study Guide* to help you learn about each of the domains covered by the CISSP exam. Once you're ready to test your knowledge, use this book to help find places where you may need to study more or to practice for the exam itself.

Since this is a companion to the *CISSP Study Guide*, this book is designed to be similar to taking the CISSP exam. It contains multipart scenarios as well as standard multiple-choice and matching questions like you may encounter on the certification exam. The book is broken up into 12 chapters: 8 domain-centric chapters with 100 or more questions about each domain, and 4 chapters that contain 125-question practice tests to simulate taking the exam.

CISSP Certification

The CISSP certification is offered by the International Information System Security Certification Consortium (ISC2), a global nonprofit organization. ISC2's mission statement says that "ISC2 strengthens the influence, diversity and vitality of the field through advocacy, expertise and workforce empowerment that accelerates cyber safety and security in an interconnected world." ISC2 achieves this mission by delivering the world's leading information security certification program, the CISSP. ISC2 also offers additional certifications including the following:

- Certified in Cybersecurity (CC)
- Systems Security Certified Practitioner (SSCP)
- Certified Cloud Security Professional (CCSP)
- Governance, Risk and Compliance Certification (CGRC)
- Certified Secure Software Lifecycle Professional (CSSLP)
- Information Systems Security Architecture Professional (ISSAP)
- Information Systems Security Engineering Professional (ISSEP)
- Information Systems Security Management Professional (ISSMP)

The CISSP certification covers eight domains of information security knowledge. These domains are meant to serve as the broad knowledge foundation required to succeed in the information security profession.

- Security and Risk Management
- Asset Security
- Security Architecture and Engineering
- Communication and Network Security
- Identity and Access Management (IAM)
- Security Assessment and Testing
- Security Operations
- Software Development Security

The CISSP domains are periodically updated by ISC2. The most recent revision on April 15, 2024, slightly modified the weighting for Security and Risk Management from 15% to 16%, while decreasing the focus on Software Development Security from 11% to 10%. It also added or expanded coverage of topics such as intellectual property, privacy laws and regulations, software bills of materials, end-of-life support, SASE, operational technology, high-performance computing, intermediate distribution frame, Compute Express Link, and a variety of other topics.

Complete details on the CISSP CBK are contained in the 2024 CISSP Detailed Content Outline. It includes a full outline of exam topics, which can be found on the ISC2 website at www.isc2.org.

Taking the CISSP Exam

The English version of the CISSP exam uses a technology called *computerized adaptive testing* (CAT). With this format, you will face an exam containing between 100 to 150 questions with a three-hour time limit. You will not have the opportunity to skip back and forth because the computer selects the next questions that it asks you based upon your answers to previous questions. If you're doing well on the exam, it will get more difficult as you progress. Don't let that unnerve you!

You can find more information about computerized adaptive testing directly from ISC2 at www.isc2.org/certifications/cissp/cissp-cat.

The computerized adaptive testing version of the exam is offered in English, Chinese, German, Japanese, and Spanish. Unlike earlier versions of the exam, the CISSP exam will no longer be offered in linear exam format after April 15th, 2024.

While it's impossible to directly simulate a CAT exam in book form, as you work through these practice exams you might want to use 80% as a goal to help you get a sense of whether you're ready to sit for the actual exam. When you're ready, you can schedule an exam at a location near you through the ISC2 website.

Questions on the CISSP exam are provided in both multiple-choice form and what ISC2 calls *advanced innovative* questions, which are drag-and-drop and hotspot questions, both of which are offered in a computer-based testing environment. Innovative questions are scored the same as traditional multiple-choice questions and have only one right answer.

ISC2 exam policies are subject to change. Please be sure to check www.isc2.org for the current policies before you register and take the exam.

Computer-Based Testing Environment

CISSP exams are administered in a computerized adaptive testing (CAT) format. You'll start the registration for your exam through your ISC2 login at www.isc2.org/register-for-exam. You may take the exam at a Pearson VUE authorized center in the language of your choice. It is offered in English, Chinese, German, Japanese, and Spanish.

You'll take the exam in a computer-based testing center located near your home or office. The centers administer many different exams, so you may find yourself sitting in the same room as a student taking a school entrance examination and a healthcare professional earning a medical certification. If you'd like to become more familiar with the testing environment, the Pearson VUE website offers a virtual tour of a testing center.

```
https://home.pearsonvue.com/Test-takers/
Pearson-Professional-Center-tour.aspx
```

When you take the exam, you'll be seated at a computer that has the exam software already loaded and running. It's a pretty straightforward interface that allows you to navigate through the exam. You can download a practice exam and tutorial from the Pearson VUE website.

```
https://home.pearsonvue.com
```

Like all exams, the CISSP certification from ISC2 is updated periodically and may eventually be retired or replaced. At some point after ISC2 is no longer offering this exam, the old editions of our books and online tools will be retired. If you have purchased this book after the exam was retired, or are attempting to register in the Sybex online learning environment after the exam was retired, please know that we make no guarantees that this exam's online Sybex tools will be available once the exam is no longer available.

Exam Retake Policy

If you don't pass the CISSP exam, you shouldn't panic. Many individuals don't reach the bar on their first attempt but gain valuable experience that helps them succeed the second time around. When you retake the exam, you'll have the benefit of familiarity with the exam environment and CISSP CAT exam format. You'll also have time to study the areas where you felt less confident.

After your first exam attempt, you must wait 30 days before retaking the computer-based exam. If you're not successful on that attempt, you may re-test after 60 days. If you don't pass after your third attempt, you can re-test after 90 days for that and any subsequent attempts. You can't take the test more than 4 times within a 12-month period. You can obtain more information about ISC2 and its other certifications from its website at www.isc2.org.

Work Experience Requirement

Candidates who want to earn the CISSP credential must not only pass the exam but also demonstrate that they have at least five years of work experience in the information security field. Your work experience must cover activities in at least two of the eight domains of the CISSP exam outline and must be paid, full-time or qualified part-time employment or paid or unpaid internship. Volunteer experiences are not acceptable to meet the CISSP experience requirement.

You may be eligible to waive one of the five years of the work experience requirement based upon your educational achievements. If you hold a bachelor's degree or four-year equivalent, you may be eligible for a degree waiver that covers one of those years. Similarly, if you hold one of the information security certifications on the current ISC2 approved credential list (www.isc2.org/certifications/cissp/cissp-experience-requirements), you may also waive a year of the experience requirement. You may not combine these two programs. Holders of both a certification and an undergraduate degree must still demonstrate at least four years of experience.

If you haven't yet completed your work experience requirement, you may still attempt the CISSP exam. Individuals who pass the exam are designated Associates of ISC2 and have six years to complete the work experience requirement.

Recertification Requirements

Once you've earned your CISSP credential, you'll need to maintain your certification by paying maintenance fees and participating in continuing professional education (CPE). As long as you maintain your certification in good standing, you will not need to retake the CISSP exam.

Currently, the annual maintenance fees for the CISSP credential are $135 per year. This fee covers the renewal for all ISC2 certifications held by an individual.

The CISSP CPE requirement mandates earning at least 120 CPE credits during each three-year renewal cycle. Associates of ISC2 must earn at least 15 CPE credits each year. ISC2 provides an online portal where certificate holders may submit CPE completion for review and approval. The portal also tracks annual maintenance fee payments and progress toward recertification.

Using This Book to Practice

This book is composed of 12 chapters. Each of the first eight chapters covers a domain, with a variety of questions that can help you test your knowledge of real-world, scenario, and security best-practices. The final four chapters are complete practice exams that can serve as timed practice tests to help determine whether you're ready for the CISSP exam.

We recommend taking the first practice exam to help identify where you may need to spend more study time and then using the domain-specific chapters to test your domain knowledge where it is weak. Once you're ready, take the other practice exams to make sure you've covered all the material and are ready to attempt the CISSP exam.

Using the Online Practice Tests

All the questions in this book are also available in Sybex's online practice test tool. To get access to this online format, go to www.wiley.com/go/sybextestprep and start by registering your book. You'll receive a PIN and instructions on where to create an online test bank account. Once you have access, you can use the online version to create your own sets of practice tests from the book questions and practice in a timed and graded setting.

How to Contact the Publisher

If you believe you have found a mistake in this book, please bring it to our attention. At John Wiley & Sons, we understand how important it is to provide our customers with accurate content, but even with our best efforts an error may occur.

In order to submit your possible errata, please email it to our Customer Service Team at wileysupport@wiley.com with the subject line "Possible Book Errata Submission."

Chapter

1

Security and Risk Management (Domain 1)

SUBDOMAINS

✓ 1.1 Understand, adhere to, and promote professional ethics

✓ 1.2 Understand and apply security concepts

✓ 1.3 Evaluate, apply, and sustain security governance principles

✓ 1.4 Understand legal, regulatory, and compliance issues that pertain to information security in a holistic context

✓ 1.5 Understand requirements for investigation types (i.e., administrative, criminal, civil, regulatory, industry standards)

✓ 1.6 Develop, document, and implement security policy, standards, procedures, and guidelines

✓ 1.7 Identify, analyze, assess, prioritize, and implement Business Continuity (BC) requirements

✓ 1.8 Contribute to and enforce personnel security policies and procedures

✓ 1.9 Understand and apply risk management concepts

✓ 1.10 Understand and apply threat modeling concepts and methodologies

✓ 1.11 Apply Supply Chain Risk Management (SCRM) concepts

✓ 1.12 Establish and maintain a security awareness, education, and training program

1. Alyssa is responsible for her organization's security awareness program. She is concerned that changes in technology may make the content outdated. What control can she put in place to protect against this risk?

  A. Gamification

  B. Computer-based training

  C. Content reviews

  D. Live training

2. Gavin is creating a report for management on the results of his most recent risk assessment. In his report, he would like to identify the remaining level of risk to the organization after adopting security controls. What term best describes this current level of risk?

  A. Inherent risk

  B. Residual risk

  C. Control risk

  D. Mitigated risk

3. Francine is a security specialist for an online service provider in the United States. She recently received a claim from a copyright holder that a user is storing information on her service that violates the third party's copyright. What law governs the actions that Francine must take?

  A. Copyright Act

  B. Lanham Act

  C. Digital Millennium Copyright Act

  D. Gramm-Leach-Bliley Act

4. FlyAway Travel has offices in both the European Union (EU) and the United States and transfers personal information between those offices regularly. They have recently received a request from an EU customer requesting that their account be terminated. Under the General Data Protection Regulation (GDPR), which requirement for processing personal information states that individuals may request that their data no longer be disseminated or processed?

  A. The right to access

  B. Privacy by Design

  C. The right to erasure

  D. The right of data portability

5. After conducting a qualitative risk assessment of her organization, Sally recommends purchasing cybersecurity breach insurance. What type of risk response behavior is she recommending?

  A. Accept

  B. Transfer

  C. Reduce

  D. Reject

6. Which one of the following elements of information is not considered personally identifiable information that would trigger most United States state data breach laws?

   A. Student identification number

   B. Social Security number

   C. Driver's license number

   D. Credit card number

7. Renee is purchasing a new software product and is working with the vendor on the negotiation of a license agreement that will specify customized terms of use and a discounted price. What type of agreement would normally be used to document the results of this negotiation?

   A. Perpetual license

   B. Subscription license

   C. Enterprise license agreement

   D. End-user license agreement

8. Henry recently assisted one of his co-workers in preparing for the CISSP® exam. During this process, Henry disclosed confidential information about the content of the exam, in violation of Canon IV of the Code of Ethics: "Advance and protect the profession." Who may bring ethics charges against Henry for this violation?

   A. Anyone may bring charges.

   B. Any certified or licensed professional may bring charges.

   C. Only Henry's employer may bring charges.

   D. Only the affected employee may bring charges.

9. Wanda is working with one of her organization's European Union business partners to facilitate the exchange of customer information. Wanda's organization is located in the United States. What would be the best method for Wanda to use to ensure GDPR compliance?

   A. Binding corporate rules

   B. Privacy Shield

   C. Standard contractual clauses

   D. Safe harbor

10. Yolanda is the chief privacy officer for a financial institution and is researching privacy requirements related to customer checking accounts. Which one of the following laws is most likely to apply to this situation?

    A. GLBA

    B. SOX

    C. HIPAA

    D. FERPA

11. Tim's organization recently received a contract to conduct sponsored research as a government contractor. What law now likely applies to the information systems involved in this contract?

   A. FISMA

   B. PCI DSS

   C. HIPAA

   D. GISRA

12. Chris is advising travelers from his organization who will be visiting many different countries overseas. He is concerned about compliance with export control laws. Which of the following technologies is most likely to trigger these regulations?

   A. Memory chips

   B. Office productivity applications

   C. Hard drives

   D. Encryption software

13. Bobbi is investigating a security incident and discovers that an attacker began with a normal user account but managed to exploit a system vulnerability to provide that account with administrative rights. What type of attack took place under the STRIDE threat model?

   A. Spoofing

   B. Repudiation

   C. Tampering

   D. Elevation of privilege

14. You are completing your business continuity planning effort and have decided that you want to accept one of the risks. What should you do next?

   A. Implement new security controls to reduce the risk level.

   B. Design a disaster recovery plan.

   C. Repeat the business impact assessment.

   D. Document your decision-making process.

15. You are completing a review of the controls used to protect a media storage facility in your organization and would like to properly categorize each control that is currently in place. Which of the following control categories accurately describe a fence around a facility? (Select all that apply.)

   A. Physical

   B. Detection

   C. Deterrent

   D. Preventive

16. Tony is developing a business continuity plan and is having difficulty prioritizing resources because of the difficulty of combining information about tangible and intangible assets. What would be the most effective risk assessment approach for him to use?

A. Quantitative risk assessment

B. Qualitative risk assessment

C. Neither quantitative nor qualitative risk assessment

D. Combination of quantitative and qualitative risk assessment

17. Vincent believes that a former employee took trade secret information from his firm and brought it with him to a competitor. He wants to pursue legal action. Under what law could he pursue charges?

A. Copyright law

B. Lanham Act

C. Glass-Steagall Act

D. Economic Espionage Act

18. Which one of the following principles imposes a standard of care upon an individual that is broad and equivalent to what one would expect from a reasonable person under the circumstances?

A. Due diligence

B. Separation of duties

C. Due care

D. Least privilege

19. Brenda's organization recently completed the acquisition of a competitor firm. Which one of the following tasks would be LEAST likely to be part of the organizational processes addressed during the acquisition?

A. Consolidation of security functions

B. Integration of security tools

C. Protection of intellectual property

D. Documentation of security policies

20. Kelly believes that an employee engaged in the unauthorized use of computing resources for a side business. After consulting with management, she decides to launch an administrative investigation. What is the burden of proof that she must meet in this investigation?

A. Preponderance of the evidence.

B. Beyond a reasonable doubt.

C. Beyond the shadow of a doubt.

D. There is no standard.

21. Keenan Systems recently developed a new manufacturing process for microprocessors. The company wants to license the technology to other companies for use but wants to prevent unauthorized use of the technology. What type of intellectual property protection is best suited for this situation?

    A. Patent

    B. Trade secret

    C. Copyright

    D. Trademark

22. Which one of the following actions might be taken as part of a business continuity plan?

    A. Restoring from backup tapes

    B. Implementing RAID

    C. Relocating to a cold site

    D. Restarting business operations

23. When developing a business impact analysis, the team should first create a list of assets. What should happen next?

    A. Identify vulnerabilities in each asset.

    B. Determine the risks facing the asset.

    C. Develop a value for each asset.

    D. Identify threats facing each asset.

24. Mike recently implemented an intrusion prevention system designed to block common network attacks from affecting his organization. What type of risk management strategy is Mike pursuing?

    A. Risk acceptance

    B. Risk avoidance

    C. Risk mitigation

    D. Risk transference

25. Laura has been asked to perform a security controls assessment (SCA). What type of organization is she most likely in?

    A. Higher education

    B. Banking

    C. Government

    D. Healthcare

26. Carl is a federal agent investigating a computer crime case. He identified an attacker who engaged in illegal conduct and wants to pursue a case against that individual that will lead to imprisonment. What standard of proof must Carl meet?

    A. Beyond the shadow of a doubt

    B. Preponderance of the evidence

    C. Beyond a reasonable doubt

    D. Majority of the evidence

27. ISC2 uses the logo shown here to represent itself online and in a variety of forums. What type of intellectual property protection can it use to protect its rights in this logo?

Source: ISC2, Inc.

A. Copyright

B. Patent

C. Trade secret

D. Trademark

28. Mary is helping a computer user who sees the following message appear on his computer screen. What type of attack has occurred?

Source: CryptoLocker

   A. Availability

   B. Confidentiality

   C. Disclosure

   D. Distributed

29. Which one of the following organizations would not be automatically subject to the privacy and security requirements of HIPAA if they engage in electronic transactions?

   A. Healthcare provider

   B. Health and fitness application developer

   C. Health information clearinghouse

   D. Health insurance plan

30. John's network begins to experience symptoms of slowness. Upon investigation, he realizes that the network is being bombarded with TCP SYN packets and believes that his organization is the victim of a denial-of-service attack. What principle of information security is being violated?

   A. Availability

   B. Integrity

   C. Confidentiality

   D. Denial

31. Renee is designing a long-term security plan for her organization and has a three- to five-year planning horizon. Her primary goal is to align the security function with the broader plans and objectives of the business. What type of plan is she developing?

   A. Operational

   B. Tactical

   C. Summary

   D. Strategic

32. Gina is working to protect a logo that her company will use for a new product they are launching. She has questions about the intellectual property protection process for this logo. What U.S. government agency would be best able to answer her questions?

   A. USPTO

   B. Library of Congress

   C. NSA

   D. NIST

33. The Acme Widgets Company is putting new controls in place for its accounting department. Management is concerned that a rogue accountant may be able to create a new false vendor and then issue checks to that vendor as payment for services that were never rendered. What security control can best help prevent this situation?

A. Mandatory vacation

B. Segregation of duties

C. Defense in depth

D. Job rotation

34. Which one of the following categories of organizations is most likely to be covered by the provisions of FISMA?

A. Banks

B. Defense contractors

C. School districts

D. Hospitals

35. Robert is responsible for securing systems used to process credit card information. What security control framework should guide his actions?

A. HIPAA

B. PCI DSS

C. SOX

D. GLBA

36. Which one of the following individuals is normally responsible for fulfilling the operational data protection responsibilities delegated by senior management, such as validating data integrity, testing backups, and managing security policies?

A. Data custodian

B. Data owner

C. User

D. Auditor

37. Alan works for an e-commerce company that recently had some content stolen by another website and republished without permission. What type of intellectual property protection would best preserve Alan's company's rights?

A. Trade secret

B. Copyright

C. Trademark

D. Patent

38. Florian receives a flyer from a U.S. federal government agency announcing that a new administrative law will affect his business operations. Where should he go to find the text of the law?

   A. U.S. Code

   B. Supreme Court rulings

   C. Code of Federal Regulations

   D. Compendium of Laws

39. Tom enables an application firewall provided by his cloud infrastructure as a service provider that is designed to block many types of application attacks. When viewed from a risk management perspective, what metric is Tom attempting to lower by implementing this countermeasure?

   A. Impact

   B. RPO

   C. MTO

   D. Likelihood

40. Which one of the following individuals would be the most effective organizational owner for an information security program?

   A. CISSP-certified analyst

   B. Chief information officer (CIO)

   C. Manager of network security

   D. President and CEO

41. What important function do senior managers normally fill on a business continuity planning team?

   A. Arbitrating disputes about criticality

   B. Evaluating the legal environment

   C. Training staff

   D. Designing failure controls

42. You are the CISO for a major hospital system and are preparing to sign a contract with a software-as-a-service (SaaS) email vendor. You want to perform a control assessment to ensure that its business continuity planning measures are reasonable. What type of audit might you request to meet this goal?

   A. SOC 1

   B. FISMA

   C. PCI DSS

   D. SOC 2

43. Gary is analyzing a security incident and, during his investigation, encounters a user who denies having performed an action that Gary believes he did perform. What type of threat has taken place under the STRIDE model?

   A. Repudiation

   B. Information disclosure

   C. Tampering

   D. Elevation of privilege

44. Beth is the security administrator for a public school district. She is implementing a new student information system and is testing the code to ensure that students are not able to alter their own grades. What principle of information security is Beth enforcing?

   A. Integrity

   B. Availability

   C. Confidentiality

   D. Denial

45. Which one of the following issues is not normally addressed in a service-level agreement (SLA)?

   A. Confidentiality of customer information

   B. Failover time

   C. Uptime

   D. Maximum consecutive downtime

46. Joan is seeking to protect a piece of computer software that she developed under intellectual property law. Which one of the following avenues of protection would not apply to a piece of software?

   A. Trademark

   B. Copyright

   C. Patent

   D. Trade secret

For questions 47–49, please refer to the following scenario:

Juniper Content is a web content development company with 40 employees located in two offices: one in New York and a smaller office in the San Francisco Bay Area. Each office has a local area network protected by a perimeter firewall. The local area network (LAN) contains modern switch equipment connected to both wired and wireless networks.

Each office has its own file server, and the information technology (IT) team runs software every hour to synchronize files between the two servers, distributing content between the offices. These servers are primarily used to store images and other files related to web content developed by the company. The team also uses a SaaS-based email and document collaboration solution for much of their work.

You are the newly appointed IT manager for Juniper Content, and you are working to augment existing security controls to improve the organization's security.

47. Users in the two offices would like to access each other's file servers over the internet. What control would provide confidentiality for those communications?

    A. Digital signatures

    B. Virtual private network

    C. Virtual LAN

    D. Digital content management

48. You are also concerned about the availability of data stored on each office's server. You would like to add technology that would enable continued access to files located on the server even if a hard drive in a server fails. What control allows you to add robustness without adding additional servers?

    A. Server clustering

    B. Load balancing

    C. RAID

    D. Scheduled backups

49. Finally, there are historical records stored on the server that are extremely important to the business and should never be modified. You would like to add an integrity control that allows you to verify on a periodic basis that the files were not modified. What control can you add?

    A. Hashing

    B. ACLs

    C. Read-only attributes

    D. Firewalls

50. Beth is a human resources specialist preparing to assist in the termination of an employee. Which of the following is not typically part of a termination process?

A. An exit interview

B. Recovery of organizational property

C. Account termination

D. Signing an NCA

51. Frances is reviewing her organization's business continuity plan documentation for completeness. Which one of the following is not normally included in business continuity plan documentation?

A. Statement of accounts

B. Statement of importance

C. Statement of priorities

D. Statement of organizational responsibility

52. An accounting employee at Doolittle Industries was recently arrested for participation in an embezzlement scheme. The employee transferred money to a personal account and then shifted funds around between other accounts every day to disguise the fraud for months. Which one of the following controls might have best allowed the earlier detection of this fraud?

A. Separation of duties

B. Least privilege

C. Defense in depth

D. Mandatory vacation

53. Jeff would like to adopt an industry-standard approach for assessing the processes his organization uses to manage risk. What maturity model would be most appropriate for his use?

A. CMM

B. SW-CMM

C. RMM

D. COBIT

54. Chris' organization recently suffered an attack that rendered their website inaccessible to paying customers for several hours. Which information security goal was most directly impacted?

A. Confidentiality

B. Integrity

C. Availability

D. Denial

55. Yolanda is writing a document that will provide configuration information regarding the minimum level of security that every system in the organization must meet. What type of document is she preparing?

A. Policy

B. Baseline

C. Guideline

D. Procedure

56. Who should receive initial business continuity plan training in an organization?

A. Senior executives

B. Those with specific business continuity roles

C. Everyone in the organization

D. First responders

57. James is conducting a risk assessment for his organization and is attempting to assign an asset value to the servers in his data center. The organization's primary concern is ensuring that it has sufficient funds available to rebuild the data center in the event it is damaged or destroyed. Which one of the following asset valuation methods would be most appropriate in this situation?

A. Purchase cost

B. Depreciated cost

C. Replacement cost

D. Opportunity cost

58. Roger's organization suffered a breach of customer credit card records. Under the terms of PCI DSS, what organization may choose to pursue an investigation of this matter?

A. FBI

B. Local law enforcement

C. Bank

D. PCI SSC

59. Rick recently engaged critical employees in each of his organization's business units to ask for their assistance with his security awareness program. They will be responsible for sharing security messages with their peers and answering questions about cybersecurity matters. What term best describes this relationship?

A. Security champion

B. Security expert

C. Gamification

D. Peer review

60. Frank discovers a keylogger hidden on the laptop of his company's chief executive officer. What information security principle is the keylogger most likely designed to disrupt?

   A. Confidentiality

   B. Integrity

   C. Availability

   D. Denial

61. Elise is helping her organization prepare to evaluate and adopt a new cloud-based human resource management (HRM) system vendor. What would be the most appropriate minimum security standard for her to require of possible vendors?

   A. Compliance with all laws and regulations

   B. Handling information in the same manner her organization would

   C. Elimination of all identified security risks

   D. Compliance with the vendor's own policies

62. The following graphic shows the NIST risk management framework with a step missing. What is the missing step?

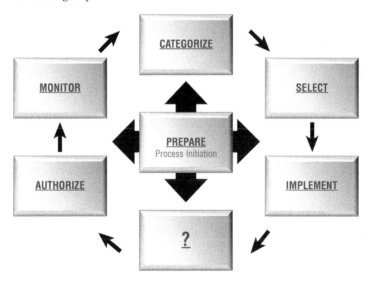

   A. Assess security controls.

   B. Determine control gaps.

   C. Remediate control gaps.

   D. Evaluate user activity.

63. HAL Systems recently decided to stop offering public NTP services because of a fear that its NTP servers would be used in amplification DDoS attacks. What type of risk management strategy did HAL pursue with respect to its NTP services?

A. Risk mitigation

B. Risk acceptance

C. Risk transference

D. Risk avoidance

64. Susan is working with the management team in her company to classify data in an attempt to apply extra security controls that will limit the likelihood of a data disclosure breach. What principle of information security is Susan trying to enforce?

A. Availability

B. Denial

C. Confidentiality

D. Integrity

65. Which one of the following components should be included in an organization's emergency response guidelines?

A. List of individuals who should be notified of an emergency incident

B. Long-term business continuity protocols

C. Activation procedures for the organization's cold sites

D. Contact information for ordering equipment

66. Chas recently completed the development of his organization's business continuity plan (BCP). Who is the ideal person to approve an organization's business continuity plan?

A. Chief information officer

B. Chief executive officer

C. Chief information security officer

D. Chief operating officer

67. Which one of the following actions is not normally part of the project scope and planning phase of business continuity planning?

A. Structured analysis of the organization

B. Review of the legal and regulatory landscape

C. Creation of a BCP team

D. Documentation of the plan

68. Gary is implementing a new website architecture that uses multiple small web servers behind a load balancer. What principle of information security is Gary seeking to enforce?

A. Denial

B. Confidentiality

C. Integrity

D. Availability

69. Becka recently signed a contract with an alternate data processing facility that will provide her company with space in the event of a disaster. The facility includes HVAC, power, and communications circuits but no hardware. What type of facility is Becka using?

A. Cold site

B. Warm site

C. Hot site

D. Mobile site

70. Greg's company recently experienced a significant data breach involving the personal data of many of their customers. The company operates only in the United States and has facilities in several different states. The personal information relates only to residents of the United States. Which breach laws should they review to ensure that they are taking appropriate action?

A. The breach laws in the state where they are headquartered along with federal breach laws.

B. The breach laws of states they do business in or where their customers reside along with federal breach laws.

C. Only federal breach laws.

D. Breach laws only cover government agencies, not private businesses.

71. Ben is seeking a control objective framework that is widely accepted around the world and focuses specifically on information security controls. Which one of the following frameworks would best meet his needs?

A. ITIL

B. ISO 27002

C. CMM

D. PMBOK Guide

72. Matt works for a telecommunications firm and was approached by a federal agent seeking assistance with wiretapping one of Matt's clients pursuant to a search warrant. Which one of the following laws requires that communications service providers cooperate with law enforcement requests?

A. ECPA

B. CALEA

C. Privacy Act

D. HITECH Act

73. Every year, Gary receives privacy notices in the mail from financial institutions where he has accounts. What law requires the institutions to send Gary these notices?

A. FERPA

B. GLBA

C. HIPAA

D. HITECH

74. Which one of the following agreements typically requires that a vendor not disclose confidential information learned during the scope of an engagement?

A. NCA

B. SLA

C. NDA

D. RTO

75. The ISC2 Code of Ethics applies to all CISSP holders. Which of the following is not one of the four mandatory canons of the code?

A. Protect society, the common good, the necessary public trust and confidence, and the infrastructure.

B. Disclose breaches of privacy, trust, and ethics.

C. Provide diligent and competent service to the principals.

D. Advance and protect the profession.

76. Which one of the following stakeholders is not typically included on a business continuity planning team?

A. Core business function leaders

B. Information technology staff

C. CEO

D. Support departments

77. Ben is designing a messaging system for a bank and would like to include a feature that allows the recipient of a message to prove to a third party that the message did indeed come from the purported originator. What goal is Ben trying to achieve?

A. Authentication

B. Authorization

C. Integrity

D. Nonrepudiation

78. What principle of information security states that an organization should implement overlapping security controls whenever possible?

A. Least privilege

B. Separation of duties

C. Defense in depth

D. Security through obscurity

79. Ryan is a CISSP-certified cybersecurity professional working in a nonprofit organization. Which of the following ethical obligations apply to his work? (Select all that apply.)

A. ISC2 Code of Ethics

B. Organizational code of ethics

C. Federal code of ethics

D. RFC 1087

80. Ben is responsible for the security of payment card information stored in a database. Policy directs that he remove the information from the database, but he cannot do this for operational reasons. He obtained an exception to policy and is seeking an appropriate compensating control to mitigate the risk. What would be his best option?

A. Purchasing insurance

B. Encrypting the database contents

C. Removing the data

D. Objecting to the exception

81. The Domer Industries risk assessment team recently conducted a qualitative risk assessment and developed a matrix similar to the one shown here. Which quadrant contains the risks that require the most immediate attention?

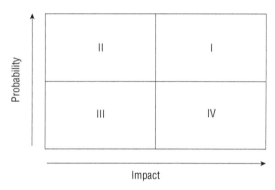

A. I

B. II

C. III

D. IV

82. Tom is planning to terminate an employee this afternoon for fraud and expects that the meeting will be somewhat hostile. He is coordinating the meeting with human resources and wants to protect the company against damage. Which one of the following steps is most important to coordinate in time with the termination meeting?

A. Informing other employees of the termination

B. Retrieving the employee's photo ID

C. Calculating the final paycheck

D. Revoking electronic access rights

83. Rolando is a risk manager with a large-scale enterprise. The firm recently evaluated the risk of California mudslides on its operations in the region and determined that the cost of responding outweighed the benefits of any controls it could implement. The company chose to take no action at this time. What risk management strategy did Rolando's organization pursue?

A. Risk avoidance

B. Risk mitigation

C. Risk transference

D. Risk acceptance

84. Helen is the owner of a U.S. website that provides information for middle and high school students preparing for exams. She is writing the site's privacy policy and would like to ensure that it complies with the provisions of the Children's Online Privacy Protection Act (COPPA). What is the cutoff age below which parents must give consent in advance of the collection of personal information from their children under COPPA?

   A. 13

   B. 15

   C. 17

   D. 18

85. Tom is considering locating a business in the downtown area of Miami, Florida. He consults the FEMA flood plain map for the region, shown here, and determines that the area he is considering lies within a 100-year flood plain. What is the ARO of a flood in this area?

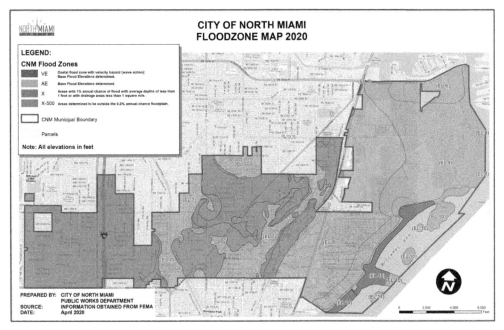

Source: The City of North Miami

   A. 100

   B. 1

   C. 0.1

   D. 0.01

86. You discover that a user on your network has been using the Wireshark tool, as shown here. Further investigation revealed that he was using it for illicit purposes. What pillar of information security has most likely been violated?

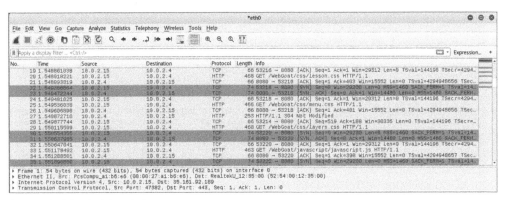

Source: The Wireshark Foundation

A. Integrity

B. Denial

C. Availability

D. Confidentiality

87. Alan is performing threat modeling and decides that it would be useful to decompose the system into the core elements shown here. What tool is he using?

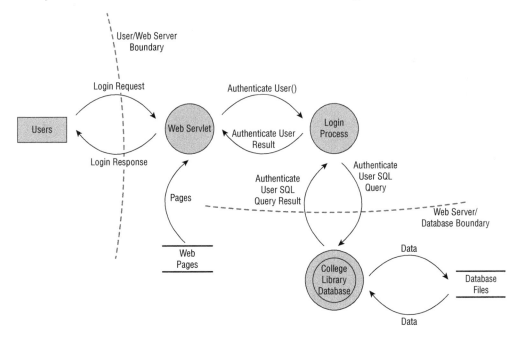

A. Vulnerability assessment

B. Fuzzing

C. Reduction analysis

D. Data modeling

88. Shahla is reviewing the privacy laws that apply to a new enterprise that her company will be launching in South Africa. This is the company's first expansion into that country, and the enterprise will involve handling the personal information of residents of South Africa. What law will likely affect this operation?

    A. PIPL

    B. PCI DSS

    C. PIPEDA

    D. POPIA

89. Which type of business impact assessment tool is most appropriate when attempting to evaluate the impact of a failure on customer confidence?

    A. Quantitative

    B. Qualitative

    C. Annualized loss expectancy

    D. Reduction

90. Ryan is a security risk analyst for an insurance company. He is currently examining a scenario in which a malicious hacker might use a SQL injection attack to deface a web server due to a missing patch in the company's web application. In this scenario, what is the threat?

    A. Unpatched web application

    B. Web defacement

    C. Malicious hacker

    D. Operating system

For questions 91–93, please refer to the following scenario:

Henry is the risk manager for Atwood Landing, a resort community in the midwestern United States. The resort's main data center is located in northern Indiana in an area that is prone to tornados. Henry recently undertook a replacement cost analysis and determined that rebuilding and reconfiguring the data center would cost $10 million.

    Henry consulted with tornado experts, data center specialists, and structural engineers. Together, they determined that a typical tornado would cause approximately $5 million of damage to the facility. The meteorologists determined that Atwood's facility lies in an area where they are likely to experience a tornado once every 200 years.

91. Based upon the information in this scenario, what is the exposure factor for the effect of a tornado on Atwood Landing's data center?

    A. 10%

    B. 25%

    C. 50%

    D. 75%

92. Based upon the information in this scenario, what is the annualized rate of occurrence for a tornado at Atwood Landing's data center?

    A. 0.0025

    B. 0.005

    C. 0.01

    D. 0.015

93. Based upon the information in this scenario, what is the annualized loss expectancy for a tornado at Atwood Landing's data center?

    A. $25,000

    B. $50,000

    C. $250,000

    D. $500,000

94. John is analyzing an attack against his company in which the attacker found comments embedded in HTML code that provided the clues needed to exploit a software vulnerability. Using the STRIDE model, what type of attack did he uncover?

    A. Spoofing

    B. Repudiation

    C. Information disclosure

    D. Elevation of privilege

95. Chris is worried that the laptops that his organization has recently acquired were modified by a third party to include keyloggers before they were delivered. Where should he focus his efforts to prevent this?

    A. His supply chain

    B. His vendor contracts

    C. His post-purchase build process

    D. The original equipment manufacturer (OEM)

96. In her role as a developer for an online bank, Lisa is required to submit her code for testing and review. After it passes through this process and it is approved, another employee moves the code to the production environment. What security management does this process describe?

    A. Regression testing

    B. Code review

    C. Change management

    D. Fuzz testing

97. After completing the first year of his security awareness program, Charles reviews the data about how many staff completed training compared to how many were assigned the training to determine whether he hit the 95% completion rate he was aiming for. What is this type of measure called?

   A. A KPI

   B. A metric

   C. An awareness control

   D. A return on investment rate

98. Which of the following is not typically included in a prehire screening process?

   A. A drug test

   B. A background check

   C. Social media review

   D. Fitness evaluation

99. Which of the following would normally be considered a supply chain risk? (Select all that apply.)

   A. Adversary tampering with hardware prior to being shipped to the end customer

   B. Adversary hacking into a web server run by the organization in an IaaS environment

   C. Adversary using social engineering to compromise an employee of a SaaS vendor to gain access to customer accounts

   D. Adversary conducting a denial-of-service attack using a botnet

100. Match the following numbered laws or industry standards to their lettered description:

Laws and industry standards:

   1. GLBA

   2. PCI DSS

   3. HIPAA

   4. SOX

Descriptions:

   A. A U.S. law that requires covered financial institutions to provide their customers with a privacy notice on a yearly basis

   B. A U.S. law that requires internal controls assessments, including IT transaction flows for publicly traded companies

   C. An industry standard that covers organizations that handle payment cards

   D. A U.S. law that provides data privacy and security requirements for medical information

Chapter 2

Asset Security (Domain 2)

SUBDOMAINS

✓ 2.1 Identify and classify information and assets

✓ 2.2 Establish information and asset handling requirements

✓ 2.3 Provision information and assets securely

✓ 2.4 Manage data lifecycle

✓ 2.5 Ensure appropriate asset retention (e.g., End of Life (EOL), End of Support)

✓ 2.6 Determine data security controls and compliance requirements

1. Angela wants to implement data security controls that are part of the NIST 800-53 Security and Privacy controls. As part of the process, she works to determine which controls are appropriate to her organization's business processes and data handling needs. What term best describes the action that she has performed?

    A. Scoping

    B. Bounds checking

    C. Data stewardship

    D. Tailoring

2. Control Objectives for Information and Related Technology (COBIT) is a framework for information technology (IT) management and governance. Which data management role is most likely to select and apply COBIT to balance the need for security controls against business requirements?

    A. Business owners

    B. Data processors

    C. Data owners

    D. Data stewards

3. Nadia's company is operating a hybrid cloud environment with some on-site systems and some cloud-based systems. She has satisfactory monitoring on-site but needs to apply security policies to both the activities her users engage in and to report on exceptions with her growing number of cloud services. What type of tool is best suited to this purpose?

    A. A NGFW

    B. A CASB

    C. An IDS

    D. A SOAR

4. When media is labeled based on the classification of the data it contains, what rule is typically applied regarding labels?

    A. The data is labeled based on its integrity requirements.

    B. The media is labeled based on the highest classification level of the data it contains.

    C. The media is labeled with all levels of classification of the data it contains.

    D. The media is labeled with the lowest level of classification of the data it contains.

5. Which one of the following administrative processes assists organizations in assigning appropriate levels of security control to sensitive information?

    A. Data classification

    B. Remanence

    C. Transmitting data

    D. Clearing

6. How can a data retention policy help to reduce liabilities?

   A. By ensuring that unneeded data isn't retained

   B. By ensuring that incriminating data is destroyed

   C. By ensuring that data is securely wiped so it cannot be restored for legal discovery

   D. By reducing the cost of data storage required by law

7. Staff in an information technology (IT) department who are delegated responsibility for day-to-day tasks hold what data role?

   A. Business owner

   B. User

   C. Data processor

   D. Custodian

8. Helen's company uses a simple data life cycle, as shown here. What stage should come first in the company's data life cycle?

   ?   Data   Data   Data   Data
                Analysis   Usage   Retention   Destruction

   A. Data policy creation

   B. Data labeling

   C. Data collection

   D. Data analysis

9. Ben has been tasked with identifying security controls for systems covered by his organization's information classification system. Why might Ben choose to use a security baseline?

   A. It applies in all circumstances, allowing consistent security controls.

   B. They are approved by industry standards bodies, preventing liability.

   C. They provide a good starting point that can be tailored to organizational needs.

   D. They ensure that systems are always in a secure state.

10. Megan wants to prepare media to allow for its reuse in an environment operating at the same sensitivity level. Which of the following is the best option to meet her needs?

   A. Clearing

   B. Erasing

   C. Purging

   D. Sanitization

11. Mikayla wants to identify data that should be classified that already exists in her environment. What type of tool is best suited to identifying data like Social Security numbers, credit card numbers, and similar well-understood data formats?

   A. Manual searching

   B. A sensitive data scanning tool

   C. An asset metadata search tool

   D. A SOAR

12. What issue is common to spare sectors and bad sectors on hard drives as well as overprovisioned space on modern SSDs?

   A. They can be used to hide data.

   B. They can only be degaussed.

   C. They are not addressable, resulting in data remanence.

   D. They may not be cleared, resulting in data remanence.

13. Naomi knows that commercial data is typically classified based on different criteria than government data. Which of the following is not a common criterion for commercial data classification?

   A. Useful lifespan

   B. Data value

   C. Impact to national security

   D. Regulatory or legal requirements

For questions 14–16, please refer to the following scenario:

Your organization regularly handles three types of data: information that it shares with customers, information that it uses internally to conduct business, and trade secret information that offers the organization significant competitive advantages. Information shared with customers is used and stored on web servers, while both the internal business data and the trade secret information are stored on internal file servers and employee workstations.

14. The organization leverages memory-resident databases to improve system performance for both customer data and internal business data. What term best describes data that is resident in system memory?

   A. Data at rest

   B. Buffered data

   C. Data in use

   D. Data in motion

15. What technique could you use to mark your trade secret information in case it was released or stolen and you need to identify it?

   A. Classification

   B. Symmetric encryption

   C. Watermarks

   D. Metadata

16. What type of encryption is best suited for use on the file servers for the proprietary data, and how might you secure the data when it is in motion?

   A. TLS at rest and AES in motion

   B. AES at rest and TLS in motion

   C. VPN at rest and TLS in motion

   D. DES at rest and AES in motion

17. What does labeling data allow a DLP system to do?

   A. The DLP system can detect labels and apply appropriate protections based on rules.

   B. The DLP system can adjust labels based on changes in the classification scheme.

   C. The DLP system can modify labels to permit requested actions.

   D. The DLP system can delete unlabeled data.

18. Why is it cost effective to purchase high-quality media to contain sensitive data?

   A. Expensive media is less likely to fail.

   B. The value of the data often far exceeds the cost of the media.

   C. Expensive media is easier to encrypt.

   D. More expensive media typically improves data integrity.

19. Chris is responsible for workstations throughout his company and knows that some of the company's workstations are used to handle both proprietary information and highly sensitive trade secrets. Which option best describes what should happen at the end of their life (EOL) for workstations he is responsible for?

   A. Erasing

   B. Clearing

   C. Sanitization

   D. Destruction

20. Fred wants to classify his organization's data using common labels: private, sensitive, public, and proprietary. Which of the following should he apply to his highest classification level based on common industry practices?

   A. Private

   B. Sensitive

   C. Public

   D. Proprietary

21. What scenario describes data at rest?

    A. Data in an IPsec tunnel

    B. Data in an e-commerce transaction

    C. Data stored on a hard drive

    D. Data stored in RAM

22. If you are selecting a security standard for a Windows 11 system that processes credit cards, what security standard is your best choice?

    A. Microsoft's Windows 11 security baseline

    B. The CIS Windows 11 baseline

    C. PCI DSS

    D. The NSA Windows 11 Secure Host Baseline

For questions 23–25, please refer to the following scenario:

The Center for Internet Security (CIS) works with subject-matter experts from a variety of industries to create lists of security controls for operating systems, mobile devices, server software, and network devices. Your organization has decided to use the CIS benchmarks for your systems. Answer the following questions based on this decision.

23. The CIS benchmarks are an example of what practice?

    A. Conducting a risk assessment

    B. Implementing data labeling

    C. Implementing proper system ownership

    D. Using security baselines

24. Adjusting the CIS benchmarks to your organization's mission and your specific IT systems would involve what two processes?

    A. Scoping and selection

    B. Scoping and tailoring

    C. Baselining and tailoring

    D. Tailoring and selection

25. How should you determine which controls from the baseline should be applied to a given system or software package?

    A. Consult the custodians of the data.

    B. Select based on the data classification of the data it stores or handles.

    C. Apply the same controls to all systems.

    D. Consult the business owner of the process the system or data supports.

26. The company that Henry works for operates in the EU and collects data about their customers. They send that data to a third party to analyze and provide reports to help the company make better business decisions. What term best describes the third-party analysis company?

    A. The data controller

    B. The data owner

    C. The data subject

    D. The data processor

27. The government defense contractor that Selah works for has recently shut down a major research project and is planning on reusing the hundreds of thousands of dollars of systems and data storage tapes used for the project for other purposes. When Selah reviews the company's internal processes, she finds that she can't reuse the tapes and that the manual says they should be destroyed. Why isn't Selah allowed to degauss and then reuse the tapes to save her employer money?

    A. Data permanence may be an issue.

    B. Data remanence is a concern.

    C. The tapes may suffer from bitrot.

    D. Data from tapes can't be erased by degaussing.

28. Information maintained about an individual that can be used to distinguish or trace their identity is known as what type of information?

    A. Personally identifiable information (PII)

    B. Personal health information (PHI)

    C. Social Security number (SSN)

    D. Secure identity information (SII)

29. Which of the following information security risks to data at rest would result in the greatest reputational impact on an organization?

    A. Improper classification

    B. Data breach

    C. Decryption

    D. An intentional insider threat

30. Full disk encryption like Microsoft's BitLocker is used to protect data in what state?

    A. Data in transit

    B. Data at rest

    C. Unlabeled data

    D. Labeled data

31. The company that Katie works for provides its staff with mobile phones for employee use, with new phones issued every two years. What scenario best describes this type of practice when the phones themselves are still usable and receiving operating system updates?

   A. EOL

   B. Planned obsolescence

   C. EOS

   D. Device risk management

32. What is the primary purpose of data classification?

   A. It quantifies the cost of a data breach.

   B. It prioritizes IT expenditures.

   C. It allows compliance with breach notification laws.

   D. It identifies the value of the data to the organization.

33. Fred's organization allows downgrading of systems for reuse after projects have been finished and the systems have been purged. What concern should Fred raise about the reuse of the systems from his Top Secret classified project for a future project classified as Secret?

   A. The Top Secret data may be commingled with the Secret data, resulting in a need to relabel the system.

   B. The cost of the sanitization process may exceed the cost of new equipment.

   C. The data may be exposed as part of the sanitization process.

   D. The organization's DLP system may flag the new system due to the difference in data labels.

34. Which of the following concerns should not be part of the decision when classifying data?

   A. The cost to classify the data

   B. The sensitivity of the data

   C. The amount of harm that exposure of the data could cause

   D. The value of the data to the organization

35. Which of the following is the least effective method of removing data from media?

   A. Degaussing

   B. Purging

   C. Erasing

   D. Clearing

For questions 36–38, please refer to the following scenario:

The healthcare company that Amanda works for handles HIPAA data as well as internal business data, protected health information, and day-to-day business communications. Its internal policy uses the following requirements for securing HIPAA data at rest and in transit:

Classification	Handling Requirements
Confidential (HIPAA)	Encrypt at rest and in transit.
	Full disk encryption is required for all workstations.
	Files can be sent only in encrypted form, and passwords must be transferred under separate cover.
	Printed documents must be labeled with "HIPAA handling required."
Private (PII)	Encrypt at rest and in transit.
	PHI must be stored on secure servers, and copies should not be kept on local workstations.
	Printed documents must be labeled with "Private."
Sensitive (business confidential)	Encryption is recommended but not required.
Public	Information can be sent unencrypted.

36. What encryption technology would be appropriate for HIPAA documents in transit?

- **A.** BitLocker
- **B.** DES
- **C.** TLS
- **D.** SSL

37. Amanda's employer asks Amanda to classify patient data that is not medical data but that includes data such as phone numbers and addresses. The company's data owner believes that exposure of the data could cause damage (but not exceptional damage) to the organization. How should Amanda classify the data?

- **A.** Public
- **B.** Sensitive
- **C.** Private
- **D.** Confidential

38. What technology could Amanda's employer implement to help prevent confidential data from being emailed out of the organization?

A. DLP

B. IDS

C. A firewall

D. UDP

39. Jacob's organization uses the U.S. government's data classification system, which includes Top Secret, Secret, Confidential, and Unclassified ratings (from most sensitive to least). Jacob encounters a system that contains Secret, Confidential, and Top Secret data. How should it be classified?

A. Top Secret

B. Confidential

C. Secret

D. Mixed classification

40. Elle is planning her organization's asset retention efforts and wants to establish when the company will remove assets from use. Which of the following is typically the last event in a manufacturer or software provider's life cycle?

A. End of life

B. End of support

C. End of sales

D. General availability

41. Alice has been asked to ensure that her organization's controls assessment procedures match the specific systems that the company uses. What activity best matches this task?

A. Asset management

B. Compliance

C. Scoping

D. Tailoring

42. Chris is responsible for his organization's security standards and has guided the selection and implementation of a security baseline for Windows PCs in his organization. How can Chris most effectively make sure that the workstations he is responsible for are being checked for compliance and that settings are being applied as necessary?

A. Assign users to spot-check baseline compliance.

B. Use Microsoft Group Policy.

C. Create start-up scripts to apply policy at system start.

D. Periodically review the baselines with the data owner and system owners.

43. Frank is reviewing his company's data life cycle and wants to place appropriate controls around the data collection phase. Which of the following ensures that data subjects agree to the processing of their data?

    A. Retention

    B. Consent

    C. Certification

    D. Remanence

44. As a DBA, Amy's data role in her organization includes technical implementations of the data policies and standards, as well as managing the data structures that the data is stored in. What data role best fits what Amy does?

    A. Data custodian

    B. Data owner

    C. Data processor

    D. Data user

45. The company Jim works for suffered from a major data breach in the past year and now wants to ensure that it knows where data is located and if it is being transferred, is being copied to a thumb drive, or is in a network file share where it should not be. Which of the following solutions is best suited to tagging, monitoring, and limiting where files are transferred to?

    A. DRM

    B. DLP

    C. A network IPS

    D. Antivirus

46. What security measure can provide an additional security control in the event that backup tapes are stolen or lost?

    A. Keep multiple copies of the tapes.

    B. Replace tape media with hard drives.

    C. Use appropriate security labels.

    D. Use AES-256 encryption.

47. Joe works at a major pharmaceutical research and development company and has been tasked with writing his organization's data retention policy. As part of its legal requirements, the organization must comply with the U.S. Food and Drug Administration's Code of Federal Regulations Title 21. To do so, it is required to retain records with electronic signatures. Why would a signature be part of a retention requirement?

    A. It ensures that someone has reviewed the data.

    B. It provides confidentiality.

    C. It ensures that the data has been changed.

    D. It validates who approved the data.

48. Susan wants to manage her data's life cycle based on retention rules. What technique can she use to ensure that data that has reached the end of its life cycle can be identified and disposed of based on her organization's disposal processes?

A. Rotation

B. DRM

C. DLP

D. Tagging

49. Ben has been asked to scrub data to eliminate any information that is no longer needed by his organization. What phase of the data life cycle is Ben most likely operating in?

A. Data retention

B. Data maintenance

C. Data remanence

D. Data collection

50. Steve wants to ensure that assets in his organization are properly secured. What should he do to make sure security practices match the data security requirements for each device in his organization?

A. Sanitization

B. Asset tagging

C. Tailoring

D. Encryption

51. Alex works for a government agency that is required to meet U.S. federal government requirements for data security. To meet these requirements, Alex has been tasked with making sure data is identifiable by its classification level when it is created to help with data asset inventory processes. What should Alex do to the data?

A. Classify the data.

B. Encrypt the data.

C. Label the data.

D. Apply DRM to the data.

52. Ben is following the National Institute of Standards and Technology (NIST) Special Publication 800-88 guidelines for sanitization and disposition as shown here. He is handling information that his organization classified as sensitive, which is a moderate security categorization in the NIST model. If the media is going to be sold as surplus, what process does Ben need to follow?

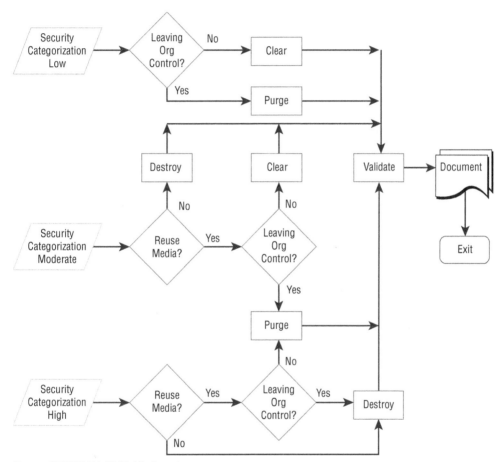

Source: NIST SP 800-88 / Public Domain.

    A. Destroy, validate, document

    B. Clear, purge, document

    C. Purge, document, validate

    D. Purge, validate, document

53. What methods are often used to protect data in transit?

    A. Telnet, ISDN, UDP

    B. BitLocker, FileVault

    C. AES, Serpent, IDEA

    D. TLS, VPN, IPsec

54. Which one of the following data roles bears ultimate organizational responsibility for data?

    A. System owners

    B. Business owners

    C. Data owners

    D. Mission owners

55. Shandra wants to secure an encryption key. Which location would be the most difficult to protect, if the key was kept and used in that location?

    A. On a local network

    B. On disk

    C. In memory

    D. On a public network

For questions 56–58, please refer to the following scenario:

Chris has recently been hired into a new organization. The organization that Chris belongs to uses the following classification process:

1. Criteria are set for classifying data.

2. Data owners are established for each type of data.

3. Data is classified.

4. Required controls are selected for each classification.

5. Baseline security standards are selected for the organization.

6. Controls are scoped and tailored.

7. Controls are applied and enforced.

8. Access is granted and managed.

56. If Chris is one of the data owners for the organization, what steps in this process is he most likely responsible for?

    A. He is responsible for steps 3, 4, and 5.

    B. He is responsible for steps 1, 2, and 3.

    C. He is responsible for steps 5, 6, and 7.

    D. All of the steps are his direct responsibility.

57. Chris manages a team of system administrators. What data role are they fulfilling if they conduct steps 6, 7, and 8 of the classification process?

   A. They are system owners and administrators.

   B. They are administrators and custodians.

   C. They are data owners and administrators.

   D. They are custodians and users.

58. If Chris's company operates in the European Union and has been contracted to handle the data for a third party, what role is his company operating in when it uses this process to classify and handle data?

   A. Business owners

   B. Mission owners

   C. Data processors

   D. Data administrators

For questions 59–62, please refer to the following scenario:

Eric has been put in charge of his organization's IT service management effort, and part of that effort includes creating an inventory of both tangible and intangible assets. As a security professional, you have been asked to provide Eric with security-related guidance on each of the following topics. Your goal is to provide Eric with the best answer from each of the options, knowing that in some cases more than one of the answers could be acceptable.

59. Eric needs to identify all of the active systems and devices on the network. Which of the following techniques will give him the most complete list of connected devices?

   A. Query Active Directory for a list of all computer objects.

   B. Perform a port scan of all systems on the network.

   C. Ask all staff members to fill out a form listing all of their systems and devices.

   D. Use network logs to identify all connected devices and track them down from there.

60. Eric knows that his inventory is accurate only at the moment it was completed. How can he best ensure that it remains up-to-date?

   A. Perform a point-in-time query of network-connected devices and update the list based on what is found.

   B. Ensure that procurement and acquisition processes add new devices to the inventory before they are deployed.

   C. Require every employee to provide an updated inventory of devices they are responsible for on a quarterly basis.

   D. Manually verify every device in service at each organizational location on a yearly basis.

61. Eric knows that his organization has more than just physical assets. In fact, his organization's business involves significant intellectual property assets, including designs and formulas. Eric needs to track and inventory those assets as well. How can he most effectively ensure that he can identify and manage data throughout his organization based on its classification or type?

A. Track file extensions for common data types.

B. Ensure that data is collected in specific network share locations based on the data type and group that works with it.

C. Use metadata tagging based on data type or security level.

D. Automatically tag data by file extension type.

62. Eric has been tasked with identifying intangible assets but needs to provide his team with a list of the assets they will be inventorying. Which of the following is not an example of an intangible asset?

A. Patents

B. Databases

C. Formulas

D. Employees

63. Which of the following is not a common requirement for the collection of data under data privacy laws and statutes?

A. Only data that is needed is collected.

B. Data should be obtained lawfully and via fair methods.

C. Data should be collected only with the consent of the individual whose data is being collected.

D. Data should be collected from all individuals equally.

64. Susan works in an organization that labels all removable media with the classification level of the data it contains, including public data. Why would Susan's employer label all media instead of labeling only the media that contains data that could cause harm if it was exposed?

A. It is cheaper to order all prelabeled media.

B. It prevents sensitive media from not being marked by mistake.

C. It prevents reuse of public media for sensitive data.

D. Labeling all media is required by HIPAA.

65. Data stored in RAM is best characterized as what type of data?

A. Data at rest

B. Data in use

C. Data in transit

D. Data at large

66. What issue is the validation portion of the NIST SP 800-88 sample certificate of sanitization (shown here) intended to help prevent?

CERTIFICATE OF SANITIZATION			
PERSON PERFORMING SANITIZATION			
Name:		Title:	
Organization:	Location:		Phone:
MEDIA INFORMATION			
Make/ Vendor:	Model Number:		
Serial Number:			
Media Property Number:			
Media Type:	Source *(ie user name or PC property number)*:		
Classification:	Data Backed Up: ☐ Yes ☐ No ☐ Unknown		
Backup Location:			
SANITIZATION DETAILS			
Method Type: ☐ Clear ☐ Purge ☐ Damage ☐ Destruct			
Method Used: ☐ Degauss ☐ Overwrite ☐ Block Erase ☐ Crypto Erase ☐ Other:			
Method Details:			
Tool Used *(include version)*:			
Verification Method: ☐ Full ☐ Quick Sampling ☐ Other:			
Post Sanitization Classification:			
Notes:			
MEDIA DESTINATION			
☐ Internal Reuse ☐ External Reuse ☐ Recycling Facility ☐ Manufacturer ☐ Other *(specify in details area)*			
Details:			
SIGNATURE			
I attest that the information provided on this statement is accurate to the best of my knowledge.			
Signature:		Date:	
VALIDATION			
Name:		Title:	
Organization:	Location:		Phone:
Signature:		Date:	

Source: Certificate of Sanitization / NIST / Public Domain.

A. Destruction

B. Reuse

C. Data remanence

D. Attribution

67. Why is declassification rarely chosen as an option for media reuse?

    A. Purging is sufficient for sensitive data.

    B. Sanitization is the preferred method of data removal.

    C. It is more expensive than new media and may still fail.

    D. Clearing is required first.

68. Incineration, crushing, shredding, and disintegration all describe what stage in the life cycle of media?

    A. Sanitization

    B. Degaussing

    C. Purging

    D. Destruction

69. What term is used to describe information like prescriptions and X-rays?

    A. PHI

    B. Proprietary data

    C. PID

    D. PII

70. Why might an organization use unique screen backgrounds or designs on workstations that deal with data of different classification levels?

    A. To indicate the software version in use

    B. To promote a corporate message

    C. To promote availability

    D. To indicate the classification level of the data or system

71. Charles has been asked to downgrade the media used for storage of private data for his organization. What process should Charles follow?

    A. Degauss the drives, and then relabel them with a lower classification level.

    B. Pulverize the drives, and then reclassify them based on the data they contain.

    C. Follow the organization's purging process, and then downgrade and replace labels.

    D. Relabel the media, and then follow the organization's purging process to ensure that the media matches the label.

72. Which of the following tasks is not performed by a system owner per NIST SP 800-18?

    A. Develops a system security plan

    B. Establishes rules for appropriate use and protection of data

    C. Identifies and implements security controls

    D. Ensures that system users receive appropriate security training

73. NIST SP 800-60 provides a process shown in the following diagram to assess information systems. What process does this diagram show?

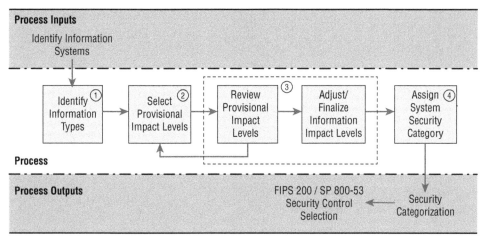

Source: NIST SP 800-60 / Public Domain.

A. Selecting a standard and implementing it

B. Categorizing and selecting controls

C. Baselining and selecting controls

D. Categorizing and sanitizing

The following diagram shows a typical workstation and server and their connections to each other and the Internet. For questions 74–76, please refer to this diagram.

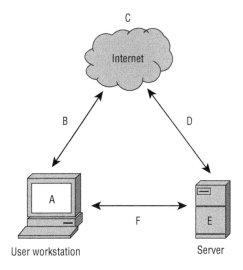

74. Which letters on this diagram are locations where you might find data at rest?

   A. A, B, and C

   B. C and E

   C. A and E

   D. B, D, and F

75. What would be the best way to secure data at points B, D, and F?

   A. AES-256

   B. SSL

   C. TLS

   D. 3DES

76. What is the best way to secure files that are sent from workstation A via the Internet service (C) to remote server E?

   A. Use AES at rest at point A, and use TLS in transit via B and D.

   B. Encrypt the data files and send them.

   C. Use 3DES and TLS to provide double security.

   D. Use full-disk encryption at A and E, and use SSL at B and D.

77. Susan needs to provide a set of minimum security requirements for email. What steps should she recommend for her organization to ensure that the email remains secure?

   A. All email should be encrypted.

   B. All email should be encrypted and labeled.

   C. Sensitive email should be encrypted and labeled.

   D. Only highly sensitive email should be encrypted.

78. How can a data retention policy reduce liabilities?

   A. By reducing the amount of storage in use

   B. By limiting the number of data classifications

   C. By reducing the amount of data that may need to be produced for lawsuits

   D. By reducing the legal penalties for noncompliance

79. What data role does a system that is used to process data have?

   A. Mission owner

   B. Data owner

   C. Data processor

   D. Custodian

80. Which one of the following is not considered PII under U.S. federal government regulations?

   A. Name

   B. Social Security number

   C. Student ID number

   D. ZIP code

81. What type of health information is the Health Insurance Portability and Accountability Act required to protect?

   A. PII

   B. PHI

   C. SHI

   D. HPHI

82. The system that Ian has built replaces data in a database field with a randomized string of characters that remains the same for each instance of that data. What technique has he used?

   A. Data masking

   B. Tokenization

   C. Anonymization

   D. DES

83. Juanita's company processes credit cards and wants to select appropriate data security standards. What data security standard is she most likely to need to use and comply with?

   A. CC-Comply

   B. PCI-DSS

   C. GLBA

   D. GDPR

84. What is the best method to sanitize a solid-state drive (SSD)?

   A. Clearing

   B. Zero fill

   C. Disintegration

   D. Degaussing

For questions 85–87, please refer to the following scenario:

As shown in the following security life-cycle diagram (loosely based on the NIST reference architecture), NIST uses a five-step process for risk management. Using your knowledge of data roles and practices, answer the following questions based on the NIST framework process.

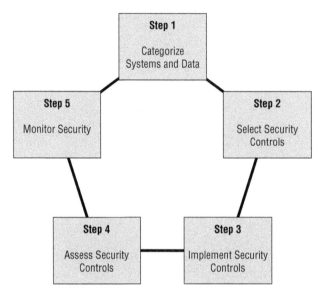

85. What data role will own responsibility for step 1, the categorization of information systems; to whom will they delegate step 2; and what data role will be responsible for step 3?

    A. Data owners, system owners, custodians

    B. Data processors, custodians, users

    C. Business owners, administrators, custodians

    D. System owners, business owners, administrators

86. If the systems that are being assessed all handle credit card information (and no other sensitive data), at what step would the PCI DSS first play an important role?

    A. Step 1

    B. Step 2

    C. Step 3

    D. Step 4

87. What data security role is primarily responsible for step 5?

   A. Data owners

   B. Data processors

   C. Custodians

   D. Users

88. Susan's organization performs a secure disk wipe process on hard drives before they are sent to a third-party organization to be shredded. What issue is her organization attempting to avoid?

   A. Data retention that is longer than defined in policy

   B. Mishandling of drives by the third party

   C. Classification mistakes

   D. Data permanence

89. Mike wants to track hardware assets as devices and equipment are moved throughout his organization. What type of system can help do this without requiring staff to individually check bar codes or serial numbers?

   A. A visual inventory

   B. Wi-Fi MAC address tracking

   C. RFID tags

   D. Steganography

90. Retaining and maintaining information for as long as it is needed is known as what?

   A. Data storage policy

   B. Data storage

   C. Asset maintenance

   D. Record retention

91. Which of the following activities is not a consideration during data classification?

   A. Who can access the data

   B. What the impact would be if the data was lost or breached

   C. How much the data cost to create

   D. What protection regulations may be required for the data

92. What type of encryption is typically used for data at rest?

   A. Asymmetric encryption

   B. Symmetric encryption

   C. DES

   D. OTP

93. Which data role is tasked with applying rights that provide appropriate access to staff members?

    A. Data processors

    B. Business owners

    C. Custodians

    D. Administrators

94. What element of asset security is often determined by identifying an asset's owner?

    A. It identifies the individual(s) responsible for protecting the asset.

    B. It provides a law enforcement contact in case of theft.

    C. It helps establish the value of the asset.

    D. It determines the security classification of the asset.

95. Fred is preparing to send backup tapes off-site to a secure third-party storage facility. What steps should Fred take before sending the tapes to that facility?

    A. Ensure that the tapes are handled the same way the original media would be handled based on their classification.

    B. Increase the classification level of the tapes because they are leaving the possession of the company.

    C. Purge the tapes to ensure that classified data is not lost.

    D. Decrypt the tapes in case they are lost in transit.

96. Which of the following does not describe data in motion?

    A. Data on a backup tape that is being shipped to a storage facility

    B. Data in a TCP packet

    C. Data in an e-commerce transaction

    D. Data in files being copied between locations

97. A new law is passed that would result in significant financial harm to your company if the data that it covers was stolen or inadvertently released. What should your organization do about this?

    A. Select a new security baseline.

    B. Relabel the data.

    C. Encrypt all of the data at rest and in transit.

    D. Review its data classifications and classify the data appropriately.

98. Which of the following data roles are typically found inside of a company instead of as a third-party contracting relationship? (Select all that apply.)

    A. Data owners

    B. Data controllers

    C. Data custodians

    D. Data processors

99. What commercial data classification is most appropriate for data contained on corporate websites?

   A. Private

   B. Sensitive

   C. Public

   D. Proprietary

100. Match each of the numbered data elements shown here with one of the lettered categories. You may use the categories once, more than once, or not at all. If a data element matches more than one category, choose the one that is most specific.

Data elements:

   1. Medical records

   2. Trade secrets

   3. Social Security numbers

   4. Driver's license numbers

Categories:

   A. Proprietary data

   B. Protected health information

   C. Personally identifiable information

101. Michelle wants to ensure that her organization's policies are enforced across all of the cloud services that it has adopted. What type of tool would be best suited to ensuring her organization's policies are enforced, regardless of the cloud service her users are accessing?

   A. A SIEM

   B. A DLP

   C. A CASB

   D. A NGFW

102. Devices in Adam's organization are no longer receiving updates, and hardware support contracts cannot be extended. How should Adam describe the devices that are impacted by this?

   A. End of support

   B. End of development

   C. End of life

   D. End of sales

103. Gary is responsible for the procurement, management, and life cycle of network devices in his organization. What role best describes him?

   A. Data owner

   B. Asset custodian

   C. Data custodian

   D. Asset owner

104. Jessica has adopted the CIS benchmark for Windows 11 workstations for her organization. She has modified what settings are called for in the benchmark to fit her organization's needs as well. What has she done?

   A. Tailoring

   B. Scoping

   C. Editing

   D. Defining

105. Why is data location a significant concern for data owners, controllers, and custodians?

   A. It prevents the data from being lost.

   B. Geographic location may impact compliance requirements.

   C. Geographic location may drive storage costs.

   D. It ensures that the proper data custodian works with it.

Chapter

3

Security Architecture and Engineering (Domain 3)

SUBDOMAINS

✓ 3.1 Research, implement, and manage engineering processes using secure design principles

✓ 3.2 Understand the fundamental concepts of security models (e.g., Biba, Star Model, Bell-LaPadula)

✓ 3.3 Select controls based upon system security requirements

✓ 3.4 Understand security capabilities of Information Systems (e.g., memory protection, Trusted Platform Module (TPM), encryption/decryption)

✓ 3.5 Assess and mitigate the vulnerabilities of security architectures, designs, and solution elements

✓ 3.6 Select and determine cryptographic solutions

✓ 3.7 Understand methods of cryptanalytic attacks

✓ 3.8 Apply security principles to site and facility design

✓ 3.9 Design site and facility security controls

✓ 3.10 Manage the information system lifecycle

1. Matthew is the security administrator for a consulting firm and must enforce access controls that restrict users' access based upon their previous activity. For example, once a consultant accesses data belonging to Acme Cola, a consulting client, they may no longer access data belonging to any of Acme's competitors. What security model best fits Matthew's needs?

    A. Clark-Wilson

    B. Biba

    C. Bell-LaPadula

    D. Brewer-Nash

2. Referring to the figure shown here, what is the earliest stage of a fire where it is possible to use detection technology to identify it?

    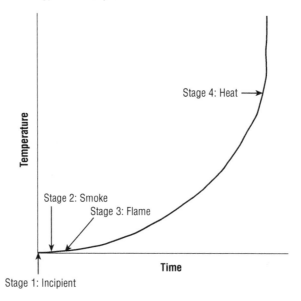

    A. Incipient

    B. Smoke

    C. Flame

    D. Heat

3. Ralph is designing a physical security infrastructure for a new computing facility that will remain largely unstaffed. He plans to implement motion detectors in the facility but would also like to include a secondary verification control for physical presence. Which one of the following would best meet his needs?

    A. CCTV

    B. IPS

    C. Turnstiles

    D. Faraday cages

4. Harry would like to retrieve a lost encryption key from a database that uses m of n control, with m = 4 and n = 8. What is the minimum number of escrow agents required to retrieve the key?

A. 2

B. 4

C. 8

D. 12

5. Fran's company is considering purchasing a web-based email service from a vendor and eliminating its own email server environment as a cost-saving measure. What type of cloud computing environment is Fran's company considering?

A. SaaS

B. IaaS

C. CaaS

D. PaaS

6. Bob is a security administrator with the U.S. federal government and wants to choose a digital signature approach that is an approved part of the federal Digital Signature Standard under FIPS 186-5. Which one of the following encryption algorithms is not an acceptable choice for use in digital signatures?

A. EdDSA

B. HAVAL

C. RSA

D. ECDSA

7. Harry would like to access a document owned by Sally and stored on a file server. Applying the subject/object model to this scenario, who or what is the subject of the resource request?

A. Harry

B. Sally

C. Server

D. Document

8. Michael is responsible for forensic investigations and is investigating a medium-severity security incident that involved the defacement of a corporate website. The web server in question ran on a virtualization platform, and the marketing team would like to get the website up and running as quickly as possible. What would be the most reasonable next step for Michael to take?

A. Keep the website offline until the investigation is complete.

B. Take the virtualization platform offline as evidence.

C. Take a snapshot of the compromised system and use that for the investigation.

D. Ignore the incident and focus on quickly restoring the website.

9. Helen is a software engineer and is developing code that she would like to restrict to running within an isolated sandbox for security purposes. What software development technique is Helen using?

   A. Bounds

   B. Input validation

   C. Confinement

   D. TCB

10. What concept describes the degree of confidence that an organization has that its controls satisfy security requirements?

    A. Trust

    B. Credentialing

    C. Verification

    D. Assurance

11. What type of security vulnerability are developers most likely to introduce into code when they seek to facilitate their own access, for testing purposes, to software they developed?

    A. Maintenance hook

    B. Cross-site scripting

    C. SQL injection

    D. Buffer overflow

12. In the figure shown here, Sally is blocked from reading the file due to the Biba integrity model. Sally has a Secret security clearance, and the file has a Confidential classification. What principle of the Biba model is being enforced?

    A. Simple Security Property

    B. Simple Integrity Property

    C. *-Security Property

    D. *-Integrity Property

13. Tom is responsible for maintaining the security of systems used to control industrial processes located within a power plant. What term is used to describe these systems?

    A. POWER

    B. SCADA

    C. HAVAL

    D. COBOL

14. Sonia recently removed an encrypted hard drive from a laptop and moved it to a new device because of a hardware failure. She is having difficulty accessing encrypted content on the drive despite that she knows the user's password. What hardware security feature is likely causing this problem?

A. TCB

B. TPM

C. NIACAP

D. RSA

15. Chris wants to verify that a software package that he downloaded matches the original version. What hashing tool should he use if he believes that technically sophisticated attackers may have replaced the software package with a version containing a backdoor?

A. MD5

B. 3DES

C. SHA1

D. SHA 256

For questions 16–19, please refer to the following scenario:

Alice and Bob would like to use an asymmetric cryptosystem to communicate with each other. They are located in different parts of the country but have exchanged encryption keys by using digital certificates signed by a mutually trusted certificate authority.

16. If Alice wants to send Bob a message that is encrypted for confidentiality, what key does she use to encrypt the message?

A. Alice's public key

B. Alice's private key

C. Bob's public key

D. Bob's private key

17. When Bob receives the encrypted message from Alice, what key does he use to decrypt the message's plaintext content?

A. Alice's public key

B. Alice's private key

C. Bob's public key

D. Bob's private key

18. Which one of the following keys would Bob not possess in this scenario?

A. Alice's public key

B. Alice's private key

C. Bob's public key

D. Bob's private key

19. Alice would also like to digitally sign the message that she sends to Bob. What key should she use to create the digital signature?

    A. Alice's public key

    B. Alice's private key

    C. Bob's public key

    D. Bob's private key

20. What name is given to the random value added to a password in an attempt to defeat rainbow table attacks?

    A. Hash

    B. Salt

    C. Extender

    D. Rebar

21. Which one of the following is not an attribute of a typical hashing algorithm?

    A. They require a cryptographic key.

    B. They are irreversible.

    C. It is very difficult to find two messages with the same hash value.

    D. They take variable-length input.

22. What type of fire suppression system fills with water after a valve opens when the initial stages of a fire are detected and then requires a sprinkler head heat activation before dispensing water?

    A. Wet pipe

    B. Dry pipe

    C. Deluge

    D. Preaction

23. Susan would like to configure IPsec in a manner that provides confidentiality for the content of packets. What component of IPsec provides this capability?

    A. AH

    B. ESP

    C. IKE

    D. ISAKMP

24. Which one of the following cryptographic goals protects against the risks posed when a device is lost or stolen?

    A. Nonrepudiation

    B. Authentication

    C. Integrity

    D. Confidentiality

25. Joanna wants to review the status of the industrial control systems her organization uses for building control. What type of systems should she inquire about access to?

A. SCADA

B. DSS

C. BAS

D. ICS-CSS

26. In the figure shown here, Harry's request to write to the data file is blocked. Harry has a Secret security clearance, and the data file has a Confidential classification. What principle of the Bell-LaPadula model blocked this request?

A. Simple Security Property

B. Simple Integrity Property

C. *-Security Property

D. Discretionary Security Property

27. Florian and Tobias would like to begin communicating using a symmetric cryptosystem, but they have no prearranged secret and are not able to meet in person to exchange keys. What algorithm can they use to securely exchange the secret key?

A. IDEA

B. Diffie-Hellman

C. RSA

D. MD5

28. Carl's organization recently underwent a user access review. At the conclusion of the review, the auditors noted several cases of privilege creep. What security principle was violated?

A. Fail securely

B. Keep it simple and secure

C. Trust but verify

D. Least privilege

29. Matt's organization recently adopted a zero trust network architecture. Under this approach, which one of the following criteria would be LEAST appropriate to use when granting a subject access to resources?

A. Password

B. Two-factor authentication

C. IP address

D. Biometric scan

30. Colin is the chief privacy officer for a nonprofit organization and is assisting with the team's transition to a Privacy by Design approach. Under this approach, which is not one of the Privacy by Design principles?

A. Proactive, not reactive

B. Privacy as the default setting

C. End-to-end security

D. Defense in depth

31. What cryptographic principle stands behind the idea that cryptographic algorithms should be open to public inspection?

A. Security through obscurity

B. Kerckhoffs' principle

C. Defense in depth

D. Heisenburg principle

32. Ryan is developing a physical access plan for his organization's data center and wants to implement the security control indicated by the arrow in this diagram. What is the name of this control?

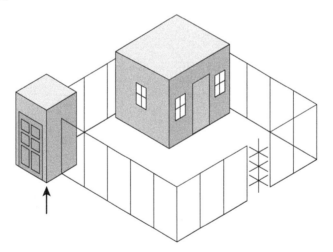

A. Access control vestibule

B. Turnstile

C. Intrusion prevention system

D. Portal

33. Which one of the following does not describe a standard physical security requirement for wiring closets?

A. Place only in areas monitored by security guards.

B. Do not store flammable items in the closet.

C. Use sensors on doors to log entries.

D. Perform regular inspections of the closet.

34. In the figure shown here, Sally is blocked from writing to the data file by the Biba integrity model. Sally has a Secret security clearance, and the file is classified Top Secret. What principle is preventing her from writing to the file?

A. Simple Security Property

B. Simple Integrity Property

C. *-Security Property

D. *-Integrity Property

35. Lana recently implemented a new process in her organization where managers who are responsible for granting users access to a system are not permitted to participate in access reviews. What principle is she enforcing?

A. Two-person control

B. Least privilege

C. Privilege creep

D. Segregation of duties

36. Which of the following statements about system development are correct? (Select all that apply.)

A. Systems should be designed to operate in a secure manner if the user performs no other configuration.

B. Systems should be designed to fall back to a secure state if they experience an error.

C. Systems should be designed to incorporate security as a design feature.

D. Systems should be designed in a manner that keeps their functionality as simple as possible.

37. Alan is reviewing a system that has been assigned the EAL1 evaluation assurance level under the Common Criteria. What is the degree of assurance that he may have about the system?

A. It has been functionally tested.

B. It has been structurally tested.

C. It has been formally verified, designed, and tested.

D. It has been methodically designed, tested, and reviewed.

38. Jake works for a research organization that is seeking to deploy a grid computing system that will perform cycle scavenging on user workstations to conduct research tasks that require high-performance computing. What is the most significant risk associated with this operation?

A. Data confidentiality

B. Isolation breach

C. Data integrity

D. Data availability

39. Eimear's software development team uses an approach that creates many discrete software objects and then binds them together using APIs. What term best describes this architecture?

A. Microservices

B. Function-as-a-service

C. Containerization

D. Virtualization

40. Adam recently configured permissions on an NTFS filesystem to describe the access that different users may have to a file by listing each user individually. What did Adam create?

A. An access control list

B. An access control entry

C. Role-based access control

D. Mandatory access control

41. Betty is concerned about the use of buffer overflow attacks against a custom application developed for use in her organization. What security control would provide the strongest defense against these attacks?

A. Firewall

B. Intrusion detection system

C. Parameter checking

D. Vulnerability scanning

42. Which one of the following combinations of controls best embodies the defense-in-depth principle?

   A. Encryption of email and network intrusion detection

   B. Cloud access security brokers (CASBs) and security awareness training

   C. Data loss prevention and multifactor authentication

   D. Network firewall and host firewall

43. James is working with a Department of Defense system that is authorized to simultaneously handle information classified at the Secret and Top Secret levels. What type of system is he using?

   A. Single state

   B. Unclassified

   C. Compartmented

   D. Multistate

44. Kyle is being granted access to a military computer system that uses System High mode. What is not true about Kyle's security clearance requirements?

   A. Kyle must have a clearance for the highest level of classification processed by the system, regardless of his access.

   B. Kyle must have access approval for all information processed by the system.

   C. Kyle must have a valid need to know for all information processed by the system.

   D. Kyle must have a valid security clearance.

45. Gary intercepts a communication between two individuals and suspects that they are exchanging secret messages. The content of the communication appears to be the image shown here. What type of technique may the individuals use to hide messages inside this image?

Source: Matt65 / Wikimedia Commons / Public domain.

   A. Visual cryptography

   B. Steganography

   C. Cryptographic hashing

   D. Transport layer security

46. Philip is developing a new security tool that will be used by individuals in many different subsidiaries of his organization. He chooses to use Docker to deploy the tool to simplify configuration. What term best describes this approach?

   A. Virtualization

   B. Abstraction

   C. Simplification

   D. Containerization

47. In the ring protection model shown here, what ring contains the operating system's kernel?

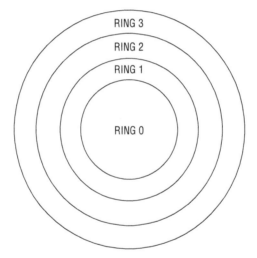

   A. Ring 0

   B. Ring 1

   C. Ring 2

   D. Ring 3

48. In an infrastructure-as-a-service environment where a vendor supplies a customer with access to storage services, who is normally responsible for removing sensitive data from drives that are taken out of service?

   A. Customer's security team

   B. Customer's storage team

   C. Customer's vendor management team

   D. Vendor

49. During a system audit, Casey notices that the private key for her organization's web server has been stored in a public Amazon S3 storage bucket for more than a year. Which one of the following actions should she take first?

   A. Remove the key from the bucket.

   B. Notify all customers that their data may have been exposed.

   C. Request a new certificate using a new key.

   D. Nothing, because the private key should be accessible for validation.

50. Which one of the following systems assurance processes provides an independent third-party evaluation of a system's controls that may be trusted by many different organizations?

   A. Certification

   B. Definition

   C. Verification

   D. Accreditation

51. Darcy's organization is deploying serverless computing technology to better meet the needs of developers and users. In a serverless model, who is normally responsible for configuring operating system security controls?

   A. Software developer

   B. Cybersecurity professional

   C. Cloud architect

   D. Vendor

52. Harold is assessing the susceptibility of his environment to hardware failures and would like to identify the expected lifetime of a piece of hardware. What measure should he use for this?

   A. MTTR

   B. MTTF

   C. RTO

   D. MTO

53. Chris is designing a cryptographic system for use within his company. The company has 1,000 employees, and they plan to use an asymmetric encryption system. They would like the system to be set up so that any pair of arbitrary users may communicate privately. How many total keys will they need?

   A. 500

   B. 1,000

   C. 2,000

   D. 499,500

54. Gary is concerned about applying consistent security settings to the many mobile devices used throughout his organization. What technology would best assist with this challenge?

  A. MDM

  B. IPS

  C. IDS

  D. SIEM

55. Alice sent a message to Bob. Bob would like to demonstrate to Charlie that the message he received definitely came from Alice. What goal of cryptography is Bob attempting to achieve?

  A. Authentication

  B. Confidentiality

  C. Nonrepudiation

  D. Integrity

56. Rhonda is considering the use of new identification cards for physical access control in her organization. She comes across a military system that uses the card shown here. What type of card is this?

  A. Smart card

  B. Proximity card

  C. Magnetic stripe card

  D. Phase three card

57. Gordon is concerned about the possibility that hackers may be able to use the Van Eck radiation phenomenon to remotely read the contents of computer monitors in a restricted work area within his facility. What technology would protect against this type of attack?

A. TCSEC

B. SCSI

C. GHOST

D. TEMPEST

58. Jorge believes that an attacker has obtained the hash of the Kerberos service account from one of his organization's Active Directory servers. What type of attack would this enable?

A. Golden ticket

B. Kerberoasting

C. Pass the ticket

D. Brute force

59. Sherry conducted an inventory of the cryptographic technologies in use within her organization and found the following algorithms and protocols in use. Which one of these technologies should she replace because it is no longer considered secure?

A. MD5

B. AES

C. PGP

D. WPA3

60. Robert is investigating a security breach and discovers the Mimikatz tool installed on a system in his environment. What type of attack has likely taken place?

A. Password cracking

B. Pass the hash

C. MAC spoofing

D. ARP poisoning

61. Tom is a cryptanalyst and is working on breaking a cryptographic algorithm's secret key. He has a copy of an intercepted message that is encrypted, and he also has a copy of the decrypted version of that message. He wants to use both the encrypted message and its decrypted plaintext to retrieve the secret key for use in decrypting other messages. What type of attack is Tom engaging in?

A. Chosen ciphertext

B. Chosen plaintext

C. Known plaintext

D. Brute force

62. A hacker recently violated the integrity of data in James's company by modifying a file using a precise timing attack. The attacker waited until James verified the integrity of a file's contents using a hash value and then modified the file between the time that James verified the integrity and read the contents of the file. What type of attack took place?

A. Social engineering

B. TOCTOU

C. Data diddling

D. Parameter checking

63. Carl is deploying a set of video sensors that will be placed in remote locations as part of a research project. Because of connectivity limitations, he would like to perform as much image processing and computation as possible on the device itself before sending results back to the cloud for further analysis. What computing model would best meet his needs?

A. Serverless computing

B. Edge computing

C. IaaS computing

D. SaaS computing

64. What action can you take to prevent accidental data disclosure due to wear leveling on an SSD device before reusing the drive?

A. Reformatting

B. Disk encryption

C. Degaussing

D. Physical destruction

65. Johnson Widgets strictly limits access to total sales volume information, classifying it as a competitive secret. However, shipping clerks have unrestricted access to order records to facilitate transaction completion. A shipping clerk recently pulled all of the individual sales records for a quarter from the database and totaled them up to determine the total sales volume. What type of attack occurred?

A. Social engineering

B. Inference

C. Aggregation

D. Data diddling

66. What physical security control broadcasts false emanations constantly to mask the presence of true electromagnetic emanations from computing equipment?

A. Faraday cage

B. Copper-infused windows

C. Shielded cabling

D. White noise

67. In a software-as-a-service cloud computing environment, who is normally responsible for ensuring that appropriate firewall controls are in place to protect the application?

    A. Customer's security team

    B. Vendor

    C. Customer's networking team

    D. Customer's infrastructure management team

68. Alice has read permissions on an object, and she would like Bob to have those same rights. Which one of the rules in the Take-Grant protection model would allow her to complete this operation?

    A. Create rule

    B. Remove rule

    C. Grant rule

    D. Take rule

69. As part of his incident response process, Charles securely wipes the drive of a compromised machine and reinstalls the operating system (OS) from original media. Once he is done, he patches the machine fully and applies his organization's security templates before reconnecting the system to the network. Almost immediately after the system is returned to service, he discovers that it has reconnected to the same botnet it was part of before. Where should Charles look for the malware that is causing this behavior?

    A. The operating system partition

    B. The system BIOS or firmware

    C. The system memory

    D. The installation media

70. Lauren implements ASLR to help prevent system compromises. What technique has she used to protect her system?

    A. Encryption

    B. Mandatory access control

    C. Memory address randomization

    D. Discretionary access control

71. Alan intercepts an encrypted message and wants to determine what type of algorithm was used to create the message. He first performs a frequency analysis and notes that the frequency of letters in the message closely matches the distribution of letters in the English language. What type of cipher was most likely used to create this message?

    A. Substitution cipher

    B. AES

    C. Transposition cipher

    D. 3DES

72. In a zero trust network architecture, what component is responsible for making policy decisions based upon rules and external data sources?

   A. Policy engine

   B. Policy administrator

   C. Policy enforcement point

   D. Subject

73. Grace would like to implement application control technology in her organization. Users often need to install new applications for research and testing purposes, and she does not want to interfere with that process. At the same time, she would like to block the use of known malicious software. What type of application control would be appropriate in this situation?

   A. Blacklisting

   B. Graylisting

   C. Whitelisting

   D. Bluelisting

74. Warren is designing a physical intrusion detection system for use in a sensitive media storage facility and wants to include technology that issues an alert if the communications lines for the alarm system are unexpectedly cut. What technology would meet this requirement?

   A. Heartbeat sensor

   B. Emanation security

   C. Motion detector

   D. Faraday cage

75. John and Gary are negotiating a business transaction, and John must demonstrate to Gary that he has access to a system. He engages in an electronic version of the "magic door" scenario shown here. What technique is John using?

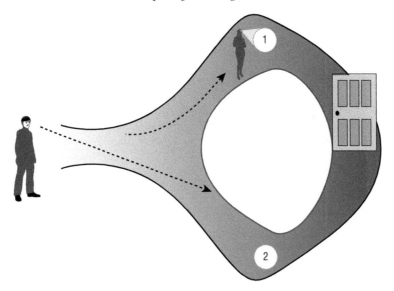

A. Split-knowledge proof

B. Zero-knowledge proof

C. Logical proof

D. Mathematical proof

76. After scanning all of the systems on his wireless network, Mike notices that one system is identified as an iOS device running a massively out-of-date version of Apple's mobile operating system. When he investigates further, he discovers that the device is an original iPad and that it cannot be updated to a current secure version of the operating system. What would be the best option for handling this device?

A. Retire or replace the device.

B. Isolate the device on a dedicated wireless network.

C. Install a firewall on the tablet.

D. Reinstall the OS.

77. Tonya believes that an attacker was able to eavesdrop on legitimate HTTPS communications between her users and remote web servers by engaging in a DNS poisoning attack. After conducting DNS poisoning, what technique would an attacker likely use to conduct this eavesdropping?

A. Man-in-the-middle

B. Brute-force

C. Timing

D. Meet-in-the-middle

78. Howard is choosing a cryptographic algorithm for his organization, and he would like to choose an algorithm that supports the creation of digital signatures. Which one of the following algorithms would meet his requirement?

A. RSA

B. 3DES

C. AES

D. Blowfish

79. Laura is responsible for securing her company's web-based applications and wants to conduct an educational program for developers on common web application security vulnerabilities. Where can she turn for a concise listing of the most common web application issues?

A. CVE

B. NSA

C. OWASP

D. CSA

80. The Bell-LaPadula and Biba models implement state machines in a fashion that uses what specific state machine model?

  A. Information flow

  B. Noninterference

  C. Cascading

  D. Feedback

81. During a third-party vulnerability scan and security test, Danielle's employer recently discovered that the embedded systems that were installed to manage her company's new buildings have a severe remote access vulnerability. The manufacturer has gone out of business, and there is no patch or update for the devices. What should Danielle recommend that her employer do about the hundreds of devices that are vulnerable?

  A. Identify a replacement device model and replace every device.

  B. Turn off all of the devices.

  C. Move the devices to a secure and isolated network segment.

  D. Reverse engineer the devices and build an in-house patch.

82. What type of motion detector senses changes in the electromagnetic fields in monitored areas?

  A. Infrared

  B. Wave pattern

  C. Capacitance

  D. Photoelectric

83. Mike has been tasked with preventing an outbreak of malware like Mirai, a botnet that targeted IP-based cameras and routers. What type of systems should be protected in his organization?

  A. Servers

  B. SCADA

  C. Mobile devices

  D. Internet of Things (IoT) devices

84. Which one of the following statements is correct about the Biba model of access control?

  A. It addresses confidentiality and integrity.

  B. It addresses integrity and availability.

  C. It prevents covert channel attacks.

  D. It focuses on protecting objects from integrity threats.

85. In Transport Layer Security, what type of key is used to encrypt the actual content of communications between a web server and a client?

  A. Ephemeral session key

  B. Client's public key

  C. Server's public key

  D. Server's private key

86. Beth would like to include technology in a secure area of her data center to protect against unwanted electromagnetic emanations. What technology would assist her with this goal?

A. Heartbeat sensor

B. Faraday cage

C. Piggybacking

D. WPA2

87. In a virtualized computing environment, what component is responsible for enforcing separation between guest machines?

A. Guest operating system

B. Hypervisor

C. Kernel

D. Protection manager

88. Rick is an application developer who works primarily in Python. He recently decided to evaluate a new service where he provides his Python code to a vendor who then executes it on their server environment. What type of cloud computing environment is this service?

A. SaaS

B. PaaS

C. IaaS

D. CaaS

89. A component failure in the primary HVAC system leads to a high temperature alarm in the data center that Kim manages. After resolving the issue, what should Kim consider to prevent future issues like this?

A. A closed loop chiller

B. Redundant cooling systems

C. Swamp coolers

D. Relocating the data center to a colder climate

90. Tommy is planning to implement a power conditioning UPS for a rack of servers in his data center. Which one of the following conditions will the UPS be unable to protect against if it persists for an extended period of time?

A. Fault

B. Blackout

C. Sag

D. Noise

91. Which one of the following humidity values is within the acceptable range for a data center operation?

   A. 0%

   B. 10%

   C. 15%

   D. 40%

92. Kristen's organization suffered a ransomware infection and has lost access to critical business data. She is considering paying the ransom to regain access to her data. Which of the following statements about this payment are correct? (Select all that apply.)

   A. Payment of the ransom may be illegal.

   B. Payment of the ransom may result in further demands for payments.

   C. Payment of the ransom guarantees access to the decryption key.

   D. Payment of the ransom may cause a data breach.

93. Alex's employer creates most of their work output as PDF files. Alex is concerned about limiting the audience for the PDF files to those individuals who have paid for them. What technology can he use to most effectively control the access to and distribution of these files?

   A. EDM

   B. Encryption

   C. Digital signatures

   D. DRM

94. As part of his team's forensic investigation process, Matt signs out drives and other evidence from an evidence storage facility before working with them. What type of documentation is he creating?

   A. Criminal

   B. Chain of custody

   C. Civil

   D. CYA

95. Todd believes that a digital certificate used by his organization has been compromised, and he wants to add it to the certificate revocation list (CRL). What element of the certificate goes on the CRL?

   A. Serial number

   B. Public key

   C. Digital signature

   D. Private key

96. Alison is examining a digital certificate presented to her by her bank's website. Which one of the following requirements is not necessary for her to trust the digital certificate?

A. She knows that the server belongs to the bank.

B. She trusts the certificate authority.

C. She verifies that the certificate is not listed on a CRL.

D. She verifies the digital signature on the certificate.

97. Which one of the following is an example of a covert timing channel when used to exfiltrate information from an organization?

A. Sending an electronic mail message

B. Posting a file on a peer-to-peer file sharing service

C. Typing with the rhythm of Morse code

D. Writing data to a shared memory space

98. Which one of the following would be a reasonable application for the use of self-signed digital certificates?

A. Digital commerce website

B. Banking application

C. Internal scheduling application

D. Customer portal

99. Ron is investigating a security incident that took place at a highly secure government facility. He believes that encryption keys were stolen during the attack and finds evidence that the attackers used dry ice to freeze an encryption component. What type of attack was likely attempted?

A. Side channel attack

B. Brute-force attack

C. Timing attack

D. Fault injection attack

100. Match the following numbered security models with the appropriate lettered security descriptions:

Security models:

    1. Clark-Wilson

    2. Bell-LaPadula

    3. Biba

Descriptions:

    A. This model blocks lower-classified objects from accessing higher-classified objects, thus ensuring confidentiality.

    B. The * property of this model can be summarized as "no write-up."

    C. This model uses security labels to grant access to objects via transformation procedures and a restricted interface model.

101. Match each of these following numbered architecture security concepts with the appropriate lettered description:

Architectural security concepts:

    1. Time of check

    2. Covert channel

    3. Time of use

    4. Maintenance hooks

    5. Parameter checking

    6. Race condition

Descriptions:

    A. A method used to pass information over a path not normally used for communication

    B. The exploitation of the reliance of a system's behavior on the sequence of events that occur externally

    C. The time at which the subject checks whether an object is available

    D. The time at which a subject can access an object

    E. An access method known only to the developer of the system

    F. A method that can help prevent buffer overflow attacks

Chapter

4

Communication and Network Security (Domain 4)

SUBDOMAINS

✓ 4.1 Apply secure design principles in network architectures

✓ 4.2 Secure network components

✓ 4.3 Implement secure communication channels according to design

1. Gary wants to distribute a large file and prefers a peer-to-peer content delivery network (CDN). Which of the following is the most common example of this type of technology?

    A. CloudFlare

    B. BitTorrent

    C. Amazon CloudFront

    D. Akamai Edge

2. What is the purpose of a virtual domain (VDOM)?

    A. They combine multiple virtual instances into a single domain.

    B. They divide a firewall device or appliance into two or more virtual firewalls.

    C. They create a virtual domain controller.

    D. They allow the hosting of multiple domain names for a single host.

3. Ben has connected his laptop to his tablet PC using an 802.11ac connection. What wireless network mode has he used to connect these devices?

    A. Infrastructure mode

    B. Wired extension mode

    C. Ad hoc mode

    D. Stand-alone mode

4. Selah's and Nick's PCs simultaneously send traffic by transmitting at the same time. What network term describes the range of systems on a network that could be affected by this same issue?

    A. The subnet

    B. The supernet

    C. A collision domain

    D. A broadcast domain

5. Sarah is manually reviewing a packet capture of TCP traffic and finds that a system is setting the RST flag in the TCP packets it sends repeatedly during a short period of time. What does this flag mean in the TCP packet header?

    A. RST flags mean "Rest." The server needs traffic to briefly pause.

    B. RST flags mean "Relay-set." The packets will be forwarded to the address set in the packet.

    C. RST flags mean "Resume Standard." Communications will resume in their normal format.

    D. RST means "Reset." The TCP session will be disconnected.

6. Gary is deploying a wireless network and wants to deploy the fastest possible wireless technology. Which one of the following wireless networking standards should he use?

A. 802.11ac

B. 802.11g

C. 802.11n

D. 802.11ax

7. Michele wants to replace FTP traffic with a secure replacement. What secure protocol should she select instead?

A. TFTP

B. HFTPS

C. SecFTP

D. SFTP

8. Jake has been told that there is a layer 3 problem with his network. Which of the following is associated with layer 3 in the OSI model?

A. IP addresses

B. TCP and UDP protocols

C. MAC addresses

D. Sending and receiving bits via hardware

9. Frank is responsible for ensuring that his organization has reliable, supported network hardware. Which of the following is not a common concern for network administrators as they work to ensure their network continues to be operational?

A. If the devices have vendor support

B. If the devices are under warranty

C. If major devices support redundant power supplies

D. If all devices support redundant power supplies

10. Brian is analyzing his network traffic and is focused on the variance of the delay between packets of data that are sent between two of his sites. What is he analyzing?

A. Latency

B. Jitter

C. Throughput

D. Signal-to-noise ratio

11. Which one of the following protocols is commonly used to provide back-end authentication services for a VPN?

A. HTTPS

B. RADIUS

C. ESP

D. AH

12. Isaac wants to ensure that his VoIP session initialization is secure. What protocol should he ensure is enabled and required?

   A. SVOIP

   B. PBSX

   C. SIPS

   D. SRTP

For questions 13–15, please refer to the following scenario and diagram:

Chris is designing layered network security for his organization.

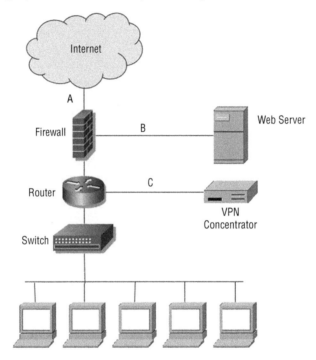

13. What type of firewall design is shown in the diagram?

   A. A single-tier firewall

   B. A two-tier firewall

   C. A three-tier firewall

   D. A four-tier firewall

14. If the VPN grants remote users the same access to network and system resources as local workstations have, what security issue should Chris raise?

   A. VPN users will not be able to access the web server.

   B. There is no additional security issue; the VPN concentrator's logical network location matches the logical network location of the workstations.

   C. Web server traffic is not subjected to stateful inspection.

   D. VPN users should only connect from managed PCs.

15. Chris wants to implement security controls in his data center at the level of individual services and workloads. He plans to use firewall rules and other controls as well as on-demand access to services as part of his security design. What design concept is he implementing?

   A. Converged protocols

   B. Physical segmentation

   C. Edge network-based design

   D. Micro-segmentation

16. As part of his segmentation approach, Chris also wants to segment network routes. What type of solution should he select?

   A. VPCs

   B. VRF

   C. VLANs

   D. A CDN

17. Ben has configured his network to not broadcast an SSID. Why might Ben disable SSID broadcast, and how could his SSID be discovered?

   A. Disabling SSID broadcast prevents attackers from discovering the encryption key. The SSID can be recovered from decrypted packets.

   B. Disabling SSID broadcast hides networks from unauthorized personnel. The SSID can be discovered using a wireless sniffer.

   C. Disabling SSID broadcast prevents issues with beacon frames. The SSID can be recovered by reconstructing the BSSID.

   D. Disabling SSID broadcast helps avoid SSID conflicts. The SSID can be discovered by attempting to connect to the network.

18. Chuck is in charge of a commercial data center that handles many customers who host their servers there. He wants to be able to configure his data center network to adjust to traffic pattern changes and to manage bandwidth and other options. What technology should he implement to allow central, programmatic control of his network?

   A. SDN

   B. SD-WAN

   C. Proxy routing

   D. Agile networking

19. Susan wants to access her company's SAN via Ethernet and knows that she can access it as a block-level storage device. What converged protocol is she most likely to use?

A. CXL

B. SDWAN

C. iSCSI

D. Zigbee

20. Melissa wants to leverage a cloud service provider's edge services. What will peering allow her to do in this scenario?

A. Ensure that a copy of any data stored in the cloud is also replicated in her local data center.

B. Provide a direct path from her on-premises network to the cloud provider's services.

C. Control traffic flows via software-defined routes.

D. Host copies of her sites at multiple locations hosted by her cloud computing service provider.

21. Jake wants to describe traffic sent between servers in his data center. What common terminology should he use to describe this?

A. North/South

B. Privilege/Unprivileged

C. East/West

D. Store/Forward

22. During a security assessment, Jim discovers that the organization he is working with uses a multilayer protocol to handle SCADA systems and recently connected the SCADA network to the rest of the organization's production network. What concern should he raise about serial data transfers carried via TCP/IP?

A. SCADA devices that are now connected to the network can be attacked over the network.

B. Serial data over TCP/IP cannot be encrypted.

C. Serial data cannot be carried in TCP packets.

D. TCP/IP's throughput can allow for easy denial-of-service attacks against serial devices.

23. Ben provides networking and security services for a small chain of coffee shops. The coffee shop chain wants to provide secure, free wireless for customers. Which of the following is the best option available to Ben to allow customers to connect securely to his wireless network without needing a user account if Ben does not need to worry about protocol support issues?

A. Use WPA2 in PSK mode.

B. Use WPA3 in SAE mode.

C. Use WPA2 in Enterprise mode.

D. Use a captive portal.

24. Alicia's company has implemented multifactor authentication using SMS messages to provide a numeric code. What is the primary security concern that Alicia may want to express about this design?

   A.   SMS messages are not encrypted.

   B.   SMS messages can be spoofed by senders.

   C.   SMS messages may be received by more than one phone.

   D.   SMS messages may be stored on the receiving phone.

25. What speed and frequency range are used by 802.11ac?

   A.   5 GHz only

   B.   900 MHz and 2.4 GHz

   C.   2.4 GHz and 5 GHz

   D.   2.4 GHz only

26. The Address Resolution Protocol (ARP) and the Reverse Address Resolution Protocol (RARP) operate at what layer of the OSI model?

   A.   Layer 1

   B.   Layer 2

   C.   Layer 3

   D.   Layer 4

27. Which of the following is a converged protocol that allows storage mounts over TCP, and which is frequently used as a lower-cost alternative to Fibre Channel?

   A.   MPLS

   B.   SDN

   C.   VoIP

   D.   iSCSI

28. Chris is building an Ethernet network and knows that he needs to span a distance of more than 150 meters with his 1000BaseT network. What network technology should he use to help with this?

   A.   Install a repeater, a switch, or a concentrator before 100 meters.

   B.   Use Category 7 cable, which has better shielding for higher speeds.

   C.   Install a gateway to handle the distance.

   D.   Use STP cable to handle the longer distance at high speeds.

For questions 29–31, please refer to the following scenario and diagram:

Selah's organization has used a popular messaging service for a number of years. Recently, concerns have been raised about the use of messaging.

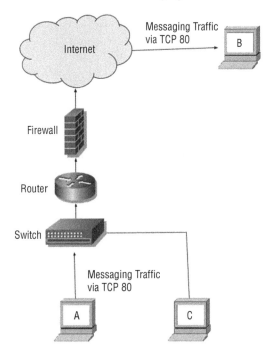

29. What protocol is the messaging traffic most likely to use based on the diagram?
    A. SLACK
    B. HTTP
    C. SMTP
    D. HTTPS

30. What security concern does sending internal communications from A to B raise?
    A. The firewall does not protect system B.
    B. System C can see the broadcast traffic from system A to B.
    C. It is traveling via an unencrypted protocol.
    D. Messaging does not provide nonrepudation.

31. How could Selah's company best address a desire for secure messaging for users of internal systems A and C?

    A. Use a third-party messaging service.

    B. Implement and use a locally hosted service.

    C. Use HTTPS.

    D. Discontinue use of messaging and instead use email, which is more secure.

32. Which of the following drawbacks is a concern when multilayer protocols are allowed?

    A. A range of protocols may be used at higher layers.

    B. Covert channels are allowed.

    C. Filters cannot be bypassed.

    D. Encryption can't be incorporated at multiple layers.

33. Which of the following is not an example of a converged protocol?

    A. MIME

    B. FCoE

    C. iSCSI

    D. VoIP

34. Chris uses a cellular hot spot to provide Internet access when he is traveling. If he leaves the hot spot connected to his PC while his PC is on his organization's corporate network, what security issue might he cause?

    A. Traffic may not be routed properly, exposing sensitive data.

    B. His system may act as a bridge from the Internet to the local network.

    C. His system may be a portal for a reflected DDoS attack.

    D. Security administrators may not be able to determine his IP address if a security issue occurs.

35. Sarah has been asked to improve the observability of her network. Which of the following is not a common step to improve observability?

    A. Aggregate and centralize data.

    B. Enable alerts for critical errors.

    C. Implement logging using a standardized format.

    D. Avoid feedback loops.

36. What features can IPsec provide for secure communication?

    A. Encryption, access control, nonrepudiation, and message authentication

    B. Protocol convergence, content distribution, micro-segmentation, and network virtualization

    C. Encryption, authorization, nonrepudiation, and message integrity checking

    D. Micro-segmentation, network virtualization, encryption, and message authentication

37. Casey has been asked to determine if Zigbee network traffic can be secured in transit. What security mechanism does Zigbee use to protect data traffic?

A. 3DES encryption

B. AES encryption

C. ROT13 encryption

D. Blowfish encryption

38. Sue modifies her MAC address to one that is allowed on a network that uses MAC filtering to provide security. What is the technique Sue used, and what nonsecurity issue could her actions cause?

A. Broadcast domain exploit, address conflict

B. Spoofing, token loss

C. Spoofing, address conflict

D. Sham EUI creation, token loss

39. Joanna wants to deploy 4G LTE as an out-of-band management solution for devices at remote sites. Which of the following security capabilities is not commonly available from 4G service providers?

A. Encryption capabilities

B. Device-based authentication

C. Dedicated towers and antennas for secure service subscribers

D. SIM-based authentication

40. SMTP, HTTP, and SNMP all occur at what layer of the OSI model?

A. Layer 4

B. Layer 5

C. Layer 6

D. Layer 7

41. Mark's organization hosts their infrastructure in a cloud IaaS environment. They operate in a private, isolated, and secure cloud that they configure. What term best describes this?

A. VLAN

B. VPC

C. SDN

D. CXL

42. Selah wants to provide port-based authentication on her network to ensure that clients must authenticate before using the network. What technology is an appropriate solution for this requirement?

A. 802.11a

B. 802.3

C. 802.15.1

D. 802.1x

43. Ben has deployed a 1000BaseT gigabit network and needs to run a cable across a large building. If Ben is running his link directly from a switch to another switch in that building, what is the maximum distance Ben can cover according to the 1000BaseT specification?

  A.   2 kilometers

  B.   500 meters

  C.   185 meters

  D.   100 meters

44. What security control does MAC cloning attempt to bypass for wired networks?

  A.   Port security

  B.   VLAN hopping

  C.   802.1q trunking

  D.   Etherkiller prevention

45. The company that Kathleen works for has moved to remote work for most employees and wants to ensure that the multimedia collaboration platform that they use for voice, video, and text-based collaboration is secure. Which of the following security options will provide the best user experience while providing appropriate security for communications?

  A.   Require software-based VPN to the corporate network for all use of the collaboration platform.

  B.   Require the use of SIPS and SRTP for all communications.

  C.   Use TLS for all traffic for the collaboration platform.

  D.   Deploy secure VPN endpoints to each remote location and use a point-to-point VPN for communications.

46. Chris wants to use a low-power, personal area network (PAN) wireless protocol for a device he is designing. Which of the following wireless protocols is best suited to creating small, low-power devices that can connect to each other at relatively short distances across buildings or rooms?

  A.   Wi-Fi

  B.   Zigbee

  C.   NFC

  D.   Infrared

47. Olga wants to provide out-of-band management for her SCADA devices, which are deployed across her organization's large physical infrastructure in multiple distinct production facilities. Which of the following is an appropriate solution to meet her needs?

  A.   Administrative access via a web client installed on each system that requires Windows-based domain authentication

  B.   Administrative access via nonstandard ports using a secure protocol like SSH

  C.   Administrative access via a second, physically separate Ethernet network with access controlled via VPN and multifactor authentication

  D.   Administrative access via physical access to the devices when needed

48. Cameron is worried about distributed denial-of-service attacks against his company's primary web application. Which of the following options will provide the most resilience against large-scale DDoS attacks?

   A. A CDN

   B. Increasing the number of servers in the web application server cluster

   C. Contract for DDoS mitigation services via the company's ISP

   D. Increasing the amount of bandwidth available from one or more ISPs

49. There are four common VPN protocols. Which group listed contains all of the common VPN protocols?

   A. PPTP, LTP, L2TP, IPsec

   B. PPP, L2TP, IPsec, VNC

   C. PPTP, L2F, L2TP, IPsec

   D. PPTP, L2TP, IPsec, SPAP

50. Wayne wants to deploy a secure voice communication network. Which of the following techniques should he consider? (Select all that apply.)

   A. Use a dedicated VLAN for VoIP phones and devices.

   B. Require the use of SIPS and SRTP.

   C. Require the use of VPN for all remote VoIP devices.

   D. Implement a VoIP IPS.

51. Which OSI layer includes electrical specifications, protocols, and interface standards?

   A. The Transport layer

   B. The Device layer

   C. The Physical layer

   D. The Data Link layer

52. Ben is designing a Wi-Fi network and has been asked to choose the most secure option for the network. Which wireless security standard should he choose?

   A. WPA2

   B. WPA

   C. WEP

   D. WPA3

53. What mode of switching is best suited to low-latency, high-throughput data transfer?

   A. Store-and-forward switching

   B. Blind switching

   C. Forward switching

   D. Cut-through switching

54. Segmentation, sequencing, and error checking all occur at what layer of the OSI model that is associated with SSL, TLS, and UDP?

A. The Transport layer

B. The Network layer

C. The Session layer

D. The Presentation layer

55. The Windows `ipconfig` command displays the following information:

`BC-5F-F4-7B-4B-7D`

What term describes this, and what information can usually be gathered from it?

A. The IP address, the network location of the system

B. The MAC address, the network interface card's manufacturer

C. The MAC address, the media type in use

D. The IPv6 client ID, the network interface card's manufacturer

56. Chris wants to ensure that traffic sent via his backhaul networks provided by third-party telecom providers is secure. Which of the following options is best suited to ensuring that all traffic sent through the connection is secure?

A. Use TLS for all web services.

B. Use an on-demand, client-based VPN.

C. Use a point-to-point VPN.

D. Tunnel traffic via SSH.

57. Ben is troubleshooting a network and discovers that the NAT router he is connected to has the 192.168.x.x subnet as its internal network and that its external IP is 192.168.1.40. What problem is he encountering?

A. 192.168.x.x is a nonroutable network and will not be carried to the Internet.

B. 192.168.1.40 is not a valid address because it is reserved by RFC 1918.

C. Double NATing is not possible using the same IP range.

D. The upstream system is unable to de-encapsulate his packets, and he needs to use PAT instead.

58. What is the default subnet mask for a Class B network?

A. 255.0.0.0

B. 255.255.0.0

C. 255.254.0.0

D. 255.255.255.0

59. Kim wants to protect her Zoom meetings from Zoom bombing. What security option should she enable?

    A. Require HTTPS connections.

    B. Turn on the waiting room.

    C. Randomize meeting links.

    D. Require a meeting passcode.

60. Olivia wants to use a network fault management tool that can provide real-time fault detection. What capabilities are most commonly associated with this type of monitoring?

    A. SNMP and ICMP-based monitoring and diagnostic data retrieval

    B. Netflow and syslog-based monitoring

    C. SNMP and Netflow-based monitoring

    D. ICMP and syslog-based monitoring

61. Selah's organization has deployed VoIP phones on the same switches that the desktop PCs are on. What security issue could this create, and what solution would help?

    A. VLAN hopping; use physically separate switches.

    B. VLAN hopping; use encryption.

    C. Caller ID spoofing; MAC filtering.

    D. Denial-of-service attacks; use a firewall between networks.

For questions 62–65, please refer to the following scenario:

Susan is designing her organization's new network infrastructure for a branch office.

62. Susan wants to use a set of nonroutable IP addresses for the location's internal network addresses. Using your knowledge of secure network design principles and IP networking, which of the following IP ranges are usable for that purpose? (Select all that apply.)

    A. 172.16.0.0/12

    B. 192.168.0.0/16

    C. 128.192.0.0/24

    D. 10.0.0.0/8

63. Susan knows that she will need to implement a Wi-Fi network for her customers and wants to gather information about the customers, such as their email address, without having to provide them with a wireless network password or key. What type of solution would provide this combination of features?

    A. NAC

    B. A captive portal

    C. Pre-shared keys

    D. WPA3's SAE mode

64. With her wireless network set up, Susan moves on to ensuring that her network will remain operational even if disruptions occur. What is the simplest way she can ensure that her network devices, including her router, access points, and network switches, stay on if a brownout or other temporary power issue occurs?

A. Purchase and install a generator with an automatic start.

B. Deploy dual power supplies for all network devices.

C. Install UPS systems to cover all network devices that must remain online.

D. Contract with multiple different power companies for redundant power.

65. Susan wants to provide 100 gigabit network connections to devices in the facility where the new branch will operate. What connectivity options does she have for structured wiring that can meet those speeds? (Select all that apply.)

A. Cat5e

B. Fiber

C. Cat6

D. Coaxial cable

66. Data streams occur at what three layers of the OSI model?

A. Application, Presentation, and Session

B. Presentation, Session, and Transport

C. Physical, Data Link, and Network

D. Data Link, Network, and Transport

67. Lucca wants to protect endpoints that are in production use but that are no longer supported and cannot be patched from network attacks. What should he do to best protect these devices?

A. Install a firewall on the device.

B. Disable all services and open ports on the devices.

C. Place a hardware network security device in front of the devices.

D. Unplug the devices from the network because they cannot be properly secured.

68. Selah's networking team has been asked to identify a technology that will allow them to separate the routing process for the network from the packet switching process while increasing centralization?

A. A network that follows the 5-4-3 rule

B. A converged network

C. A software-defined network

D. A hypervisor-based network

69. Jason knows that protocols using the OSI model rely on encapsulation as data moves from layer to layer. What is added at each layer as data flows up the OSI layers such as from layer 3 to 4 and layer 4 to 5?

A. Information is added to the header.

B. Information is added to the main body of the data.

C. The data is encrypted with a new secret key.

D. A security envelope that provides perfect forward secrecy.

70. During a troubleshooting process, the support technician that Alyssa is talking to states that the problem is a layer 3 problem. Which of the following possible issues is not a layer 3 problem?

A. A TTL mismatch

B. An MTU mismatch

C. An incorrect ACL

D. A broken network cable

71. During a review of her organization's network, Angela discovered that it was suffering from broadcast storms and that contractors, guests, and organizational administrative staff were on the same network segment. What design change should Angela recommend?

A. Require encryption for all users.

B. Install a firewall at the network border.

C. Enable spanning tree loop detection.

D. Segment the network based on functional requirements.

72. Lisa wants to explain the difference between network throughput and bandwidth to her team. Which of the following best describes the difference between the two terms?

A. Bandwidth describes the number of parallel data channels available to a network, and throughput describes how many can be used at once.

B. Bandwidth is the maximum amount of data that can be sent via a channel or connection, and throughput is the actual amount of data that is sent via the channel or connection in a given period of time.

C. Bandwidth and throughput are the same and can be used interchangeably.

D. Bandwidth is a measure of the amount of data sent over a given period of time, and throughput is the maximum amount of data that could be sent via the channel.

For questions 73–75, please refer to the following scenario:

Ben is an information security professional at an organization that is replacing its physical servers with cloud-hosted virtual machines. As the organization builds its virtual environment, it is moving toward a hybrid cloud operational model with some systems and services remaining in its local data center and others hosted in the cloud. The following diagram shows the local data center and cloud VPC's network IP ranges, which you should consider as you answer the questions.

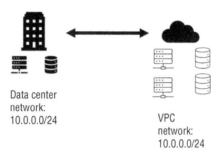

Data center
network:
10.0.0.0/24

VPC
network:
10.0.0.0/24

73. Ben wants to ensure that the instance-to-instance (system-to-system) traffic in his cloud-hosted infrastructure-as-a-service environment is secure. What can he do to fully ensure that the virtualized network traffic is not being captured and analyzed?

   A. Prevent the installation of a packet sniffer on all hosts.

   B. Disable promiscuous mode for all virtual network interfaces.

   C. Disallow the use of any virtual taps.

   D. Encrypt all traffic between hosts.

74. What issue is most likely to occur due to the subnets configured for the data center and VPC?

   A. IP address conflicts

   B. Routing loops

   C. MAC address conflicts

   D. All of the above

75. Ben wants to use multiple Internet service providers (ISPs) to connect to his cloud VPC to ensure reliable access and bandwidth. What technology can he use to manage and optimize those connections?

   A. FCoE

   B. VXLAN

   C. SD-WAN

   D. LiFi

76. Traffic entering and leaving a network through a WAN link is often described as what sort of traffic?

A. Foreign/domestic

B. North/south

C. East/west

D. Trusted/untrusted

77. What converged protocol is designed to allow high-speed communication to devices like CPUs, GPUs, and accelerators?

A. CXL

B. VoIP

C. CDN

D. iSCSI

78. Mark is concerned about the physical security of his network cables. What type of network connection would be the hardest to tap without specialized equipment?

A. Wi-Fi

B. Bluetooth

C. Cat5/Cat6 twisted pair

D. Fiber optic

79. Rich wants to connect his network to a building a half-mile away from his current location. There are trees and terrain features along the way, but a road passes between the trees to the other location. What type of transmission media is best suited to this type of deployment?

A. Ethernet cable with repeaters every 200 to 300 yards

B. A Wi-Fi directional antenna

C. Fiber-optic cable

D. A LiFi system

80. What challenge is most common for endpoint security system deployments?

A. Compromises

B. The volume of data

C. Monitoring encrypted traffic on the network

D. Handling non-TCP protocols

81. What type of address is 127.0.0.1?

A. A public IP address

B. An RFC 1918 address

C. An APIPA address

D. A loopback address

82. Susan is writing a best practices statement for her organizational users who need to use Bluetooth. She knows that there are many potential security issues with Bluetooth and wants to provide the best advice she can. Which of the following sets of guidance should Susan include?

    A. Use Bluetooth's built-in strong encryption, change the default PIN on your device, turn off discovery mode, and turn off Bluetooth when it's not in active use.

    B. Use Bluetooth only for those activities that are not confidential, change the default PIN on your device, turn off discovery mode, and turn off Bluetooth when it's not in active use.

    C. Use Bluetooth's built-in strong encryption, use extended (eight digits or longer) Bluetooth PINs, turn off discovery mode, and turn off Bluetooth when it's not in active use.

    D. Use Bluetooth only for those activities that are not confidential, use extended (eight digits or longer) Bluetooth PINs, turn off discovery mode, and turn off Bluetooth when it's not in active use.

83. What type of networking device is most commonly used to assign endpoint systems to VLANs?

    A. Firewall

    B. Router

    C. Switch

    D. Hub

84. Srini is building a high-performance computing cluster that requires very high bandwidth and very low latency. What converged protocol is he most likely to select for this purpose?

    A. iSCSI

    B. VoIP

    C. Infiniband over Ethernet

    D. CXL

85. Michelle is told that the organization that she is joining uses an SD-WAN controller architecture to manage their WAN connections. What can she assume about how the network is managed and controlled? (Select all that apply.)

    A. The network uses predefined rules to optimize performance.

    B. The network conducts continuous monitoring to support better performance.

    C. The network uses self-learning techniques to respond to changes in the network.

    D. All connections are managed by the organization's primary Internet service provider.

86. Which of the following shows the layers of the OSI model in correct order, from layer 1 to layer 7? Place the layers of the OSI model shown here in the appropriate order, from layer 1 to layer 7.

    A. Layer 1 = Data Link; Layer 2 = Physical; Layer 3 = Network; Layer 4 = Transport; Layer 5 = Session; Layer 6 = Presentation; Layer 7 = Applications

    B. Layer 1 = Physical; Layer 2 = Data Link; Layer 3 = Network; Layer 4 = Transport; Layer 5 = Session; Layer 6 = Presentation; Layer 7 = Applications

    C. Layer 1 = Physical; Layer 2 = Data Link; Layer 3 = Network; Layer 4 = Transport; Layer 5 = Session; Layer 6 = Applications; Layer 7 = Presentation

    D. Layer 1 = Physical; Layer 2 = Data Link; Layer 3 = Network; Layer 4 = Session; Layer 5 = Transport; Layer 6 = Presentation; Layer 7 = Applications

87. Valerie enables port security on the switches on her network. What type of attack is she most likely trying to prevent?

    A. IP spoofing

    B. MAC aggregation

    C. CAM table flooding

    D. VLAN hopping

88. Alaina wants to ensure that systems are compliant with her network security settings before they are allowed on the network and wants to ensure that she can test and validate system settings as soon as possible. What type of NAC system should she deploy?

    A. A pre-admit, clientless NAC system

    B. A postadmission, client-based NAC system

    C. A pre-admit, client-based NAC system

    D. A postadmission, clientless NAC system

89. Derek wants to deploy redundant core routers, as shown in the diagram. What model of high availability clustering will provide him with the greatest throughput?

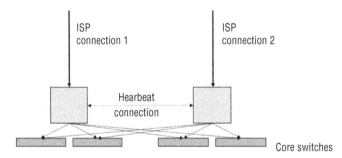

    A. Active/active

    B. Line interactive

    C. Active/passive

    D. Nearline

90. Angela needs access to manage IoT devices at multiple sites that her organization manages. What solution should she suggest to ensure access and security for the devices?

A. VPNs to protected VLANs

B. An IDS located at the network edge protecting a network using only private IP addresses

C. A DLP system configured to prevent attacks against IoT devices

D. An iSCSI-based security solution accessed using a VPN and jump boxes

91. What is a frequent concern for systems that require high-performing Internet connectivity when satellite Internet is the only available option?

A. Security

B. Compatibility with protocols like LiFi

C. Compatibility with protocols like Zigbee

D. Latency

92. What layer of an SDN implementation uses programs to communicate needs for resources via APIs?

A. The data plane

B. The control plane

C. The application plane

D. The monitoring plane

93. Which of the following is not a drawback of multilayer protocols?

A. They can allow filters and rules to be bypassed.

B. They can operate at higher OSI levels.

C. They can allow covert channels.

D. They can allow network segment boundaries to be bypassed.

94. Place the following layers of the TCP/IP model in order, starting with the Application layer and moving down the stack.

1. Application layer

2. Network Access layer

3. Internet layer

4. Transport layer

A. 1, 2, 3, 4

B. 1, 4, 2, 3

C. 1, 4, 3, 2

D. 4, 1, 3, 2

95. Aadita's company wants to ensure that their website is highly available and resistant to potential denial-of-service attacks. What type of solution would be best suited to this if the company operates an e-commerce site that serves multiple countries and regions with a very large number of customers?

   A. A load-balanced web server cluster

   B. A CDN

   C. Micro-segmentation of virtual servers

   D. A VPC

96. What are two primary advantages that 5G networks have over 4G networks? (Select all that apply.)

   A. Anti-jamming features

   B. Enhanced subscriber identity protection

   C. Mutual authentication capabilities

   D. Multifactor authentication

97. What function does VXLAN perform in a data center environment? (Select all that apply.)

   A. It removes limitations due to maximum distance for Ethernet cables.

   B. It allows multiple subnets to exist in the same IP space with hosts using the same IP addresses.

   C. It tunnels layer 2 connections over a layer 3 network, stretching them across the underlying layer 3 network.

   D. All of the above.

98. Chris is setting up a hotel network and needs to ensure that systems in each room or suite can connect to each other, but systems in other suites or rooms cannot. At the same time, he needs to ensure that all systems in the hotel can reach the Internet. What solution should he recommend as the most effective business solution?

   A. Per-room VPNs

   B. VLANs

   C. Port security

   D. Firewalls

99. During a forensic investigation, Charles is able to determine the Media Access Control (MAC) address of a system that was connected to a compromised network. Charles knows that MAC addresses are tied back to a manufacturer or vendor and are part of the fingerprint of the system. To which OSI layer does a MAC address belong?

   A. The Application layer

   B. The Session layer

   C. The Physical layer

   D. The Data Link layer

100. Mikayla is reviewing her organization's VoIP environment configuration and finds a diagram that shows the following design. What concern should she express?

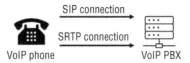

SIP connection

SRTP connection

VoIP phone   VoIP PBX

    A. The voice connection is unencrypted and could be listened to.

    B. There are no security issues in this diagram.

    C. The session initialization connection is unencrypted and could be viewed.

    D. Both the session initialization and voice data connection are unencrypted and could be captured and analyzed.

101. Jake's company keeps their certificate signing server disconnected from the network to prevent it from being compromised by network attacks. What is this type of solution called?

    A. Store-and-forward

    B. Out-of-band

    C. In-band

    D. Air-gapping

Chapter

5

Identity and Access Management (Domain 5)

SUBDOMAINS

✓ **5.1 Control physical and logical access to assets**

✓ **5.2 Design identification and authentication strategy (e.g., people, devices, and services)**

✓ **5.3 Federated identity with a third-party service**

✓ **5.4 Implement and manage authorization mechanisms**

✓ **5.5 Manage the identity and access provisioning lifecycle**

✓ **5.6 Implement authentication systems**

1. Henry uses his organizationally provided credentials to log into his workstation and is then able to use services across the organization and in the cloud. What identity solution has his organization implemented?

   A. An access control list

   B. Single sign-on

   C. Multifactor authentication

   D. Role-based access control

2. Jim's organization-wide implementation of IDaaS offers broad support for cloud-based applications. Jim's company does not have internal identity management staff and does not use centralized identity services. Instead, they rely upon Active Directory for AAA services. Which of the following options should Jim recommend to best handle the company's on-site identity needs?

   A. Integrate on-site systems using OAuth.

   B. Use an on-premises third-party identity service.

   C. Integrate on-site systems using SAML.

   D. Design an internal solution to handle the organization's unique needs.

3. What role does a policy enforcement point play in a zero trust environment?

   A. It makes decisions for the policy engine.

   B. It is the workstation or mobile device used by the end user.

   C. It deploys role-based access controls based on local policy.

   D. It receives authorization requests and sends them to the policy decision point.

4. Voice pattern recognition is what type of authentication factor?

   A. Something you know

   B. Something you have

   C. Something you are

   D. Somewhere you are

5. If Susan's organization requires her to log in with her username, a PIN, a password, and a retina scan, how many distinct authentication factor types has she used?

   A. One

   B. Two

   C. Three

   D. Four

6. Charles wants to deploy a credential management system (CMS). He wants to keep the keys as secure as possible. Which of the following is the best design option for his CMS implementation?

   A. Use AES-256 instead of 3DES.

   B. Use long keys.

   C. Use an HSM.

   D. Change passphrases regularly.

7. Brian is a researcher at a major university. As part of his research, he logs into a computing cluster hosted at another institution using his own university's credentials. Once logged in, he is able to access the cluster and use resources based on his role in a research project, as well as using resources and services in his home organization. What has Brian's home university implemented to make this happen?

   A. Domain stacking

   B. Federated identity management

   C. Domain nesting

   D. Hybrid login

8. When Sally attempts to authenticate to her organization's services, she knows that the organization uses a mobile device management tool to check her location and whether she's logging in from her company-issued mobile device. What type of authentication is this?

   A. Context-aware

   B. Knowledge-based

   C. Identity factoring

   D. Zero trust

9. What major issue often results from decentralized access control?

   A. Access outages may occur.

   B. Control is not consistent.

   C. Control is too granular.

   D. Training costs are high.

10. Callback to a landline phone number is an example of what type of factor?

   A. Something you know

   B. Somewhere you are

   C. Something you have

   D. Something you are

11. What common behavior drives the NIST recommendation that passwords should not expire?

    A. Attackers would not have enough time to compromise passwords if they expired.

    B. Users often make minimal changes to passwords to handle change requirements.

    C. Password expiration leads to too little support overhead.

    D. Re-hashing passwords when changes are required is computationally intensive.

12. What three functions make up the AAA model?

    A. Access control, authentication, and authorization

    B. Access, administration, and authorization

    C. Authentication, authorization, and accounting

    D. Accounting, auditing, and assessment

13. What directory-based technology underlies Microsoft Active Directory single sign-on?

    A. LDAP

    B. zero trust

    C. Shibboleth

    D. RADIUS

14. Sameer's organization needs to perform identity proofing for new customers. What type of authentication is best suited to identity proofing in this scenario?

    A. Cognitive passwords

    B. Knowledge-based authentication

    C. Palm scans

    D. USB tokens

15. What type of access controls allow the owner of a file to grant other users access to it using an access control list?

    A. Role-based

    B. Nondiscretionary

    C. Rule-based

    D. Discretionary

16. Alex's job requires him to see protected health information (PHI) to ensure proper treatment of patients. His access to their medical records does not provide access to patient addresses or billing information. What access control concept best describes this control?

    A. Separation of duties

    B. Constrained interfaces

    C. Context-dependent control

    D. Need to know

For questions 17–19, please use your knowledge of password policies and their application.

17. Ifemoa wants to ensure that users in her organization cannot change their password to a previously used password. What setting should she configure?

   A. Password length

   B. Maximum password age

   C. An MFA requirement

   D. Password history

18. With a password history set, Ifeoma wants to prevent users from resetting their password multiple times to allow them to return to their original password. What setting should she apply?

   A. A password complexity requirement

   B. A maximum password age

   C. A minimum password age

   D. A password length requirement

19. With her organization's password behavior under control, Ifeoma wants to ensure that a lost password will not result in easy compromise of her company's accounts. Which of the following controls provides the best protection against password loss or exposure-related compromise?

   A. MFA

   B. SSO

   C. Federation

   D. Password rotation

20. Jacob is planning his organization's biometric authentication system and is considering retina scans. What concern may be raised about retina scans by others in his organization?

   A. Retina scans can reveal information about medical conditions.

   B. Retina scans are painful because they require a puff of air in the user's eye.

   C. Retina scanners are the most expensive type of biometric device.

   D. Retina scanners have a high false positive rate and will cause support issues.

21. Mandatory access control is based on what type of model?

   A. Discretionary

   B. Group-based

   C. Lattice-based

   D. Rule-based

22. Greg wants to control access to iPads used throughout his organization as point-of-sale terminals. Which of the following methods should he use to allow logical access control for the devices in a shared environment?

    A. Use a shared PIN for all point-of-sale terminals to make them easier to use.

    B. Use OAuth to allow cloud logins for each user.

    C. Issue a unique PIN to each user for the iPad they are issued.

    D. Use Active Directory and user accounts for logins to the iPads using the AD user ID and password.

23. What is the best way to provide accountability for the use of identities?

    A. Logging

    B. Authorization

    C. Digital signatures

    D. Type 1 authentication

24. Jim has worked in human relations, payroll, and customer service roles in his company over the past few years. What type of process should his company perform to ensure that he has appropriate rights?

    A. Re-provisioning

    B. Account review

    C. Privilege creep

    D. Account revocation

25. Biba is what type of access control model?

    A. MAC

    B. DAC

    C. Role BAC

    D. ABAC

26. Which of the following is a client-server protocol designed to allow network access servers to authenticate remote users by sending access request messages to a central server?

    A. Kerberos

    B. EAP

    C. RADIUS

    D. OAuth

27. Henry is working with a web application development team on their authentication and authorization process for his company's new application. The team wants to make session IDs as secure as possible. Which of the following is not a best practice that Henry should recommend?

   A. The session ID token should be predictable.

   B. The session ID should have at least 64 bits of entropy.

   C. The session length should be at least 128 bits.

   D. The session ID should be meaningless.

28. Angela uses her smartphone's built-in biometric authentication and an application provided by her employer to log into her account. What type of authentication has she used?

   A. Extended

   B. Passwordless

   C. Alternative

   D. SPOT

29. What type of access control best describes NAC's posture assessment capability?

   A. A mandatory access control

   B. A risk-based access control

   C. A discretionary access control

   D. A role-based access control

30. When an application or system allows a logged-in user to perform specific actions, it is an example of what?

   A. Roles

   B. Group management

   C. Logins

   D. Authorization

31. Alex has been employed by his company for more than a decade and has held a number of positions in the company. During an audit, it is discovered that he has access to shared folders and applications because of his former roles. What issue has Alex's company encountered?

   A. Excessive provisioning

   B. Unauthorized access

   C. Privilege creep

   D. Account review

32. Geoff wants to prevent privilege escalation attacks in his organization. Which of the following practices is most likely to prevent horizontal privilege escalation?

    A. Multifactor authentication

    B. Limiting permissions for groups and accounts

    C. Disabling unused ports and services

    D. Sanitizing user inputs to applications

33. Jim's Microsoft Exchange environment includes servers that are located in local data centers at multiple business offices around the world as well as an Office 365 deployment for employees who are not located at one of those offices. Identities are created and used in both environments and will work in both. What type of federated system is Jim running?

    A. A primary cloud system

    B. A primary on-premises system

    C. A hybrid system

    D. A multitenant system

34. What type of access control scheme is shown in the following table?

Highly Sensitive	Red	Blue	Green
Confidential	Purple	Orange	Yellow
Internal Use	Black	Gray	White
Public	Clear	Clear	Clear

    A. RBAC

    B. DAC

    C. MAC

    D. TBAC

35. Michelle's company is creating a new division by splitting the marketing and communications departments into two separate groups. She wants to create roles that provide access to resources used by each group. What should she do to maintain the appropriate security and rights for each group?

    A. Put both the marketing and communications teams into the existing group because they will have similar access requirements.

    B. Keep the marketing team in the existing group and create a new communications group based on their specific needs.

    C. Keep the communications' team in the existing group and create a new marketing group based on their specific needs.

    D. Create two new groups, assess which rights they need to perform their roles, and then add additional rights if required.

36. When a subject claims an identity, what process is occurring?

   A. Login

   B. Identification

   C. Authorization

   D. Token presentation

37. Which of the following is a common account setting for a service account?

   A. Disable password expiration.

   B. Set maximum password age to 90 days.

   C. Set minimum password age to 1 day.

   D. Disable complexity requirements.

38. Susan's organization is updating its password policy and wants to use the strongest possible passwords. What password requirement will have the highest impact in preventing brute-force attacks?

   A. Change the maximum age from 1 year to 180 days.

   B. Increase the minimum password length from 8 characters to 16 characters.

   C. Increase the password complexity so that at least three character classes (such as uppercase, lowercase, numbers, and symbols) are required.

   D. Retain a password history of at least four passwords to prevent reuse.

39. Alaina is performing a regularly scheduled review for service accounts. Which of the following events should she be most concerned about?

   A. An interactive login for the service account

   B. A password change for the service account

   C. Limitations placed on the service account's rights

   D. Local use of the service account

40. When might an organization using biometrics choose to allow a higher FRR instead of a higher FAR?

   A. When security is more important than usability

   B. When false rejection is not a concern due to data quality

   C. When the CER of the system is not known

   D. When the CER of the system is very high

41. After recent reports of undesired access to workstations after hours, Derek has been asked to find a way to ensure that maintenance staff cannot log into workstations in business offices. The maintenance staff members do have systems in their break rooms and their offices for the organization, which they still need access to. What should Derek do to meet this need?

A. Require multifactor authentication and allow only office staff to have multifactor tokens.

B. Use rule-based access control to prevent logins after hours in the business area.

C. Use role-based access control by setting up a group that contains all maintenance staff and then give that group rights to log into only the designated workstations.

D. Use geofencing to only allow logins in maintenance areas.

42. Nick wants to do session management for his web application. Which of the following are common web application session management techniques or methods? (Select all that apply.)

A. IP tracking

B. Cookies

C. URL rewriting

D. TLS tokens

For questions 43–45, please use your knowledge of SAML integrations and security architecture design and refer to the following scenario and diagram:

Alex is in charge of SAML integration with a major third-party partner that provides a variety of business productivity services for his organization.

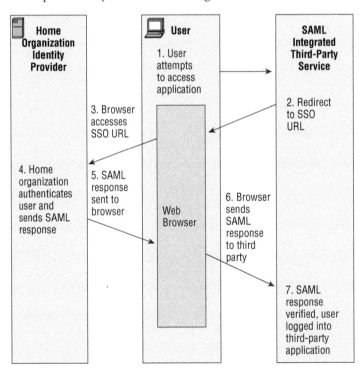

43. Alex is concerned about eavesdropping on the SAML traffic and also wants to ensure that forged assertions will not be successful. What should he do to prevent these potential attacks?

   A. Use SAML's secure mode to provide secure authentication.

   B. Implement TLS using a strong cipher suite, which will protect against both types of attacks.

   C. Implement TLS using a strong cipher suite and use digital signatures.

   D. Implement TLS using a strong cipher suite and message hashing.

44. If Alex's organization is one that is primarily made up of off-site, traveling users, what availability risk does integration of critical business applications to on-site authentication create, and how could he solve it?

   A. Third-party integration may not be trustworthy; use SSL and digital signatures.

   B. If the home organization is offline, traveling users won't be able to access third-party applications; implement a hybrid cloud/local authentication system.

   C. Local users may not be properly redirected to the third-party services; implement a local gateway.

   D. Browsers may not properly redirect; use host files to ensure that issues with redirects are resolved.

45. What solution can best help address concerns about third parties that control SSO redirects as shown in step 2 in the diagram?

   A. An awareness campaign about trusted third parties

   B. TLS

   C. Handling redirects at the local site

   D. Implementing an IPS to capture SSO redirect attacks

46. Susan has been asked to recommend whether her organization should use a MAC scheme or a DAC scheme. If flexibility and scalability are important requirements for implementing access controls, which scheme should she recommend and why?

   A. MAC, because it provides greater scalability and flexibility because you can simply add more labels as needed

   B. DAC, because allowing individual administrators to make choices about the objects they control provides scalability and flexibility

   C. MAC, because compartmentalization is well suited to flexibility and adding compartments will allow it to scale well

   D. DAC, because a central decision process allows quick responses and will provide scalability by reducing the number of decisions required and flexibility by moving those decisions to a central authority

47. Which of the following tools is not typically used to verify that a provisioning process was followed in a way that ensures that the organization's security policy is being followed?

   A. Log review

   B. Manual review of permissions

   C. Signature-based detection

   D. Review the audit trail

48. Jessica wants to adopt an open standard to provide authentication, authorization, and attribute information as part of her cloud identity federation efforts. What standard should she adopt to leverage the flexibility of XML as part of her efforts?

   A. SAML

   B. SOAP

   C. OAuth

   D. OpenID Connect

49. During a penetration test, Chris recovers a file containing hashed passwords for the system he is attempting to access. What type of attack is most likely to succeed against the hashed passwords?

   A. A brute-force attack

   B. A pass-the-hash attack

   C. A rainbow table attack

   D. A salt recovery attack

50. Google's identity integration with a variety of organizations and applications across domains is an example of which of the following?

   A. PKI

   B. Federation

   C. Single sign-on

   D. Provisioning

51. Amanda starts at her new job and finds that she has access to a variety of systems that she does not need to accomplish her job. What problem has she encountered?

   A. Privilege creep

   B. Rights collision

   C. Least privilege

   D. Excessive privileges

52. When Chris verifies an individual's identity and adds a unique identifier like a user ID to an identity system, what process has occurred?

   A. Identity proofing

   B. Registration

   C. Directory management

   D. Session management

53. Selah wants to provide accountability for actions performed via her organization's main line-of-business application. What controls are most frequently used to provide accountability in a situation like this? (Select all that apply.)

A. Enable audit logging.

B. Provide every staff member with a unique account and enable multifactor authentication.

C. Enable time- and location-based login requirements.

D. Provide every staff member with a unique account and require a self-selected password.

54. Charles wants to provide authorization services as part of his web application. What standard should he use if he wants to integrate easily with other web identity providers?

A. OpenID

B. TACACS+

C. RADIUS

D. OAuth

55. The company that Cameron works for uses a system that allows users to request privileged access to systems when necessary. Cameron requests access, and the request is pre-approved due to his role. He is then able to access the system to perform the task. Once he is done, the rights are removed. What type of system is he using?

A. Zero trust

B. Federated identity management

C. Single sign-on

D. Just-in-time access

56. Elle is responsible for building a banking website. She needs proof of the identity of the users who register for the site. How should she validate user identities?

A. Require users to create unique questions that only they will know.

B. Require new users to bring their driver's license or passport in person to the bank.

C. Use information that both the bank and the user have such as questions pulled from their credit report.

D. Call the user on their registered phone number to verify that they are who they claim to be.

57. Susan's organization is part of a federation that allows users from multiple organizations to access resources and services at other federated sites. When Susan wants to use a service at a partner site, which identity provider is used?

A. Susan's home organization's identity provider.

B. The service provider's identity provider.

C. Both their identity provider and the service provider's identity provider.

D. The service provider creates a new identity.

58. A new customer at a bank that uses fingerprint scanners to authenticate its users is surprised when he scans his fingerprint and is logged into another customer's account. What type of biometric factor error occurred?

- **A.** A registration error
- **B.** A Type 1 error
- **C.** A Type 2 error
- **D.** A time of use, method of use error

59. What type of access control is typically used by firewalls?

- **A.** Discretionary access controls
- **B.** Rule-based access controls
- **C.** Task-based access control
- **D.** Mandatory access controls

60. When you input a user ID and password, you are performing what important identity and access management activity?

- **A.** Authorization
- **B.** Validation
- **C.** Authentication
- **D.** Login

61. Kathleen works for a data center hosting facility that provides physical data center space for individuals and organizations. Until recently, each client was given a magnetic-strip-based keycard to access the section of the facility where their servers are located, and they were also given a key to access the cage or rack where their servers reside. In the past month, a number of servers have been stolen, but the logs for the passcards show only valid IDs. What is Kathleen's best option to make sure that the users of the passcards are who they are supposed to be?

- **A.** Add a reader that requires a PIN for passcard users.
- **B.** Add a camera system to the facility to observe who is accessing servers.
- **C.** Add a biometric factor.
- **D.** Replace the magnetic stripe keycards with smartcards.

62. Theresa wants to allow her staff to securely store and manage passwords for systems including service accounts and other rarely used administrative credentials. What type of tool should she implement to enable this?

- **A.** Single sign-on
- **B.** A federated identity system
- **C.** A password vault
- **D.** A multifactor authentication system

63. Olivia wants to limit the commands that a user can run via `sudo` to limit the potential for privilege escalation attacks. What Linux file should she modify to allow this?

    A. The bash `.bin` configuration file

    B. The `sudoers` file

    C. The bash `.allowed` configuration file

    D. The `sudont` file

64. Which objects and subjects have a label in a MAC model?

    A. Objects and subjects that are classified as Confidential, Secret, or Top Secret have a label.

    B. All objects have a label, and all subjects have a compartment.

    C. All objects and subjects have a label.

    D. All subjects have a label and all objects have a compartment.

For questions 65–67, please refer to the following scenario and diagram:

Chris is the identity architect for a growing e-commerce website that wants to leverage social identity. To do this, he and his team intend to allow users to use their existing Google accounts as their primary accounts when using the e-commerce site. This means that when a new user initially connects to the e-commerce platform, they are given the choice between using their Google account using OAuth 2.0 or creating a new account on the platform using their own email address and a password of their choice.

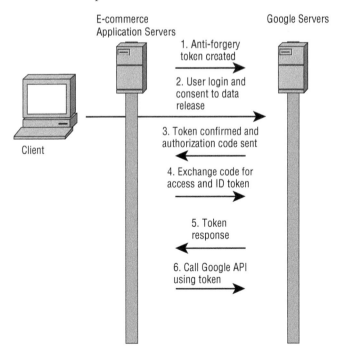

65. When the e-commerce application creates an account for a Google user, where should that user's password be stored?

    A. The password is stored in the e-commerce application's database.

    B. The password is stored in memory on the e-commerce application's server.

    C. The password is stored in Google's account management system.

    D. The password is never stored; instead, a salted hash is stored in Google's account management system.

66. Which of the following is responsible for user authentication for Google users?

    A. The e-commerce application.

    B. Both the e-commerce application and Google servers.

    C. Google servers.

    D. The diagram does not provide enough information to determine this.

67. What type of attack is the creation and exchange of state tokens intended to prevent?

    A. XSS

    B. CSRF

    C. SQL injection

    D. XACML

68. Questions like "What is your pet's name?" are examples of what type of identity proofing?

    A. Knowledge-based authentication

    B. Dynamic knowledge-based authentication

    C. Out-of-band identity proofing

    D. A Type 3 authentication factor

69. Madhuri creates a table that includes assigned privileges, objects, and subjects to manage access control for the systems she is responsible for. Each time a subject attempts to access an object, the systems check the table to ensure that the subject has the appropriate rights to the object. What type of access control system is Madhuri using?

    A. A capability table

    B. An access control list

    C. An access control matrix

    D. A subject/object rights management system

70. During a review of support tickets, Ben's organization discovered that password changes accounted for more than a quarter of its help desk's cases. Which of the following options would be most likely to decrease that number significantly?

    A. Two-factor authentication

    B. Biometric authentication

    C. Self-service password reset

    D. Passphrases

71. Brian's large organization has used RADIUS for AAA services for its network devices for years and has recently become aware of security issues with the unencrypted information transferred during authentication. How should Brian implement encryption for RADIUS?

   A. Use the built-in encryption in RADIUS.

   B. Implement RADIUS over its native UDP using TLS for protection.

   C. Implement RADIUS over TCP using TLS for protection.

   D. Use an AES256 pre-shared cipher between devices.

72. Jim wants to allow cloud-based applications to act on his behalf to access information from other sites. Which of the following tools can allow that?

   A. Kerberos

   B. OAuth

   C. OpenID

   D. LDAP

73. Ben's organization has had an issue with unauthorized access to applications and workstations during the lunch hour when employees aren't at their desk. What are the best types of session management solutions for Ben to recommend to help prevent this type of access?

   A. Use session IDs for all access and verify system IP addresses of all workstations.

   B. Set session timeouts for applications and use password-protected screensavers with inactivity timeouts on workstations.

   C. Use session IDs for all applications, and use password-protected screensavers with inactivity timeouts on workstations.

   D. Set session timeouts for applications and verify system IP addresses of all workstations.

74. What type of authentication scenario is shown in the following diagram?

A. Hybrid federation

B. On-premise federation

C. Cloud federation

D. Kerberos federation

75. Chris wants to control access to his facility while still identifying individuals. He also wants to ensure that the individuals are the people who are being admitted without significant ongoing costs. Which solutions from the following options would meet all of these requirements? (Select all that apply.)

A. Security guards and photo identification badges

B. RFID badges and readers with PIN pads

C. Magstripe badges and readers with PIN pads

D. Security guards and magstripe readers

76. A device like Yubikey or Titan Security Key is what type of Type 2 authentication factor?

A. A token

B. A biometric identifier

C. A smart card

D. A PIV

77. What authentication technology can be paired with OAuth to perform identity verification and obtain user profile information using a RESTful API?

A. SAML

B. Shibboleth

C. OpenID Connect

D. Higgins

78. Jim wants to implement an access control scheme that will ensure that users cannot delegate access. He also wants to enforce access control at the operating system level. What access control mechanism best fits these requirements?

A. Role-based access control

B. Discretionary access control

C. Mandatory access control

D. Attribute-based access control

79. Jesse wants to access a resource protected by a zero trust solution. What component of the system will he connect through to conduct a transaction?

A. The constrained interface

B. The policy engine

C. The policy decision point

D. A policy enforcement point

80. Ben uses a software-based token that changes its code every minute. What type of token is he using?

   A. Asynchronous

   B. Smart card

   C. Synchronous

   D. Static

81. Which of the following is not a commonly used single sign-on solution for internal networks?

   A. Kerberos

   B. SENTRY

   C. RADIUS

   D. TACACS+

82. Michelle works for a financial services company and wants to register customers for her web application. What type of authentication mechanism could she use for the initial login if she wants to quickly and automatically verify that the person is who they claim to be without having a previous relationship with them?

   A. Request their Social Security number.

   B. Use knowledge-based authentication.

   C. Perform manual identity verification.

   D. Use a biometric factor.

83. Megan's company wants to use Google accounts to allow users to quickly adopt their web application. What common cloud federation technologies will Megan need to implement? (Select all that apply.)

   A. Kerberos

   B. OpenID

   C. OAuth

   D. RADIUS

84. Session ID length and session ID entropy are both important to prevent what type of attack?

   A. Denial of service

   B. Cookie theft

   C. Session guessing

   D. Man-in-the-middle attacks

85. Naomi's organization employs an access control system that evaluates the security readiness of a device before granting network access. The system checks whether the device is fully patched, if the latest antimalware scans are clean, and if the firewall is active. If there are potential issues that may indicate a compromise, she is not permitted to connect and must contact support. What type of access control scheme best describes this type of process?

A. MAC

B. Rule-based access control

C. Role-based access control

D. Risk-based access control

86. Isabelle wants to prevent privilege escalation attacks via her organization's service accounts. Which of the following security practices is best suited to this?

A. Remove unnecessary rights.

B. Disable interactive login for service accounts.

C. Limit when accounts can log in.

D. Use meaningless or randomized names for service accounts.

87. In the NIST zero trust model, what component includes the Policy Engine and the Policy Administrator as shown here?

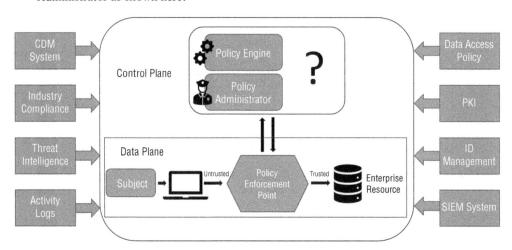

A. The control plane module

B. The policy decision point

C. The enterprise management console

D. The zero trust engine

88. Jim's organization has joined a federation and has begun to allow users from other organizations in the federation to use their services. What services will the members of other organizations be able to use?

A. All of the services provided by Jim's company

B. Only the services their own organization provides

C. Services that Jim's company grants access to on a per-user or per-organization basis

D. Only services that they pay for that Jim's company provides

89. Kristen wants to control access to an application in her organization based on a combination of staff member's job titles, the permissions each group of titles need for the application, and the time of day and location. What type of control scheme should she select?

A. ABAC

B. DAC

C. MAC

D. Role BAC

90. When Alex sets the permissions shown here as one of many users on a Linux server, what type of access control model is he leveraging?

```
$ chmod 731 alex.txt
$ ls -la
total 12
drwxr-xr-x 2 alex root 4096 Feb 27 19:26 .
drwxr-xr-x 3 root root 4096 Feb 27 19:25 ..
-rwx-wx--x 1 alex alex   15 Feb 27 19:26 alex.txt
$
```

A. Role-based access control

B. Rule-based access control

C. Mandatory access control (MAC)

D. Discretionary access control (DAC)

91. Joanna leads her organization's identity management team and wants to ensure that roles are properly updated when staff members change to new positions. What issue should she focus on for those staff members to avoid future issues with role definition?

A. Registration

B. Privilege creep

C. Deprovisioning

D. Accountability

92. What type of authorization mechanism is shown in the following chart?

Group	Privileges
System administrators	Superuser on a desktop, domain administrator
Application administrators	Sudo privileges on application servers
Database administrators	Sudo privileges on database servers
Users	User rights on desktop workstations

   A. RBAC

   B. ABAC

   C. MAC

   D. DAC

93. Samantha wants to log all sudo activity under individual user accounts. What first step should she take to ensure that she captures privileged use like this?

   A. Prevent the use of sudo su -.

   B. Add all users to the sudoers file.

   C. Remove all users from the sudoers.

   D. Disable sudo.

94. Brian wants to explain the benefits of an on-premises federation approach for identity to his organization's leadership. Which of the following is not a common benefit of a federated identity system?

   A. Ease of account management

   B. Single sign-on

   C. Prevention of brute-force attacks

   D. Increased productivity

95. The bank that Aaron works for wants to allow customers to use a new add-on application from a third-party partner they are working with. Since not every customer will want or need an account, Aaron has suggested that the bank use a SAML-based workflow that creates an account when a user downloads the app and tries to log in. What type of provisioning system has he suggested?

   A. JIT

   B. OpenID

   C. OAuth

   D. Kerberos

96. What authentication protocol does Windows use by default for Active Directory systems?

   A. RADIUS

   B. Kerberos

   C. OAuth

   D. TACACS+

97. Valerie needs to control access to applications that are deployed to mobile devices in a BYOD environment. What type of solution will best allow her to exercise control over the applications while ensuring that they do not leave remnant data on the devices used by her end users?

   A. Deploy the applications to the BYOD devices and require unique PINs on every device.

   B. Deploy the application to desktop systems and require users to use remote desktop to access them using enterprise authentication.

   C. Deploy the applications to the BYOD devices using application containers and require unique PINs on every device.

   D. Use a virtual hosted application environment that requires authentication using enterprise credentials.

98. Match the following authorization mechanisms with their descriptions:

   1. Role-BAC

   2. Rule BAC

   3. DAC

   4. ABAC

   5. MAC

   A. An access control model enforced by the operating system.

   B. Permissions or rights are granted based on parameters like an IP address, time, or other specific details that match requirements.

   C. Sometimes called policy-based access control, this model uses information about the subject to assign permissions.

   D. A model where subjects with the proper rights can assign or pass those rights to other subjects.

   E. Used to assign permissions based on job or function.

99. Match each of the numbered authentication techniques with the appropriate lettered category. Each technique should be matched with exactly one category. Each category may be used once, more than once, or not at all.

Authentication technique:

1. Password

2. ID card

3. Retinal scan

4. Smartphone token

5. Fingerprint analysis

Category:

A. Something you have

B. Something you know

C. Something you are

100. Match the following identity and access controls with the asset type they are best suited to protect. Each only has one option.

1. Information assets

2. Systems

3. Mobile devices

4. Facilities

5. Partner applications

A. Discretionary access controls

B. Badge readers

C. Federated identity management

D. Biometric authentication

E. User accounts with multifactor authentication

Chapter

6

Security Assessment and Testing (Domain 6)

SUBDOMAINS

✓ **6.1 Design and validate assessment, test, and audit strategies**

✓ **6.2 Conduct security controls testing**

✓ **6.3 Collect security process data (e.g., technical, and administrative)**

✓ **6.4 Analyze test output and generate report**

✓ **6.5 Conduct or facilitate security audits**

1. During a port scan, Susan discovers a system running services on TCP and UDP 137–139 and TCP 445, as well as TCP 1433. What type of system is she likely to find if she connects to the machine?

   A. A Linux email server

   B. A Windows SQL server

   C. A Linux file server

   D. A Windows workstation

2. Which of the following is a method used to automatically design new software tests and to ensure the quality of tests?

   A. Code auditing

   B. Static code analysis

   C. Regression testing

   D. Mutation testing

3. During a port scan, Naomi found TCP port 443 open on a system. Which tool is best suited to scanning the service that is most likely running on that port?

   A. zzuf

   B. Nikto

   C. Metasploit

   D. Sqlmap

4. What message logging standard is commonly used by network devices, Linux and Unix systems, and many other enterprise devices?

   A. Syslog

   B. Netlog

   C. Eventlog

   D. Remote Log Protocol (RLP)

5. Alex wants to use an automated tool to fill web application forms to test for format string vulnerabilities. What type of tool should he use?

   A. A black box

   B. A brute-force tool

   C. A fuzzer

   D. A static analysis tool

6. Susan needs to scan a system for vulnerabilities, and she wants to use an open-source tool to test the system remotely. Which of the following tools will meet her requirements and allow vulnerability scanning?

   A. Nmap

   B. OpenVAS

   C. MBSA

   D. Nessus

7. Morgan is implementing a vulnerability management system that uses standards-based components to score and evaluate the vulnerabilities it finds. Which of the following is most commonly used to provide a severity score for vulnerabilities?

   A. CCE

   B. CVSS

   C. CPE

   D. OVAL

8. Jim has been contracted to perform a penetration test of a bank's primary branch. To make the test as real as possible, he has not been given any information about the bank other than its name and address. What type of penetration test has Jim agreed to perform?

   A. A crystal-box penetration test

   B. A gray-box penetration test

   C. A black-box penetration test

   D. A white-box penetration test

9. In a response to a request for proposal, Susan receives an SSAE 18 SOC report. If she wants a report that includes details on operating effectiveness, what should Susan ask for as follow-up, and why?

   A. A SOC 2 Type II report, because Type I does not cover operating effectiveness

   B. A SOC 1 Type I report, because SOC 2 does not cover operating effectiveness

   C. A SOC 2 Type I report, because SOC 2 Type II does not cover operating effectiveness

   D. A SOC 3 report, because SOC 1 and SOC 2 reports are outdated

10. During a wireless network penetration test, Susan runs aircrack-ng against the network intending to capture a password as part of the four-way handshake and then crack the password offline. What might cause her to fail in her password-cracking efforts if the target is using WPA3 in Personal network mode?

    A. WPA3 uses complex passwords.

    B. WPA3 uses SAE and does not transfer the password over the air.

    C. WPA3 requires multifactor, making a password alone insufficient.

    D. The password crack will work due to flaws in WPA3.

11. A zero-day vulnerability is announced for the popular Apache web server in the middle of a workday. In Jacob's role as an information security analyst, he needs to quickly scan his network to determine what servers are vulnerable to the issue. What is Jacob's best route to quickly identify vulnerable systems?

    A. Immediately run Nessus against all of the servers to identify which systems are vulnerable.

    B. Review the CVE database to find the vulnerability information and patch information.

    C. Create a custom IDS or IPS signature.

    D. Identify affected versions and check systems for that version number using an automated scanner.

12. What type of testing is used to ensure that separately developed software modules properly exchange data?

    A. Fuzzing

    B. Dynamic testing

    C. Interface testing

    D. API checksums

13. Selah wants to provide security assessment information to customers who want to use her organization's cloud services. Which of the following options should she select to ensure that the greatest number of customers are satisfied with the assessment information?

    A. Use an internal audit team to self-assess against internal metrics.

    B. Use a third-party auditor.

    C. Use internal technical staff who know the systems.

    D. Use an internal audit team to self-assess against a common standard like COBIT.

14. Yasmine has been asked to consider a breach and attack simulation system. What type of system should she look for?

    A. A ticket and change management system designed to help manage incidents

    B. A system that runs incident response simulations for blue teams to test their skills

    C. A system that combines red and blue team techniques with automation

    D. A security operations and response (SOAR) system

15. Monica wants to gather information about security awareness in her organization. What technique is most frequently used to assess the broad range elements that make up security awareness?

    A. Phishing simulations

    B. Gamified applications

    C. Assessment tests

    D. Surveys

16. Jim has been contracted to conduct a gray-box penetration test, and his clients have provided him with the following information about their networks so that he can scan them:

    Data center: 10.10.10.0/24

    Sales: 10.10.11.0/24

    Billing: 10.10.12.0/24

    Wireless: 192.168.0.0/16

    What problem will Jim encounter if he is contracted to conduct a scan from off-site?

    A. The IP ranges are too large to scan efficiently.

    B. The IP addresses provided cannot be scanned.

    C. The IP ranges overlap and will cause scanning issues.

    D. The IP addresses provided are RFC 1918 addresses.

17. Mark's company has been notified of a flaw in their web application. The anonymous individual has notified them that they have two weeks to fix it before the details of the flaw are published along with example exploit code. What industry norm is the individual who contacted Mark's company violating?

A. Zero-day reporting

B. Ethical disclosure

C. Ethical hacking

D. The ISC2 vulnerability disclosure ethics statement

For questions 18–20, please refer to the following scenario:

The company that Jennifer works for has implemented a central logging infrastructure, as shown here. Use this diagram and your knowledge of logging systems to answer the following questions.

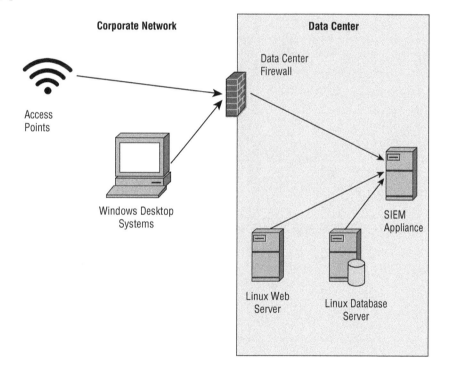

18. Jennifer needs to ensure that all Windows systems provide identical logging information to the SIEM. How can she best ensure that all Windows desktops have the same log settings?

A. Perform periodic configuration audits.

B. Use Group Policy.

C. Use Local Policy.

D. Deploy a Windows syslog client.

19. During normal operations, Jennifer's team uses the SIEM appliance to monitor for exceptions received via syslog. What system shown does not natively have support for syslog events?

   A. Enterprise wireless access points

   B. Windows desktop systems

   C. Linux web servers

   D. Enterprise firewall devices

20. What technology should an organization use for each of the devices shown in the diagram to ensure that logs can be time sequenced across the entire infrastructure?

   A. Syslog

   B. NTP

   C. Logsync

   D. SNAP

21. During a penetration test, Michelle needs to identify systems, but she hasn't gained sufficient access on the system she is using to generate raw packets. What type of scan should she run to verify the most open services?

   A. A TCP connect scan

   B. A TCP SYN scan

   C. A UDP scan

   D. An ICMP scan

22. During a port scan using nmap, Joseph discovers that a system shows two ports open that cause him immediate worry:

21/open

23/open

What services are likely running on those ports?

   A. SSH and FTP

   B. FTP and Telnet

   C. SMTP and Telnet

   D. POP3 and SMTP

23. Aaron wants to validate his compliance with PCI-DSS. His company is a large commercial organization with millions of dollars in transactions a year. What is the most common method of conducting this type of testing for large organizations?

   A. Self-assessment

   B. To conduct a thirty-party assessment using COBIT

   C. To partner with another company and trade assessments between the organizations

   D. To conduct a third-party assessment using a qualified security assessor

24. What method is commonly used to assess how well software testing covered the potential uses of an application?

- **A.** A test coverage analysis
- **B.** A source code review
- **C.** A fuzz analysis
- **D.** A code review report

25. Testing that is focused on functions that a system should not allow is an example of what type of testing?

- **A.** Use case testing
- **B.** Manual testing
- **C.** Misuse case testing
- **D.** Dynamic testing

26. What type of monitoring uses simulated traffic to a website to monitor performance?

- **A.** Log analysis
- **B.** Synthetic transaction monitoring
- **C.** Passive monitoring
- **D.** Simulated transaction analysis

27. Derek wants to ensure that his organization tracks all changes to accounts through their life cycle. What type of tool should he invest in for his organization?

- **A.** A directory service like LDAP
- **B.** An IAM system
- **C.** A SIEM
- **D.** An EDR system

28. Jim uses a tool that scans a system for available services and then connects to them to collect banner information to determine what version of the service is running. It then provides a report detailing what it gathers, basing results on service fingerprinting, banner information, and similar details it gathers combined with CVE information. What type of tool is Jim using?

- **A.** A port scanner
- **B.** A service validator
- **C.** A vulnerability scanner
- **D.** A patch management tool

29. Emily builds a script that sends data to a web application that she is testing. Each time the script runs, it sends a series of transactions with data that fits the expected requirements of the web application to verify that it responds to typical customer behavior. What type of transactions is she using, and what type of test is this?

   A. Synthetic, passive monitoring

   B. Synthetic, use case testing

   C. Actual, dynamic monitoring

   D. Actual, fuzzing

30. What passive monitoring technique records all user interaction with an application or website to ensure quality and performance?

   A. Client-server testing

   B. Real user monitoring

   C. Synthetic user monitoring

   D. Passive user recording

31. Earlier this year, the information security team at Jim's employer identified a vulnerability in the web server that Jim is responsible for maintaining. He immediately applied the patch and is sure that it installed properly, but the vulnerability scanner has continued to incorrectly flag the system as vulnerable. To prevent the issue from being flagged incorrectly in the future, what is the next step?

   A. Uninstall and reinstall the patch.

   B. Ask the information security team to flag the system as patched and not vulnerable to that particular flaw.

   C. Update the version information in the web server's configuration.

   D. Review the vulnerability report and use alternate remediation options.

32. Angela wants to test a web browser's handling of unexpected data using an automated tool. What tool should she choose?

   A. Nmap

   B. zzuf

   C. Nessus

   D. Nikto

33. Kara wants to conduct a security audit of her cloud IaaS vendor's systems, infrastructure, and practices. What type of audit is she most likely to be able to conduct?

   A. A third-party audit.

   B. She cannot conduct an audit.

   C. An internal audit.

   D. She may request the vendor's third-party audit results.

34. Why should passive scanning be conducted in addition to implementing wireless security technologies like wireless intrusion detection systems?

A. It can help identify rogue devices.

B. It can test the security of the wireless network via scripted attacks.

C. Their short dwell time on each wireless channel can allow them to capture more packets.

D. They can help test wireless IDS or IPS systems.

35. Paul is reviewing the approval process for a penetration test and wants to ensure that it has appropriate management review. Who should he ensure has approved the request for a penetration test for a business system?

A. The change advisory board

B. Senior management

C. The systems administrator for the system

D. The service owner

36. What term describes software testing that is intended to uncover new bugs introduced by patches or configuration changes?

A. Nonregression testing

B. Evolution testing

C. Smoke testing

D. Regression testing

37. Which of the following tools cannot identify a target's operating system for a penetration tester?

A. Nmap

B. Nessus

C. Nikto

D. Sqlmap

38. Susan needs to predict high-risk areas for her organization and wants to use metrics to assess risk trends as they occur. What should she do to handle this?

A. Perform yearly risk assessments.

B. Hire a penetration testing company to regularly test organizational security.

C. Identify and track key risk indicators.

D. Monitor logs and events using a SIEM device.

39. What major difference separates synthetic and passive monitoring?

A. Synthetic monitoring works only after problems have occurred.

B. Passive monitoring cannot detect functionality issues.

C. Passive monitoring works only after problems have occurred.

D. Synthetic monitoring cannot detect functionality issues.

For questions 40–42, please refer to the following scenario. Chris uses the standard penetration testing methodology shown here. Use this methodology and your knowledge of penetration testing to answer questions about tool usage during a penetration test.

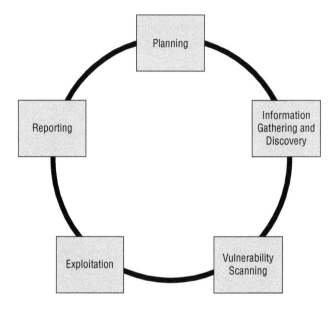

40. What task is the most important during Phase 1, planning?

- **A.** Building a test lab
- **B.** Getting authorization
- **C.** Gathering appropriate tools
- **D.** Determining if the test is white, black, or gray box

41. Which of the following tools is most likely to be used during discovery?

- **A.** Nessus
- **B.** John
- **C.** Nmap
- **D.** Nikto

42. Which of these concerns is the most important to address during planning to ensure that the reporting phase does not cause problems?

- **A.** Which CVE format to use
- **B.** How the vulnerability data will be stored and sent
- **C.** Which targets are off-limits
- **D.** How long the report should be

43. What four types of coverage criteria are commonly used when validating the work of a code testing suite?

　　A. Input, statement, branch, and condition coverage

　　B. Function, statement, branch, and condition coverage

　　C. API, branch, bounds, and condition coverage

　　D. Bounds, branch, loop, and condition coverage

44. As part of his role as a security manager, Jacob provides the following chart to his organization's management team. What type of measurement is he providing for them?

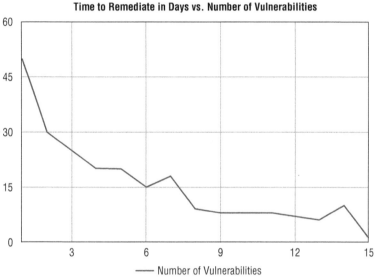

　　A. A coverage rate measure

　　B. A key performance indicator

　　C. A time to live metric

　　D. A business criticality indicator

45. What does using unique user IDs for all users provide when reviewing logs?

　　A. Confidentiality

　　B. Integrity

　　C. Availability

　　D. Accountability

46. Which of the following is not an interface that is typically tested during the software testing process?

   A. APIs

   B. Network interfaces

   C. UIs

   D. Physical interfaces

47. Alan's organization uses the Security Content Automation Protocol (SCAP) to standardize its vulnerability management program. Which component of SCAP can Alan use to reconcile the identity of vulnerabilities generated by different security assessment tools?

   A. OVAL

   B. XCCDF

   C. CVE

   D. SCE

48. Susan is reviewing software testing coverage data and sees the information shown here. What can she determine about this testing process? (Select all answers that apply.)

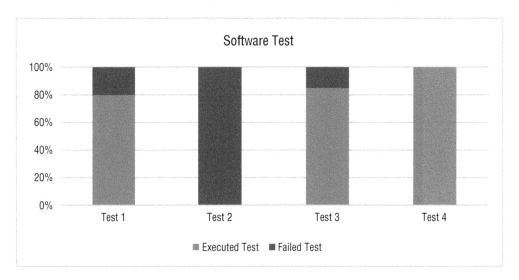

   A. The testing does not have full coverage.

   B. Test 4 completed with no failures.

   C. Test 2 failed to run successfully.

   D. The testing needs to be run a fifth time.

49. Which of the following strategies is not a reasonable approach for remediating a vulnerability identified by a vulnerability scanner?

   A. Install a patch.

   B. Use a workaround fix.

    C. Update the banner or version number.

    D. Use an application layer firewall or IPS to prevent attacks against the identified vulnerability.

50. During a penetration test, Selah calls her target's help desk claiming to be the senior assistant to an officer of the company. She requests that the help desk reset the officer's password because of an issue with his laptop while traveling and persuades them to do so. What type of attack has she successfully completed?

    A. Zero knowledge

    B. Help-desk spoofing

    C. Social engineering

    D. Black box

51. In this image, what issue may occur due to the log handling settings?

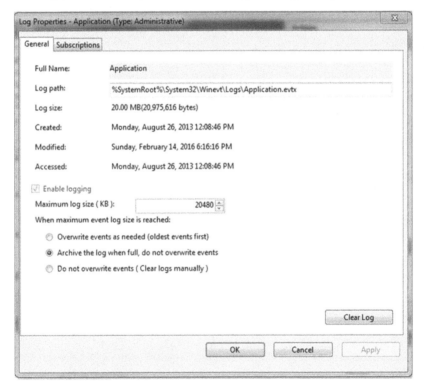

Source: Microsoft Corporation

    A. Log data may be lost when the log is archived.

    B. Log data may be overwritten.

    C. Log data may not include needed information.

    D. Log data may fill the system disk.

52. Which of the following is not a hazard associated with penetration testing?

    A. Application crashes

    B. Denial of service

    C. Blackouts

    D. Data corruption

53. Which NIST special publication covers the assessment of security and privacy controls?

    A. 800-12

    B. 800-53A

    C. 800-34

    D. 800-86

54. Michelle wants to assess her organization's disaster recovery readiness. What type of test could she run to most effectively assess readiness without the potential for disruption?

    A. Conduct a tabletop exercise.

    B. Conduct a failover test.

    C. Conduct a simulation.

    D. Conduct a plan review.

55. Lucca wants to conduct an audit of a hybrid cloud environment. What potential challenge should he identify for his management team?

    A. On-premises audits are difficult to complete.

    B. Hybrid audits cannot be conducted by third parties.

    C. Underlying cloud infrastructure may not be auditable.

    D. There are no differences between hybrid and cloud audits.

56. If Kara's primary concern is preventing administrative connections to the server, which port should she block?

    A. 22

    B. 80

    C. 443

    D. 1433

57. During a third-party audit, Jim's company receives a finding that states, "The administrator should review backup success and failure logs on a daily basis and take action in a timely manner to resolve reported exceptions." What potential problem does this finding indicate?

    A. Administrators will not know if the backups succeeded or failed.

    B. The backups may not be properly logged.

    C. The backups may not be usable.

    D. The backup logs may not be properly reviewed.

58. Jim is helping his organization decide on audit standards for use throughout their international organization. Which of the following is not an IT standard that Jim's organization is likely to use as part of its audits?

  A. COBIT

  B. SSAE-18

  C. ITIL

  D. ISO 27001

59. Nicole wants to conduct a standards-based audit of her organization. Which of the following is commonly used to describe common requirements for information systems?

  A. IEC

  B. COBIT

  C. FISA

  D. DMCA

60. Kelly's team conducts regression testing on each patch they release. What key performance measure should they maintain to measure the effectiveness of their testing?

  A. Time to remediate vulnerabilities

  B. A measure of the rate of defect recurrence

  C. A weighted risk trend

  D. A measure of the specific coverage of their testing

61. Which of the following types of code review is not typically performed by a human?

  A. Software inspections

  B. Pair programming

  C. Static program analysis

  D. Software walk-throughs

For questions 62–64, please refer to the following scenario:

Susan is the lead of a quality assurance team at her company. The team has been tasked with the testing for a major release of their company's core software product.

62. Susan's team of software testers are required to test every code path, including those that will be used only when an error condition occurs. What type of testing environment does her team need to ensure complete code coverage?

  A. White box

  B. Gray box

  C. Black box

  D. Dynamic

63. As part of the continued testing of their new application, Susan's quality assurance team has designed a set of test cases for a series of black-box tests. These functional tests are then run, and a report is prepared explaining what has occurred. What type of report is typically generated during this testing to indicate test metrics?

A. A test coverage report

B. A penetration test report

C. A code coverage report

D. A line coverage report

64. As part of their code coverage testing, Susan's team runs the analysis in a nonproduction environment using logging and tracing tools. Which of the following type of code issues is most likely to be missed during testing due to this change in the operating environment?

A. Improper bounds checking

B. Input validation

C. A race condition

D. Pointer manipulation

65. Robin recently conducted a vulnerability scan and found a critical vulnerability on a server that handles sensitive information. What should Robin do next?

A. Patching

B. Reporting

C. Remediation

D. Validation

66. The automated code testing and integration that Andrea ran as part of her organization's CI/CD pipeline errored out. What should Andrea do with the code if the company needs the code to go live immediately?

A. Manually bypass the test.

B. Review error logs to identify the problem.

C. Rerun the test to see if it works.

D. Send the code back to the developer for a fix.

67. Michelle wants to compare vulnerabilities she has discovered in her data center based on how exploitable they are, if exploit code exists, and how hard they are to remediate. What scoring system should she use to compare vulnerability metrics like these?

A. CSV

B. NVD

C. VSS

D. CVSS

68. During a port scan of his network, Alex finds that a number of hosts respond on TCP ports 80, 443, 515, and 9100 in offices throughout his organization. What type of devices is Alex likely discovering?

    A. Web servers

    B. File servers

    C. Wireless access points

    D. Printers

69. Nikto, Burp Suite, and Wapiti are all examples of what type of tool?

    A. Web application vulnerability scanners

    B. Code review tools

    C. Vulnerability scanners

    D. Port scanners

70. Frank's team is testing a new API that his company's developers have built for their application infrastructure. Which of the following is not a common API issue that you would expect Frank's team to find?

    A. Improper encryption

    B. Object-level authorization issues

    C. User authentication issues

    D. Lack of rate limiting

71. Jim is working with a penetration testing contractor who proposes using Metasploit as part of her penetration testing effort. What should Jim expect to occur when Metasploit is used?

    A. Systems will be scanned for vulnerabilities.

    B. Systems will have known vulnerabilities exploited.

    C. Services will be probed for buffer overflow and other unknown flaws.

    D. Systems will be tested for zero-day exploits.

72. Susan needs to ensure that the interactions between the components of her e-commerce application are all handled properly. She intends to verify communications, error handling, and session management capabilities throughout her infrastructure. What type of testing is she planning to conduct?

    A. Misuse case testing

    B. Fuzzing

    C. Regression testing

    D. Interface testing

73. Jim is designing his organization's log management systems and knows that he needs to carefully plan to handle the organization's log data. Which of the following is not a factor that Jim should be concerned with?

A. The volume of log data

B. A lack of sufficient log sources

C. Data storage security requirements

D. Network bandwidth

74. Ryan's organization wants to ensure that proper account management is occurring but does not have a central identity and access management tool in place. Ryan has a limited amount of time to do his verification process. What is his best option to test the account management process as part of an internal audit?

A. Validate all accounts changed in the past 90 days.

B. Select high-value administrative accounts for validation.

C. Validate all account changes in the past 180 days.

D. Validate a random sample of accounts.

75. When a Windows system is rebooted, what type of log is generated?

A. Error

B. Warning

C. Information

D. Failure audit

76. During a review of access logs, Alex notices that Michelle logged into her workstation in New York at 8 a.m. daily, but then she was recorded as logging into her department's main web application shortly after 3 a.m. daily. What common logging issue has Alex likely encountered?

A. Inconsistent log formatting

B. Modified logs

C. Inconsistent timestamps

D. Multiple log sources

77. What type of vulnerability scan accesses configuration information from the systems it is run against as well as information that can be accessed via services available via the network?

A. Authenticated scans

B. Web application scans

C. Unauthenticated scans

D. Port scans

78. Brian has discovered a vulnerability in a website and has notified the company that owns the website about the issue. What has he done?

A. A penetration test

B. Ethical disclosure

C. A web application test

D. OSINT

For questions 79–80, please refer to the following scenario:

Ben's organization has begun to use STRIDE to assess its software and has identified threat agents and the business impacts that these threats could have. Now they are working to identify appropriate controls for the issues they have identified.

79. Ben's team is attempting to categorize a transaction identification issue that is caused by using a symmetric key shared by multiple servers. What STRIDE category should this fall into?

A. Information disclosure

B. Denial of service

C. Tampering

D. Repudiation

80. Ben wants to use a third-party service to help assess denial-of-service attack vulnerabilities due to the amount of traffic during denial-of-service attacks. What type of engagement should he suggest to his organization?

A. A social engineering engagement

B. A penetration test

C. Load or stress testing

D. Testing using a fuzzer

81. Chris is troubleshooting an issue with his organization's SIEM reporting. After analyzing the issue, he believes that the timestamps on log entries from different systems are inconsistent. What protocol can he use to resolve this issue?

A. SSH

B. FTP

C. TLS

D. NTP

82. Ryan is considering the use of fuzz testing in his web application testing program. Which one of the following statements about fuzz testing should Ryan consider when making his decision?

A. Fuzzers only find complex faults.

B. Testers must manually generate input.

C. Fuzzers may not fully cover the code.

D. Fuzzers can't reproduce errors.

83. Ken is designing a testing process for software developed by his team. He is designing a test that verifies that every line of code was executed during the test. What type of analysis is Ken performing?

A. Branch coverage

B. Condition coverage

C. Function coverage

D. Statement coverage

For questions 84–86, please refer to the following scenario. During a port scan, Ben uses nmap's default settings and sees the following results.

```
Nmap scan report for 192.168.184.130
Host is up (1.0s latency).
Not shown: 977 closed ports
PORT     STATE SERVICE
21/tcp   open  ftp
22/tcp   open  ssh
23/tcp   open  telnet
25/tcp   open  smtp
53/tcp   open  domain
80/tcp   open  http
111/tcp  open  rpcbind
139/tcp  open  netbios-ssn
445/tcp  open  microsoft-ds
512/tcp  open  exec
513/tcp  open  login
514/tcp  open  shell
1099/tcp open  rmiregistry
1524/tcp open  ingreslock
2049/tcp open  nfs
2121/tcp open  ccproxy-ftp
3306/tcp open  mysql
5432/tcp open  postgresql
5900/tcp open  vnc
6000/tcp open  X11
6667/tcp open  irc
8009/tcp open  ajp13
8180/tcp open  unknown

Nmap done: 1 IP address (1 host up) scanned in 54.69 seconds
```

84. If Ben is conducting a penetration test, what should his next step be after receiving these results?

A. Connect to the web server using a web browser.

B. Connect via Telnet to test for vulnerable accounts.

C. Identify interesting ports for further scanning.

D. Use sqlmap against the open databases.

85. Based on the scan results, what operating system (OS) was the system that was scanned most likely running?

A. Windows Desktop

B. Linux

C. Network device

D. Windows Server

86. Ben's manager expresses concern about the coverage of his scan. Why might his manager have this concern?

- **A.** Ben did not test UDP services.
- **B.** Ben did not discover ports outside the "well-known ports."
- **C.** Ben did not perform OS fingerprinting.
- **D.** Ben tested only a limited number of ports.

87. Lucca is reviewing his organization's disaster recovery process data and notes that the MTD for the business's main website is two hours. What does he know about the RTO for the site when he does testing and validation?

- **A.** It needs to be less than two hours.
- **B.** It needs to be at least two hours.
- **C.** The MTD is too short and needs to be longer.
- **D.** The RTO is too short and needs to be longer.

88. Diana has engaged third-party auditors and wants to release an audit attestation to third parties without including details of the audit. What type of SSAE 18 SOC report should she request?

- **A.** SOC 1
- **B.** SOC 2
- **C.** SOC 3
- **D.** SOC 4

89. While reviewing the software testing output for her organization's new application, Madhuri notices that the application has produced errors that included directory and file information shown to the web application tester. What issue should she include in her report about the application?

- **A.** It does not perform proper exception handling.
- **B.** The software does not handle misuse case testing properly.
- **C.** Debugging statements need to be removed.
- **D.** The code was not fully tested due to errors.

90. What action might a pen tester perform to identify potential exploitable services to gain an initial foothold in a network?

- **A.** Data gathering
- **B.** Port scanning
- **C.** Getting permission
- **D.** Planning

91. The president of Josh's company is concerned about a significant increase in cryptographic malware that is impacting other companies in their industry. She has asked John to ensure that the company's data will be recoverable if malware strikes and encrypts their production systems. What process does Josh need to undertake to be able to tell her that the company is covered?

A. Encrypt all sensitive data.

B. Hash all of the organization's data to detect cryptographic malware.

C. Perform backup verification.

D. Use anti-encryption technology to prevent the malware from encrypting drives.

92. Joanna is her organization's CISO, and in her security operations oversight role she wants to ensure that management oversight is happening for security-related changes. What system should she focus on to track this type of data in most organizations?

A. The SIEM system

B. The IPS system

C. The CMS tool

D. The ITSM tool

93. Henry wants to validate that his backups are working. Which of the following options is the best way for him to ensure that the backups will be useful in a true disaster recovery scenario?

A. Periodically restore a random file to ensure that the backups are working.

B. Review configurations and settings on a regular schedule to validate backup settings.

C. Review the backup logs to ensure no errors are occurring.

D. Regularly perform full restores from backups to validate their success.

94. What type of vulnerabilities will not be found by a vulnerability scanner?

A. Local vulnerabilities

B. Service vulnerabilities

C. Zero-day vulnerabilities

D. Vulnerabilities that require authentication

95. Jacinda wants to measure the effectiveness of her security training as one of her security metrics. Which of the following measures are the most useful for assessing the effectiveness of security awareness training? (Select all that apply.)

A. How many people took the training

B. The level of security awareness before and after the training

C. The length of the training in hours

D. The number of training events each individual attended this year

96. Elaine has discovered a previously unknown critical vulnerability in a product that her organization uses. Her organization has a strong commitment to ethical disclosure, and Elaine wants to follow common ethical disclosure practices. What should she do first?

　A. Build an in-house remediation or control and then publicly disclose the vulnerability to prompt the vendor to patch it quickly.

　B. Build an in-house remediation or control and then notify the vendor of the issue.

　C. Notify the vendor and give them a reasonable amount of time to fix the issue.

　D. Publicly disclose the vulnerability so that the vendor will patch it in an appropriate amount of time.

For questions 97–99, please refer to the following scenario. NIST Special Publication 800-115, the Technical Guide to Information Security Testing and Assessment, provides NIST's process for penetration testing. Use this image as well as your knowledge of penetration testing to answer the questions.

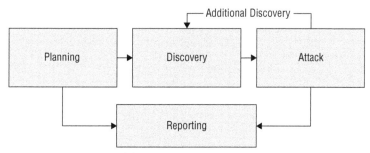

Source: NIST SP 800-115 / Public Domain.

97. Which of the following is not a part of the discovery phase?

　A. Hostname and IP address information gathering

　B. Service information capture

　C. Dumpster diving

　D. Privilege escalation

98. NIST specifies four attack phase steps: gaining access, escalating privileges, system browsing, and installing additional tools. Once attackers install additional tools, what phase will a penetration tester typically return to?

　A. Discovery

　B. Gaining access

　C. Escalating privileges

　D. System browsing

99. Which of the following is not a typical part of a penetration test report?

    A. A list of identified vulnerabilities

    B. All sensitive data that was gathered during the test

    C. Risk ratings for each issue discovered

    D. Mitigation guidance for issues identified

100. Alex is using nmap to perform port scanning of a system, and he receives three different port status messages in the results. Match each of the numbered status messages with the appropriate lettered description. You should use each item exactly once.

Status message:

    1. Open

    2. Closed

    3. Filtered

Description:

    A. The port is accessible on the remote system, but no application is accepting connections on that port.

    B. The port is not accessible on the remote system.

    C. The port is accessible on the remote system, and an application is accepting connections on that port.

Chapter

7

Security Operations (Domain 7)

SUBDOMAINS

✓ 7.1 Understand and comply with investigations

✓ 7.2 Conduct logging and monitoring activities

✓ 7.3 Perform Configuration Management (CM) (e.g., provisioning, baselining, automation)

✓ 7.4 Apply foundational security operations concepts

✓ 7.5 Apply resource protection

✓ 7.6 Conduct incident management

✓ 7.7 Operate and maintain detection and preventative measures

✓ 7.8 Implement and support patch and vulnerability management

✓ 7.9 Understand and participate in change management processes

✓ 7.10 Implement recovery strategies

✓ 7.11 Implement Disaster Recovery (DR) processes

✓ 7.12 Test Disaster Recovery Plan (DRP)

✓ 7.13 Participate in Business Continuity (BC) planning and exercises

✓ 7.14 Implement and manage physical security

✓ 7.15 Address personnel safety and security concerns

1. Mary is reviewing the availability controls for the system architecture shown here. What technology is shown that provides fault tolerance for the database servers?

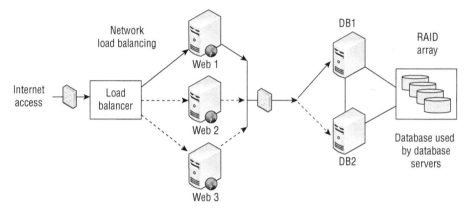

   A. Failover cluster

   B. UPS

   C. Tape backup

   D. Cold site

2. Joe is the security administrator for an ERP system. He is preparing to create accounts for several new employees. What default access should he give to all of the new employees as he creates the accounts?

   A. Read only

   B. Editor

   C. Administrator

   D. No access

3. Tim is configuring a privileged account management solution for his organization. Which one of the following is not a privileged administrative activity that should be automatically sent to a log of superuser actions?

   A. Purging log entries

   B. Restoring a system from backup

   C. Logging into a workstation

   D. Managing user accounts

4. When one of the employees of Alice's company calls in for support, she uses a code word that the company agreed to use if employees were being forced to perform an action. What is this scenario called?

   A. Social engineering

   B. Duress

   C. Force majeure

   D. Stockholm syndrome

5. Jordan is preparing to bring evidence into court after a cybersecurity incident investigation. He is responsible for preparing the physical artifacts, including affected servers and mobile devices. What type of evidence consists entirely of tangible items that may be brought into a court of law?

   A. Documentary evidence

   B. Parol evidence

   C. Testimonial evidence

   D. Real evidence

6. Lauren wants to ensure that her users only run software that her organization has approved. What technology should she deploy?

   A. Blacklisting

   B. Configuration management

   C. Whitelisting

   D. Graylisting

7. Colin is responsible for managing his organization's use of cybersecurity deception technologies. Which one of the following should he use on a honeypot system to consume an attacker's time while alerting administrators?

   A. Honeynet

   B. Pseudo-flaw

   C. Warning banner

   D. Darknet

8. Toni responds to the desk of a user who reports slow system activity. Upon checking outbound network connections from that system, Toni notices a large amount of social media traffic originating from the system. The user does not use social media, and when Toni checks the accounts in question, she sees they contain strange messages that appear encrypted. What is the most likely cause of this traffic?

   A. Other users are relaying social media requests through the user's computer.

   B. The user's computer is part of a botnet.

   C. The user is lying about her use of social media.

   D. Someone else is using the user's computer when she is not present.

9. John deploys his website to multiple regions using load balancers around the world through his cloud infrastructure as a service provider. What availability concept is he using?

   A. Multiple processing sites

   B. Warm sites

   C. Cold sites

   D. A honeynet

10. Jim would like to identify compromised systems on his network that may be participating in a botnet. He plans to do this by watching for connections made to known command-and-control servers. Which one of the following techniques would be most likely to provide this information if Jim has access to a list of known servers?

A. NetFlow records

B. IDS logs

C. Authentication logs

D. RFC logs

For questions 11–15, please refer to the following scenario:

Gary was recently hired as the first chief information security officer (CISO) for a local government agency. The agency recently suffered a security breach and is attempting to build a new information security program. Gary would like to apply some best practices for security operations as he is designing this program.

11. As Gary decides what access permissions he should grant to each user, what principle should guide his decisions about default permissions?

A. Segregation of duties

B. Least privilege

C. Privilege creep

D. Separation of privileges

12. As Gary designs the program, he uses the matrix shown here. What principle of information security does this matrix most directly help enforce?

Roles/Tasks	Application Programmer	Security Administrator	Database Administrator	Database Server Administrator	Budget Analyst	Accounts Receivable	Accounts Payable	Deploy Patches	Verify Patches
Application Programmer		X	X	X					
Security Administrator	X		X	X	X	X	X	X	
Database Administrator	X	X		X					
Database Server Administrator	X	X	X						
Budget Analyst		X				X	X		
Accounts Receivable		X			X		X		
Accounts Payable		X			X	X			
Deploy Patches		X							X
Verify Patches								X	
	Potential Areas of Conflict								

    A. Segregation of duties

    B. Privilege creep

    C. Two-person control

    D. Defense in depth

13. Gary is preparing to create an account for a new user and assign privileges to the HR database. What two elements of information must Gary verify before granting this access?

    A. Credentials and need to know

    B. Clearance and need to know

    C. Password and clearance

    D. Password and biometric scan

14. Gary is preparing to develop controls around access to root encryption keys and would like to apply a principle of security designed specifically for very sensitive operations. Which principle should he apply?

    A. Least privilege

    B. Defense in depth

    C. Security through obscurity

    D. Two-person control

15. How often should Gary and his team conduct a review of the privileged access that a user has to sensitive systems? (Select all that apply.)

    A. On a periodic basis

    B. When a user leaves the organization

    C. When a user changes roles

    D. On a daily basis

16. Which one of the following terms is often used to describe a collection of unrelated patches released in a large collection?

    A. Hotfix

    B. Update

    C. Security fix

    D. Service pack

17. Tonya is collecting evidence from a series of systems that were involved in a cybersecurity incident. A colleague suggests that she use a write blocker for the collection process. What is the function of this device?

    A. Masking error conditions reported by the storage device

    B. Transmitting write commands to the storage device

    C. Intercepting and modifying or discarding commands sent to the storage device

    D. Preventing data from being returned by a read operation sent to the device

18. Lydia is processing access control requests for her organization. She comes across a request where the user does have the required security clearance, but there is no business justification for the access. Lydia denies this request. What security principle is she following?

   A. Need to know

   B. Least privilege

   C. Segregation of duties

   D. Two-person control

19. Helen is tasked with implementing security controls in her organization that might be used to deter fraudulent insider activity. Which one of the following mechanisms would be LEAST useful to her work?

   A. Job rotation

   B. Mandatory vacations

   C. Incident response

   D. Two-person control

20. Matt wants to ensure that critical network traffic from systems throughout his company is prioritized over web browsing and social media use at this company. What technology can he use to do this?

   A. VLANs

   B. QoS

   C. VPN

   D. ISDN

21. Tom is responding to a recent security incident and is seeking information on the approval process for a recent modification to a system's security settings. Where would he most likely find this information?

   A. Change log

   B. System log

   C. Security log

   D. Application log

22. Staff from Susan's company often travel internationally and require connectivity to corporate systems for their work. Susan believes that these users may be targeted for corporate espionage activities because of the technologies that her company is developing and wants to include advice in the security training provided to international travelers. What practice should Susan recommend that they adopt for connecting to networks while they travel?

   A. Only connect to public Wi-Fi.

   B. Use a VPN for all connections.

   C. Only use websites that support TLS.

   D. Do not connect to networks while traveling.

23. Ricky is seeking a list of information security vulnerabilities in applications, devices, and operating systems. Which one of the following threat intelligence sources would be most useful to him?

A. OWASP

B. CIS

C. Microsoft Security Bulletins

D. CVE

24. Which of the following would normally be considered an example of a disaster when performing disaster recovery planning? (Select all that apply.)

A. Hacking incident

B. Flood

C. Fire

D. Terrorism

25. Glenda would like to conduct a disaster recovery test and is seeking a test that will allow a review of the plan with no disruption to normal information system activities and as minimal a commitment of time as possible. What type of test should she choose?

A. Tabletop exercise

B. Parallel test

C. Full interruption test

D. Read-through

26. Which one of the following is not an example of a backup tape rotation scheme?

A. Grandfather-Father-Son

B. Meet-in-the-Middle

C. Tower of Hanoi

D. Six Cartridge Weekly

27. Helen is implementing a new security mechanism for granting employees administrative privileges in the accounting system. She designs the process so that both the employee's manager and the accounting manager must approve the request before the access is granted. What information security principle is Helen enforcing?

A. Least privilege

B. Two-person control

C. Job rotation

D. Segregation of duties

28. Frank is considering the use of different types of evidence in an upcoming criminal matter. Which one of the following is not a requirement for evidence to be admissible in court?

   A. The evidence must be relevant.

   B. The evidence must be material.

   C. The evidence must be tangible.

   D. The evidence must be competently acquired.

29. Harold recently completed leading the postmortem review of a security incident. What documentation should he prepare next?

   A. A lessons learned document

   B. A risk assessment

   C. A remediation list

   D. A mitigation checklist

30. Beth is creating a new cybersecurity incident response team (CSIRT) and would like to determine the appropriate team membership. Which of the following groups would she normally include? (Select all that apply.)

   A. Information security

   B. Law enforcement

   C. Senior management

   D. Public affairs

31. Sam is responsible for backing up his company's primary file server. He configured a backup schedule that performs full backups every Monday evening at 9 p.m. and differential backups on other days of the week at that same time. Files change according to the information shown here. How many files will be copied in Wednesday's backup?

> File Modifications
> Monday 8 a.m. - File 1 created
> Monday 10 a.m. - File 2 created
> Monday 11 a.m. - File 3 created
> Monday 4 p.m. - File 1 modified
> Monday 5 p.m. - File 4 created
> Tuesday 8 a.m. - File 1 modified
> Tuesday 9 a.m. - File 2 modified
> Tuesday 10 a.m. - File 5 created
> Wednesday 8 a.m. - File 3 modified
> Wednesday 9 a.m. - File 6 created

   A. 2

   B. 3

   C. 5

   D. 6

32. Which one of the following security tools is not capable of generating an active response to a security event?

  A. IPS

  B. Firewall

  C. IDS

  D. Antivirus software

33. Scott is responsible for disposing of disk drives that have been pulled from his company's SAN as they are retired. Which of the following options should he avoid if the data on the SAN is considered highly sensitive by his organization?

  A. Destroy them physically.

  B. Sign a contract with the SAN vendor that requires appropriate disposal and provides a certification process.

  C. Reformat each drive before it leaves the organization.

  D. Use a secure wipe tool like DBAN.

34. Which of the following topics is least likely to be included in a company's user security training and awareness program?

  A. Insider threat

  B. Social media impact

  C. 2FA fatigue

  D. Secure router configuration guidelines

35. Which one of the following types of agreements is the most formal document that contains expectations about availability and other performance parameters between a service provider and a customer?

  A. Service-level agreement (SLA)

  B. Operational-level agreement (OLA)

  C. Memorandum of understanding (MOU)

  D. Statement of work (SOW)

36. As the CIO of a large organization, Clara would like to adopt standard processes for managing IT activities. Which one of the following frameworks focuses on IT service management and includes topics such as change management, configuration management, and service-level agreements?

  A. ITIL

  B. PMBOK

  C. PCI DSS

  D. TOGAF

37. Richard is experiencing issues with the quality of network service on his organization's network. The primary symptom is that packets are consistently taking too long to travel from their source to their destination. What term describes the issue Richard is facing?

   A. Jitter

   B. Packet loss

   C. Interference

   D. Latency

38. Joe wants to test a program he suspects may contain malware. What technology can he use to isolate the program while it runs?

   A. ASLR

   B. Sandboxing

   C. Clipping

   D. Process isolation

39. Which one of the following is an example of a non-natural disaster?

   A. Hurricane

   B. Flood

   C. Mudslide

   D. Transformer explosion

40. Anne wants to gather information about security settings as well as build an overall view of her organization's assets by gathering data about a group of Windows 11 workstations spread throughout her company. What Windows tool is best suited to this type of configuration management task?

   A. ConfigMgr

   B. Group Policy

   C. SCOM

   D. A custom PowerShell script

41. Javier is verifying that only IT system administrators have the ability to log on to servers used for administrative purposes. What principle of information security is he enforcing?

   A. Need to know

   B. Least privilege

   C. Two-person control

   D. Transitive trust

42. Which one of the following is not a basic preventive measure that you can take to protect your systems and applications against attack?

   A. Implement intrusion detection and prevention systems.

   B. Maintain current patch levels on all operating systems and applications.

   C. Remove unnecessary accounts and services.

   D. Conduct forensic imaging of all systems.

43. Chas is a cybersecurity manager who is concerned that the cloud provider his organization relies upon for disaster recovery may not be able to meet their needs in the event that a disaster strikes multiple customers simultaneously. What type of agreement should Chas enter into with this provider?

   A. Nondisclosure agreement

   B. Resource capacity agreement

   C. Mutual assistance agreement

   D. Business partnership agreement

44. Which one of the following is an example of a computer security incident?

   A. Failure of a backup to complete properly

   B. System access recorded in a log

   C. Unauthorized vulnerability scan of a file server

   D. Update of antivirus signatures

45. Roland is a physical security specialist in an organization that has a large amount of expensive lab equipment that often moves around the facility. Which one of the following technologies would provide the most automation of an inventory control process in a cost-effective manner?

   A. IPS

   B. Wi-Fi

   C. RFID

   D. Ethernet

46. Connor's company recently experienced a denial-of-service attack that Connor believes came from an inside source. If true, what type of event has the company experienced?

   A. Espionage

   B. Confidentiality breach

   C. Sabotage

   D. Integrity breach

47. Evan detects an attack against a server in his organization and examines the TCP flags on a series of packets, shown in the following diagram. What type of attack most likely took place?

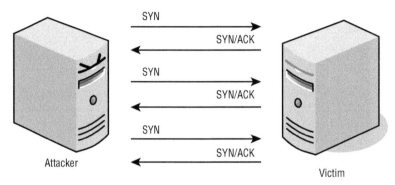

A. SYN flood

B. Ping flood

C. Smurf

D. Fraggle

48. Florian is building a disaster recovery plan for his organization and would like to determine the amount of time that a particular IT service may be down without causing serious damage to business operations. What variable is Florian calculating?

A. RTO

B. MTD

C. RPO

D. SLA

49. Which of the following would normally be classified as zero-day attacks?

A. An attacker who is new to the world of hacking

B. A database attack that places the date 00/00/0000 in data tables in an attempt to exploit flaws in business logic

C. An attack previously unknown to the security community

D. An attack that sets the operating system date and time to 00/00/0000 and 00:00:00

50. Rob is conducting a forensic investigation and is looking for elements of trace digital evidence. Which one of the following principles applies most closely to his work?

A. Kerckhoff's principle

B. Principle of least privilege

C. Defense-in-depth principle

D. Locard's principle

51. During an incident investigation, investigators meet with a system administrator who may have information about the incident but is not a suspect. What type of conversation is taking place during this meeting?

   A. Interview

   B. Interrogation

   C. Both an interview and an interrogation

   D. Neither an interview nor an interrogation

52. What technique has been used to protect the intellectual property shown here?

Source: Bruce Jaffe / USGS / Public domain

   A. Steganography

   B. Clipping

   C. Sampling

   D. Watermarking

53. You are working to evaluate the risk of flood to an area as part of a business continuity planning (BCP) effort. You consult the flood maps from the Federal Emergency Management Agency (FEMA). According to those maps, the area lies within a 200-year flood plain. What is the annualized rate of occurrence (ARO) of a flood in that region?

   A. 200

   B. 0.01

   C. 0.02

   D. 0.005

54. Which one of the following individuals poses the greatest risk to security in most well-defended organizations?

   A. Political activist

   B. Malicious insider

   C. Script kiddie

   D. Thrill attacker

55. Veronica is considering the implementation of a database recovery mechanism recommended by a consultant. In the recommended approach, an automated process will move database backups from the primary facility to an off-site location each night. What type of database recovery technique is the consultant describing?

   A. Remote journaling

   B. Remote mirroring

   C. Electronic vaulting

   D. Transaction logging

56. When designing an access control scheme, Hilda set up roles so that the same person does not have the ability to provision a new user account and assign superuser privileges to an account. What information security principle is Hilda following?

   A. Least privilege

   B. Segregation of duties

   C. Job rotation

   D. Security through obscurity

57. Patrick was asked to implement a threat-hunting program for his organization. Which one of the following is the basic assumption of a threat-hunting program that he should use as he plans his work?

   A. Security controls were designed using a defense-in-depth strategy.

   B. Audits may uncover control deficiencies.

   C. Attackers may already be present on the network.

   D. Defense mechanisms may contain unpatched vulnerabilities.

58. Brian is developing the training program for his organization's disaster recovery program and would like to make sure that participants understand when disaster activity concludes. Which one of the following events marks the completion of a disaster recovery process?

   A. Securing property and life safety

   B. Restoring operations in an alternate facility

   C. Restoring operations in the primary facility

   D. Standing down first responders

59. Melanie suspects that someone is using malicious software to steal computing cycles from her company. Which one of the following security tools would be in the best position to detect this type of incident?

A. NIDS

B. Firewall

C. HIDS

D. DLP

60. Brandon observes that an authorized user of a system on his network recently misused his account to exploit a system vulnerability against a shared server that allowed him to gain root access to that server. What type of attack took place?

A. Denial-of-service

B. Privilege escalation

C. Reconnaissance

D. Brute force

61. Carla has worked for her company for 15 years and has held a variety of different positions. Each time she changed positions, she gained new privileges associated with that position, but no privileges were ever taken away. What concept describes the sets of privileges she has accumulated?

A. Entitlement

B. Privilege creep

C. Transitivity

D. Isolation

62. During what phase of the incident response process do administrators take action to limit the effect or scope of an incident?

A. Detection

B. Response

C. Mitigation

D. Recovery

For questions 63–66, please refer to the following scenario:

Ann is a security professional for a midsize business and typically handles log analysis and security monitoring tasks for her organization. One of her roles is to monitor alerts originating from the organization's intrusion detection system. The system typically generates several dozen alerts each day, and many of those alerts turn out to be false alarms after her investigation.

This morning, the intrusion detection system alerted because the network began to receive an unusually high volume of inbound traffic. Ann received this alert and began looking into the origin of the traffic.

63. At this point in the incident response process, what term best describes what has occurred in Ann's organization?

    A. Security occurrence

    B. Security incident

    C. Security event

    D. Security intrusion

64. Ann continues her investigation and realizes that the traffic generating the alert is abnormally high volumes of inbound UDP traffic on port 53. What service typically uses this port?

    A. DNS

    B. SSH/SCP

    C. SSL/TLS

    D. HTTP

65. As Ann analyzes the traffic further, she realizes that the traffic is coming from many different sources and has overwhelmed the network, preventing legitimate uses. The inbound packets are responses to queries that she does not see in outbound traffic. The responses are abnormally large for their type. What type of attack should Ann suspect?

    A. Reconnaissance

    B. Malicious code

    C. System penetration

    D. Denial of service

66. Now that Ann understands that an attack has taken place that violates her organization's security policy, what term best describes what has occurred in Ann's organization?

    A. Security occurrence

    B. Security incident

    C. Security event

    D. Security intrusion

67. Frank is seeking to introduce a hacker's laptop in court as evidence against the hacker. The laptop does contain logs that indicate the hacker committed the crime, but the court ruled that the search of the apartment that resulted in police finding the laptop was unconstitutional. What admissibility criteria prevents Frank from introducing the laptop as evidence?

A. Materiality

B. Relevance

C. Hearsay

D. Competence

68. Gordon suspects that a hacker has penetrated a system belonging to his company. The system does not contain any regulated information, and Gordon wants to conduct an investigation on behalf of his company. He has permission from his supervisor to conduct the investigation. Which of the following statements is true?

A. Gordon is legally required to contact law enforcement before beginning the investigation.

B. Gordon may not conduct his own investigation.

C. Gordon's investigation may include examining the contents of hard disks, network traffic, and any other systems or information belonging to the company.

D. Gordon may ethically perform "hack back" activities after identifying the perpetrator.

69. Which one of the following tools provides an organization with the greatest level of protection against a software vendor going out of business?

A. Service-level agreement

B. Escrow agreement

C. Mutual assistance agreement

D. PCI DSS compliance agreement

70. Fran is considering new human resources policies for her bank that will deter fraud. She plans to implement a mandatory vacation policy. What is typically considered the shortest effective length of a mandatory vacation?

A. Two days

B. Four days

C. One week

D. One month

71. Which of the following events would constitute a security incident? (Select all that apply.)

A. An attempted network intrusion

B. A successful database intrusion

C. A malware infection

D. A successful attempt to access a file

E. A violation of a confidentiality policy

F. An unsuccessful attempt to remove information from a secured area

72. Amanda is configuring her organization's firewall to implement egress filtering. Which one of the following traffic types should be blocked by her organization's egress filtering policy? (Select all that apply.)

A. Traffic rapidly scanning many IP addresses on port 22

B. Traffic with a broadcast destination

C. Traffic with a source address from an external network

D. Traffic with a destination address on an external network

73. Allie is responsible for reviewing authentication logs on her organization's network. She does not have the time to review all logs, so she decides to choose only records where there have been four or more invalid authentication attempts. What technique is Allie using to reduce the size of the pool?

A. Sampling

B. Random selection

C. Clipping

D. Statistical analysis

74. You are performing an investigation into a potential bot infection on your network and want to perform a forensic analysis of the information that passed between different systems on your network and those on the Internet. You believe that the information was likely encrypted. You are beginning your investigation after the activity concluded. What would be the best and easiest way to obtain the source of this information?

A. Packet captures

B. NetFlow data

C. Intrusion detection system logs

D. Centralized authentication records

75. Which one of the following tools helps system administrators by providing a standard, secure template of configuration settings for operating systems and applications?

A. Security guidelines

B. Security policy

C. Baseline configuration

D. Running configuration

76. What type of disaster recovery test activates the alternate processing facility and uses it to conduct transactions but leaves the primary site up and running?

A. Full interruption test

B. Parallel test

C. Read-through

D. Tabletop exercise

77. During which phase of the incident response process would an analyst receive an intrusion detection system alert and verify its accuracy?

A. Response

B. Mitigation

C. Detection

D. Reporting

78. Kevin is developing a continuous security monitoring strategy for his organization. Which one of the following is not normally used when determining assessment and monitoring frequency?

A. Threat intelligence

B. System categorization/impact level

C. Security control operational burden

D. Organizational risk tolerance

79. Hunter is reviewing his organization's monitoring strategy and identifying new technologies that they might deploy. His assessment reveals that the firm is not doing enough to monitor employee activity on endpoint devices. Which one of the following technologies would best meet his needs?

A. EDR

B. IPS

C. IDS

D. UEBA

80. Bruce is seeing quite a bit of suspicious activity on his network. After consulting records in his SIEM, it appears that an outside entity is attempting to connect to all of his systems using a TCP connection on port 22. What type of scanning is the outsider likely engaging in?

A. FTP scanning

B. Telnet scanning

C. SSH scanning

D. HTTP scanning

81. Dylan believes that a database server in his environment was compromised using a SQL injection attack. Which one of the following actions would Dylan most likely take during the remediation phase of the attack?

A. Rebuilding the database from backups

B. Adding input validation to a web application

C. Reviewing firewall logs

D. Reviewing database logs

82. Roger recently accepted a new position as a security professional at a company that runs its entire IT infrastructure within an IaaS environment. Which one of the following would most likely be the responsibility of Roger's firm?

  A. Configuring the network firewall

  B. Applying hypervisor updates

  C. Patching operating systems

  D. Wiping drives prior to disposal

83. What technique can application developers use to test applications in an isolated virtualized environment before allowing them on a production network?

  A. Penetration testing

  B. Sandboxing

  C. White-box testing

  D. Black-box testing

84. Gina is the firewall administrator for a small business and recently installed a new firewall. After seeing signs of unusually heavy network traffic, she checked the intrusion detection system, which reported that a SYN flood attack was underway. What firewall configuration change can Gina make to most effectively prevent this attack?

  A. Block SYN from known IPs.

  B. Block SYN from unknown IPs.

  C. Enable SYN-ACK spoofing at the firewall.

  D. Disable TCP.

85. Nancy is leading an effort to modernize her organization's antimalware protection and would like to add endpoint detection and response (EDR) capabilities. Which of the following actions are normally supported by EDR systems? (Select all that apply.)

  A. Analyzing endpoint memory, filesystem, and network activity for signs of malicious activity

  B. Automatically isolating possible malicious activity to contain the potential damage

  C. Conducting simulated phishing campaigns

  D. Integration with threat intelligence sources

86. Alan is assessing the potential for using machine learning and artificial intelligence in his cybersecurity program. Which of the following activities is most likely to benefit from this technology?

  A. Intrusion detection

  B. Account provisioning

  C. Firewall rule modification

  D. Media sanitization

87. Timber Industries recently had a dispute with a customer. During a meeting with his account representative, the customer stood up and declared, "There is no other solution. We will have to take this matter to court." He then left the room. When does Timber Industries have an obligation to begin preserving evidence?

   A. Immediately

   B. Upon receipt of a notice of litigation from opposing attorneys

   C. Upon receipt of a subpoena

   D. Upon receipt of a court order

88. Candace is designing a backup strategy for her organization's file server. She would like to perform a backup every weekday that has the smallest possible storage footprint. What type of backup should she perform?

   A. Incremental backup

   B. Full backup

   C. Differential backup

   D. Transaction log backup

89. Darcy is a computer security specialist who is assisting with the prosecution of a hacker. The prosecutor requests that Darcy give testimony in court about whether, in her opinion, the logs and other records in a case are indicative of a hacking attempt. What type of evidence is Darcy being asked to provide?

   A. Expert opinion

   B. Direct evidence

   C. Real evidence

   D. Documentary evidence

90. Which one of the following techniques is not commonly used to remove unwanted remnant data from magnetic tapes?

   A. Physical destruction

   B. Degaussing

   C. Overwriting

   D. Reformatting

91. Sally is building a new server for use in her environment and plans to implement RAID level 1 as a storage availability control. What is the minimum number of physical hard disks that she needs to implement this approach?

   A. One

   B. Two

   C. Three

   D. Five

92. Jerome is conducting a forensic investigation and is reviewing database server logs to investigate query contents for evidence of SQL injection attacks. What type of analysis is he performing?

   A. Hardware analysis

   B. Software analysis

   C. Network analysis

   D. Media analysis

93. Quigley Computing regularly ships tapes of backup data across the country to a secondary facility. These tapes contain confidential information. What is the most important security control that Quigley can use to protect these tapes?

   A. Locked shipping containers

   B. Private couriers

   C. Data encryption

   D. Media rotation

94. Carolyn is concerned that users on her network may be storing sensitive information, such as Social Security numbers, on their hard drives without proper authorization or security controls. What third-party security service can she implement to best detect this activity?

   A. IDS

   B. IPS

   C. DLP

   D. TLS

95. Gavin is the disaster recovery team leader for his organization, which is currently in the response phase of an incident that has severe customer impact. Gavin just received a phone call from a reporter asking for details on the root cause and an estimated recovery time. Gavin has this information at his fingertips. What should he do?

   A. Provide the information to the reporter.

   B. Request a few minutes to gather the information and return the call.

   C. Refer the matter to the public relations department.

   D. Refuse to provide any information.

96. Pauline is reviewing her organization's emergency management plans. What should be the highest priority when creating these plans?

   A. Protection of mission-critical data

   B. Preservation of operational systems

   C. Collection of evidence

   D. Preservation of safety

97. Barry is the CIO of an organization that recently suffered a serious operational issue that required activation of the disaster recovery plan. He would like to conduct a lessons learned session to review the incident. Who would be the best facilitator for this session?

    A. Barry, as chief information officer

    B. Chief information security officer

    C. Disaster recovery team leader

    D. External consultant

98. Brent is reviewing the controls that will protect his organization in the event of a sustained period of power loss. Which one of the following solutions would best meet his needs?

    A. Redundant servers

    B. Uninterruptible power supply (UPS)

    C. Generator

    D. RAID

99. Match each of the numbered terms with its correct lettered definition:

Terms:

    1. Honeypot

    2. Honeynet

    3. Pseudo-flaw

    4. Darknet

Definitions:

    A. An intentionally designed vulnerability used to lure in an attacker

    B. A network set up with intentional vulnerabilities

    C. A system set up with intentional vulnerabilities

    D. A monitored network without any hosts

100. Match each of the numbered types of recovery capabilities to their correct lettered definition:

Terms:

    1. Hot site

    2. Cold site

    3. Warm site

    4. Service bureau

Definitions:

A. An organization that can provide on-site or off-site IT services in the event of a disaster

B. A site with dedicated storage and real-time data replication, often with shared equipment that allows restoration of service in a very short time

C. A site that relies on shared storage and backups for recovery

D. A rented space with power, cooling, and connectivity that can accept equipment as part of a recovery effort

Chapter

8

Software Development Security (Domain 8)

SUBDOMAINS

✓ 8.1 Understand and integrate security into the Software Development Life Cycle (SDLC)

✓ 8.2 Identify and apply security controls in software development ecosystems

✓ 8.3 Assess the effectiveness of software security

✓ 8.4 Assess security impact of acquired software

✓ 8.5 Define and apply secure coding guidelines and standards

1. Susan provides a public RESTful API for her organization's data but wants to limit its use to trusted partners. She intends to use API keys. What other recommendation would you give Susan to limit the potential abuse of the service?

   A. Limit request rates.

   B. Force HTTP-only requests.

   C. Avoid tokens due to bandwidth constraints.

   D. Blacklist HTTP methods such as GET, POST, and PUT.

2. Darren is conducting a threat-hunting exercise and would like to look for botnet indicators of compromise. Which of the following are common ways that attackers leverage botnets? (Select all that apply.)

   A. Mining cryptocurrency

   B. Conducting brute-force attacks

   C. Scanning for vulnerable systems

   D. Conducting man-in-the-middle attacks

3. Which one of the following statements is not true about code review?

   A. Code review should be a peer-driven process that includes multiple developers.

   B. Code review may be automated.

   C. Code review occurs during the design phase.

   D. Code reviewers may expect to review several hundred lines of code per hour.

4. Kathleen is reviewing the Ruby code shown here. What security technique is this code using?

   ```
   insert_new_user = db.prepare "INSERT INTO users (name, userid, gender,
   usertype) VALUES (?, ? ,?,?)"
   insert_new_user.execute 'davids', '194567', 'male', 'admin'
   ```

   A. Parameterization

   B. Typecasting

   C. Gem cutting

   D. Stored procedures

5. Jessica is reviewing her organization's change management process and would like to verify that changes to software include acceptance testing. Which process is responsible for achieving this goal?

   A. Request control

   B. Change control

   C. Release control

   D. Configuration control

6. Ashley is investigating an attack that compromised an account of one of her users. In the attack, the attacker forced the submission of an authenticated request to a third-party site by exploiting trust relationships in the user's browser. What type of attack most likely took place?

A. XSS

B. CSRF

C. SQL injection

D. Session hijacking

7. Arnold is creating a new software package and is making use of the OpenSSL library. What term best describes the library he is using?

A. Open source

B. COTS

C. Third-party

D. Managed

8. Jaime is a technical support analyst and is asked to visit a user whose computer is displaying the error message shown here. What state has this computer entered?

```
A problem has been detected and Windows has been shut down to prevent damage
to your computer.

The problem seems to be caused by the following file: SPCMDCON.SYS

PAGE_FAULT_IN_NONPAGED_AREA

If this is the first time you've seen this stop error screen,
restart your computer. If this screen appears again, follow
these steps:

Check to make sure any new hardware or software is properly installed.
If this is a new installation, ask your hardware or software manufacturer
for any windows updates you might need.

If problems continue, disable or remove any newly installed hardware
or software. Disable BIOS memory options such as caching or shadowing.
If you need to use Safe Mode to remove or disable components, restart
your computer, press F8 to select Advanced Startup Options, and then
select Safe Mode.

Technical information:

*** STOP: 0x00000050 (0xFD3094C2,0x00000001,0xFBFE7617,0x00000000)


***   SPCMDCON.SYS - Address FBFE7617 base at FBFE5000, DateStamp 3d6dd67c
```

A. Fail open

B. Irrecoverable error

C. Memory exhaustion

D. Fail secure

9. Joshua is developing a software threat modeling program for his organization. Which of the following are appropriate goals for the program? (Select all that apply.)

A. To reduce the number of security-related design flaws

B. To reduce the number of security-related coding flaws

C. To reduce the severity of non-security-related flaws

D. To reduce the number of threat vectors

10. In the diagram shown here, which is an example of a method?

Account
Balance: currency = 0 Owner: string
AddFunds(deposit: currency) RemoveFunds(withdrawal: currency)

A. Account

B. Owner

C. AddFunds

D. Balance

11. Wanda is reviewing the application development documentation used by her organization and finds the life-cycle illustration shown here. What application development method is her organization using?

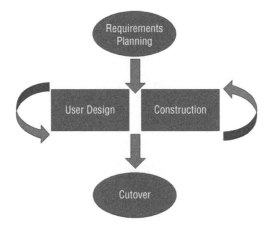

A. Waterfall

B. Spiral

C. Agile

D. RAD

12. Which one of the following testing methodologies typically works without access to source code?

A. Dynamic testing

B. Static testing

C. White-box testing

D. Code review

13. Lucca is analyzing a web application that his organization acquired from a third-party vendor. Lucca determined that the application contains a flaw that causes users who are logged in to be able to take actions they should not be able to in their role. What type of security vulnerability should this be classified as?

A. Data validation

B. Session management

C. Authorization

D. Error handling

14. Bobby is investigating how an authorized database user is gaining access to information outside his normal clearance level. Bobby believes that the user is making use of a type of function that summarizes data. What term describes this type of function?

A. Inference

B. Polymorphic

C. Aggregate

D. Modular

15. Taylor would like to better protect the applications developed by her organization against buffer overflow attacks. Which of the following controls would best provide this protection?

A. Encryption

B. Input validation

C. Firewall

D. Intrusion prevention system

16. Kayla recently completed a thorough risk analysis and mitigation review of the software developed by her team and identified three persistent issues:

- Cross-site scripting
- SQL injection
- Buffer overflows

What is the most significant deficiency in her team's work identified by these issues?

A. Lack of API security

B. Improper error handling

C. Improper or missing input validation

D. Source code design issues

For questions 17–20, please refer to the following scenario:

Robert is a consultant who helps organizations create and develop mature software development practices. He prefers to use the Software Capability Maturity Model (SW-CMM) to evaluate the current and future status of organizations using both independent review and self-assessments. He is currently working with two different clients.

Acme Widgets is not well organized with its software development practices. It does have a dedicated team of developers who do "whatever it takes" to get software out the door, but it does not have any formal processes.

Beta Particles is a company with years of experience developing software using formal, documented software development processes. It uses a standard model for software development but does not have quantitative management of those processes.

17. What phase of the SW-CMM should Robert report as the current status of Acme Widgets?
    A. Defined
    B. Repeatable
    C. Initial
    D. Managed

18. Robert is working with Acme Widgets on a strategy to advance their software development practices. What SW-CMM stage should be their next target milestone?
    A. Defined
    B. Repeatable
    C. Initial
    D. Managed

19. What phase of the SW-CMM should Robert report as the current status of Beta Particles?
    A. Defined
    B. Repeatable
    C. Optimizing
    D. Managed

20. Robert is also working with Beta Particles on a strategy to advance their software development practices. What SW-CMM stage should be their next target milestone?
    A. Defined
    B. Repeatable
    C. Optimizing
    D. Managed

21. Which one of the following database keys is used to enforce referential integrity relationships between tables?

    A. Primary key

    B. Candidate key

    C. Foreign key

    D. Master key

22. Brynn believes that a system in her organization may have been compromised by a macro virus. Which one of the following files is most likely to be the culprit?

    A. `projections.doc`

    B. `command.com`

    C. `command.exe`

    D. `loopmaster.exe`

23. Victor created a database table that contains information on his organization's employees. The table contains the employee's user ID, three different telephone number fields (home, work, and mobile), the employee's office location, and the employee's job title. There are 16 records in the table. What is the degree of this table?

    A. 3

    B. 4

    C. 6

    D. 16

24. Carrie is analyzing the application logs for her web-based application and comes across the following string:

`../../../../../../../../etc/passwd`

What type of attack was likely attempted against Carrie's application?

    A. Command injection

    B. Session hijacking

    C. Directory traversal

    D. Brute-force

25. When should a design review take place when following an SDLC approach to software development?

    A. After the code review

    B. After user acceptance testing

    C. After the development of functional requirements

    D. After the completion of unit testing

26. Tracy is preparing to apply a patch to her organization's enterprise resource planning system. She is concerned that the patch may introduce flaws that did not exist in prior versions, so she plans to conduct a test that will compare previous responses to input with those produced by the newly patched application. What type of testing is Tracy planning?

A. Unit testing

B. Acceptance testing

C. Regression testing

D. Vulnerability testing

27. What term is used to describe the level of confidence that software is free from vulnerabilities, either intentionally designed into the software or accidentally inserted at any time during its life cycle, and that the software functions in the intended manner?

A. Validation

B. Accreditation

C. Confidence interval

D. Assurance

28. Victor recently took a new position at an online dating website and is responsible for leading a team of developers. He realized quickly that the developers are having issues with production code because they are working on different projects that result in conflicting modifications to the production code. What process should Victor invest in improving?

A. Request control

B. Release control

C. Change control

D. Configuration control

29. Tom is assessing security risks related to a database he manages. Examining user access controls, he determines that users have access to individual records in a table that match their clearances, but if they pull multiple records, that collection of facts has a higher classification than the classification of any of those facts standing alone and exceeds the permitted access. What type of issue has Tom identified?

A. Inference

B. SQL injection

C. Multilevel security

D. Aggregation

30. Ron leads a team of software developers who find themselves often re-creating code that performs common functions. What software development tool could he use to best address this situation?

A. Code repositories

B. Code libraries

C. IDEs

D. DAST

31. Vivian would like to hire a software tester to come in and evaluate a new web application from a user's perspective. Which of the following tests best simulates that perspective?

A. Black box

B. Gray box

C. Blue box

D. White box

32. Referring to the database transaction shown here, what would happen if no account exists in the Accounts table with account number 1001?

```
BEGIN TRANSACTION

UPDATE accounts
SET balance = balance + 250
WHERE account_number = 1001;

UPDATE accounts
SET balance = balance - 250
WHERE account_number = 2002;

COMMIT TRANSACTION
```

A. The database would create a new account with this account number and give it a $250 balance.

B. The database would ignore that command and still reduce the balance of the second account by $250.

C. The database would roll back the transaction, ignoring the results of both commands.

D. The database would generate an error message.

33. Brandon is a software developer seeking to integrate his software with a popular social media site. The site provides him with software libraries that he can use to better integrate his code as well as other tools that make his work easier. What term best describes the service he is using?

A. SDK

B. DLP

C. IDE

D. API

34. Kim is troubleshooting an application firewall that serves as a supplement to the organization's network and host firewalls and intrusion prevention system, providing added protection against web-based attacks. The issue the organization is experiencing is that the firewall technology suffers somewhat frequent restarts that render it unavailable for 10 minutes at a time. What configuration might Kim consider to maintain availability during that period at the lowest cost to the company?

A. High availability cluster

B. Failover device

C. Fail open

D. Redundant disks

35. What type of security issue arises when an attacker can deduce a more sensitive piece of information by analyzing several pieces of information classified at a lower level?

   A. SQL injection

   B. Multilevel security

   C. Parameterization

   D. Inference

36. Greg is battling a malware outbreak in his organization. He used specialized malware analysis tools to capture samples of the malware from three different systems and noticed that the code is changing slightly from infection to infection. Greg believes that this is the reason that antivirus software is having a tough time defeating the outbreak. What type of malware should Greg suspect is responsible for this security incident?

   A. Stealth virus

   B. Polymorphic virus

   C. Multipartite virus

   D. Encrypted virus

For questions 37–40, please refer to the following scenario:

Linda is reviewing posts to a user forum on her company's website, and when she browses a certain post, a message pops up in a dialog box on her screen reading "Alert." She reviews the source code for the post and finds the following code snippet:

```
<script>alert('Alert');</script>
```

37. What vulnerability definitely exists on Linda's message board?

   A. Cross-site scripting

   B. Cross-site request forgery

   C. SQL injection

   D. Improper authentication

38. What was the likely motivation of the user who posted the message on the forum containing this code?

   A. Reconnaissance

   B. Theft of sensitive information

   C. Credential stealing

   D. Social engineering

39. Linda communicates with the vendor and determines that no patch is available to correct this vulnerability. Which one of the following devices would best help her defend the application against further attack?

   A. VPN

   B. WAF

   C. DLP

   D. IDS

40. In further discussions with the vendor, Linda finds that they are willing to correct the issue but do not know how to update their software. What technique would be most effective in mitigating the vulnerability of the application to this type of attack?

A. Bounds checking

B. Peer review

C. Input validation

D. OS patching

41. Hannah is a software developer working on creating statistical software using the R programming language. She uses the RStudio tool, shown here, to assist her in writing this code. What term best describes this tool?

    A. SDK

    B. IDE

    C. API

    D. DLP

42. Which of the following configurations within the Scaled Agile Framework (SAFe) is specifically designed to support enterprises in building and maintaining large integrated solutions with the collaboration of hundreds of practitioners?

    A. Large Solution SAFe

    B. Portfolio SAFe

    C. Essential SAFe

    D. Full SAFe

43. Alan is deploying Java code to a variety of machines in his environment and must install the JVM on those machines first. What term best describes the JVM in this case?

    A. Repository

    B. Change manager

    C. Runtime

    D. Sandbox

44. Christine is nearing the final stages of testing a new software package. Which one of the following types of software testing usually occurs last and is executed against test scenarios?

    A. Unit testing

    B. Integration testing

    C. User acceptance testing

    D. System testing

45. Alexis' organization recently moved to a CI/CD approach for software development where they intend to speed up the deployment of code supporting their website. What is the most reasonable frequency that they can expect to achieve using this type of approach?

    A. Monthly deployments

    B. Weekly deployments

    C. Daily deployments

    D. Hundreds of daily deployments

46. Amber is conducting a threat intelligence project and would like to find a source of information on threats to her organization's web applications. Which of the following organizations is widely considered as the definitive source for information on web-based attack vectors?

    A. ISC2

    B. ISACA

    C. OWASP

    D. Mozilla Foundation

47. Chris is a software developer, and he is actively writing code for an application. What phase of the Agile process is he in?

    A. Planning

    B. Sprints

    C. Deployment

    D. Testing

48. Alyssa's team recently implemented a new system that gathers information from a variety of different log sources, analyzes that information, and then triggers automated playbooks in response to security events. What term best describes this technology?

    A. SIEM

    B. Log repositories

    C. IPS

    D. SOAR

49. Chris is reviewing the code of an open-source application that he is planning to use in his organization. He finds the code excerpt shown here:

```
int myarray[10];
myarray[10] = 8;
```

What type of attack is taking place?

    A. Mismatched data types

    B. Overflow

    C. SQL injection

    D. Covert channel

50. Which one of the following database issues occurs when one transaction writes a value to the database that overwrites a value that was needed by transactions with earlier precedence?

    A. Dirty read

    B. Incorrect summary

    C. Lost update

    D. SQL injection

51. Belinda would like to better protect users of her organization's web application from cookie-stealing attacks. Which one of the following is the most effective control against this type of session hijacking attack?

    A. TLS

    B. Complex session cookies

    C. SSL

    D. Expiring cookies frequently

52. In a software configuration management program, what is the primary role of the CAB?

A. Approve the credentials of developers.

B. Facilitate lessons learned sessions.

C. Review and approve/reject code changes.

D. Prioritize software development efforts.

53. Which one of the following tools is commonly used by software developers to interact with and manage code that is stored in code repositories?

A. grep

B. git

C. lsof

D. gcc

54. While evaluating a potential security incident, Harry comes across a log entry from a web server request showing that a user entered the following input into a form field:

CARROT'&1=1;--

What type of attack was attempted?

A. Buffer overflow

B. Cross-site scripting

C. SQL injection

D. Cross-site request forgery

55. Which one of the following is not an effective control against SQL injection attacks?

A. Escaping

B. Client-side input validation

C. Parameterization

D. Limiting database permissions

56. Jason is reviewing the documentation for a software development project and comes across the diagram shown here. What type of diagram is he examining?

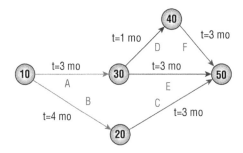

A. WBS chart

B. PERT chart

C. Gantt chart

D. Wireframe diagram

57. In what software testing technique does the evaluator retest a large number of scenarios each time that the software changes to verify that the results are consistent with a standard baseline?

A. Orthogonal array testing

B. Pattern testing

C. Matrix testing

D. Regression testing

58. Haley is reviewing code created by her organization for its possible exposure to web application vulnerabilities. Which one of the following conditions may make an application most vulnerable to a cross-site scripting (XSS) attack?

A. Input validation

B. Reflected input

C. Unpatched server

D. Promiscuous firewall rules

59. Roger is conducting a software test for a tax preparation application developed by his company. End users will access the application over the web, but Roger is conducting his test on the back end, evaluating the source code on the web server. What type of test is Roger conducting?

A. White box

B. Gray box

C. Blue box

D. Black box

60. Which of the following statements is true about heuristic-based antimalware software?

A. It has a lower false positive rate than signature detection.

B. It requires frequent definition updates to detect new malware.

C. It has a higher likelihood of detecting zero-day exploits than signature detection.

D. It monitors systems for files with content known to be viruses.

61. Martin is inspecting a system where the user reported unusual activity, including disk activity when the system is idle and abnormal CPU and network usage. He suspects that the machine is infected by a virus, but scans come up clean. What malware technique might be in use here that would explain the clean scan results?

A. File infector virus

B. MBR virus

C. Service injection virus

D. Stealth virus

62. Tomas discovers a line in his application log that appears to correspond with an attempt to conduct a directory traversal attack. He believes the attack was conducted using URL encoding. The line reads as follows:

```
%252E%252E%252F%252E%252E%252Fetc/passwd
```

What character is represented by the %252E value?

A. .

B. ,

C. ;

D. /

63. An attacker posted a message to a public discussion forum that contains an embedded malicious script that is not displayed to the user but executes on the user's system when read. What type of attack is this?

A. Persistent XSRF

B. Nonpersistent XSRF

C. Persistent XSS

D. Nonpersistent XSS

64. Which one of the following is not a principle of the Agile software development process?

A. Welcome changing requirements, even late in the development process.

B. Maximizing the amount of work not done is essential.

C. Clear documentation is the primary measure of progress.

D. Build projects around motivated individuals.

65. Gavin is an internal auditor tasked with examining the change management practices of his organization. He would like to review a series of changes made to a software package to determine whether they were properly documented. Where should he turn for a description of each proposed change?

A. CAB

B. RFC

C. SOAR

D. SIEM

66. Neal is working with a DynamoDB database. The database is not structured like a relational database but allows Neal to store data using a key-value store. What type of database is DynamoDB?

A. Relational database

B. Graph database

C. Hierarchical database

D. NoSQL database

67. In the transaction shown here, what would happen if the database failed in between the first and second update statements?

```
BEGIN TRANSACTION

UPDATE accounts
SET balance = balance + 250
WHERE account_number = 1001;

UPDATE accounts
SET balance = balance - 250
WHERE account_number = 2002;

COMMIT TRANSACTION
```

A. The database would credit the first account with $250 in funds but then not reduce the balance of the second account.

B. The database would ignore the first command and only reduce the balance of the second account by $250.

C. The database would roll back the transaction, ignoring the results of both commands.

D. The database would successfully execute both commands.

68. Tareck's organization makes use of a significant amount of COTS software. He recently discovered a significant buffer overflow vulnerability in the code of a COTS software package that is crucial to his business. What is the most likely way that Tareck can get this corrected?

A. Work with his software development team to modify the code.

B. Notify the vendor and request a patch.

C. Deploy an intrusion prevention system.

D. Update firewall rules.

69. Which one of the following statements is true about software testing?

A. Static testing works on runtime environments.

B. Static testing performs code analysis.

C. Dynamic testing uses automated tools, but static testing does not.

D. Static testing is a more important testing technique than dynamic testing.

70. David is working on developing a project schedule for a software development effort, and he comes across the chart shown here. What type of chart is this?

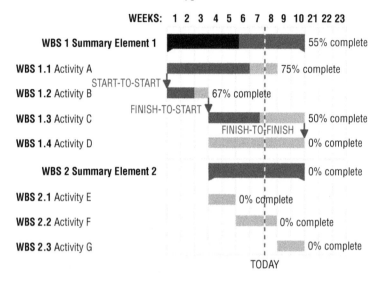

A. Work breakdown structure

B. Functional requirements

C. PERT chart

D. Gantt chart

71. Barry is a software tester who is working with a new gaming application developed by his company. He is playing the game on a smartphone to conduct his testing in an environment that best simulates a normal end user, but he is referencing the source code as he conducts his test. What type of test is Barry conducting?

A. White box

B. Black box

C. Blue box

D. Gray box

72. Miguel recently completed a penetration test of the applications that his organization uses to handle sensitive information. During his testing, he discovered a condition where an attacker can exploit a timing condition to manipulate software into allowing him to perform an unauthorized action. Which one of the following attack types fits this scenario?

A. SQL injection

B. Cross-site scripting

C. Pass the hash

D. TOC/TOU

73. What part of the security review process are the input parameters shown in the diagram used for?

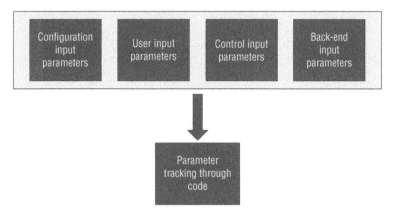

A. SQL injection review

B. Sprint review

C. Fagan inspection

D. Attack surface identification

74. What application security process can be described in these three major steps?

1. Decomposing the application

2. Determining and ranking threats

3. Determining countermeasures and mitigation

A. Fagan inspection

B. Threat modeling

C. Penetration testing

D. Code review

75. Which one of the following approaches to failure management is the most conservative from a security perspective?

A. Fail open

B. Fail mitigation

C. Fail clear

D. Fail closed

76. What software development model is shown here?

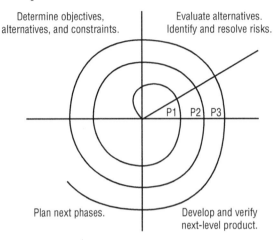

Determine objectives, alternatives, and constraints.

Evaluate alternatives. Identify and resolve risks.

Plan next phases.

Develop and verify next-level product.

P1   P2   P3

- **A.** Waterfall
- **B.** Agile
- **C.** Lean
- **D.** Spiral

77. Mark is considering replacing his organization's customer relationship management (CRM) solution with a new product that is available in the cloud. This new solution is completely managed by the vendor, and Mark's company will not have to write any code or manage any physical resources. What type of cloud solution is Mark considering?

- **A.** IaaS
- **B.** CaaS
- **C.** PaaS
- **D.** SaaS

78. Which one of the following change management processes is initiated by users rather than developers?

- **A.** Change request
- **B.** Change control
- **C.** Release control
- **D.** Design review

79. Teagan would like to better protect his organization against database inference attacks. Which one of the following techniques is an effective countermeasure against these attacks?

- **A.** Input validation
- **B.** Parameterization
- **C.** Polyinstantiation
- **D.** Server-side validation

80. Ursula is a government web developer who recently created a public application that offers property records. She would like to make it available for other developers to integrate into their applications. What can Ursula create to make it easiest for developers to call her code directly and integrate the output into their applications?

    A. Object model

    B. Data dictionary

    C. API

    D. Primary key

81. Nathan recently completed a software development project where he integrated the organization's network operations stack with their development processes. As a result, developers can modify firewall rules from their code on an as-needed basis. What term best describes this ability?

    A. Agile

    B. IaC

    C. SDS

    D. DevOps

82. TJ is inspecting a system where the user reported a strange error message and the inability to access files. He sees the window shown here. What type of malware should TJ suspect?

    A. Service injection

    B. Encrypted virus

    C. SQL injection

    D. Ransomware

83. Charles is developing a mission-critical application that has a direct impact on human safety. Time and cost are less important than correctly functioning software. Which of the following software development methodologies should he choose given these requirements?

    A. Agile

    B. DevOps

    C. Spiral

    D. Waterfall

84. Which one of the following types of artificial intelligence attempts to use complex computations to replicate the partial function of the human mind?

    A. Decision support systems

    B. Expert systems

    C. Knowledge bank

    D. Neural networks

85. At which level of the Software Capability Maturity Model (SW-CMM) does an organization introduce basic life-cycle management processes?

    A. Initial

    B. Repeatable

    C. Defined

    D. Managed

86. Lucas runs the accounting systems for his company. The morning after an essential employee was fired, systems began mysteriously losing information. Lucas suspects that the fired employee tampered with the systems prior to his departure. What type of attack should Lucas suspect?

    A. Privilege escalation

    B. SQL injection

    C. Logic bomb

    D. Remote code execution

87. Which one of the following principles would not be favored in an Agile approach to software development?

    A. Processes and tools over individuals and interactions

    B. Working software over comprehensive documentation

    C. Customer collaboration over contract negotiations

    D. Responding to change over following a plan

88. What technique do API developers most commonly use to limit access to an API to authorized individuals and applications?

   A. Encryption

   B. Input validation

   C. API keys

   D. IP filters

89. Reggie recently received a letter from his company's internal auditors scheduling the kickoff meeting for an assessment of his group. Which of the following should Reggie not expect to learn during that meeting?

   A. Scope of the audit

   B. Purpose of the audit

   C. Expected timeframe

   D. Expected findings

90. Which one of the following is the proper order of steps in the waterfall model of software development?

   A. Requirements, Design, Testing, Coding, Maintenance

   B. Requirements, Design, Coding, Testing, Maintenance

   C. Design, Requirements, Coding, Testing, Maintenance

   D. Design, Requirements, Testing, Coding, Maintenance

91. Renee is a software developer who writes code in Node.js for her organization. The company is considering moving from a self-hosted Node.js environment to one where Renee will run her code on application servers managed by a cloud vendor. What type of cloud solution is Renee's company considering?

   A. IaaS

   B. CaaS

   C. PaaS

   D. SaaS

92. Tom is writing a software program that calculates the sales tax for online orders placed from various jurisdictions. The application includes a user-defined field that allows the entry of the total sale amount. Tom would like to ensure that the data entered in this field is a properly formatted dollar amount. What technique should he use?

   A. Limit check

   B. Fail open

   C. Fail secure

   D. Input validation

93. Brian is helping implement a new software testing methodology for his organization and would like to review the completeness of his toolkit. Which of the following would be considered dynamic application security testing (DAST) tools? (Select all that apply.)

A. Code review

B. Fuzzing

C. Static analysis

D. Web application vulnerability scanning

94. What approach to technology management integrates the three components of technology management shown in this illustration?

A. Agile

B. Lean

C. DevOps

D. ITIL

95. Olivia is conducting a risk analysis of a web application that her organization obtained from a third party and is concerned that it might contain vulnerabilities. Which one of the following activities might she take to best mitigate the risk?

A. Deploy a WAF.

B. Implement strong encryption.

C. Purchase an insurance policy.

D. Discontinue use of the software.

96. Which one of the following database concurrency issues occurs when one transaction reads information that was written to a database by a second transaction that never committed?

A. Lost update

B. SQL injection

C. Incorrect summary

D. Dirty read

97. What software development concept was pioneered by the Defense Department in the 1990s as an effort to bring together diverse product development teams?

A. Integrated product team

B. Agile methodology

C. Scrum approach

D. User stories

98. Frank is working to select a new cloud service that will provide block storage for a server being built by his team. What category of cloud service is Frank planning to use?

A. SaaS

B. IaaS

C. FaaS

D. PaaS

99. Match the numbered code testing methods to their lettered definition:

Code testing methods:

1. Regression testing

2. Integration testing

3. Unit testing

4. System testing

Definitions:

A. Testing on a complete integrated product

B. A testing method that focuses on modules or smaller sections of code for testing

C. A testing method that is used to verify that previously tested software performs the same way after changes are made

D. A testing method used to validate how software modules work together

100. Match the following numbered terms to their lettered definitions:

1. Session hijacking

2. Cross-site scripting

3. Cross-site request forgery

4. SQL injection

A. An attack that injects a malicious script into otherwise trusted websites

B. An attack that is designed to execute commands against a database via an insecure web application

C. An exploitation method that often involves cookies or keys to gain unauthorized access to a computer or service

D. An attack that forces a user to execute unwanted actions in a website or application they are currently logged into

Chapter

9

Practice Test 1

1. Lisa is attempting to prevent her network from being targeted by IP spoofing attacks as well as preventing her network from being the source of those attacks. Which of the following rules are best practices that Lisa should configure at her network border? (Select all that apply.)

   A. Block packets with internal source addresses from entering the network.

   B. Block packets with external source addresses from leaving the network.

   C. Block packets with public IP addresses from entering the network.

   D. Block packets with private IP addresses from exiting the network.

2. Ed has been tasked with identifying a service that will provide a low-latency, high-performance, and high-availability way to host content for his employer. What type of solution should he seek out to ensure that his employer's customers around the world can access their content quickly, easily, and reliably?

   A. A hot site

   B. A CDN

   C. Redundant servers

   D. A P2P CDN

3. Fran is building a forensic analysis workstation and is selecting a forensic disk controller to include in the setup. Which of the following are functions of a forensic disk controller? (Select all that apply.)

   A. Preventing the modification of data on a storage device

   B. Returning data requested from the device

   C. Reporting errors sent by the device to the forensic host

   D. Blocking read commands sent to the device

4. Mike is building a fault-tolerant server and wants to implement RAID 1. How many physical disks are required to build this solution?

   A. 1

   B. 2

   C. 3

   D. 5

5. Darren is troubleshooting an authentication issue for a Kerberized application used by his organization. He believes the issue is with the generation of session keys. What Kerberos service should he investigate first?

   A. KDC

   B. TGT

   C. AS

   D. TGS

6. Evelyn believes that one of her organization's vendors has breached a contractual obligation to protect sensitive data and would like to conduct an investigation into the circumstances. Based upon the results of the investigation, it is likely that Evelyn's organization will sue the vendor for breach of contract. What term best describes the type of investigation that Evelyn is conducting?

   A. Administrative investigation

   B. Criminal investigation

   C. Civil investigation

   D. Regulatory investigation

7. Ivan is installing a motion detector to protect a sensitive work area that uses high-frequency microwave signal transmissions to identify potential intruders. What type of detector is he installing?

   A. Infrared

   B. Heat-based

   C. Wave pattern

   D. Capacitance

8. Susan sets up a firewall that keeps track of the status of the communication between two systems and allows a remote system to respond to a local system only after the local system starts communication. What type of firewall is Susan using?

   A. A static packet filtering firewall

   B. An application-level gateway firewall

   C. A stateful packet inspection firewall

   D. A circuit-level gateway firewall

For questions 9–11, please refer to the following scenario:

Ben owns a coffeehouse and wants to provide wireless Internet service for his customers. Ben's network is simple and uses a single consumer-grade wireless router and a cable modem connected via a commercial cable data contract.

9. How can Ben provide access control for his customers without having to provision user IDs before they connect while also gathering useful contact information for his business purposes?

   A. WPA2-PSK.

   B. A captive portal.

   C. Require customers to use a publicly posted password like "BensCoffee."

   D. WPA3 SAE.

10. Ben intends to run an open (unencrypted) wireless network for his customers. How should he connect his wireless business devices?

    A. Run WPA3 on the same SSID.

    B. Set up a separate SSID using WPA3.

    C. Run the open network in Enterprise mode.

    D. Set up a separate wireless network using WEP.

11. After implementing the solution from the first question, Ben receives a complaint about users in his cafe hijacking other customers' web traffic, including using their usernames and passwords. How is this possible?

    A. The password is shared by all users, making traffic vulnerable.

    B. A malicious user has installed a Trojan on the router.

    C. A user has ARP spoofed the router, making all traffic broadcast to all users.

    D. Open networks are unencrypted, making traffic easily sniffable.

12. Kevin is reviewing and updating the security documentation used by his organization. He would like to document some best practices for securing IoT devices that his team has developed over the past year. The practices are generalized in nature and do not cover specific devices. What type of document would be best for this purpose?

    A. Policy

    B. Standard

    C. Guideline

    D. Procedure

13. Tom is tuning his security monitoring tools in an attempt to reduce the number of alerts received by administrators without missing important security events. He decides to configure the system to only report failed login attempts if there are five failed attempts to access the same account within a one-hour period of time. What term best describes the technique that Tom is using?

    A. Thresholding

    B. Sampling

    C. Account lockout

    D. Clipping

14. Sally has been tasked with deploying an authentication, authorization, and accounting server for wireless network services in her organization and needs to avoid using proprietary technology. What technology should she select?

    A. OAuth

    B. RADIUS

    C. XTACACS

    D. OpenID Connect

15. An accounting clerk for Christopher's Cheesecakes does not have access to the salary information for individual employees but wanted to know the salary of a new hire. He pulled total payroll expenses for the pay period before the new person was hired and then pulled the same expenses for the following pay period. He computed the difference between those two amounts to determine the individual's salary. What type of attack occurred?

A. Salami slicing

B. Data diddling

C. Inference

D. Social engineering

16. Alice would like to have read permissions on an object and knows that Bob already has those rights and would like to give them to herself. Which one of the rules in the Take-Grant protection model would allow her to complete this operation if the relationship exists between Alice and Bob?

A. Take rule

B. Grant rule

C. Create rule

D. Remote rule

17. During a log review, Danielle discovers a series of logs that show login failures:

```
Jan 31 11:39:12 ip-10-0-0-2 sshd[29092]: Invalid user admin from remotehost
passwd=aaaaaaaa
Jan 31 11:39:20 ip-10-0-0-2 sshd[29098]: Invalid user admin from remotehost
passwd=aaaaaaab
Jan 31 11:39:23 ip-10-0-0-2 sshd[29100]: Invalid user admin from remotehost
passwd=aaaaaaac
Jan 31 11:39:31 ip-10-0-0-2 sshd[29106]: Invalid user admin from remotehost
passwd=aaaaaaad
Jan 31 20:40:53 ip-10-0-0-2 sshd[30520]: Invalid user admin from remotehost
passwd=aaaaaaae
```

What type of attack has Danielle discovered?

A. A pass-the-hash attack

B. A brute-force attack

C. A man-in-the-middle attack

D. A dictionary attack

18. Ben is designing a database-driven application and would like to ensure that two executing transactions do not affect each other by storing interim results in the database. What property is he seeking to enforce?

A. Atomicity

B. Isolation

C. Consistency

D. Durability

19. Kim is the system administrator for a small business network that is experiencing security problems. She is in the office in the evening working on the problem, and nobody else is there. As she is watching, she can see that systems on the other side of the office that were previously behaving normally are now exhibiting signs of an infection one after the other. What type of malware is Kim likely dealing with?

    A. Virus

    B. Worm

    C. Trojan horse

    D. Logic bomb

20. Barb is reviewing the compliance obligations facing her organization and the types of liability that each one might incur. Which of the following laws and regulations may involve criminal penalties if violated? (Select all that apply.)

    A. FERPA

    B. HIPAA

    C. SOX

    D. PCI DSS

21. Quentin is analyzing network traffic that he collected with Wireshark on a TCP/IP network. He would like to identify all new connections that were set up during his traffic collection. If he is looking for the three packets that constitute the TCP three-way handshake used to establish a new connection, what flags should be set on the first three packets?

    A. SYN, ACK, SYN/ACK

    B. PSH, RST, ACK

    C. SYN, SYN/ACK, ACK

    D. SYN, RST, FIN

22. Daniel is selecting a mobile device management (MDM) solution for his organization and is writing the RFP. He is trying to decide what features he should include as requirements after aligning his organization's security needs with an MDM platform's capabilities. Which of the following are typical capabilities of MDM solutions? (Select all that apply.)

    A. Remotely wiping the contents of a mobile device

    B. Assuming control of a nonregistered BYOD mobile device

    C. Enforcing the use of device encryption

    D. Managing device backups

23. Jim is implementing an IDaaS solution for his organization. What type of technology is he putting in place?

    A. Identity as a service

    B. Employee ID as a service

    C. Intrusion detection as a service

    D. OAuth

24. Gina recently took the CISSP certification exam and then wrote a blog post that included the text of many of the exam questions that she experienced. What aspect of the ISC2 Code of Ethics is most directly violated in this situation?

A. Advance and protect the profession.

B. Act honorably, honestly, justly, responsibly, and legally.

C. Protect society, the common good, necessary public trust and confidence, and the infrastructure.

D. Provide diligent and competent service to principals.

25. Gordon is conducting a risk assessment for his organization and determined the amount of damage that flooding is expected to cause to his facilities each year. What metric has Gordon identified?

A. ALE

B. ARO

C. SLE

D. EF

26. Greg would like to implement application control technology in his organization. He would like to limit users to installing only approved software on their systems. What type of application control would be appropriate in this situation?

A. Blacklisting

B. Graylisting

C. Whitelisting

D. Bluelisting

27. Frank is the security administrator for a web server that provides news and information to people located around the world. His server received an unusually high volume of traffic that it could not handle and was forced to reject requests. Frank traced the source of the traffic back to a botnet. What type of attack took place?

A. Denial-of-service

B. Reconnaissance

C. Compromise

D. Malicious insider

28. In the database table shown here, which column would be the best candidate for a primary key?

Company ID	Company Name	Address	City	State	ZIP Code	Telephone	Sales Rep
1	Acme Widgets	234 Main Street	Columbia	MD	21040	(301) 555-1212	14
2	Abrams Consulting	1024 Sample Street	Miami	FL	33131	(305) 555-1995	14
3	Dome Widgets	913 Sorin Street	South Bend	IN	46556	(574) 555-5863	26

   A. Company ID

   B. Company Name

   C. ZIP Code

   D. Sales Rep

29. Gwen is a cybersecurity professional for a financial services firm that maintains records of their customers. These records include personal information about each customer, including the customer's name, Social Security number, date and place of birth, and mother's maiden name. What category best describes these records?

   A. PHI

   B. Proprietary data

   C. PII

   D. EDI

30. Bob is configuring egress filtering on his network, examining traffic destined for the Internet. His organization uses the public address range 12.8.195.0/24. Packets with which one of the following destination addresses should Bob permit to leave the network?

   A. 12.8.195.15

   B. 10.8.15.9

   C. 192.168.109.55

   D. 129.53.44.124

31. Brian is considering increasing the length of the cryptographic keys used by his organization. If he adds 8 bits to the encryption key, how many more possible keys will be added to the keyspace for the algorithm?

   A. The size of the keyspace will double.

   B. The size of the keyspace will increase by a factor of 8.

   C. The size of the keyspace will increase by a factor of 64.

   D. The size of the keyspace will increase by a factor of 256.

32. Which of the following data assets may be safely and effectively disposed of using shredding? (Select all that apply.)

   A. Paper records

   B. Credit cards

   C. Removable media

   D. SSD hard drives

33. GAD Systems is concerned about the risk of hackers stealing sensitive information stored on a file server. They choose to pursue a risk mitigation strategy. Which one of the following actions would support that strategy?

   A. Encrypting the files

   B. Deleting the files

   C. Purchasing cyber-liability insurance

   D. Taking no action

34. Viola is conducting a user account audit to determine whether accounts have the appropriate level of permissions and that all permissions were approved through a formal process. The organization has approximately 50,000 user accounts and an annual employee turnover rate of 24%. Which one of the following sampling approaches would be the most effective use of her time when choosing records for manual review?

   A. Select all records that have been modified during the past month.

   B. Ask access administrators to identify the accounts most likely to have issues and audit those.

   C. Select a random sample of records, either from the entire population or from the population of records that have changed during the audit period.

   D. Sampling is not effective in this situation, and all accounts should be audited.

35. Lila is reviewing her organization's adverse termination process. In that process, when would be the most appropriate time to revoke a user's access privileges to digital systems?

   A. At the time the user is informed of the termination

   B. At the end of the last day of employment

   C. At the time the decision is made

   D. Several days after the last day of employment

36. William is reviewing log files that were stored on a system with a suspected compromise. He finds the log file shown here. What type of log file is this?

```
217.69.133.190 - - [11/Apr/2016:09:41:48 -0400] "GET /forum/viewtopic.php?f=4&t=25630 HTTP/1.1" 503 2009 "-
" "Mozilla/5.0 (compatible; Linux x86_64; Mail.RU_Bot/2.0; +http://go.mail.ru/help/robots)"
217.69.133.190 - - [11/Apr/2016:09:41:50 -0400] "GET /forum/viewtopic.php?f=7&t=28513 HTTP/1.1" 503 2009 "-
" "Mozilla/5.0 (compatible; Linux x86_64; Mail.RU_Bot/2.0; +http://go.mail.ru/help/robots)"
188.143.234.155 - - [11/Apr/2016:09:41:50 -0400] "GET /ask-a-pci-dss-question/ HTTP/1.1" 200 6501 "-"
"Mozilla/5.0 (Windows NT 6.1; WOW64; rv:41.0) Gecko/20100101 Firefox/41.0"
217.69.133.242 - - [11/Apr/2016:09:41:51 -0400] "GET /forum/viewtopic.php?f=5&t=27086 HTTP/1.1" 503 2009 "-
" "Mozilla/5.0 (compatible; Linux x86_64; Mail.RU_Bot/2.0; +http://go.mail.ru/help/robots)"
217.69.133.245 - - [11/Apr/2016:09:41:52 -0400] "GET /forum/viewtopic.php?f=6&t=28548 HTTP/1.1" 503 2009 "-
" "Mozilla/5.0 (compatible; Linux x86_64; Mail.RU_Bot/2.0; +http://go.mail.ru/help/robots)"
217.69.133.247 - - [11/Apr/2016:09:41:54 -0400] "GET /forum/viewtopic.php?f=3&t=26497 HTTP/1.1" 503 2009 "-
" "Mozilla/5.0 (compatible; Linux x86_64; Mail.RU_Bot/2.0; +http://go.mail.ru/help/robots)"
217.69.133.247 - - [11/Apr/2016:09:41:55 -0400] "GET /forum/viewtopic.php?f=3&t=27282 HTTP/1.1" 503 2009 "-
" "Mozilla/5.0 (compatible; Linux x86_64; Mail.RU_Bot/2.0; +http://go.mail.ru/help/robots)"
217.69.133.246 - - [11/Apr/2016:09:41:56 -0400] "GET /forum/viewtopic.php?f=6&t=33830 HTTP/1.1" 503 2009 "-
" "Mozilla/5.0 (compatible; Linux x86_64; Mail.RU_Bot/2.0; +http://go.mail.ru/help/robots)"
217.69.133.190 - - [11/Apr/2016:09:41:58 -0400] "GET /forum/viewtopic.php?f=6&t=26425 HTTP/1.1" 503 2009 "-
" "Mozilla/5.0 (compatible; Linux x86_64; Mail.RU_Bot/2.0; +http://go.mail.ru/help/robots)"
217.69.133.245 - - [11/Apr/2016:09:41:59 -0400] "GET /pci-dss/pci-dss-vulnerability-scanning-requirements/
HTTP/1.1" 301 - "-" "Mozilla/5.0 (compatible; Linux x86_64; Mail.RU_Bot/2.0;
+http://go.mail.ru/help/robots)"
217.69.133.247 - - [11/Apr/2016:09:42:01 -0400] "GET /forum/viewtopic.php?f=4&t=26035 HTTP/1.1" 503 2009 "-
" "Mozilla/5.0 (compatible; Linux x86_64; Mail.RU_Bot/2.0; +http://go.mail.ru/help/robots)"
217.69.133.190 - - [11/Apr/2016:09:42:02 -0400] "GET /vulnerability-scanning/pci-dss-vulnerability-
scanning-requirements/ HTTP/1.1" 200 11007 "http://www.pcidssguru.com/pci-dss/pci-dss-vulnerability-
scanning-requirements/" "Mozilla/5.0 (compatible; Linux x86_64; Mail.RU_Bot/2.0;
+http://go.mail.ru/help/robots)"
207.46.13.18 - - [11/Apr/2016:09:42:17 -0400] "GET /category/articles/page/3/ HTTP/1.1" 200 7583 "-"
"Mozilla/5.0 (compatible; bingbot/2.0; +http://www.bing.com/bingbot.htm)"
```

A. Firewall log

B. Change log

C. Application log

D. System log

37. Roger is reviewing a list of security vulnerabilities in his organization and rating them based upon their severity. Which one of the following models would be most useful to his work?

A. CVSS

B. STRIDE

C. PASTA

D. ATT&CK

38. An attacker recently called an organization's help desk and persuaded them to reset a password for another user's account. What term best describes this attack?

A. A human Trojan

B. Social engineering

C. Phishing

D. Whaling

39. Greg is evaluating a new vendor that will be supplying networking gear to his organization. Because of the nature of his organization's work, Greg is concerned that an attacker might attempt a supply chain exploit. Assuming that both Greg's organization and the vendor operate under reasonable security procedures, which one of the following activities likely poses the greatest supply chain risk to the equipment?

A. Tampering by an unauthorized third party at the vendor's site

B. Interception of devices in transit

C. Misconfiguration by an administrator after installation

D. Tampering by an unauthorized third party at Greg's site

40. Kevin is operating in a single-level security environment and is seeking to classify information systems according to the type of information that they process. What procedure would be the best way for him to assign asset classifications?

A. Assign systems the classification of information that they most commonly process.

B. Assign systems the classification of the highest level of information that they are expected to process regularly.

C. Assign systems the classification of the highest level of information that they are ever expected to process.

D. Assign all systems the same classification level.

For questions 41–43, please refer to the following scenario:

The organization that Ben works for has a traditional on-site Active Directory environment that uses a manual provisioning process for each addition to their 350-employee company. As the company adopts new technologies, they are increasingly using software-as-a-service applications to replace their internally developed software stack.

   Ben has been tasked with designing an identity management implementation that will allow his company to use cloud services while supporting their existing systems. Using the logical diagram shown here, answer the following questions about the identity recommendations Ben should make.

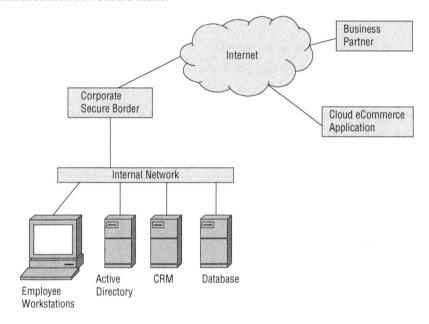

41. If availability of authentication services is the organization's biggest priority, what type of identity platform should Ben recommend?

   A. On-site

   B. Cloud-based

   C. Hybrid

   D. Outsourced

42. If Ben needs to share identity information with the business partner shown, what should he investigate?

   A. Single sign-on

   B. Multifactor authentication

   C. Federation

   D. IDaaS

43. What technology is likely to be involved when Ben's organization needs to provide authentication and authorization assertions to their cloud e-commerce application?

A. Active Directory

B. SAML

C. RADIUS

D. SPML

44. Dave is responsible for password security in his organization and would like to strengthen the security of password files. He would like to defend his organization against the use of rainbow tables. Which one of the following techniques is specifically designed to frustrate the use of rainbow tables?

A. Password expiration policies

B. Salting

C. User education

D. Password complexity policies

45. Helen recently built a new system as part of her organization's deception campaign. The system is configured in a manner that makes it vulnerable to attack and that conveys that it might contain highly sensitive information. What term best describes this system?

A. Honeynet

B. Darknet

C. Honeypot

D. Pseudoflaw

46. Nandi is evaluating a set of candidate systems to replace a biometric authentication mechanism in her organization. What metric would be the best way to compare the effectiveness of the different systems?

A. FAR

B. FRR

C. CER

D. FDR

47. Sean suspects that an individual in his company is smuggling out secret information despite his company's careful use of data loss prevention systems. He discovers that the suspect is posting photos, including the one shown here, to public Internet message boards. What type of technique may the individuals be using to hide messages inside this image?

Source: National Museum of American History / Wikimedia Commons / Public domain.

A. Watermarking

B. VPN

C. Steganography

D. Covert timing channel

48. Roger is concerned that a third-party firm hired to develop code for an internal application will embed a backdoor in the code. The developer retains rights to the intellectual property and will only deliver the software in its final form. Which one of the following languages would be least susceptible to this type of attack because it would provide Roger with code that is human-readable in its final form?

A. JavaScript

B. C

C. C++

D. Java

49. Jesse is looking at the /etc/passwd file on a system configured to use shadowed passwords. What should she expect to see in the password field of this file?

A. Plaintext passwords

B. Encrypted passwords

C. Hashed passwords

D. x

50. Rob recently received a notice from a vendor that the EOL date is approaching for a firewall platform that is used in his organization. What action should Rob take?

A. Prepare to discontinue use of the platform as soon as possible.

B. Immediately discontinue use of the device.

C. Prepare to discontinue use of the device as part of the organization's normal planning cycle.

D. No action is necessary.

51. What principle states that an individual should make every effort to complete their responsibilities in an accurate and timely manner?

A. Least privilege

B. Separation of duties

C. Due care

D. Due diligence

52. Tony is developing a data classification system for his organization. What factor should he use as the primary driver when determining the classification level of each category of information?

A. Sensitivity

B. Source

C. Likelihood of theft

D. Likelihood of data loss

53. Perry is establishing information handling requirements for his organization. He discovers that the organization often needs to send sensitive information over the Internet to a supplier and is concerned about it being intercepted. What handling requirement would best protect against this risk?

A. Require the use of transport encryption.

B. Require proper classification and labeling.

C. Require the use of data loss prevention technology.

D. Require the use of storage encryption.

54. John is developing a tangible asset inventory for his organization. Which of the following items would most likely be included in this inventory? (Select all that apply.)

A. Intellectual property

B. Server hardware

C. Files stored on servers

D. Mobile devices

55. Maria is analyzing a security incident where she believes that an attacker gained access to a fiber-optic cable and installed a tap on that cable. What layer of the OSI model did this attack occur at?

A. Transport

B. Network

C. Data Link

D. Physical

56. Bert is considering the use of an infrastructure-as-a-service (IaaS) cloud computing partner to provide virtual servers. Which one of the following would be a vendor responsibility in this scenario?

A. Maintaining the hypervisor

B. Managing operating system security settings

C. Maintaining the host firewall

D. Configuring server access control

57. When Ben records data and then replays it against his test website to verify how it performs based on a real production workload, what type of performance monitoring is he undertaking?

A. Passive

B. Proactive

C. Reactive

D. Replay

58. Kailey is reviewing a set of old records maintained by her organization and wants to dispose of them securely. She is unsure how long the organization should keep the records because they involve tax data. How can Kailey determine whether the records may be disposed?

A. Consult the organization's records retention policy.

B. Consult IRS requirements.

C. Retain the records for at least seven years.

D. Retain the records permanently.

59. Alan is considering the use of new identification cards in his organization that will be used for physical access control. He comes across a sample card and is unsure of the technology. He breaks it open and sees the following internal construction. What type of card is this?

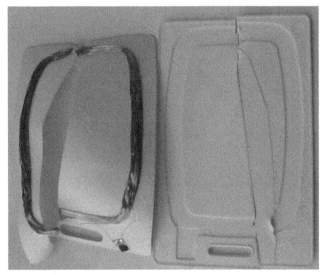

Source: Arkrishna / Wikimedia Commons / Public domain.

A. Smart card

B. Proximity card

C. Magnetic stripe

D. Phase-two card

60. Mark is planning a disaster recovery test for his organization. He would like to perform a live test of the disaster recovery facility but does not want to disrupt operations at the primary facility. What type of test should Mark choose?

A. Full interruption test

B. Read-through

C. Parallel test

D. Tabletop exercise

61. Which one of the following is not a principle of the Agile approach to software development?

A. The best architecture, requirements, and designs emerge from self-organizing teams.

B. Deliver working software infrequently, with an emphasis on creating accurate code over longer timelines.

C. Welcome changing requirements, even late in the development process.

D. Simplicity is essential.

62. During a security audit, Susan discovers that the organization is using hand geometry scanners as the access control mechanism for their secure data center. What recommendation should Susan make about the use of hand geometry scanners?

A. They have a high FRR and should be replaced.

B. A second factor should be added because they are not a good way to reliably distinguish individuals.

C. The hand geometry scanners provide appropriate security for the data center and should be considered for other high-security areas.

D. They may create accessibility concerns, and an alternate biometric system should be considered.

63. Colleen is conducting a business impact assessment for her organization. What metric provides important information about the amount of time that the organization may be without a service before causing irreparable harm?

A. MTD

B. ALE

C. RPO

D. RTO

64. Bailey is concerned that users around her organization are using sensitive information in a variety of cloud services and would like to enforce security policies consistently across those services. What security control would be best suited for her needs?

A. DRM

B. IPS

C. CASB

D. DLP

65. Matt is designing a set of information handling requirements for his organization and would like to draw upon common industry practices. Which of the following practices should Matt implement? (Select all that apply.)

A. Labeling both paper and electronic documents with their classification level

B. Automatically granting senior executives full access to all classified information

C. Automatically granting visitors access to information classified at the lowest level of sensitivity

D. Encrypting sensitive information in transit and at rest

66. Jerry is investigating an attack where the attacker stole an authentication token from a user's web session and used it to impersonate the user on the site. What term best describes this attack?

A. Masquerading

B. Replay

C. Spoofing

D. Modification

67. Lisa wants to integrate with a cloud identity provider that uses OAuth 2.0, and she wants to select an appropriate authentication framework. Which of the following best suits her needs?

   A. OpenID Connect

   B. SAML

   C. RADIUS

   D. Kerberos

68. Owen recently designed a security access control structure that prevents a single user from simultaneously holding the role required to create a new vendor and the role required to issue a check. What principle is Owen enforcing?

   A. Two-person control

   B. Least privilege

   C. Separation of duties

   D. Job rotation

69. Denise is preparing for a trial relating to a contract dispute between her company and a software vendor. The vendor is claiming that Denise made a verbal agreement that amended their written contract. What rule of evidence should Denise raise in her defense?

   A. Real evidence rule

   B. Best evidence rule

   C. Parol evidence rule

   D. Testimonial evidence rule

70. While Lauren is monitoring traffic on two ends of a network connection, she sees traffic that is inbound to a public IP address show up inside the production network. It is headed for an internal host with an RFC 1918 reserved destination address. What technology should she expect is in use at the network border?

   A. NAT

   B. VLANs

   C. G/NAT

   D. BGP

71. Which of the following statements about SSAE-18 are correct? (Select all that apply.)

   A. It mandates a specific control set.

   B. It is an attestation standard.

   C. It is used for external audits.

   D. It uses a framework, including SOC 1, SOC 2, and SOC 3 reports.

72. Elliott is using an asymmetric cryptosystem and would like to add a digital signature to a message. What key should he use to encrypt the message digest?

A. Elliott's private key

B. Elliott's public key

C. Recipient's private key

D. Recipient's public key

73. Greg is building a disaster recovery plan for his organization and would like to determine the amount of time that it should take to restore a particular IT service after an outage. What variable is Greg calculating?

A. MTD

B. RTO

C. RPO

D. SLA

74. What business process typically requires sign-off from a manager before modifications are made to a system?

A. SDN

B. Release management

C. Change management

D. Versioning

75. Jen is selecting a fire suppression system for her organization's data center and would like to narrow down the list of potential vendors. Which one of the following suppression systems would be LEAST appropriate for use?

A. Dry pipe

B. Wet pipe

C. Pre-action

D. FM-200

76. The company Chris works for has notifications posted at each door reminding employees to be careful to not allow people to enter when they do. Which type of control is this?

A. Detective

B. Physical

C. Preventive

D. Directive

77. Seth is designing the physical security controls for a new facility being constructed by his organization. He would like to deter attacks to the extent possible. Which of the following controls serve as deterrents? (Select all that apply.)

A. Motion detectors

B. Guard dogs

C. Access control vestibules

D. Lighting

78. Thomas recently signed an agreement for a serverless computing environment where his organization's developers will be able to write functions in Python and deploy them on the cloud provider's servers for execution. The cloud provider will manage the servers. What term best describes this model?

A. SaaS

B. PaaS

C. IaaS

D. Containerization

79. An attacker has intercepted a large amount of data that was all encrypted with the same algorithm and encryption key. With no further information, which of the following cryptanalytic attacks are possible? (Select all that apply.)

A. Known plaintext

B. Chosen ciphertext

C. Frequency analysis

D. Brute force

For questions 80–82, please refer to the following scenario:

Alex has been with the university he works at for more than 10 years. During that time, he has been a system administrator and a database administrator, and he has worked in the university's help desk. He is now a manager for the team that runs the university's web applications. Using the provisioning diagram shown here, answer the following questions.

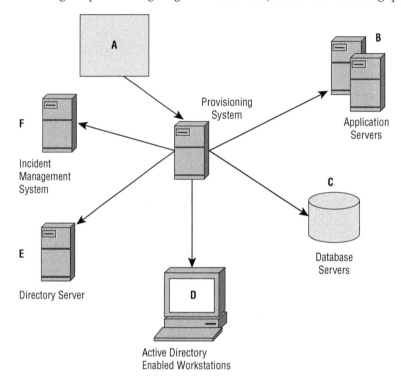

80. If Alex hires a new employee and the employee's account is provisioned after HR manually inputs information into the provisioning system based on data Alex provides via a series of forms, what type of provisioning has occurred?

   A. Discretionary account provisioning

   B. Workflow-based account provisioning

   C. Automated account provisioning

   D. Self-service account provisioning

81. Alex has access to B, C, and D in the diagram. What concern should he raise to the university's identity management team?

   A. The provisioning process did not give him the rights he needs.

   B. He has excessive privileges.

   C. Privilege creep may be taking place.

   D. Logging is not properly enabled.

82. When Alex changes roles, what should occur?

   A. He should be de-provisioned, and a new account should be created.

   B. He should have his new rights added to his existing account.

   C. He should be provisioned for only the rights that match his role.

   D. He should have his rights set to match those of the person he is replacing.

83. Robert is reviewing a system that has been assigned the EAL2 evaluation assurance level under the Common Criteria. What is the highest level of assurance that he may have about the system?

   A. It has been functionally tested.

   B. It has been structurally tested.

   C. It has been formally verified, designed, and tested.

   D. It has been semiformally designed and tested.

84. Adam is processing an access request for an end user. What two items should he verify before granting the access?

   A. Separation and need to know

   B. Clearance and endorsement

   C. Clearance and need to know

   D. Second factor and clearance

85. During what phase of the electronic discovery reference model does an organization ensure that potentially discoverable information is protected against alteration or deletion?

   A. Identification

   B. Preservation

   C. Collection

   D. Processing

86. Dana is selecting a hash function for use in her organization and would like to balance a concern for a cryptographically strong hash with the speed and efficiency of the algorithm. Which one of the following hash functions would best meet her needs?

   A. MD5

   B. RIPEMD

   C. SHA-2

   D. SHA-3

87. Harry would like to access a document owned by Sally stored on a file server. Applying the subject/object model to this scenario, who or what is the object of the resource request?

   A. Harry

   B. Sally

   C. File server

   D. Document

88. What is the process that occurs when the Session layer removes the header from data sent by the Transport layer in the OSI model?

   A. Encapsulation

   B. Packet unwrapping

   C. De-encapsulation

   D. Payloading

89. Rob is reviewing his organization's campus for physical security using the Crime Prevention Through Environmental Design (CPTED) framework. Which one of the following is NOT a strategy in this framework?

   A. Natural intrusion detection

   B. Natural access control

   C. Natural surveillance

   D. Natural territorial reinforcement

90. Shahla's organization handles personally identifiable information as part of its routine business. The organization currently operates only in the United States but is considering an expansion into Canada. What new law is most likely to affect the organization if they undertake this expansion?

   A. PIPL

   B. POPIA

   C. PIPEDA

   D. CCPA

91. What type of risk assessment uses tools such as the one shown here?

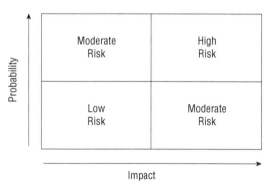

   A. Quantitative

   B. Loss expectancy

   C. Financial

   D. Qualitative

92. MAC models use three types of environments. Which of the following is not a mandatory access control design?

A. Hierarchical

B. Bracketed

C. Compartmentalized

D. Hybrid

93. Mandy is the team leader for a project team of six people (including herself). She would like to provide those people with the ability to communicate privately, such that any pair of people can exchange communications that are not subject to interception by anyone else (team member or nonteam member). The team is using an asymmetric encryption algorithm. How many keys are required to implement these requirements?

A. 6

B. 12

C. 15

D. 36

94. Sally is wiring a gigabit Ethernet network. What cabling choices should she make to ensure she can use her network at the full 1000 Mbps she wants to provide to her users?

A. Cat 5 and Cat 6

B. Cat 5e and Cat 6

C. Cat 4e and Cat 5e

D. Cat 6 and Cat 7

95. Ursula is seeking to expand the reach and scalability of her organization's website. She would like to position copies of her data around the world in locations close to website visitors to reduce loading time and the burden on her servers. What type of cloud service would best meet her needs?

A. IaaS

B. Containerization

C. CDN

D. SaaS

96. Robert is the network administrator for a small business and recently installed a new firewall. After seeing signs of unusually heavy network traffic, he checked his intrusion detection system, which reported that a smurf attack was underway. What firewall configuration change can Robert make to most effectively prevent this attack?

A. Block the source IP address of the attack.

B. Block inbound UDP traffic.

C. Block the destination IP address of the attack.

D. Block inbound ICMP traffic.

97. Which one of the following types of firewalls does not have the ability to track connection status between different packets?

    A. Stateful inspection

    B. Application proxy

    C. Packet filter

    D. Next generation

98. Frances is concerned that equipment failures within her organization's servers will lead to a loss of power to those servers. Which one of the following controls would best address this risk?

    A. Redundant power sources

    B. Backup generators

    C. Dual power supplies

    D. Uninterruptible power supplies

99. Peter is reviewing the remote access technologies used by his organization and would like to eliminate the use of any techniques that do not include built-in encryption. Which of the following approaches should he retain? (Select all that apply.)

    A. RDP

    B. Telnet

    C. SSH

    D. Dial-up

100. Matthew is experiencing issues with the quality of network service on his organization's network. The primary symptom is that packets are occasionally taking too long to travel from their source to their destination. The length of this delay changes for individual packets. What term describes the issue Matthew is facing?

    A. Latency

    B. Jitter

    C. Packet loss

    D. Interference

101. Gavin is an internal auditor working to assess his organization's cybersecurity posture. Which of the following would be appropriate recipients of the reports he generates from his work? (Select all that apply.)

    A. Managers

    B. Individual contributors

    C. Suppliers

    D. Board members

102. Kim is conducting testing of a web application developed by her organization and would like to ensure that it is accessible from all commonly used web browsers. What type of testing should she conduct?

A. Regression testing

B. Interface testing

C. Fuzzing

D. White-box testing

103. Kathleen is implementing an access control system for her organization and builds the following arrays:

Reviewers: Update files, delete files

Submitters: Upload files

Editors: Upload files, update files

Archivists: Delete files

What type of access control system has Kathleen implemented?

A. Role-based access control

B. Task-based access control

C. Rule-based access control

D. Discretionary access control

104. Alan is installing a fire suppression system that will activate after a fire breaks out and protect the equipment in the data center from extensive damage. What metric is Alan attempting to lower?

A. Likelihood

B. RTO

C. RPO

D. Impact

105. Alan's Wrenches recently developed a new manufacturing process for its product. They plan to use this technology internally and not share it with others. They would like it to remain protected for as long as possible. What type of intellectual property protection is best suited for this situation?

A. Patent

B. Copyright

C. Trademark

D. Trade secret

106. Ben wants to interface with the National Vulnerability Database using a standardized protocol. What option should he use to ensure that the tools he builds work with the data contained in the NVD?

A. XACML

B. SCML

C. VSML

D. SCAP

107. Ron's organization does not have the resources to conduct penetration testing that uses time-intensive manual techniques, but he would like to achieve some of the benefits of penetration testing. Which one of the following techniques could he engage in that requires the least manual effort?

A. White-box testing

B. Black-box testing

C. Gray-box testing

D. Breach and attack simulation

108. In the figure shown here, Harry's request to read the data file is blocked. Harry has a Secret security clearance, and the data file has a Top Secret classification. What principle of the Bell–LaPadula model blocked this request?

A. Simple Security Property

B. Simple Integrity Property

C. *-Security Property

D. Discretionary Security Property

109. Norm is starting a new software project with a vendor that uses an SDLC approach to development. When he arrives on the job, he receives a document that has the sections shown here. What type of planning document is this?

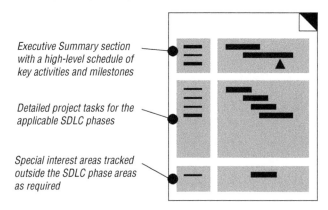

Executive Summary section with a high-level schedule of key activities and milestones

Detailed project tasks for the applicable SDLC phases

Special interest areas tracked outside the SDLC phase areas as required

    A. Functional requirements

    B. Work breakdown structure

    C. Test analysis report

    D. Project plan

110. Kolin is searching for a network security solution that will allow him to help reduce zero-day attacks while using identities to enforce a security policy on systems before they connect to the network. What type of solution should Kolin implement?

    A. A firewall

    B. A NAC system

    C. An intrusion detection system

    D. Port security

111. Gwen comes across an application that is running under a service account on a web server. The service account has full administrative rights to the server. What principle of information security does this violate?

    A. Need to know

    B. Separation of duties

    C. Least privilege

    D. Job rotation

112. Ed is developing a set of key performance and risk indicators for his organization's information security program. Which of the following are commonly used indicators? (Select all that apply.)

A. Number of scheduled audits

B. Time to resolve vulnerabilities

C. Number of malicious site visit attempts

D. Number of account compromises

113. Kara is documenting the results of a vulnerability scan. After reviewing one finding, she determined that the vulnerability did exist. The team then implemented a configuration change that corrected the issue. How should Kara classify this vulnerability in her report?

A. True positive

B. True negative

C. False positive

D. False negative

For questions 114–116, please refer to the following scenario:

During a web application vulnerability scanning test, Steve runs Nikto against a web server he believes may be vulnerable to attacks. Using the Nikto output shown here, answer the following questions.

```
- Nikto v2.1.4
---------------------------------------------------------------------------
+ Target IP:          192.168.184.130
+ Target Hostname:    192.168.184.130
+ Target Port:        80
+ Start Time:         2016-02-15 18:40:54
---------------------------------------------------------------------------
+ Server: Apache/2.2.8 (Ubuntu) DAV/2
+ Retrieved x-powered-by header: PHP/5.2.4-2ubuntu5.10
+ Apache/2.2.8 appears to be outdated (current is at least Apache/2.2.19). Apache 1.3.
42 (final release) and 2.0.64 are also current.
+ DEBUG HTTP verb may show server debugging information. See http://msdn.microsoft.com
/en-us/library/e8z01xdh%28VS.80%29.aspx for details.
+ OSVDB-877: HTTP TRACE method is active, suggesting the host is vulnerable to XST
+ OSVDB-3233: /phpinfo.php: Contains PHP configuration information
+ OSVDB-3268: /doc/: Directory indexing found.
+ OSVDB-48: /doc/: The /doc/ directory is browsable. This may be /usr/doc.
+ OSVDB-12184: /index.php?=PHPB8B5F2A0-3C92-11d3-A3A9-4C7B08C10000: PHP reveals potent
ially sensitive information via certain HTTP requests that contain specific QUERY stri
ngs.
+ OSVDB-3092: /phpMyAdmin/changelog.php: phpMyAdmin is for managing MySQL databases, a
nd should be protected or limited to authorized hosts.
+ OSVDB-3092: /phpMyAdmin/: phpMyAdmin is for managing MySQL databases, and should be
protected or limited to authorized hosts.
+ OSVDB-3268: /test/: Directory indexing found.
+ OSVDB-3092: /test/: This might be interesting...
+ OSVDB-3268: /icons/: Directory indexing found.
+ OSVDB-3233: /icons/README: Apache default file found.
+ /phpMyAdmin/: phpMyAdmin directory found
+ 6456 items checked: 1 error(s) and 15 item(s) reported on remote host
+ End Time:           2016-02-15 18:41:36 (42 seconds)
---------------------------------------------------------------------------
+ 1 host(s) tested
```

114. Why does Nikto flag the `/test` directory?

    A. The `/test` directory allows administrative access to PHP.

    B. It is used to store sensitive data.

    C. Test directories often contain scripts that can be misused.

    D. It indicates a potential compromise.

115. Why does Nikto identify directory indexing as an issue?

    A. It lists files in a directory.

    B. It may allow for XDRF.

    C. Directory indexing can result in a denial-of-service attack.

    D. Directory indexing is off by default, potentially indicating compromise.

116. Nikto lists OSVDB-877, noting that the system may be vulnerable to XST. What would this type of attack allow an attacker to do?

    A. Use cross-site targeting.

    B. Steal a user's cookies.

    C. Counter SQL tracing.

    D. Modify a user's TRACE information.

117. Who would be the most appropriate supervisor for an organization's chief audit executive (CAE)?

    A. CIO

    B. CISO

    C. CEO

    D. CFO

118. Ursula believes that many individuals in her organization are storing sensitive information on their laptops in a manner that is unsafe and potentially violates the organization's security policy. What control can she use to identify the presence of these files?

    A. Network DLP

    B. Network IPS

    C. Endpoint DLP

    D. Endpoint IPS

119. In what cloud computing model does the customer build a cloud computing environment in their own data center or build an environment in another data center that is for the customer's exclusive use?

    A. Public cloud

    B. Private cloud

    C. Hybrid cloud

    D. Shared cloud

120. Which one of the following technologies is designed to prevent a web server going offline from becoming a single point of failure in a web application architecture?

    A. Load balancing

    B. Dual-power supplies

    C. IPS

    D. RAID

121. Alice wants to send Bob a message with the confidence that Bob will know the message was not altered while in transit. What security goal is Alice trying to achieve?

    A. Confidentiality

    B. Nonrepudiation

    C. Authentication

    D. Integrity

122. What network topology is shown here?

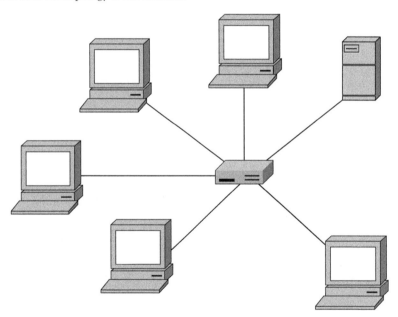

    A. A ring

    B. A bus

    C. A star

    D. A mesh

123. Monica is developing a software application that calculates an individual's body mass index for use in medical planning. She would like to include a control on the field where the physician enters an individual's weight to ensure that the weight falls within an expected range. What type of control should Monica use?

A. Fail open

B. Fail secure

C. Limit check

D. Buffer bounds

124. Match the following numbered types of testing methodologies with the lettered correct level of knowledge:

Testing methodologies:

1. Black box

2. White box

3. Gray box

Level of knowledge:

A. Full knowledge of the system

B. Partial or incomplete knowledge

C. No prior knowledge of the system

125. Match the following lettered factors to their numbered type:

Factors:

A. A PIN

B. A token

C. A fingerprint

D. A password

E. A smart card

F. A retinal scan

G. A security question/answer

Types:

1. Something you know

2. Something you have

3. Something you are

Chapter
10

Practice Test 2

1. James is building a disaster recovery plan for his organization and would like to determine the amount of acceptable data loss after an outage. What variable is James determining?

   A. SLA

   B. RTO

   C. MTD

   D. RPO

2. In his role, Chris is expected to protect the interests of the organization, as well as the customers whose information he is charged to protect. What term describes the preparation and research undertaken before decisions and actions are made?

   A. Due care

   B. Compliance

   C. Due diligence

   D. Regulatory action

3. Ade is part of a penetration testing exercise. As part of the process his role is to act as a defender. What color is frequently used to describe defenders in penetration testing exercises?

   A. Red teams

   B. Yellow teams

   C. Green teams

   D. Blue teams

4. Sharif's U.S.-based company wants to build a data center with AI-focused GPU-based computation nodes in China. What concern about regulations should Sharif express about the hardware needed?

   A. AI hardware may not be legal in China.

   B. The total dollar value of the hardware may exceed what can be shipped to China.

   C. Export controls may limit what hardware can be imported to China.

   D. There may be ethical issues with the use of AI hardware across international borders.

5. Tony wants to conduct a disaster recovery plan test exercise for his organization. What type of exercise should he conduct if he wants it to be the most realistic event possible and is able to disrupt his organization's operations to conduct the exercise?

   A. Read-through

   B. Full interruption

   C. Walk-through

   D. Simulation

6. Brian's organization has a remote facility that it could move operations to in an emergency. While the facility has basic utilities, no additional work has been done to prepare it for data-center operations. What type of site is this?

   A. A hot site

   B. A warm site

   C. A cold site

   D. A frozen site

7. Ben works in an organization that uses a formal data governance program. He is consulting with an employee working on a project that created an entirely new class of data and wants to work with the appropriate individual to assign a classification level to that information. Who is responsible for the assignment of information to a classification level?

   A. Data creator

   B. Data owner

   C. CISO

   D. Data custodian

8. James wants to ensure that his company's backups will survive a disaster that strikes the data center. Which of the following options is the best solution to this concern?

   A. Off-site backups

   B. A grandfather/father/son backup tiering system

   C. Redundant backup systems

   D. Snapshots to a SAN or NAS

9. Gabe is concerned about the security of passwords used as a cornerstone of his organization's information security program. Which one of the following controls would provide the greatest improvement in Gabe's ability to authenticate users?

   A. More complex passwords

   B. User education against social engineering

   C. Multifactor authentication

   D. Addition of security questions based on personal knowledge

10. The separation of network infrastructure from the control layer, combined with the ability to centrally program a network design in a vendor-neutral, standards-based implementation, is an example of what important concept?

    A. MPLS, a way to replace long network addresses with shorter labels and support a wide range of protocols

    B. FCoE, a converged protocol that allows common applications over Ethernet

    C. SDN, a converged architecture that allows network virtualization

    D. CDN, a converged protocol that makes common network designs accessible

11. Susan is preparing to decommission her organization's archival DVD-ROMs that contain Top Secret data. How should she ensure that the data cannot be exposed?

    A. Degauss

    B. Zero wipe

    C. Pulverize

    D. Secure erase

12. Susan is worried about a complex change and wants to ensure that the organization can recover if the change does not go as planned. What should she require in her role on the organization's change advisory board (CAB)?

    A. She should reject the change due to risk.

    B. She should require a second change review.

    C. She should ensure a backout plan exists.

    D. She should ensure a failover plan exists.

13. Angie is configuring egress monitoring on her network to provide added security. Which one of the following packet types should Angie allow to leave the network headed for the Internet?

    A. Packets with a source address from Angie's public IP address block.

    B. Packets with a destination address from Angie's public IP address block.

    C. Packets with a source address outside Angie's address block.

    D. Packets with a source address from Angie's private address block.

14. Michele's company operates a private cloud inside of an environment provided by their IaaS service provider. What term describes these isolated pools of resources that organizations can configure to serve their purposes?

    A. A VLAN

    B. A VPC

    C. An SDN

    D. A CDN

15. Theresa is implementing a new access control system and wants to ensure that developers do not have the ability to move code from development systems into the production environment. She wants to ensure that a developer who checks in code cannot then approve their own code as part of the process. What information security principle is she most directly enforcing?

    A. Separation of duties

    B. Two-person control

    C. Least privilege

    D. Job rotation

16. Which one of the following tools may be used to achieve the goal of nonrepudiation?

   A. Digital signature

   B. Symmetric encryption

   C. Firewall

   D. IDS

17. In this diagram of the TCP three-way handshake, what should system A send to system B in step 3?

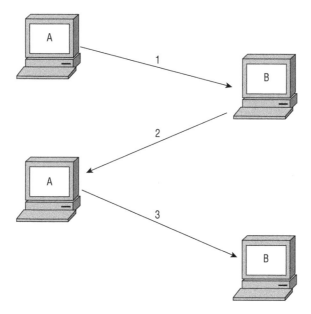

   A. ACK

   B. SYN

   C. FIN

   D. RST

18. What RADIUS alternative is commonly used for Cisco network gear and supports two-factor authentication?

   A. RADIUS+

   B. TACACS+

   C. XTACACS

   D. Kerberos

19. What two types of attacks are VoIP call managers and VoIP phones most likely to be susceptible to?

    A. DoS and malware

    B. Worms and Trojans

    C. DoS and host OS attacks

    D. Host OS attacks and buffer overflows

20. Vivian works for a chain of retail stores and would like to use a software product that restricts the software used on point-of-sale terminals to those packages on a preapproved list. What approach should Vivian use?

    A. Antivirus

    B. Heuristic

    C. Whitelist

    D. Blacklist

For questions 21–23, please refer to the following scenario:

Hunter is the facilities manager for DataTech, a large data center management firm. He is evaluating the installation of a flood prevention system at one of DataTech's facilities. The facility and contents are valued at $100 million. Installing the new flood prevention system would cost $10 million.

    Hunter consulted with flood experts and determined that the facility lies within a 200-year flood plain and that, if a flood occurred, it would likely cause $20 million in damage to the facility.

21. Based on the information in this scenario, what is the exposure factor for the effect of a flood on DataTech's data center?

    A. 2%

    B. 20%

    C. 100%

    D. 200%

22. Based on the information in this scenario, what is the annualized rate of occurrence for a flood at DataTech's data center?

    A. 0.002

    B. 0.005

    C. 0.02

    D. 0.05

23. Based on the information in this scenario, what is the annualized loss expectancy for a flood at DataTech's data center?

   A. $40,000

   B. $100,000

   C. $400,000

   D. $1,000,000

24. Which accounts are typically assessed during an account management assessment?

   A. A random sample

   B. Highly privileged accounts

   C. Recently generated accounts

   D. Accounts that have existed for long periods of time

25. Cloud computing uses a shared responsibility model for security, where the vendor and customer both bear some responsibility for security. The division of responsibility depends upon the type of service used. Place the cloud service offerings listed here in order from the case where the customer bears the LEAST responsibility to where the customer bears the MOST responsibility.

   1. IaaS

   2. SaaS

   3. PaaS

   A. 1, 2, 3

   B. 2, 1, 3

   C. 3, 2, 1

   D. 2, 3, 1

26. Jill wants to use a breach attack system to test her organization's security. Which of the following is not typically part of a BAS solution's portfolio of testing platforms?

   A. User-owned mobile devices

   B. Software agents

   C. Software-as-a-service platforms

   D. Virtual machines

27. An emergency button under the desk is a common example of what type of physical security system?

   A. An airgap button

   B. A keylogger

   C. A pushbutton lock

   D. A duress system

28. Henry runs Nikto against an Apache web server and receives the output shown here.

```
- Nikto v2.1.6
--------------------------------------------------------------
+ Target IP:        10.0.2.7
+ Target Hostname:  10.0.2.7
+ Target Port:      80
+ Start Time:       2020-04-26 21:54:21 (GMT-4)
--------------------------------------------------------------
+ Server: Apache/2.2.14 (Ubuntu) mod_mono/2.4.3 PHP/5.3.2-1ubuntu4.30 with Suhosin-Patch
proxy_html/3.0.1 mod_python/3.3.1 Python/2.6.5 mod_ssl/2.2.14 OpenSSL/0.9.8k
Phusion_Passenger/4.0.38 mod_perl/2.0.4 Perl/v5.10.1
+ Server may leak inodes via ETags, header found with file /, inode: 286483, size: 28067,
mtime: Thu Jul 30 22:55:52 2015
+ The anti-clickjacking X-Frame-Options header is not present.
+ The X-XSS-Protection header is not defined. This header can hint to the user agent to protect
against some forms of XSS
```

Which of the following statements is the least important to include in his report?

A. The missing clickjacking x-frame options could be used to redirect input to a malicious site or frame.

B. Cross-site scripting protections should be enabled, but aren't.

C. Inode information leakage from a Linux system is a critical vulnerability allowing direct access to the filesystem using node references.

D. The server is a Linux server.

29. George is assisting a prosecutor with a case against a hacker who attempted to break into the computer systems at George's company. He provides system logs to the prosecutor for use as evidence, but the prosecutor insists that George testify in court about how he gathered the logs. What rule of evidence requires George's testimony?

A. Testimonial evidence rule

B. Parol evidence rule

C. Best evidence rule

D. Hearsay rule

30. Which of the following is not a valid use for key risk indicators (KRIs)?

A. Provide warnings before issues occur.

B. Provide real-time incident response information.

C. Provide historical views of past incidents.

D. Provide insight into risk tolerance for the organization.

31. Which one of the following malware types uses built-in propagation mechanisms that exploit system vulnerabilities to spread?

A. Trojan horse

B. Worm

C. Logic bomb

D. Virus

32. As part of your company's security team, you have been asked to advise on how to ensure that media is not improperly used or stored. What solution will help staff members in your organization to handle media appropriately?

   A. Labeling with sensitivity levels

   B. Encrypting the sensitive media

   C. Dual control media systems

   D. A clear desk policy

33. Alaina wants to use a broadly adopted threat modeling framework for her organization's threat intelligence efforts. Which of the following would you advise her to adopt if she wants to use pre-existing tools to help her threat modeling team integrate both internally created intelligence and external threat feed data?

   A. The Diamond Model of Intrusion Analysis

   B. ATT&CK

   C. Microsoft's Threat-JUMP modeling system

   D. Threat-EN

34. Which one of the following is not a principle of the Agile approach to software development?

   A. The most efficient method of conveying information is electronic.

   B. Working software is the primary measure of progress.

   C. Simplicity is essential.

   D. Businesspeople and developers must work together daily.

35. Harry is concerned that accountants within his organization will modify data to cover up fraudulent activity in accounts that they normally access. Which one of the following controls would best defend against this type of attack?

   A. Encryption

   B. Access controls

   C. Integrity verification

   D. Firewalls

36. CAPEC, STIX, and TAXII are all used for what purpose?

   A. Federated authentication

   B. Vulnerability scanning

   C. Threat intelligence feeds

   D. Risk assessment and relative ranking

37. Meena wants to ensure that her supply chain risks are well managed. Which of the following is not a common practice she should include in her supply chain risk management (SCRM) plan?

A. Using contractual controls such as insurance and liability limitations where appropriate

B. Relying on a single vendor to provide vendor stability

C. Ensuring multiple suppliers exist for critical components

D. Validating the financial stability of potential suppliers

Using the following table and your knowledge of the auditing process, answer questions 38–40.

	Report Content	Audience
SOC 1	Internal controls for financial reporting	Users and auditors
SOC 2	Confidentiality, integrity, availability, security, and privacy controls	Auditors, regulators, management, partners, and others under NDA
SOC 3	Confidentiality, integrity, availability, security, and privacy controls	Publicly available, often used for a website seal

38. As they prepare to migrate their data center to an infrastructure-as-a-service (IaaS) provider, Susan's company wants to understand the effectiveness of their new provider's security, integrity, and availability controls. What SOC report would provide them with the most detail, including input from the auditor on the effectiveness of controls at the IaaS provider?

A. SOC 1.

B. SOC 2.

C. SOC 3.

D. None of the SOC reports is suited to this, and they should request another form of report.

39. Susan wants to ensure that the audit report that her organization requested includes input from an external auditor and information about control implementation over a period of time. What type of report should she request?

A. SOC 2, Type 1

B. SOC 3, Type 1

C. SOC 2, Type 2

D. SOC 3, Type 2

40. When Susan requests a SOC 2 report, she receives a SOC 1 report. What issue should Susan raise?

   A. SOC 1 reports only reveal publicly available information.

   B. SOC 1 reports cover financial data.

   C. SOC 1 reports cover only a point in time.

   D. SOC 1 reports use only a three-month period for testing.

41. Which group is best suited to evaluate an organization's administrative controls and provide credible reports to a third party?

   A. Internal auditors

   B. Penetration testers

   C. External auditors

   D. Employees who design, implement, and monitor the controls

42. Bell–LaPadula is an example of what type of access control model?

   A. DAC

   B. RBAC

   C. MAC

   D. ABAC

43. Martha is the information security officer for a small college and is responsible for safeguarding the privacy of student records. What law most directly applies to her situation?

   A. HIPAA

   B. HITECH

   C. COPPA

   D. FERPA

44. What U.S. federal law mandates the security of protected health information?

   A. FERPA

   B. SAFE Act

   C. GLBA

   D. HIPAA

45. Gurvinder wants to test a potentially malicious file while observing what it does when executed. What type of tool should he identify to allow him to do this?

   A. A SIEM

   B. A SOAR

   C. A SAST tool

   D. A sandboxing tool

46. Susan is configuring her network devices to use syslog. What should she set to ensure that she is notified about issues but does not receive normal operational issue messages?

A. The facility code

B. The log priority

C. The security level

D. The severity level

47. What RAID level is commonly used for distributed parity, allowing for resilience while being space efficient?

A. RAID 0

B. RAID 1

C. RAID 3

D. RAID 5

48. Isaac recently purchased a 48-port switch from his switch vendor. The switch vendor has announced that the model of the switch that Isaac purchased will reach its end of life next year. What does this tell Isaac about the devices?

A. The devices will stop being sold next year.

B. The devices will stop functioning next year.

C. The devices will no longer be supported next year.

D. The devices will be supported for a minimum of three more years.

49. Surveys, interviews, and audits are all examples of ways to measure what important part of an organization's security posture?

A. Code quality

B. Service vulnerabilities

C. Awareness

D. Attack surface

50. Sharon wants to help her company's developers understand the risks of API calls that allow over-consumption of resources like CPU, memory, or network bandwidth. What is the primary risk created by unconstrained API calls in this scenario?

A. Inability to attribute actions to an account

B. Denial of service

C. Malicious access to files

D. The potential for request forgery attacks

51. What type of authenticator generates dynamic passwords using time- or algorithm-based methods?

A. A biometric scanner

B. A smart card

C. A token

D. A CAC

52. Fred's new employer has hired him for a position with access to their trade secrets and confidential internal data. What legal tool should they use to help protect their data if he chooses to leave to work at a competitor?

A. A stop-loss order

B. An NDA

C. An AUP

D. Encryption

53. Mark's company is involved in a civil case. What evidentiary standard is he likely to need to meet?

A. The real evidence standard

B. Beyond a reasonable doubt

C. Preponderance of evidence

D. The documentary evidence standard

54. How many possible keys exist when using a cryptographic algorithm that has an 8-bit binary encryption key?

A. 16

B. 128

C. 256

D. 512

55. What activity is being performed when you apply security controls based on the specific needs of the IT system that they will be applied to?

A. Standardizing

B. Baselining

C. Scoping

D. Editing

56. Dawson is preparing to hire a new staff member for a role that requires very high levels of integrity and trust. Which of the following is most commonly used as part of the hiring process to determine if an employee is likely to be trustworthy?

A. Signing an NDA

B. A background check

C. Signing a noncompete

D. A COA

57. Ben's job is to ensure that data is labeled with the appropriate sensitivity label. Since Ben works for the U.S. government, he has to apply the labels Unclassified, Confidential, Secret, and Top Secret to systems and media. If Ben is asked to label a system that handles Secret, Confidential, and Unclassified information, how should he label it?

   A. Mixed classification

   B. Confidential

   C. Top Secret

   D. Secret

58. Susan has discovered that the smart card–based locks used to keep the facility she works at secure are not effective because staff members are propping the doors open. She places signs on the doors reminding staff that leaving the door open creates a security issue, and she adds alarms that will sound if the doors are left open for more than five minutes. What type of controls has she put into place?

   A. Physical

   B. Administrative

   C. Compensating

   D. Recovery

59. Ben's organization has purchased cybersecurity insurance. What type of risk treatment has the organization engaged in?

   A. Acceptance

   B. Avoidance

   C. Mitigation

   D. Transfer

60. Brad wants to engage third-party auditors to assess a vendor that his company will be signing a contract with. If Brad wants to assess the vendor's security policies and controls as well as the effectiveness of those controls as implemented over time, what SOC level and type should he request the auditors perform?

   A. A SOC 1, Type 2

   B. A SOC 2, Type 1

   C. A SOC 1, Type 1

   D. A SOC 2, Type 2

61. Lucca's manager does not want to adopt an open-source software package for their organization's web application stack. What software security advantage is the most important when considering open-source software packages?

   A. The fact that the code is not compiled

   B. The fact the code is free

   C. The ability to inspect the code

   D. The ability to change the code

62. As part of hiring a new employee, Kathleen's identity management team creates a new user object and ensures that the user object is available in the directories and systems where it is needed. What is this process called?

A. Registration

B. Provisioning

C. Population

D. Authenticator loading

63. What phase of the change management process for software occurs when changes are finalized?

A. Request control

B. Configuration control

C. Release control

D. Change control

64. Alice is designing a cryptosystem for use by six users and would like to use a symmetric encryption algorithm. She wants any two users to be able to communicate with each other without worrying about eavesdropping by a third user. How many symmetric encryption keys will she need to generate?

A. 6

B. 12

C. 15

D. 30

65. Which one of the following intellectual property protection mechanisms has the shortest duration in the United States?

A. Copyright

B. Patent

C. Trademark

D. Trade secret

66. Gordon is working on a business continuity plan for a manufacturing company's IT operations, which is located in North Dakota. The company is currently assessing the risk of an earthquake and has decided to adopt a risk acceptance strategy. Which of the following actions is in line with this strategy?

A. Purchasing earthquake insurance

B. Relocating the data center to a safer area

C. Documenting the decision-making process

D. Reengineering the facility to withstand the shock of an earthquake

67. Carol would like to implement a control that protects her organization from the momentary loss of power to the data center. Which control is most appropriate for her needs?

  A. Redundant servers

  B. RAID

  C. UPS

  D. Generator

68. Ben has encountered problems with users in his organization reusing passwords, despite a requirement that they change passwords every 30 days. What type of password setting should Ben employ to help prevent this issue?

  A. Longer minimum age

  B. Increased password complexity

  C. Implement password history

  D. Implement password length requirements

69. Chris is conducting a risk assessment for his organization and has determined the amount of damage that a single flood could be expected to cause to his facilities. What metric has Chris identified?

  A. ALE

  B. SLE

  C. ARO

  D. AV

70. The removal of a hard drive from a PC before it is retired and sold as surplus is an example of what type of action?

  A. Purging

  B. Sanitization

  C. Degaussing

  D. Destruction

71. During which phase of the incident response process would an organization determine whether it is required to notify law enforcement officials or other regulators of the incident?

  A. Detection

  B. Recovery

  C. Remediation

  D. Reporting

72. Every 90 days, the staff in Charles's department at his bank switch tasks as part of the organization's normal processes to ensure that an individual does not exploit their privileges. What security practice is his organization engaging in?

   A. Dual control

   B. Job rotation

   C. Cross-training

   D. Offboarding

73. Michelle oversees her organization's endpoint security, focusing on mobile device management and the recovery of lost or stolen devices. Which of the following recommendations will most effectively ensure data protection if a device is stolen?

   A. Mandatory passcodes and application management

   B. Full device encryption and mandatory passcodes

   C. Remote wipe and GPS tracking

   D. GPS tracking and full device encryption

74. Susan's SMTP server does not authenticate senders before accepting and relaying emails. What is this security configuration issue known as?

   A. An email gateway

   B. An SMTP relay

   C. An X.400-compliant gateway

   D. An open relay

For questions 75–77, please refer to the following scenario:

The large business that Jack works for has been using noncentralized logging for years. They have recently started to implement centralized logging, however, and as they reviewed logs, they discovered a breach that appeared to have involved a malicious insider.

75. When the breach was discovered and the logs were reviewed, it was discovered that the attacker had purged the logs on the system that they compromised. How can this be prevented in the future?

   A. Encrypt local logs.

   B. Require administrative access to change logs.

   C. Enable log rotation.

   D. Send logs to a secure log server.

76. How can Jack detect issues such as this using his organization's new centralized logging?

   A. Deploy and use an IDS.

   B. Send logs to a central logging server.

   C. Deploy and use a SIEM tool.

   D. Use syslog.

77. How can Jack best ensure accountability for actions taken on systems in his environment?

A. Log review and require digital signatures for each log.

B. Require authentication for all actions taken and capture logs centrally.

C. Log the use of administrative credentials and encrypt log data in transit.

D. Require authorization and capture logs centrally.

78. Ed's organization has 5 IP addresses allocated to them by their ISP but needs to connect more than 100 computers and network devices to the Internet. What technology can he use to connect his entire network via the limited set of IP addresses he can use?

A. IPsec

B. PAT

C. SDN

D. IPX

79. What type of attack would the following precautions help prevent?

- Requesting proof of identity
- Requiring callback authorizations on voice-only requests
- Not changing passwords via voice communications

A. DoS attacks

B. Worms

C. Social engineering

D. Shoulder surfing

80. The CIS benchmarks are an example of what sort of compliance tool?

A. A security baseline

B. A compliance standard

C. A secure provisioning tool

D. A security automation tool

81. Residual data is another term for what type of data left after attempts have been made to erase it?

A. Leftover data

B. MBR

C. Bitrot

D. Remnant data

82. Which one of the following disaster recovery test types involves the actual activation of the disaster recovery facility?

A. Simulation test

B. Tabletop exercise

C. Parallel test

D. Checklist review

83. What access control system lets owners decide who has access to the objects they own?

   A. Role-based access control

   B. Task-based access control

   C. Discretionary access control

   D. Rule-based access control

84. Using a trusted channel and link encryption are both ways to prevent what type of access control attack?

   A. Brute-force

   B. Spoofed login screens

   C. Man-in-the-middle attacks

   D. Dictionary attacks

85. Which one of the following is not one of the canons of the ISC2 Code of Ethics?

   A. Protect society, the common good, necessary public trust and confidence, and the infrastructure.

   B. Act honorably, honestly, justly, responsibly, and legally.

   C. Provide diligent and competent service to principals.

   D. Maintain competent records of all investigations and assessments.

86. Which one of the following components should be included in an organization's emergency response guidelines?

   A. Immediate response procedures

   B. Long-term business continuity protocols

   C. Activation procedures for the organization's cold sites

   D. Contact information for ordering equipment

87. Ben is working on integrating a federated identity management system and needs to exchange authentication and authorization information for browser-based single sign-on. What technology is his best option?

   A. HTML

   B. XACML

   C. SAML

   D. SPML

88. What is the minimum interval at which an organization should conduct business continuity plan refresher training for those with specific business continuity roles?

   A. Weekly

   B. Monthly

   C. Semiannually

   D. Annually

89. What three types of interfaces are typically tested during software testing?

    A. Network, physical, and application interfaces

    B. APIs, UIs, and physical interfaces

    C. Network interfaces, APIs, and UIs

    D. Application, programmatic, and user interfaces

90. Amanda's company has been looking for ways to reduce their costs for network switches and routers and has started to acquire devices from the gray market. Which of the following is not a typical concern for gray-market devices?

    A. API vulnerabilities

    B. Product tampering

    C. Implants

    D. Counterfeits

91. Andre has implemented virtual routing and forwarding (VRF) on his router. Which of the following descriptions best explains what this allows him to do?

    A. VRF is used to support VPCs.

    B. VRF is like a VPN at layer 3.

    C. VRF is like a VLAN at layer 3.

    D. VRF is used to support multilayer protocols.

92. Ben is selecting an encryption algorithm for use in an organization with 10,000 employees. He must facilitate communication between any two employees within the organization. Which one of the following algorithms would allow him to meet this goal with the least time dedicated to key management?

    A. RSA

    B. IDEA

    C. 3DES

    D. Skipjack

93. Grace uses her cloud service provider's function-as-a-service (FaaS) environment to deploy her organization's new application. What term should she use to describe this to her organization's leadership?

    A. ICS

    B. A VPC

    C. Embedded

    D. Serverless

94. What type of log file is shown here?

```
2015-08-09 16:39:01 ALLOW UDP 172.30.0.64 172.30.0.2 62166 53 0 - - - - - - - SEND
2015-08-09 16:39:01 ALLOW UDP 172.30.0.64 172.30.0.2 62167 53 0 - - - - - - - SEND
2015-08-09 16:39:01 ALLOW UDP 172.30.0.64 172.30.0.2 62168 53 0 - - - - - - - SEND
2015-08-09 16:39:01 ALLOW UDP 172.30.0.64 172.30.0.2 62169 53 0 - - - - - - - SEND
2015-08-09 16:39:01 ALLOW UDP 172.30.0.64 172.30.0.2 62170 53 0 - - - - - - - SEND
2015-08-09 16:39:01 ALLOW UDP 172.30.0.64 172.30.0.2 62171 53 0 - - - - - - - SEND
2015-08-09 16:39:01 ALLOW UDP 172.30.0.64 172.30.0.2 62172 53 0 - - - - - - - SEND
2015-08-09 16:39:01 ALLOW UDP 172.30.0.64 172.30.0.2 62173 53 0 - - - - - - - SEND
2015-08-09 16:39:01 ALLOW UDP 172.30.0.64 172.30.0.2 62174 53 0 - - - - - - - SEND
2015-08-09 16:39:01 ALLOW UDP 172.30.0.64 172.30.0.2 62175 53 0 - - - - - - - SEND
2015-08-09 16:39:01 ALLOW UDP 172.30.0.64 172.30.0.2 62176 53 0 - - - - - - - SEND
2015-08-09 16:39:39 ALLOW TCP 54.172.251.189 172.30.0.64 53355 80 0 - 0 0 0 - - - RECEIVE
2015-08-09 16:39:44 ALLOW TCP 54.172.251.189 172.30.0.64 53356 80 0 - 0 0 0 - - - RECEIVE
2015-08-09 16:39:44 ALLOW TCP 127.0.0.1 127.0.0.1 49178 47001 0 - 0 0 0 - - - SEND
2015-08-09 16:39:44 ALLOW TCP 127.0.0.1 127.0.0.1 49178 47001 0 - 0 0 0 - - - RECEIVE
2015-08-09 16:39:47 ALLOW TCP 172.30.0.64 169.254.169.254 49179 80 0 - 0 0 0 - - - SEND
2015-08-09 16:40:37 ALLOW TCP 54.172.251.189 172.30.0.64 53362 80 0 - 0 0 0 - - - RECEIVE
2015-08-09 16:40:47 ALLOW TCP 172.30.0.64 169.254.169.254 49180 80 0 - 0 0 0 - - - SEND
2015-08-09 16:40:55 ALLOW UDP fe80::11ef:7f4f:afb5:7f70 ff02::1:2 546 547 0 - - - - - - - SEND
```

- **A.** Application
- **B.** Web server
- **C.** System
- **D.** Firewall

95. Which one of the following activities transforms a zero-day vulnerability into a less dangerous attack vector?

- **A.** Discovery of the vulnerability
- **B.** Implementation of transport-layer encryption
- **C.** Reconfiguration of a firewall
- **D.** Release of a security patch

96. Elle's organization has had to shift to remote work. Each staff member needs access to specific applications, and due to the quick shift, staff members are working from systems that may be home systems or borrowed laptops. What is the best option for remote access in a situation like the one that Elle is facing?

- **A.** An IPsec VPN
- **B.** A dedicated fiber connection to each remote work location
- **C.** An HTML5-based VPN
- **D.** Use of remote desktop to connect to an existing workstation at the company's office building

97. Sameer's company has begun to deploy computation and storage capabilities to their industrial plants to gather and process data where it is created. What term best describes this type of deployment?

- **A.** Cloud computing
- **B.** Edge computing
- **C.** Hybrid cloud
- **D.** Microservices

For questions 98–101, please refer to the following scenario:

Matthew and Richard are friends located in different physical locations who would like to begin communicating with each other using cryptography to protect the confidentiality of their communications. They exchange digital certificates to begin this process and plan to use an asymmetric encryption algorithm for the secure exchange of email messages.

98. When Matthew sends Richard a message, what key should he use to encrypt the message?

A. Matthew's public key

B. Matthew's private key

C. Richard's public key

D. Richard's private key

99. When Richard receives the message from Matthew, what key should he use to decrypt the message?

A. Matthew's public key

B. Matthew's private key

C. Richard's public key

D. Richard's private key

100. Matthew would like to enhance the security of his communication by adding a digital signature to the message. What goal of cryptography are digital signatures intended to enforce?

A. Secrecy

B. Availability

C. Confidentiality

D. Nonrepudiation

101. When Matthew adds a digital signature to the message, what encryption key does he use to create the digital signature?

A. Matthew's public key

B. Matthew's private key

C. Richard's public key

D. Richard's private key

102. When Jim logs into a system, his password is compared to a hashed value stored in a database. What is this process?

A. Identification

B. Hashing

C. Tokenization

D. Authentication

103. What is the top priority for security professionals when considering facility design?

  A. Limiting access to only approved personnel

  B. Ensuring that the structure supports least privilege

  C. Ensuring the safety of personnel

  D. Limiting the potential for weather or other natural disasters to impact operations

104. Which of the following types of controls does not describe an access control vestibule?

  A. Deterrent

  B. Preventive

  C. Compensating

  D. Physical

105. Sally's organization needs to be able to prove that certain staff members sent emails, and she wants to adopt a technology that will provide that capability without changing their existing email system. What is the technical term for the capability Sally needs to implement as the owner of the email system, and what tool could she use to do it?

  A. Integrity; IMAP

  B. Repudiation; encryption

  C. Nonrepudiation; digital signatures

  D. Authentication; DKIM

106. Which one of the following background checks is not normally performed during normal pre-hire activities?

  A. Credit check

  B. Reference verification

  C. Criminal records check

  D. Medical records check

107. Naomi's organization limits data access to only those users with roles that require it for their job. What key security operations practice does this describe?

  A. Least privilege

  B. Privileged account management

  C. Job rotation

  D. Privilege escalation

108. In the OSI model, when a packet changes from a data stream to a segment or a datagram, what layer has it traversed?

  A. The Transport layer

  B. The Application layer

  C. The Data Link layer

  D. The Physical layer

109. Tommy handles access control requests for his organization. A user approaches him and explains that he needs access to the human resources database in order to complete a head-count analysis requested by the CFO. What has the user demonstrated successfully to Tommy?

- **A.** Clearance
- **B.** Separation of duties
- **C.** Need to know
- **D.** Isolation

110. Sharif wants to improve his organization's security awareness. He implements a process that gives points for identifying phishing emails and rewards departments based on their point scores. What awareness technique is he using?

- **A.** Security champions
- **B.** Gamification
- **C.** Social engineering
- **D.** Awareness training

111. What type of tool is most frequently used to match assets to users and owners in enterprises?

- **A.** An enterprise content management tool
- **B.** Barcoded property tags
- **C.** RFID-based property tags
- **D.** A system inventory

112. Alice would like to add another object to a security model and grant herself rights to that object. Which one of the rules in the Take-Grant protection model would allow her to complete this operation?

- **A.** Take rule
- **B.** Grant rule
- **C.** Create rule
- **D.** Remove rule

113. Which of the following concerns should not be on Amanda's list of potential issues when penetration testers suggest using Metasploit during their testing?

- **A.** Metasploit can only test vulnerabilities it has plug-ins for.
- **B.** Penetration testing only covers a point-in-time view of the organization's security.
- **C.** Tools like Metasploit can cause denial-of-service issues.
- **D.** Penetration testing cannot test process and policy.

114. Colin's organization has decommissioned multifunction photocopier/printer devices used throughout its administrative headquarters. What concern would be most likely to drive physical destruction of the device rather than allowing them to be sold as surplus?

A. Data remanence

B. Asset inventory

C. Asset management

D. Compliance

115. Which ITU-T standard should Alex expect to see in use when he uses his smartcard to provide a certificate to an upstream authentication service?

A. X.500

B. SPML

C. X.509

D. SAML

116. What type of websites are regulated under the terms of COPPA?

A. Financial websites not run by financial institutions

B. Healthcare websites that collect personal information

C. Websites that collect information from children

D. Financial websites run by financial institutions

117. Tracy recently accepted an IT compliance position at a federal government agency that works very closely with the Department of Defense on classified government matters. Which one of the following laws is least likely to pertain to Tracy's agency?

A. HIPAA

B. FISMA

C. HSA

D. CFAA

118. Henry's organization wants to meet federal security standards for the cloud services it provides. What program should he investigate to meet this goal?

A. COBIT

B. SABSA

C. FedRAMP

D. PCI

119. What two important factors does accountability for access control rely on?

A. Identification and authorization

B. Authentication and authorization

C. Identification and authentication

D. Accountability and authentication

120. What part of the CIA triad does a checksum support?

    A. Availability

    B. Integrity

    C. Confidentiality

    D. Authenticity

121. Scott's organization has configured their external IP address to be 192.168.1.25. When traffic is sent to their ISP, it never reaches its destination. What problem is Scott's organization encountering?

    A. BGP is not set up properly.

    B. They have not registered their IP with their ISP.

    C. The IP address is a private, nonroutable address.

    D. 192.168.1.25 is a reserved address for home routers.

122. Jack's organization merges updates to their main application multiple times a day and then deploys it as code that is checked in and tested through their software development pipeline. What type of model is this?

    A. Waterfall

    B. CI/CD

    C. SCM

    D. IDE

123. Sue's organization recently failed a security assessment because their network was a single flat broadcast domain, and sniffing traffic was possible between different functional groups. What solution should she recommend to help prevent the issues that were identified?

    A. Use VLANs.

    B. Change the subnet mask for all systems.

    C. Deploy gateways.

    D. Turn on port security.

124. Which of the following terms best describes the IP address 10.14.124.240?

    A. Public IP address

    B. Private IP address

    C. APIPA address

    D. Loopback address

125. Jim is performing a security assessment of his company and would like to use a testing tool to perform a web vulnerability scan. Which of the following tools is best suited for identifying this form of vulnerability?

    A. Nmap

    B. Hydra

    C. Metasploit

    D. Nikto

Chapter

11

Practice Test 3

1. Fred's data role requires him to maintain system security plans and to ensure that system users and support staff get the training they need about security practices and acceptable use. What is the role that Fred is most likely to hold in the organization?

    A. Data owner

    B. System owner

    C. User

    D. Custodian

2. Sally is using IPsec's ESP component in transport mode. What important information should she be aware of about transport mode?

    A. Transport mode provides full encryption of the entire IP packet.

    B. Transport mode adds a new, unencrypted header to ensure that packets reach their destination.

    C. Transport mode does not encrypt the header of the packet.

    D. Transport mode provides no encryption; only tunnel mode provides encryption.

3. Which one of the following is not an essential process area for the Repeatable phase of the Software Capability Maturity Model (SW-CMM)?

    A. Software Project Planning

    B. Software Quality Management

    C. Software Project Tracking

    D. Software Subcontract Management

4. Ben wants to provide predictive information about his organization's risk exposure in an automated way as part of an ongoing organizational risk management plan. What should he use to do this?

    A. KRIs

    B. Quantitative risk assessments

    C. KPIs

    D. Penetration tests

5. In the image shown here, what does system B send to system A at step 2 of the three-way TCP handshake?

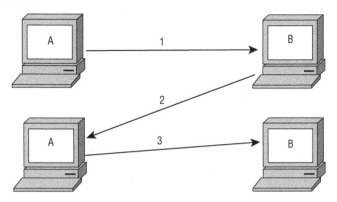

A. SYN

B. ACK

C. FIN/ACK

D. SYN/ACK

6. Chris is conducting reconnaissance on a remote target and discovers that pings are allowed through his target's border firewall. What can he learn by using pings to probe the remote network?

A. Which systems respond to pings, a rough network topology, and potentially the location of additional firewalls

B. A list of all of the systems behind the target's firewall

C. The hostnames and time to live (TTL) for each pingable system and the ICMP types allowed through the firewall

D. Router advertisements, echo request responses, and potentially which hosts are tarpitted

7. Jake is conducting a review of his organization's identity and access management program. During his review, he is verifying the privileges assigned to each user and ensuring that they match with business requirements. What element of the program is he reviewing?

A. Identification

B. Accounting

C. Authorization

D. Authentication

8. Faith is looking at the `/etc/passwd` file on a system configured to use shadowed passwords. When she examines a line in the file for a user with interactive login permissions, what should she expect to see in the password field?

    A. Plaintext password

    B. Hashed password

    C. x

    D. *

9. Berta is analyzing the logs of the Windows Firewall on one of her servers and comes across the entries shown in this figure. What type of attack do these entries indicate?

    ```
    2016-04-21 05:14:52 DROP TCP 192.168.250.4 192.168.42.14 4004 21  - - - - - - RECEIVE
    2016-04-21 05:14:53 DROP TCP 192.168.250.4 192.168.42.14 4005 22  - - - - - - RECEIVE
    2016-04-21 05:14:54 DROP TCP 192.168.250.4 192.168.42.14 4006 23  - - - - - - RECEIVE
    2016-04-21 05:14:56 DROP TCP 192.168.250.4 192.168.42.14 4007 25  - - - - - - RECEIVE
    2016-04-21 05:14:59 DROP TCP 192.168.250.4 192.168.42.14 4008 53  - - - - - - RECEIVE
    2016-04-21 05:15:02 DROP TCP 192.168.250.4 192.168.42.14 4009 80  - - - - - - RECEIVE
    2016-04-21 05:15:03 DROP TCP 192.168.250.4 192.168.42.14 4010 110 - - - - - - RECEIVE
    2016-04-21 05:15:04 DROP TCP 192.168.250.4 192.168.42.14 4011 111 - - - - - - RECEIVE
    ```

    A. SQL injection

    B. Port scan

    C. Teardrop

    D. Land

10. Danielle is testing tax software, and part of her testing process requires her to input a variety of actual tax forms to verify that the software produces the right answers. What type of testing is Danielle performing?

    A. Use-case testing

    B. Dynamic testing

    C. Fuzzing

    D. Misuse testing

11. After 10 years working in her organization, Cassandra is moving into her fourth role, this time as a manager in the accounting department. What issue is likely to show up during an account review if her organization does not have strong account maintenance practices?

    A. An issue with least privilege

    B. Privilege creep

    C. Account creep

    D. Account termination

12. IP addresses like 10.10.10.10 and 172.19.24.21 are both examples of what type of IP address?

    A. Public IP addresses

    B. Prohibited IP addresses

    C. Private IP addresses

    D. Class B IP ranges

13. Ben is reviewing the password recovery mechanism used by his website and discovers that the approach uses cognitive authentication through the use of security questions. What is the major issue with this approach?

A. It prevents the use of tokens.

B. The question's answer may be easy to find on the Internet.

C. Cognitive passwords require users to think to answer the question, and not all users may be able to solve the problems presented.

D. Cognitive passwords don't support long passwords.

14. Megan needs to create a forensic copy of a hard drive that will be used in an investigation. Which of the following tools is best suited to her work?

A. xcopy

B. dd

C. DBAN

D. ImageMagick

15. Kay is selecting an application management approach for her organization. Employees need the flexibility to install software on their systems, but Kay wants to prevent them from installing certain prohibited packages. What type of approach should she use?

A. Antivirus

B. Whitelist

C. Blacklist

D. Heuristic

16. Donna is a security administrator for a healthcare provider located in the United States and is reviewing their payment processing system. It contains data relating to the past, present, or future payment for the provision of healthcare to an individual. How would this information be classified under HIPAA?

A. PCI

B. Personal billing data

C. PHI

D. PII

17. Harold's company has a strong password policy that requires a minimum length of 12 characters and the use of both alphanumeric characters and symbols. What technique would be the most effective way for an attacker to compromise passwords in Harold's organization?

A. Brute-force attack

B. Dictionary attack

C. Rainbow table attack

D. Social engineering attack

18. While traveling, James is held at knifepoint and forced to log into his laptop. What is this called?

A. Duress

B. Antisocial engineering

C. Distress

D. Knifepoint hacking

19. Kayla recently took a position at a new start-up company that runs entirely in the cloud. The company leverages a major IaaS provider for hosting its web services and a SaaS email system. Both of these providers operate multitenant environments. What term best describes the type of cloud environment this organization uses?

A. Public cloud

B. Dedicated cloud

C. Private cloud

D. Hybrid cloud

20. Cameron is responsible for backing up his company's primary file server. He configured a backup schedule that performs full backups every Monday evening at 9 p.m. and incremental backups on other days of the week at that same time. How many files will be copied in Wednesday's backup?

> **File Modifications**
> Monday 8AM - File 1 created
> Monday 10AM - File 2 created
> Monday 11AM - File 3 created
> Monday 4PM - File 1 modified
> Monday 5PM - File 4 created
> Tuesday 8AM - File 1 modified
> Tuesday 9AM - File 2 modified
> Tuesday 10AM - File 5 created
> Wednesday 8AM - File 3 modified
> Wednesday 9AM - File 6 created

A. 1

B. 2

C. 5

D. 6

21. Susan uses a SPAN port to monitor traffic to her production website and uses a monitoring tool to identify performance issues in real time. What type of monitoring is she conducting?

A. Passive monitoring

B. Active monitoring

C. Synthetic monitoring

D. Signature-based monitoring

22. In what type of attack do attackers manage to insert themselves into a connection between a user and a legitimate website?

   A. Man-in-the-middle attack

   B. Fraggle attack

   C. Wardriving attack

   D. Meet-in-the-middle attack

23. Which one of the following would be considered an example of infrastructure-as-a-service cloud computing?

   A. Payroll system managed by a vendor and delivered over the web

   B. Application platform managed by a vendor that runs customer code

   C. Servers provisioned by customers on a vendor-managed virtualization platform

   D. Web-based email service provided by a vendor

For questions 24–26, please refer to the following scenario:

Darcy is an information security risk analyst for Roscommon Agricultural Products. She is currently trying to decide whether the company should purchase an upgraded fire suppression system for their primary data center. The data center facility has a replacement cost of $2 million.

   After consulting with actuaries, data center managers, and fire subject-matter experts, Darcy determined that a typical fire would likely require the replacement of all equipment inside the building but not cause significant structural damage. Together, they estimated that recovering from the fire would cost $750,000. They also determined that the company can expect a fire of this magnitude once every 50 years.

24. Based on the information in this scenario, what is the exposure factor for the effect of a fire on the Roscommon Agricultural Products data center?

   A. 7.5%

   B. 15.0%

   C. 27.5%

   D. 37.5%

25. Based on the information in this scenario, what is the annualized rate of occurrence for a fire at the Roscommon Agricultural Products data center?

   A. 0.002

   B. 0.005

   C. 0.02

   D. 0.05

26. Based on the information in this scenario, what is the annualized loss expectancy for a fire at the Roscommon Agricultural Products data center?

   A. $15,000

   B. $25,000

   C. $75,000

   D. $750,000

27. Which one of the following techniques uses statistical methods to select a small number of log records from a large pool for further analysis with the goal of choosing a set of records that is representative of the entire pool?

   A. Clipping

   B. Randomization

   C. Sampling

   D. Selection

28. Mike wants to ensure that third-party users of his service's API can be tracked to prevent abuse of the API. What should he implement to help with this?

   A. Session IDs

   B. An API firewall

   C. API keys

   D. An API buffer

29. Fran is a web developer who works for an online retailer. Her boss asked her to create a way that customers can easily integrate themselves with Fran's company's site. They need to be able to check inventory in real time, place orders, and check order status programmatically without having to access the web page. What can Fran create to most directly facilitate this interaction?

   A. An API

   B. A web scraper

   C. A data dictionary

   D. A call center

30. Todd's data center facility recently experienced a series of events that involved the momentary loss of power. What term best describes these events?

   A. Fault

   B. Blackout

   C. Sag

   D. Brownout

31. Lauren's team of system administrators each deals with hundreds of systems with varying levels of security requirements and finds it difficult to handle the multitude of usernames and passwords they each have. What type of solution should she recommend to ensure that passwords are properly handled and that features like logging and password rotation occur?

   A. A credential management system

   B. A strong password policy

   C. Separation of duties

   D. Single sign-on

32. Ed's Windows system can't connect to the network, and `ipconfig` shows the following:

```
Ethernet adapter Local Area Connection:

   Connection-specific DNS Suffix  . :
   Link-local IPv6 Address . . . . . : fe80::90f1:e9f0:c0f5:b0ba%11
   IPv4 Address. . . . . . . . . . . : 169.254.19.21
   Subnet Mask . . . . . . . . . . . : 255.255.0.0
   Default Gateway . . . . . . . . . :
```

What has occurred on the system?

   A. The system has been assigned an invalid IP address by its DHCP server.

   B. The system has a manually assigned IP address.

   C. The system has failed to get a DHCP address and has assigned itself an address.

   D. The subnet mask is set incorrectly, and the system cannot communicate with the gateway.

33. Gina is performing the initial creation of user accounts for a batch of new employees. What phase of the provisioning process is she conducting?

   A. Enrollment

   B. Clearance verification

   C. Background checks

   D. Initialization

34. Ravi is developing procedures for forensic investigations conducted by his organization and would like to differentiate based upon the evidentiary standards commonly used for each type of investigation. What type of forensic investigation typically has the highest evidentiary standards?

   A. Administrative

   B. Criminal

   C. Civil

   D. Industry

35. What U.S. legal protection prevents law enforcement agencies from searching an American facility or electronic system without either probable cause or consent?

A. First Amendment

B. Fourth Amendment

C. Fifth Amendment

D. Fifteenth Amendment

36. Tom believes that a customer of his Internet service provider has been exploiting a vulnerability in his system to read the email messages of other customers. If true, what law did the customer most likely violate?

A. ECPA

B. CALEA

C. HITECH

D. Privacy Act

37. In the protection ring model shown here, what ring contains user programs and applications?

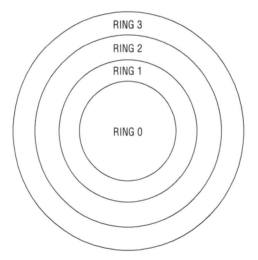

A. Ring 0

B. Ring 1

C. Ring 2

D. Ring 3

38. In virtualization platforms, what name is given to the module that is responsible for controlling access to physical resources by virtual resources?

A. Guest machine

B. SDN

C. Kernel

D. Hypervisor

39. In which cloud computing model does a customer share computing infrastructure with other customers of the cloud vendor where one customer may not know the other's identity?

A. Public cloud

B. Private cloud

C. Community cloud

D. Shared cloud

40. Justin recently participated in a disaster recovery plan test where the team sat together and discussed the response to a scenario but did not actually activate any disaster recovery controls. What type of test did he participate in?

A. Read-through

B. Full interruption test

C. Parallel test

D. Tabletop exercise

41. Susan wants to integrate her website to allow users to use accounts from sites like Google. What technology should she adopt?

A. Kerberos

B. LDAP

C. OpenID Connect

D. SESAME

42. Tom is conducting a business continuity planning effort for Orange Blossoms, a fruit orchard located in Central Florida. During the assessment process, the committee determined that there is a small risk of snow in the region but that the cost of implementing controls to reduce the impact of that risk is not warranted. They elect to not take any specific action in response to the risk. What risk management strategy is Orange Blossoms pursuing?

A. Risk mitigation

B. Risk transference

C. Risk avoidance

D. Risk acceptance

43. Paul is reviewing the contents of an audit report and discovers a finding that a manager in the accounting department has full access to perform every function in the financial system. What security principles have most likely been violated? (Select all that apply.)

A. Separation of duties

B. Job rotation

C. Management review

D. Least privilege

44. Jack's organization is a multinational nonprofit that has small offices in many developing countries throughout the world. They need to implement an access control system that allows flexibility and that can work despite poor Internet connectivity at their locations. What is the best type of access control design for Jack's organization?

A. Centralized access control

B. Mandatory access control

C. Decentralized access control

D. Rule-based access control

45. What U.S. government classification label is applied to information that, if disclosed, could cause serious damage to national security and also requires that the damage that would be caused is able to be described or identified by the classification authority?

A. Classified

B. Secret

C. Confidential

D. Top Secret

For questions 46–49, please refer to the following scenario:

Mike and Renee would like to use an asymmetric cryptosystem to communicate with each other. They are located in different parts of the country but have exchanged encryption keys by using digital certificates signed by a mutually trusted certificate authority.

46. When the certificate authority (CA) created Renee's digital certificate, what key was contained within the body of the certificate?

A. Renee's public key

B. Renee's private key

C. CA's public key

D. CA's private key

47. When the certificate authority created Renee's digital certificate, what key did it use to digitally sign the completed certificate?

A. Renee's public key

B. Renee's private key

C. CA's public key

D. CA's private key

48. When Mike receives Renee's digital certificate, what key does he use to verify the authenticity of the certificate?

A. Renee's public key

B. Renee's private key

C. CA's public key

D. CA's private key

49. Mike would like to send Renee a private message using the information gained during this exchange. What key should he use to encrypt the message?

A. Renee's public key

B. Renee's private key

C. CA's public key

D. CA's private key

50. Which one of the following tools may be used to directly violate the confidentiality of communications on an unencrypted VoIP network?

A. Nmap

B. Nessus

C. Wireshark

D. Nikto

51. Which of the following is not true about the ISC2 Code of Ethics?

A. Adherence to the code is a condition of certification.

B. Failure to comply with the code may result in revocation of certification.

C. The code applies to all members of the information security profession.

D. Members who observe a breach of the code are required to report the possible violation.

52. Which one of the following cryptographic algorithms supports the goal of nonrepudiation?

A. Blowfish

B. DES

C. AES

D. RSA

53. Microsoft's STRIDE threat assessment framework uses six categories for threats: Spoofing, Tampering, Repudiation, Information Disclosure, Denial of Service, and Elevation of Privilege. If a penetration tester is able to modify audit logs, what STRIDE categories best describe this issue?

A. Tampering and information disclosure

B. Elevation of privilege and tampering

C. Repudiation and denial of service

D. Repudiation and tampering

54. Carmen is reviewing her organization's web architecture and realizes that the web server is often under heavy load from users in different regions of the world. This load comes at unpredictable times. She would like to find a solution that minimizes the burden on her organization's servers and places content geographically closer to the user to decrease load time. What would be the best solution to Carmen's requirements?

   A. Load balancer

   B. Content delivery network

   C. TLS acceleration

   D. Web application firewall

55. Brian recently joined an organization that runs the majority of its services on a virtualization platform located in its own data center but also leverages an IaaS provider for hosting its web services and an SaaS email system. What term best describes the type of cloud environment this organization uses?

   A. Public cloud

   B. Dedicated cloud

   C. Private cloud

   D. Hybrid cloud

56. The government agency that Ben works at installed a new access control system. The system uses information such as Ben's identity, department, normal working hours, job category, and location to make authorization decisions. What type of access control system did Ben's employer adopt?

   A. Role-based access control

   B. Attribute-based access control

   C. Administrative access control

   D. System discretionary access control

57. Ben is building his organization's security awareness and training program and would like to include interactive activities that better engage users. What techniques would best help him meet this goal? (Select all that apply.)

   A. Policy reviews

   B. Gamification

   C. Classroom training

   D. Phishing simulations

58. Andrew believes that a digital certificate belonging to his organization was compromised and would like to add it to a certificate revocation list (CRL). Who must add the certificate to the CRL?

   A. Andrew

   B. The root authority for the top-level domain

   C. The CA that issued the certificate

   D. The revocation authority for the top-level domain

59. Amanda is considering the implementation of a database recovery mechanism recommended by a consultant. In the recommended approach, an automated process will move records of transactions from the primary site to a backup site on an hourly basis. What type of database recovery technique is the consultant describing?

A. Electronic vaulting

B. Transaction logging

C. Remote mirroring

D. Remote journaling

60. Ron is working to classify information used by his organization and would like to include all information that might trigger a U.S. state data breach notification law in his classification scheme. Which of the following categories of information should he include, assuming that they are connected to a specific individual? (Select all that apply.)

A. Bank account number and PIN

B. Driver's license number

C. Marital status

D. Social Security number

61. Which one of the following investigation types has the loosest standards for the collection and preservation of information?

A. Civil investigation

B. Operational investigation

C. Criminal investigation

D. Regulatory investigation

62. Sue was required to sign an NDA when she took a job at her new company. Why did the company require her to sign it?

A. To protect the confidentiality of their data

B. To ensure that Sue did not delete their data

C. To prevent Sue from directly competing with them in the future

D. To require Sue to ensure the availability for their data as part of her job

63. Susan is concerned about the FAR associated with her biometric technology. What is the best method to deal with the FAR?

A. Adjust the CER.

B. Change the sensitivity of the system to lower the FRR.

C. Add a second factor.

D. Replace the biometric system.

64. Which data role in an organization is most likely to perform backups of critical systems to ensure that their availability is preserved?

  A. Business owners

  B. Data users

  C. Data owners

  D. Data custodians

65. Ron is the CISO of a U.S. company that is entering into a business partnership with a European firm. The European firm will be sending his company customer records to run through Ron's firm's proprietary credit scoring algorithm. Under GDPR, what role will Ron's company have relative to the customer data?

  A. Data controller

  B. Data owner

  C. Data subject

  D. Data processor

66. Tonya recently introduced a new security control in her organization for emergency access to system administrator privileges. Under this procedure, two qualified administrators must agree to retrieve emergency credentials. What term best describes this process?

  A. Separation of duties

  B. Least privilege

  C. Two-person control

  D. Multifactor authentication

67. Attackers who compromise websites often acquire databases of hashed passwords. What technique can best protect these passwords against automated password cracking attacks that use precomputed values?

  A. Using the MD5 hashing algorithm

  B. Using the SHA-1 hashing algorithm

  C. Salting

  D. Double-hashing

68. Jim starts a new job as a system engineer, and he is reviewing a team document entitled "Forensic Response Guidelines." Which one of the following statements is not true?

  A. Jim must comply with the information in this document.

  B. The document contains information about forensic examinations.

  C. Jim should read the document thoroughly.

  D. The document is likely based on industry best practices.

69. Evan is reviewing his access control system to ensure that no user is able to read information that is above their security clearance level. What security model is he enforcing?

   A. Bell–LaPadula

   B. Star security property

   C. Discretionary security property

   D. Biba

70. Ben needs to verify that the most recent patch for his organization's critical application did not introduce issues elsewhere. What type of testing does Ben need to conduct to ensure this?

   A. Unit testing

   B. White box

   C. Regression testing

   D. Black box

71. Tamara recently decided to purchase cyber-liability insurance to cover her company's costs in the event of a data breach. What risk management strategy is she pursuing?

   A. Risk acceptance

   B. Risk mitigation

   C. Risk transference

   D. Risk avoidance

72. Which of the following is not one of the four canons of the ISC2 Code of Ethics?

   A. Avoid conflicts of interest that may jeopardize impartiality.

   B. Protect society, the common good, necessary public trust and confidence, and the infrastructure.

   C. Act honorably, honestly, justly, responsibly, and legally.

   D. Provide diligent and competent service to principals.

73. Jim wants to allow a partner organization's Active Directory forest (B) to access his domain forest's (A)'s resources but doesn't want to allow users in his domain to access B's resources. He also does not want the trust to flow upward through the domain tree as it is formed. What should he do?

   A. Set up a two-way transitive trust.

   B. Set up a one-way transitive trust.

   C. Set up a one-way nontransitive trust.

   D. Set up a two-way nontransitive trust.

74. Susan's team is performing code analysis by manually reviewing the code for flaws. What type of analysis are they performing?

   A. Gray box

   B. Static

   C. Dynamic

   D. Fuzzing

75. Kevin's organization recently suffered a ransomware attack, and he is considering paying the ransom. Which of the following statements are true about paying the ransom? (Select all that apply.)

   A. There is no guarantee that he will receive the decryption key.

   B. The attackers have encrypted his data but do not have access to the data itself.

   C. Restoring from backup will not recover information.

   D. Paying ransoms may be illegal.

76. What feature of a Trusted Platform Module (TPM) creates a hash summary of the system configuration to verify that changes have not been made?

   A. Remote attestation

   B. Binding

   C. Sealing

   D. RNG

77. Gary is concerned that the environmental controls in his organization's data center may not be effectively controlling humidity. Which of the following circumstances may result from humidity issues? (Select all that apply.)

   A. Static electricity damaging equipment

   B. Fires in power supplies

   C. Corrosion of equipment

   D. Physical access control failures

78. Evan recently built an alternate processing facility that includes all of the hardware and data necessary to restore operations in a matter of minutes or seconds. What type of facility has he built?

   A. Hot site

   B. Warm site

   C. Cold site

   D. Mobile site

79. Hadley is reviewing network traffic logs and is searching for syslog activity on his network. When he creates a filter to look for this traffic, which UDP port should he include?

A. 443

B. 514

C. 515

D. 445

80. Fred finds a packet that his protocol analyzer shows with both PSH and URG set. What type of packet is he looking at, and what do the flags mean?

A. A UDP packet; PSH and URG are used to indicate that the data should be sent at high speed

B. A TCP packet; PSH and URG are used to clear the buffer and indicate that the data is urgent

C. A TCP packet; PSH and URG are used to preset the header and indicate that the speed of the network is unregulated

D. A UDP packet; PSH and URG are used to indicate that the UDP buffer should be cleared and that the data is urgent

81. What code review process is shown here?

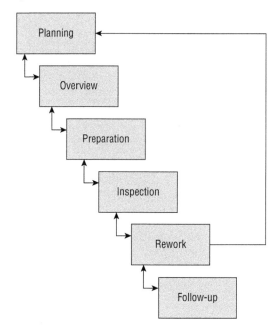

A. Static inspection

B. Fagan inspection

C. Dynamic inspection

D. Interface testing

82. During a log review, Karen discovers that the system she needs to gather logs from has the log setting shown here. What problem is Karen likely to encounter?

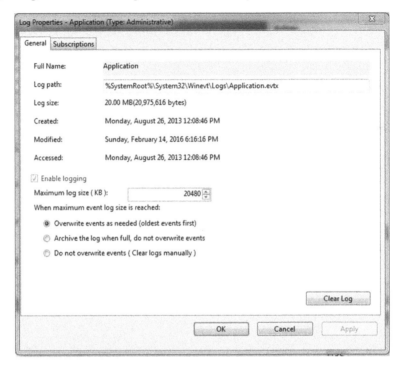

A. Too much log data will be stored on the system.

B. The system is automatically purging archived logs.

C. The logs will not contain the information needed.

D. The logs will contain only the most recent 20 MB of log data.

83. While investigating a widespread distributed denial-of-service attack, Matt types in the IP address of one of the attacking systems into his browser and sees the following page. What type of devices is the botnet likely composed of?

A. SCADA

B. Cloud infrastructure

C. Web servers

D. IoT

For questions 84–86, please refer to the following scenario:

Alejandro is an incident response analyst for a large corporation. He is on the midnight shift when an intrusion detection system alerts him to a potential brute-force password attack against one of the company's critical information systems. He performs an initial triage of the event before taking any additional action.

84. What stage of the incident response process is Alejandro currently conducting?

    A. Detection

    B. Response

    C. Recovery

    D. Mitigation

85. If Alejandro's initial investigation determines that a security incident is likely taking place, what should be his next step?

    A. Investigate the root cause.

    B. File a written report.

    C. Activate the incident response team.

    D. Attempt to restore the system to normal operations.

86. As the incident response progresses, during which stage should the team conduct a root-cause analysis?

    A. Response

    B. Reporting

    C. Remediation

    D. Lessons learned

87. Barry recently received a message from Melody that Melody encrypted using symmetric cryptography. What key should Barry use to decrypt the message?

    A. Barry's public key

    B. Barry's private key

    C. Melody's public key

    D. Shared secret key

88. After you do automated functional testing with 100% coverage of an application, what type of error is most likely to remain?

    A. Business logic errors

    B. Input validation errors

    C. Runtime errors

    D. Error handling errors

89. During what phase of the incident response process would security professionals analyze the process itself to determine whether any improvements are warranted?

A. Lessons learned

B. Remediation

C. Recovery

D. Reporting

90. What U.S. law prevents the removal of protection mechanisms placed on a copyrighted work by the copyright holder?

A. HIPAA

B. DMCA

C. GLBA

D. ECPA

91. Linda is selecting a disaster recovery facility for her organization, and she wants to retain independence from other organizations as much as possible. She would like to choose a facility that balances cost and recovery time, allowing activation in about one week after a disaster is declared. What type of facility should she choose?

A. Cold site

B. Warm site

C. Mutual assistance agreement

D. Hot site

92. Helen's organization handles large quantities of highly sensitive information. To help address this risk, she purchased a cyber-liability insurance policy. What type of risk response action is Helen taking?

A. Transfer

B. Avoid

C. Mitigate

D. Accept

93. What type of penetration testing provides detail on the scope of a penetration test—including items like what systems would be targeted—but does not provide full visibility into the configuration or other details of the systems or networks the penetration tester must test?

A. Crystal box

B. White box

C. Black box

D. Gray box

94. Joanna would like to implement multifactor authentication for access to a restricted work area in her building. Which pairing of controls would best meet her requirement?

    A. ID card and PIN

    B. Password and retinal scan

    C. ID card and access token

    D. Retinal scan and fingerprint scan

95. What network topology is used by modern-day Ethernet networks?

    A. Star

    B. Mesh

    C. Ring

    D. Bus

96. Reed would like to add capabilities to his network that allow him to hide the identities of his users from remote web servers. Which one of the following tools would best meet his needs?

    A. Proxy server

    B. Content filter

    C. Malware filter

    D. Caching server

97. Evelyn is preparing a training program that will provide cybersecurity advice to users who often travel internationally. Which of the following topics requires special training to ensure that users do not run afoul of U.S. export control laws?

    A. Encryption software

    B. Content filtering

    C. Firewall rules

    D. Phishing simulations

98. Skip needs to transfer files from his PC to a remote server. What protocol should he use instead of FTP?

    A. SCP

    B. SSH

    C. HTTP

    D. Telnet

99. Ben's New York–based commercial web service collects personal information from California residents. What does the California Online Privacy Protection Act require Ben to do to be compliant?

    A. Ben must encrypt all personal data he receives.

    B. Ben must comply with the EU GDPR.

    C. Ben must have a conspicuously posted privacy policy on his site.

    D. Ben must provide notice and choice for users of his website.

100. Grayson is reviewing his organization's password policies and would like to follow modern best practices. What is the recommended expiration period for passwords?

A. 30 days

B. 90 days

C. 180 days

D. None

101. A consortium of colleges and universities recently worked to integrate their authentication systems so that students registered at one institution may use their credentials to access services at other institutions. What term best describes this arrangement?

A. Federation

B. Identity proofing

C. Enrollment

D. Provisioning

102. Olivia is selecting a new biometric authentication technology and is considering purchasing iris scanners. What advantage do iris scans have over most other types of biometric factors?

A. Iris scanners are harder to deceive.

B. Irises don't change as much as other factors.

C. Iris scanners are cheaper than other factors.

D. Iris scans cannot be easily replicated.

103. Jen's firm received a new contract to develop information systems for use by a U.S. federal government agency. She is concerned about identifying any required security controls that must be in place. Which one of the following standards describes controls mandatory for use on U.S. government systems?

A. PCI DSS

B. ISO 27001

C. SABSA

D. NIST 800-53

104. Matthew, Richard, and Christopher would like to exchange messages with each other using symmetric cryptography. They want to ensure that each individual can privately send a message to another individual without the third person being able to read the message. How many keys do they need?

A. 1

B. 2

C. 3

D. 6

105. Colleen is responsible for protecting credit card numbers as part of her organization's efforts to comply with PCI DSS. She would like to select an appropriate control to protect those numbers while in transit over the network. Which of the following controls would best meet this need?

A. FDE

B. SSL

C. TPM

D. TLS

106. Joe is concerned about the confidentiality of email messages as they are transiting the Internet from his organization's servers to their final destination. What is the best way that Joe can ensure email confidentiality in transit?

A. Use TLS between the client and server.

B. Use SSL between the client and server.

C. Encrypt the email content.

D. Use a digital signature.

107. Brenda is analyzing the web server logs after a successful compromise of her organization's web-based order processing application. She finds an entry in the log file showing that a user entered the following information as his last name when placing an order:

`Smith';DROP TABLE orders;--`

What type of attack was attempted?

A. Buffer overflow

B. Cross-site scripting

C. Cross-site request forgery

D. SQL injection

108. Hannah's organization is implementing a new approach to user authentication that relies upon SAML. She would like to protect against eavesdropping on this traffic and also ensure that SAML traffic is not forged by an attacker. What should she do to protect against both types of attack?

A. Use SAML's secure mode to provide secure authentication.

B. Implement TLS using a strong cipher suite, which will protect against both types of attacks.

C. Implement TLS using a strong cipher suite and use digital signatures.

D. Implement TLS using a strong cipher suite and message hashing.

109. What is the goal of the BCP process?

A. RTO < MTD

B. MTD < RTO

C. RPO < MTD

D. MTD < RPO

110. During which phase of the incident response process would administrators design new security controls intended to prevent a recurrence of the incident?

   A. Reporting

   B. Recovery

   C. Remediation

   D. Lessons learned

111. Bethany received an email from one of her colleagues with an unusual attachment named `smime.p7s`. She does not recognize the attachment and is unsure what to do. What is the most likely scenario?

   A. This is an encrypted email message.

   B. This is a phishing attack.

   C. This is embedded malware.

   D. This is a spoofing attack.

For questions 112–114, please refer to the following scenario:

Kim is the database security administrator for Aircraft Systems, Inc. (ASI). ASI is a military contractor engaged in the design and analysis of aircraft avionics systems and regularly handles classified information on behalf of the government and other government contractors. Kim is concerned about ensuring the security of information stored in ASI databases.

Kim's database is a multilevel security database, and different ASI employees have different security clearances. The database contains information on the location of military aircraft containing ASI systems to allow ASI staff to monitor those systems.

112. Kim learned that the military is planning a classified mission that involves some ASI aircraft. She is concerned that employees not cleared for the mission may learn of it by noticing the movement of many aircraft to the region. Individual employees are cleared to know about the movement of an individual aircraft, but they are not cleared to know about the overall mission. What type of attack is Kim concerned about?

   A. Aggregation

   B. SQL injection

   C. Inference

   D. Multilevel security

113. What technique can Kim employ to prevent employees not cleared for the mission from learning the true location of the aircraft?

   A. Input validation

   B. Polyinstantiation

   C. Parameterization

   D. Server-side validation

114. Kim's database uniquely identifies aircrafts by using their tail number. Which one of the following terms would not necessarily accurately describe the tail number?

A. Database field

B. Foreign key

C. Primary key

D. Candidate key

115. Kim would like to create a key that enforces referential integrity for the database. What type of key does she need to create?

A. Primary key

B. Foreign key

C. Candidate key

D. Master key

116. Doug is choosing a software development life-cycle model for use in a project he is leading to develop a new business application. He has clearly defined requirements and would like to choose an approach that places an early emphasis on developing comprehensive documentation. He does not have a need for the production of rapid prototypes or iterative improvement. Which model is most appropriate for this scenario?

A. Agile

B. Waterfall

C. Spiral

D. DevOps

117. Which individual bears the ultimate responsibility for data protection tasks?

A. Data owner

B. Data custodian

C. User

D. Auditor

118. Carla is conducting a web application security test and would like to automatically generate input that is used to test the application. Which of the following tools would be best suited for this purpose?

A. Static application testing tool

B. White-box testing tool

C. Brute-force testing tool

D. Fuzz testing tool

119. Warren's organization recently completed a massive phishing awareness campaign, and he would like to measure its effectiveness. Which of the following tools would best provide this measurement?

   A. Survey

   B. Simulation

   C. Code review

   D. Third-party assessment

120. Which one of the following controls would be most effective in detecting zero-day attack attempts?

   A. Signature-based intrusion detection

   B. Anomaly-based intrusion detection

   C. Strong patch management

   D. Full-disk encryption

121. Rob believes that an individual he met on an online forum used unapproved resources to cheat on the CISSP exam. He has evidence to back up his claim. Which one of the following statements is most correct?

   A. Rob may report this situation to ISC2 as a violation of the Code of Ethics.

   B. Rob does not have standing to report this situation to ISC2 unless he is an employer of the individual in question.

   C. Rob does not have standing to report this situation to ISC2 unless he holds a professional license or certification that includes a code of ethics.

   D. Rob does not have standing to report this situation to ISC2 unless he is a member of ISC2 or holds an ISC2 certification.

122. Which one of the following components should be included in an organization's emergency response guidelines?

   A. Secondary response procedures for incident responders

   B. Long-term business continuity protocols

   C. Activation procedures for the organization's cold sites

   D. Contact information for ordering equipment

123. When Jim enters his organization's data center, he has to use a smartcard and code to enter and is allowed through one set of doors. The first set of doors closes, and he must then use his card again to get through a second set, which locks behind him. What type of control is this, and what is it called?

   A. A physical control; a one-way trapdoor

   B. A logical control; a dual-swipe authorization

   C. A directive control; a one-way access corridor

   D. A preventive access control; an access control vestibule

124. Bill implemented RAID level 5 on a server that he operates using a total of three disks. How many disks may fail without the loss of data?

A. 0

B. 1

C. 2

D. 3

125. Match the following numbered system and organization controls (SOC) levels to their matching lettered SOC report descriptions:

SOC levels:

1. SOC 1, Type 1

2. SOC 1, Type 2

3. SOC 2

4. SOC 3

SOC report descriptions:

A. A general use report that reports on controls related to compliance and/or operations

B. A report that provides predefined, standard benchmarks for controls involving confidentiality, availability, integrity, and privacy of a system and the information it contains, generally for restricted use

C. A report that provides an assessment of the risk of material misstatement of financial statement assertions affected by the service organization's processing and that includes a description of the service auditor's tests of the controls and the results of the tests and their effectiveness

D. A report that provides the auditor's opinions of financial statements about controls at the service organization and that includes a report on the opinion on the presentation of the service organization's system as well as suitability of the controls

Chapter

12

Practice Test 4

1. What type of access control is intended to discover unwanted or unauthorized activity by providing information after the event has occurred?

    A. Preventive

    B. Corrective

    C. Detective

    D. Directive

2. Which one of the following presents the most complex decoy environment for an attacker to explore during an intrusion attempt?

    A. Honeypot

    B. Darknet

    C. Honeynet

    D. Pseudo-flaw

Ben's organization is adopting biometric authentication for their high-security building's access control system. Using this chart, answer questions 3–5 about their adoption of the technology.

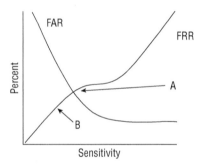

3. Ben's company is considering configuring their systems to work at the level shown by point A on the diagram. What level are they setting the sensitivity to?

    A. The FRR crossover

    B. The FAR point

    C. The CER

    D. The CFR

4. At point B, what problem is likely to occur?

    A. False acceptance will be very high.

    B. False rejection will be very high.

    C. False rejection will be very low.

    D. False acceptance will be very low.

5. What should Ben do if the FAR and FRR shown in this diagram do not provide an acceptable performance level for his organization's needs?

  A. Adjust the sensitivity of the biometric devices.

  B. Assess other biometric systems to compare them.

  C. Move the CER.

  D. Adjust the FRR settings in the software.

6. Ed is tasked with protecting information about his organization's customers, including their name, Social Security number, birthdate, and place of birth, as well as a variety of other information. What is this information known as?

  A. PHI

  B. PII

  C. Personal protected data

  D. PID

7. What software development life-cycle model is shown in the following illustration?

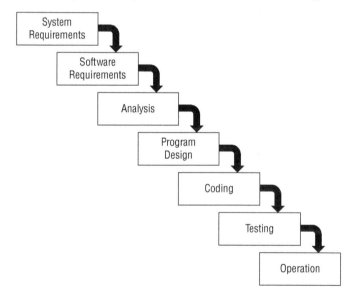

  A. Spiral

  B. Agile

  C. Boehm

  D. Waterfall

8. Encapsulation is the core concept that enables what type of protocol?

   A. Bridging

   B. Multilayer

   C. Hashing

   D. Storage

9. Amanda wants to use contacts from the existing Gmail accounts that new users already have for her application. What protocol from the following options is used to provide secure delegated access?

   A. Open ID

   B. Kerberos

   C. OAuth

   D. SAML

10. Which one of the following metrics specifies the amount of time that business continuity planners find acceptable for the restoration of service after a disaster?

   A. MTD

   B. RTO

   C. RPO

   D. MTO

11. Jill is working to procure new network hardware for her organization. She finds a gray market supplier that is importing the hardware from outside the country at a much lower price. What security concern is the most significant for hardware acquired this way?

   A. The security of the hardware and firmware

   B. Availability of support for the hardware and software

   C. Whether the hardware is a legitimate product of the actual vendor

   D. The age of the hardware

12. What process is typically used to ensure data security for workstations that are being removed from service but that will be resold or otherwise reused?

   A. Destruction

   B. Erasing

   C. Sanitization

   D. Clearing

13. Colleen is conducting a software test that is evaluating code for both security flaws and usability issues. She is working with the application from an end-user perspective and referencing the source code as she works her way through the product. What type of testing is Colleen conducting?

A. White box

B. Blue box

C. Gray box

D. Black box

14. Harold is looking for a software development methodology that will help with a major issue he is seeing in his organization. Currently, developers and operations staff do not work together and are often seen as taking problems and "throwing them over the fence" to the other team. What technology management approach is designed to alleviate this problem?

A. ITIL

B. Lean

C. ITSM

D. DevOps

15. NIST Special Publication 800-92, the Guide to Computer Security Log Management, describes four types of common challenges to log management:

- Many log sources
- Inconsistent log content
- Inconsistent timestamps
- Inconsistent log formats

Which of the following solutions is best suited to solving these issues?

A. Implement SNMP for all logging devices.

B. Implement a SIEM tool.

C. Standardize the Windows event log format for all devices and use NTP.

D. Ensure that logging is enabled on all endpoints using their native logging formats and set their local time correctly.

16. Mikayla's organization has been notified about an authentication bypass vulnerability in their product by a security researcher. The researcher has stated that they will share details about the vulnerability in question within the next 90 days if Mikayla's company fails to remediate it. However, they are also willing to collaborate with the company to help them understand the issue and provide them with full details on how to re-create the problem. What process has the researcher followed?

A. A CVE creation process

B. A bug bounty

C. Ethical disclosure

D. Blackmail

17. Carlos is investigating the compromise of sensitive information in his organization. He believes that attackers managed to retrieve personnel information on all employees from the database and finds the following user-supplied input in a log entry for a web-based personnel management system:

```
Collins'&1=1;--
```

What type of attack took place, and how could it be prevented?

   A. SQL injection, use of stored procedures

   B. Buffer overflow, automatic buffer expansion

   C. Cross-site scripting, turning on XSS prevention on the web server

   D. Cross-site request forgery, requiring signed requests

18. Which one of the following is a detailed, step-by-step document that describes the exact actions that individuals must complete?

   A. Policy

   B. Standard

   C. Guideline

   D. Procedure

19. For what purpose are the CIS benchmarks frequently used in organizations?

   A. Secure coding standards

   B. Performance testing

   C. Baselining

   D. Monitoring metrics

20. Carlos' team has detected a compromise and initiated the incident response process. What will happen next?

   A. Remediation

   B. Mitigation

   C. Reporting

   D. Lessons learned

21. Carlos is planning a design for a data center that will be constructed within a new four-story corporate headquarters. The building consists of a basement and three above-ground floors. What is the best location for the data center?

   A. Basement

   B. First floor

   C. Second floor

   D. Third floor

22. Chris is an information security professional for a major corporation, and as he is walking into the building, he notices that the door to a secure area has been left ajar. Physical security does not fall under his responsibility, but he takes immediate action by closing the door and informing the physical security team of his action. What principle is Chris demonstrating?

  A. Due care

  B. Crime prevention through environmental design

  C. Separation of duties

  D. Informed consent

23. Which one of the following investigation types always uses the beyond-a-reasonable-doubt standard of proof?

  A. Civil investigation

  B. Criminal investigation

  C. Operational investigation

  D. Regulatory investigation

24. Kristen wants to use multiple processing sites for her data but does not want to pay for a full data center. Which of the following options would you recommend as her best option if she wants to be able to quickly migrate portions of her custom application environment to facilities in multiple countries without having to wait to ship or acquire hardware?

  A. A cloud PaaS vendor

  B. A hosted data center provider

  C. A cloud IaaS vendor

  D. A data center vendor that provides rack, power, and remote hands services

25. What type of alternate processing facility contains the hardware necessary to restore operations but does not have a current copy of data?

  A. Hot site

  B. Warm site

  C. Cold site

  D. Mobile site

26. Which one of the following terms describes a period of momentary high voltage?

  A. Sag

  B. Brownout

  C. Spike

  D. Surge

27. Greg needs to label drives used for his company's medical insurance claims database. What data label from the following list best matches the type of data he is dealing with?

A. PII

B. Secret

C. Business confidential

D. PHI

28. Marco wants to deploy a network security device that can detect and stop network-based attacks without additional external intervention. What type of device should he employ and in what configuration?

A. An inline IDS

B. An IDS connected through a network tap

C. An inline IPS

D. An IPS connected through a network tap

29. Selah wants to ensure that vehicles cannot crash through her company's entryway and front lobby while still remaining accessible to pedestrians and wheelchairs or other mobility devices. What physical security control is best suited to this purpose?

A. Fences

B. Bollards

C. Walls

D. Stairs

For questions 30–34, please refer to the following scenario:

Concho Controls is a midsize business focusing on building automation systems. It hosts a set of local file servers in its on-premises data center that store customer proposals, building plans, product information, and other data that is critical to its business operations.

Tara works in the Concho Controls IT department and is responsible for designing and implementing the organization's backup strategy, among other tasks. She currently conducts full backups every Sunday evening at 8 p.m. and differential backups on Monday through Friday at noon.

Concho experiences a server failure at 3 p.m. on Wednesday. Tara rebuilds the server and wants to restore data from the backups.

30. What backup should Tara apply to the server first?

A. Sunday's full backup

B. Monday's differential backup

C. Tuesday's differential backup

D. Wednesday's differential backup

31. How many backups in total must Tara apply to the system to make the data it contains as current as possible?

   A. 1

   B. 2

   C. 3

   D. 4

32. In this backup approach, some data may be irretrievably lost. How long is the time period when any changes made will have been lost?

   A. 3 hours.

   B. 5 hours.

   C. 8 hours.

   D. No data will be lost.

33. If Tara followed the same schedule but switched the differential backups to incremental backups, how many backups in total would she need to apply to the system to make the data it contains as current as possible?

   A. 1

   B. 2

   C. 3

   D. 4

34. If Tara made the change from differential to incremental backups and we assume that the same amount of information changes each day, which one of the following files would be the largest?

   A. Monday's incremental backup.

   B. Tuesday's incremental backup.

   C. Wednesday's incremental backup.

   D. All three will be the same size.

35. The following figure shows an example of an attack where Mal, the attacker, has redirected traffic from a user's system to their own, allowing them to read TLS encrypted traffic. Which of the following terms best describes this attack?

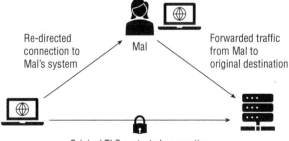

Re-directed connection to Mal's system

Mal

Forwarded traffic from Mal to original destination

Original TLS protected connection

    A. A DNS hijacking attack

    B. An ARP spoofing attack

    C. A man-in-the-middle attack

    D. A SQL injection attack

36. Bob has been tasked with writing a policy that describes how long data should be kept and when it should be purged. What concept does this policy deal with?

    A. Data remanence

    B. Record retention

    C. Data redaction

    D. Audit logging

37. Which component of IPsec provides authentication, integrity, and nonrepudiation?

    A. L2TP

    B. Encapsulating Security Payload

    C. Encryption Security Header

    D. Authentication Header

38. Renee is reviewing logs and notices that a system on her network recently received connection attempts on all 65,536 TCP ports from a single system during a short period of time. What type of attack did Renee most likely experience?

    A. Denial of service

    B. Reconnaissance

    C. Malicious insider

    D. Compromise

39. What type of Windows audit record describes events like an OS shutdown or a service being stopped?

    A. An application log

    B. A security log

    C. A system log

    D. A setup log

40. Melissa is in charge of her organization's security compliance efforts and has been told that the organization does not install Windows patches until a month has passed since the patch has been released unless there is a zero-day exploit that is being actively exploited. Why would the company delay patching like this?

    A. To minimize business impact of the installation

    B. To allow any flaws with the patch to be identified

    C. To prevent malware in the patches from being installed before it is identified

    D. To allow the patch to be distributed to all systems

41. What level of RAID is also known as disk striping?

   A. RAID 0

   B. RAID 1

   C. RAID 5

   D. RAID 10

42. Jake is updating his disaster recovery plan and wants to ensure that the third-party data center his organization contracts with can handle the scaling requirements needed in a disaster. What type of agreement should Jake sign with the hosting provider?

   A. A resource capacity agreement

   B. A cold-site agreement

   C. An NDA

   D. A business continuity agreement

43. Diana's organization teaches employees to use a pre-arranged code if they are kidnapped or under threat and contact the organization. What type of solution is this?

   A. A duress code

   B. A panic button

   C. A kidnap code

   D. A threat code

44. Fred's company wants to ensure the integrity of email messages sent via its central email servers. If the confidentiality of the messages is not critical, what solution should Fred suggest?

   A. Digitally sign and encrypt all messages to ensure integrity.

   B. Digitally sign but don't encrypt all messages.

   C. Use TLS to protect messages, ensuring their integrity.

   D. Use a hashing algorithm to provide a hash in each message to prove that it hasn't changed.

45. The leadership at Susan's company has asked her to implement an access control system that can support rule declarations like "Only allow access to salespeople from managed devices on the wireless network between 8 a.m. and 6 p.m." What type of access control system would be Susan's best choice?

   A. ABAC

   B. RBAC

   C. DAC

   D. MAC

46. Nora's company operates servers on a five-year life cycle. When they reach their end of life according to that process, the servers are sent to an e-waste recycler. Which of the following is the most effective control that Nora could implement to ensure that a data breach does not occur due to remanent data?

  A. Zero wipe the drives before the servers leave the organization.

  B. Remove the drives and shred them.

  C. Reformat the drives before the servers are sent to the e-waste company.

  D. Require certificates of disposal from the e-waste company.

47. Chris is deploying a gigabit Ethernet network using Category 6 cable between two buildings. What is the maximum distance he can run the cable according to the Category 6 standard?

  A. 50 meters

  B. 100 meters

  C. 200 meters

  D. 300 meters

48. Howard is a security analyst working with an experienced computer forensics investigator. The investigator asks him to retrieve a forensic drive controller, but Howard cannot locate a device in the storage room with this name. What is another name for a forensic drive controller?

  A. RAID controller

  B. Write blocker

  C. SCSI terminator

  D. Forensic device analyzer

49. The web application that Saria's development team is working on needs to provide secure session management that can prevent hijacking of sessions using the cookies that the application relies on. Which of the following techniques would be the best for her to recommend to prevent this?

  A. Set the Secure attribute for the cookies, thus forcing TLS.

  B. Set the Domain cookie attribute to example.com to limit cookie access to servers in the same domain.

  C. Set the Expires cookie attribute to less than a week.

  D. Set the HTTPOnly attribute to require only unencrypted sessions.

50. Ben's team has been tasked with ensuring that devices that leave his organization do not contain organizational data. They have wiped and re-formatted drives in systems that are being sent to a third-party electronics recycler as part of the process, but a journalist recently reported that organization entrusted to Ben's company was recovered from drives bought from the recycler. What issue is Ben's team encountering, and what solution should they select to prevent it most effectively?

   A. Data permanence, process certification

   B. Data remanence, drive destruction

   C. Data permanence, using a degausser

   D. Data remanence, zero fill

51. What access control scheme labels subjects and objects and allows subjects to access objects when the labels match?

   A. DAC

   B. MAC

   C. Rule-based access control (RBAC)

   D. Role-based access control (RBAC)

52. A cloud-based service that provides account provisioning, management, authentication, authorization, reporting, and monitoring capabilities is known as what type of service?

   A. PaaS

   B. IDaaS

   C. IaaS

   D. SaaS

53. Sally wants to secure her organization's VoIP systems. Which of the following attacks is one that she shouldn't have to worry about?

   A. Eavesdropping

   B. Denial-of-service

   C. XSS

   D. Caller ID spoofing

54. Marty discovers that the access restrictions in his organization allow any user to log into the workstation assigned to any other user, even if they are from completely different departments. This type of access most directly violates which information security principle?

   A. Separation of duties

   B. Two-person control

   C. Need to know

   D. Least privilege

55. Fred needs to transfer files between two servers on an untrusted network. Since he knows the network isn't trusted, he needs to select an encrypted protocol that can ensure that his data remains secure. What protocol should he choose?

   A. SSH

   B. TCP

   C. SFTP

   D. IPsec

56. Manesh wants to help his organization build secure software. Which of the following is not a common security best practice for working with security frameworks and libraries?

   A. Use internally developed libraries and frameworks whenever possible to reduce third-party threats.

   B. Identify and inventory all third-party libraries.

   C. Encapsulate libraries to prevent the use of functions that are not needed.

   D. Update libraries and components on a regular basis.

Use your knowledge of Kerberos authentication and authorization as well as the following diagram to answer questions 57–59.

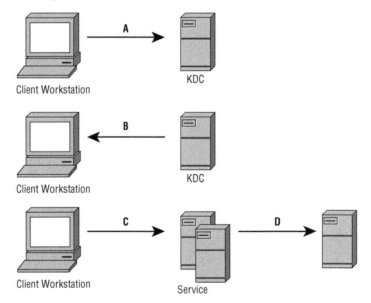

57. If the client has already authenticated to the KDC, what does the client workstation send to the KDC at point A when it wants to access a resource?

   A. It resends the password.

   B. A TGR.

   C. Its TGT.

   D. A service ticket.

58. What occurs between steps A and B?

- **A.** The KDC verifies the validity of the TGT and whether the user has the right privileges for the requested resource.
- **B.** The KDC updates its access control list based on the data in the TGT.
- **C.** The KDC checks its service listing and prepares an updated TGT based on the service request.
- **D.** The KDC generates a service ticket to issue to the client.

59. What system or systems does the service that is being accessed use to validate the ticket?

- **A.** The KDC.
- **B.** The client workstation and the KDC.
- **C.** The client workstation supplies it in the form of a client-to-server ticket and an authenticator.
- **D.** The KVS.

60. What does a service ticket (ST) provide in Kerberos authentication?

- **A.** It serves as the authentication host.
- **B.** It provides proof that the subject is authorized to access an object.
- **C.** It provides proof that a subject has authenticated through a KDC and can request tickets to access other objects.
- **D.** It provides ticket granting services.

61. Judy is preparing to conduct a business impact analysis. What should her first step be in the process?

- **A.** Identify threats to the business.
- **B.** Identify risks to the organization.
- **C.** Identify business priorities.
- **D.** Conduct likelihood analysis.

62. What is the most common risk that cellular phone hotspots create for business networks?

- **A.** They can provide attackers with an unsecured network path into your network.
- **B.** They can be used like rogue access points for man-in-the-middle attacks.
- **C.** They allow wireless data to be intercepted.
- **D.** They are unencrypted and can be easily sniffed.

63. Which one of the following fire suppression systems poses the greatest risk of accidental discharge that damages equipment in a data center?

- **A.** Wet pipe
- **B.** Dry pipe
- **C.** Deluge
- **D.** Preaction

64. Amanda's healthcare provider maintains such data as details about her health, treatments, and medical billing. What type of data is this?

    A. Protected health information

    B. Personally identifiable information

    C. Protected health insurance

    D. Individual protected data

65. What type of code review is best suited for identifying business logic flaws?

    A. Mutation fuzzing

    B. Manual testing

    C. Generational fuzzing

    D. Interface testing

66. Something you know is an example of what type of authentication factor?

    A. Type 1

    B. Type 2

    C. Type 3

    D. Type 4

67. Saria is the system owner for a healthcare organization. What responsibilities does she have related to the data that resides on or is processed by the systems she owns?

    A. She has to classify the data.

    B. She has to make sure that appropriate security controls are in place to protect the data.

    C. She has to grant appropriate access to personnel.

    D. She bears sole responsibility for ensuring that data is protected at rest, in transit, and in use.

68. During software testing, Jack diagrams how a hacker might approach the application he is reviewing and determines what requirements the hacker might have. He then tests how the system would respond to the attacker's likely behavior. What type of testing is Jack conducting?

    A. Misuse case testing

    B. Use-case testing

    C. Hacker use-case testing

    D. Static code analysis

69. Rick's risk assessment for his company's web application noted that it could suffer from SQL injection attacks. Which of the following mitigation techniques would you recommend Rick apply to help reduce this risk? (Select all that apply.)

    A. Stored procedures

    B. Escaping all user-supplied input

    C. Parameterized queries

    D. Input validation

70. Chris has been assigned to scan a system on all of its possible TCP and UDP ports. How many ports of each type must he scan to complete his assignment?

    A. 65,536 TCP ports and 32,768 UDP ports

    B. 1,024 common TCP ports and 32,768 ephemeral UDP ports

    C. 65,536 TCP and 65,536 UDP ports

    D. 16,384 TCP ports, and 16,384 UDP ports

71. CVE and the NVD both provide information about what?

    A. Vulnerabilities

    B. Markup languages

    C. Vulnerability assessment tools

    D. Penetration testing methodologies

72. Michelle wants to ensure that her company does not keep logs for longer than they need to. What type of policy should she write and implement to ensure this?

    A. An EOL policy

    B. A data classification policy

    C. An EOS policy

    D. A record retention policy

73. Beth's company uses cloud-based infrastructure that uses a combination of policies and automated security controls to ensure security. The company deploys firewalls, endpoint security tools, and management capabilities to ensure that every virtual system is protected as it is brought online. What term describes this type of implementation?

    A. Root of trust

    B. Software-defined security

    C. A policy engine

    D. Software-defined networks

74. What three important items should be considered if you are attempting to control the strength of signal for a wireless network as well as where it is accessible?

A. Antenna placement, antenna type, antenna power levels

B. Antenna design, power levels, use of a captive portal

C. Antenna placement, antenna design, use of a captive portal

D. Power levels, antenna placement, FCC minimum strength requirements

75. What is the best way to ensure that data is unrecoverable from an SSD?

A. Use the built-in erase commands.

B. Use a random pattern wipe of 1s and 0s.

C. Physically destroy the drive.

D. Degauss the drive.

76. Alice sends a message to Bob and wants to ensure that Mal, a third party, does not read the contents of the message while in transit. What goal of cryptography is Alice attempting to achieve?

A. Confidentiality

B. Integrity

C. Authentication

D. Nonrepudiation

77. Ian wants to ensure that his organization is using appropriate secure coding techniques. Which of the following is not a common practice for input validation?

A. Conduct data validation on a trusted system.

B. Validate data length.

C. Validate all client-provided data before it is processed.

D. Convert all data to the same data type.

78. The company that Gary works for processes credit cards and operates under an industry standard for credit card handling. Which of the following standards will his company need to comply with?

A. ISO27001

B. FIPS 140

C. PCI-DSS

D. ISO 27002

79. James has opted to implement a NAC solution that uses a post-admission philosophy for its control of network connectivity. What type of issues can't a strictly post-admission policy handle?

A. Out-of-band monitoring

B. Preventing an unpatched laptop from being exploited immediately after connecting to the network

C. Denying access when user behavior doesn't match an authorization matrix

D. Allowing a user access to a specific object when user behavior is allowed based on an authorization matrix

80. Ben has built an access control list that lists the objects that his users are allowed to access. When users attempt to access an object that they don't have rights to, they are denied access, even though there isn't a specific rule that prevents it. What access control principle is key to this behavior?

A. Least privilege

B. Implicit deny

C. Explicit deny

D. Final rule fall-through

81. Mary is a security risk analyst for an insurance company. She is currently examining a scenario where a hacker might be able to modify the contents of directories on the web server due to a missing patch in the company's web application. In this scenario, what is the risk?

A. Unpatched web application

B. Web defacement

C. Hacker

D. Operating system

82. The mean time to detect a compromise is what type of security measurement?

A. An MTO

B. A technical control objective

C. A compliance objective

D. A KPI

83. Val is testing her organization's software using a tool that simulates an attacker's actions against it. What type of testing is Val conducting?

A. SAST

B. LAST

C. DAST

D. FAST

84. In Jen's job as the network administrator for an industrial production facility, she is tasked with ensuring that the network is not susceptible to electromagnetic interference due to the large motors and other devices running on the production floor. What type of network cabling should she choose if this concern is more important than the cost and difficulty of installation?

    A. 10Base2

    B. 100BaseT

    C. 1000BaseT

    D. Fiber optic

For questions 85–88, please refer to the following scenario:

Jasper Diamonds is a jewelry manufacturer that markets and sells custom jewelry through its website. Bethany is the manager of Jasper's software development organization, and she is working to bring the company into line with industry-standard practices. She is developing a new change management process for the organization and wants to follow commonly accepted approaches.

85. Bethany would like to put in place controls that provide an organized framework for company employees to suggest new website features that her team will develop. What change management process facilitates this?

    A. Configuration control

    B. Change control

    C. Release control

    D. Request control

86. Bethany would also like to create a process that helps multiple developers work on code at the same time. What change management process facilitates this?

    A. Configuration control

    B. Change control

    C. Release control

    D. Request control

87. Bethany is working with her colleagues to conduct user acceptance testing. What change management process includes this task?

    A. Configuration control

    B. Change control

    C. Release control

    D. Request control

88. Bethany noticed that some problems arise when system administrators update libraries without informing developers. What change management process can assist with this problem?

    A. Configuration control

    B. Change control

    C. Release control

    D. Request control

89. Asha's team wants to ensure that all of the functions of their software are tested. What are they ensuring?

    A. Proper misuse case testing

    B. That a breach attack simulation is conducted

    C. Complete interface testing

    D. Complete coverage

90. Which one of the following is an example of risk transference?

    A. Building a guard shack

    B. Purchasing insurance

    C. Erecting fences

    D. Relocating facilities

91. What protocol takes the place of certificate revocation lists and adds real-time status verification?

    A. RTCP

    B. RTVP

    C. OCSP

    D. CSRTP

92. Xavier's company has been using an increasing number of cloud services, and he is concerned that the security policies that the company has implemented in its existing data center are not being followed in the cloud. Which of the following solutions is best suited to ensuring that policies are applied to all cloud services?

    A. A CIPS

    B. A CASB

    C. A CSG

    D. A CDLP

93. What process makes TCP a connection-oriented protocol?

    A. It works via network connections.

    B. It uses a handshake.

    C. It monitors for dropped connections.

    D. It uses a complex header.

94. Susan wants to build a security awareness program for her organization but knows that keeping staff engaged is difficult. Which of the following techniques is often associated with the use of points and scores as part of the assessment process?

A. Gamification

B. Phishing testing

C. Security champions

D. Social engineering evaluations

95. You are conducting a qualitative risk assessment for your organization. The two important risk elements that should weigh most heavily in your analysis of risk are probability and

_____.

A. Likelihood

B. History

C. Impact

D. Cost

96. Using the OSI model, what format does the Data Link layer use to format messages received from higher up the stack?

A. A data stream

B. A frame

C. A segment

D. A datagram

97. What is the maximum penalty that may be imposed by an ISC2 peer review board when considering a potential ethics violation?

A. Revocation of certification

B. Termination of employment

C. Financial penalty

D. Suspension of certification

98. Which one of the following statements about the SDLC is correct?

A. The SDLC requires the use of an iterative approach to software development.

B. The SDLC requires the use of a sequential approach to software development.

C. The SDLC does not include training for end users and support staff.

D. The waterfall methodology is compatible with the SDLC.

99. In the diagram shown here, Harry is prevented from reading a file at a higher classification level than his security clearance. What security model prevents this behavior?

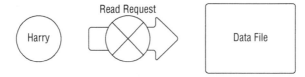

- **A.** Bell–LaPadula
- **B.** Biba
- **C.** Clark–Wilson
- **D.** Brewer–Nash

100. Sylvia's company's new application allows users to sign up for banking services. Sylvia needs to identify a way to ensure that users are who they claim to be. What is this process called?

- **A.** Proofing
- **B.** Registration
- **C.** FIM
- **D.** Single sign-on

101. Travis is concerned about the security that his organization's use of Microsoft's BitLocker provides for systems. When are the systems most secure from data loss based on the encryption state of the drive if the systems are equipped with TPM and use full-disk encryption?

- **A.** When they are booted up and running because the system monitors for drive access
- **B.** When the system is shutting down because keys are removed from memory
- **C.** When they are booting up because the TPM checks for a secure boot process
- **D.** When they are off because the drive is fully encrypted

102. Andrea wants to ensure that her virtualized networks are secure between virtual environments. She uses virtual machine clusters in multiple locations in her state with third-party Internet service providers between those locations. Which of the following solutions is best suited to protecting her traffic if she runs a flattened layer 2 network between those locations?

- **A.** TLS
- **B.** BGP
- **C.** IPsec
- **D.** AES

For questions 103–105, please refer to the following scenario:

The company that Fred works for is reviewing the security of their company-issued cell phones. They issue 4G-capable smartphones running Android and iOS and use a mobile device management solution to deploy company software to the phones. The mobile device management software also allows the company to remotely wipe the phones if they are lost.

103. What security considerations should Fred's company require for sending sensitive data over the cellular network?

  A. They should use the same requirements as data over any public network.

  B. Cellular provider networks are private networks and should not require special consideration.

  C. Encrypt all traffic to ensure confidentiality.

  D. Require the use of WAP for all data sent from the phone.

104. Fred intends to attend a major hacker conference this year and needs to connect to his employer's network during his time at the conference. What should he do when connecting to his cellular provider's 4G network while at the conference?

  A. Continue normal usage.

  B. Discontinue all usage; towers can be spoofed.

  C. Only use trusted Wi-Fi networks.

  D. Connect to his company's encrypted VPN service.

105. What are the most likely circumstances that would cause a remote wipe of a mobile phone to fail?

  A. The phone has a passcode on it.

  B. The phone cannot contact a network.

  C. The provider has not unlocked the phone.

  D. The phone is in use.

106. Elaine is developing a business continuity plan for her organization. What value should she seek to minimize?

  A. AV

  B. SSL

  C. RTO

  D. MTO

107. Warren wants to conduct an internal security audit. He wants to use a broadly accepted audit framework so that he can more easily compare the results to other organizations. Which of the following options should he select as his base audit framework?

  A. ITSM

  B. ATT&CK

  C. COBIT

  D. CIS

108. Place the list of disaster recovery test types in order of their potential operational impact on the business, starting with the least impactful and progressing through the most impactful.

1. Checklist review

2. Parallel test

3. Tabletop exercise

4. Full interruption test

A. 1, 2, 3, 4

B. 1, 3, 2, 4

C. 1, 3, 4, 2

D. 2, 1, 3, 4

109. Jack's data center design calls for dual-power supplies in every critical server. What part of the CIA triad is he addressing with this design decision?

A. Confidentiality

B. Integrity

C. Availability

D. None of the above

110. What step is missing from the IR process cycle diagram shown here?

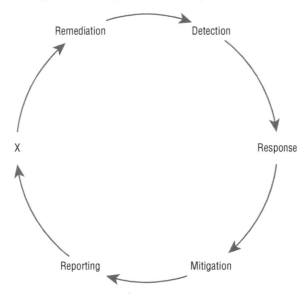

A. Forensics

B. Retribution

C. Recovery

D. Analysis

111. The company that Felipe works for has connected servers they have hosted in a third-party data center to vendor-owned systems using fiber-optic cables for a direct connection to them. What is this called?

A. Ingress

B. Peering

C. East/west

D. Egress

112. Megan wants to ensure that the new software as a service provider that her company is signing a contract with will make sure the service works all the time without disruptions. Which of the following is often part of contracts to provide that assurance?

A. An SLA

B. An RPA

C. An NDA

D. An MOU

113. Kyle wants to ensure that his organization's backups are stored securely in case of a natural disaster or other event. What type of solution should he choose if he needs to store backup tapes?

A. A cloud backup service

B. A hot site

C. A media storage facility

D. A BaaS provider

114. Norm would like to conduct a disaster recovery test for his organization and wants to choose the most thorough type of test, recognizing that it may be quite disruptive. What type of test should Norm choose?

A. Full interruption test

B. Parallel test

C. Tabletop exercise

D. Checklist review

115. Ed is building a network that supports IPv6 but needs to connect it to an IPv4 network. What type of device should Ed place between the networks?

A. A switch

B. A router

C. A bridge

D. A gateway

116. Henry's company has deployed an extensive IoT infrastructure for building monitoring that includes environmental controls, occupancy sensors, and a variety of other sensors and controllers that help manage the building. Which of the following security concerns should Henry report as the most critical in his analysis of the IoT deployment?

A. The lack of local storage space for security logs that is common to IoT devices.

B. The IoT devices may not have a separate administrative interface, allowing anybody on the same network to attempt to log into them and making brute-force attacks possible.

C. The IoT devices may not support strong encryption for communications, exposing the log and sensor data to interception on the network.

D. The long-term support and patching model for the IoT devices may create security and operational risks for the organization.

117. Isaac wants to use a connectionless protocol to transfer data because he needs to optimize the speed of transmission over reliability. Which protocol should he select?

A. ICMP

B. TCP

C. UDP

D. SNMP

118. Which one of the following actions is not required under the EU General Data Protection Regulation?

A. Organizations must allow individuals to opt out of information sharing.

B. Organizations must provide individuals with lists of employees with access to information.

C. Organizations must use proper mechanisms to protect data against unauthorized disclosure.

D. Organizations must have a dispute resolution process for privacy issues.

119. Tammy is selecting a disaster recovery facility for her organization. She would like to choose a facility that balances the time required to recover operations with the cost involved. What type of facility should she choose?

A. Hot site

B. Warm site

C. Cold site

D. Red site

120. What layer of the OSI model is associated with datagrams?

A. Session

B. Transport

C. Network

D. Data Link

121. Which one of the following is not a valid key length for the Advanced Encryption Standard?

    A. 128 bits

    B. 192 bits

    C. 256 bits

    D. 384 bits

122. Which one of the following technologies provides a function interface that allows developers to directly interact with systems without knowing the implementation details of that system?

    A. Data dictionary

    B. Object model

    C. Source code

    D. API

123. Ian wants to assess the security of his company's new SaaS provider. Which of the following options is the most likely option that he can realistically expect to be able to use to assess a major cloud provider's security?

    A. Run a vulnerability scan against the provider's external services.

    B. Request a SOC 2 Type II report.

    C. Run a vulnerability scan against the provider's internal systems.

    D. Request a SOC 1 Type II report.

124. Sharon wants to conduct a pass-the-hash attack. Which of the following is not a common means of acquiring NTLM hashes for the attack?

    A. Dumping the system's SAM

    B. Dumping credentials from active memory

    C. Capturing network traffic

    D. Downloading the hashes from a third-party site

125. Match each one of the numbered protocols with the most accurate lettered description. Use each answer exactly once.

Protocol:

    1. TCP

    2. UDP

    3. DNS

    4. ARP

Description:

    A. Performs translations between MAC addresses and IP addresses

    B. Performs translations between FQDNs and IP addresses

    C. Transports data over a network in a connection-oriented fashion

    D. Transports data over a network in a connectionless fashion

Appendix

Answers to Review Questions

Chapter 1: Security and Risk Management (Domain 1)

1. C. Alyssa should use periodic content reviews to continually verify that the content in her program meets the organization's needs and is up-to-date based upon the evolving risk landscape. She may do this using a combination of computer-based training, live training, and gamification, but those techniques do not necessarily verify that the content is updated.

2. B. The residual risk is the level of risk that remains after controls have been applied to mitigate risks. Inherent risk is the original risk that existed prior to the controls. Control risk is new risk introduced by the addition of controls to the environment. Mitigated risk is the risk that has been addressed by existing controls.

3. C. The Digital Millennium Copyright Act (DMCA) sets forth the requirements for online service providers when handling copyright complaints received from third parties. The Copyright Act creates the mechanics for issuing and enforcing copyrights but does not cover the actions of online service providers. The Lanham Act regulates the issuance of trademarks to protect intellectual property. The Gramm-Leach-Bliley Act regulates the handling of personal financial information.

4. C. The right to erasure, also known as the right to be forgotten, guarantees the data subject the ability to have their information removed from processing or use. It may be tied to consent given for data processing; if a subject revokes consent for processing, the data controller may need to take additional steps, including erasure.

5. B. Purchasing insurance is a means of transferring risk. If Sally had worked to decrease the likelihood of the events occurring, she would have been using a reduce or risk mitigation strategy, while simply continuing to function as the organization has would be an example of an acceptance strategy. Rejection, or denial of the risk, is not a valid strategy, even though it occurs!

6. A. Most state data breach notification laws are modeled after California's data breach notification law, which covers Social Security number, driver's license number, state identification card number, credit/debit card numbers, and bank account numbers (in conjunction with a PIN or password). These laws are separate and distinct from privacy laws, such as the California Consumer Privacy Act (CCPA), which regulates the handling of personal information more broadly.

7. C. Renee's situation calls for an enterprise license agreement as it typically allows customization of terms and pricing, reflecting the negotiated details between the vendor and a corporate client. The license agreement may be written as a perpetual or subscription license, but there is no information provided in the scenario about which one is being used. An end-user license agreement usually accompanies software to dictate the terms of use but is not designed for custom negotiations and pricing agreements.

8. B. This is a question about who has the standing to bring an ethics complaint. The group of individuals that has standing differs based upon the violated canon. In this case, we are examining Canon IV, which permits any certified or licensed professional who subscribes to a code of ethics to bring charges. Charges of violations of Canons I or II may be brought by anyone. Charges of violations of Canon III may be brought only by a principal with an employer/contractor relationship with the accused.

9. C. The European Union provides standard contractual clauses that may be used to facilitate data transfer. That would be the best choice in a case where two different companies are sharing data. If the data was being shared internally within a company, binding corporate rules would also be an option. The EU/U.S. Privacy Shield was a safe harbor agreement that would previously have allowed the transfer but is no longer valid.

10. A. The Gramm-Leach-Bliley Act (GLBA) contains provisions regulating the privacy of customer financial information. It applies specifically to financial institutions. Among other things, the Sarbanes Oxley (SOX) Act regulates the financial reporting activities of publicly traded companies.

The Health Insurance Portability and Accountability Act (HIPAA) regulates the handling of protected health information (PHI).

The Family Educational Rights and Privacy Act (FERPA) regulates the handling of student educational records.

11. A. The Federal Information Security Modernization Act (FISMA) specifically applies to government contractors. The Government Information Security Reform Act (GISRA) was the precursor to FISMA and expired in November 2002. HIPAA and PCI DSS apply to healthcare and payment card information, respectively. Additionally, PCI DSS is not a law, while FISMA, HIPAA, and GISRA are all laws.

12. D. The export of encryption software to certain countries is regulated under U.S. export control laws. Memory chips, office productivity applications, and hard drives are less likely to be covered by these regulations, unless they contain hardware dedicated to encryption.

13. D. In an elevation of privilege attack, the attacker transforms a limited user account into an account with greater privileges, powers, and/or access to the system. Spoofing attacks falsify an identity, while repudiation attacks attempt to deny accountability for an action. Tampering attacks attempt to violate the integrity of information or resources.

14. D. Whenever you choose to accept a risk, you should maintain detailed documentation of the risk acceptance process to satisfy auditors in the future. This should happen before implementing security controls, designing a disaster recovery plan, or repeating the business impact analysis (BIA).

15. A, C, D. A fence does not have the ability to detect intrusions. It does, however, have the ability to prevent and deter an intrusion. A fence is an example of a physical control.

16. D. Tony would see the best results by combining elements of quantitative and qualitative risk assessment. Quantitative risk assessment excels at analyzing financial risk, while qualitative risk assessment is a good tool for intangible risks. Combining the two techniques provides a well-rounded risk picture.

17. D. The Economic Espionage Act imposes fines and jail sentences on anyone found guilty of stealing trade secrets from a U.S. corporation. It gives true teeth to the intellectual property rights of trade secret owners. Copyright law does not apply in this situation because there is no indication that the information was copyrighted. The Lanham Act applies to trademark protection cases. The Glass-Steagall Act was a banking reform act that is not relevant in this situation.

18. C. The due care principle states that an individual should react in a situation using the same level of care that would be expected from any reasonable person. It is a very broad standard. The due diligence principle is a more specific component of due care that states that an individual assigned a responsibility should exercise due care to complete it accurately and in a timely manner.

19. C. The protection of intellectual property is a greater concern during a divestiture, where a subsidiary is being spun off into a separate organization, than an acquisition, where one firm has purchased another. Acquisition concerns include consolidating security functions and policies as well as integrating security tools.

20. D. Unlike criminal or civil cases, administrative investigations are an internal matter, and there is no set standard of proof that Kelly must apply. However, it would still be wise for her organization to include a standard burden of proof in their own internal procedures to ensure the thoroughness and fairness of investigations.

21. A. Patents and trade secrets can both protect intellectual property related to a manufacturing process. Trade secrets are appropriate only when the details can be tightly controlled within an organization, so a patent is the appropriate solution in this case. Copyrights are used to protect creative works, while trademarks are used to protect names, logos, and symbols.

22. B. RAID technology provides fault tolerance for hard drive failures and is an example of a business continuity action. Restoring from backup tapes, relocating to a cold site, and restarting business operations are all disaster recovery actions.

23. C. After developing a list of assets, the business impact analysis team should assign values to each asset. The other activities listed here occur only after the assets are assigned values.

24. C. Risk mitigation strategies attempt to lower the probability and/or impact of a risk occurring. Intrusion prevention systems attempt to reduce the probability of a successful attack and are, therefore, examples of risk mitigation. Risk acceptance involves making a conscious decision to accept a risk as is with no further action.

Risk avoidance alters business activities to make a risk irrelevant.

Risk transference shifts the costs of a risk to another organization, such as an insurance company.

25. C. A security controls assessment (SCA) most often refers to a formal U.S. government process for assessing security controls. This means that Laura is probably part of a government organization or contractor.

26. C. There are two steps to answering this question. First, you must realize that for the case to lead to imprisonment, it must be the result of a criminal investigation. Next, you must know that the standard of proof for a criminal investigation is normally the beyond a reasonable doubt standard.

27. D. Trademark protection extends to words and symbols used to represent an organization, product, or service in the marketplace. Copyrights are used to protect creative works.

Patents and trade secrets are used to protect inventions and similar intellectual property.

28. A. The message displayed is an example of ransomware, which encrypts the contents of a user's computer to prevent legitimate use. This is an example of an availability attack. There is no indication that the data was disclosed to others, so there is no confidentiality/disclosure risk.

There is also no indication that other systems were involved in a distributed attack.

29. B. A health and fitness application developer would not necessarily be collecting or processing healthcare data, and the terms of HIPAA do not apply to this category of business. HIPAA regulates three types of entities—healthcare providers, health information clearinghouses, and health insurance plans—as well as the business associates of any of those covered entities.

30. A. A SYN flood attack is an example of a denial-of-service attack, which jeopardizes the availability of a targeted network. SYN flood attacks do not target integrity or confidentiality.

While this is a denial-of-service attack, denial is not the correct answer because you are asked which principle is being violated, not what type of attack took place.

Denial-of-service attacks target resource availability.

31. D. Strategic plans have a long-term planning horizon of up to five years in most cases. They are designed to strategically align the security function with the business' objectives. Operational and tactical plans have shorter horizons of a year or less.

32. A. First, you must realize that a trademark is the correct intellectual property protection mechanism for a logo. Therefore, Gina should contact the U.S. Patent and Trademark Office (USPTO), which bears responsibility for the registration of trademarks. The Library of Congress Copyright Office administers the copyright program. The National Security Agency (NSA) and the National Institute of Standards and Technology (NIST) play no role in intellectual property protection.

33. B. When following the segregation of duties principle, organizations divide critical tasks into discrete components and ensure that no one individual has the ability to perform both actions. This prevents a single rogue individual from performing that task in an unauthorized manner. Mandatory vacations and job rotations are designed to detect fraud, not prevent it.

Defense in depth is not a relevant principle here because the answer is seeking an initial control.

Management may choose to add additional controls at a later date, but the primary objective here would be to implement segregation of duties.

34. B. The U.S. Federal Information Security Modernization Act (FISMA) applies to federal government agencies and contractors. Of the entities listed, a defense contractor is the most likely to have government contracts subject to FISMA.

35. B. The Payment Card Industry Data Security Standard (PCI DSS) governs the storage, processing, and transmission of payment card information. Among other things, the Sarbanes Oxley (SOX) Act regulates the financial reporting activities of publicly traded companies.

The Health Insurance Portability and Accountability Act (HIPAA) regulates the handling of protected health information (PHI). The Gramm-Leach-Bliley Act (GLBA) regulates the handling of personal financial information.

36. A. The data custodian role is assigned to an individual who is responsible for implementing the security controls defined by policy and senior management. The data owner does bear ultimate responsibility for these tasks, but the data owner is typically a senior leader who delegates operational responsibility to a data custodian.

37. B. Written works, such as website content, are normally protected by copyright law. Trade secret status would not be appropriate here because the content is online and available outside the company. Patents protect inventions, and trademarks protect words and symbols used to represent a brand, neither of which is relevant in this scenario.

38. C. The Code of Federal Regulations (CFR) contains the text of all administrative laws promulgated by federal agencies. The U.S. Code contains criminal and civil law. Supreme Court rulings contain interpretations of law and are not laws themselves. The Compendium of Laws does not exist.

39. D. Installing a device that will block attacks is an attempt to lower risk by reducing the likelihood of a successful application attack. Adding a firewall will not address the impact of a risk, the recovery point objective (RPO), or the maximum tolerable outage (MTO).

40. B. The owner of information security programs may be different from the individuals responsible for implementing the controls. This person should be as senior an individual as possible who is able to focus on the management of the security program. The president and CEO would not be an appropriate choice because an executive at this level is unlikely to have the time necessary to focus on security. Of the remaining choices, the CIO is the most senior position who would be the strongest advocate at the executive level.

41. A. Senior managers play several business continuity planning roles. These include setting priorities, obtaining resources, and arbitrating disputes among team members.

42. D. The System and Organization Controls audit program includes business continuity controls in a SOC 2, but not SOC 1, audit. Although FISMA and PCI DSS may audit business continuity, they would not apply to an email service used by a hospital.

43. A. Repudiation threats allow an attacker to deny having performed an action or activity without the other party being able to prove differently. There is no evidence that the attacker engaged in information disclosure, tampering, or elevation of privilege.

44. A. Integrity controls, such as the one Beth is implementing in this example, are designed to prevent the unauthorized modification of information. There is no evidence of an attack against availability or confidentiality.

Denial is an objective of attackers, rather than of security professionals, and is not relevant in this scenario that targets integrity.

45. A. SLAs do not normally address issues of data confidentiality. Those provisions are normally included in a nondisclosure agreement (NDA).

46. A. Trademarks protect words and images that represent a product or service and would not protect computer software.

47. B. Virtual private networks (VPNs) provide secure communications channels over otherwise insecure networks (such as the Internet) using encryption. If you establish a VPN connection between the two offices, users in one office could securely access content located on the other office's server over the Internet. Digital signatures are used to provide nonrepudiation, not confidentiality. Virtual LANs (VLANs) provide network segmentation on local networks but do not cross the Internet. Digital content management solutions are designed to manage web content, not access shared files located on a file server.

48. C. RAID uses additional hard drives to protect the server against the failure of a single drive or two, based on the RAID level selected. Load balancing and server clustering do add robustness but require the addition of a server. Scheduled backups protect against data loss but do not provide immediate access to data in the event of a hard drive failure.

49. A. Hashing allows you to computationally verify that a file has not been modified between hash evaluations. ACLs and read-only attributes are useful controls that may help you prevent unauthorized modification, but they cannot verify that files were not modified. Firewalls are network security controls and do not verify file integrity.

50. D. Signing a noncompete (NCA) or NDA agreement is typically done at hiring. Exit interviews, recovery of organizational property, and account termination are all common elements of a termination process. During the exit interview, the team may choose to review employment agreements and policies that remain in force, such as a noncompete or nondisclosure agreement.

51. A. Business continuity plan documentation normally includes the continuity planning goals, a statement of importance, a statement of priorities, a statement of organizational responsibility, a statement of urgency and timing, risk assessment and risk acceptance and mitigation documentation, a vital records program, emergency response guidelines, and documentation for maintaining and testing the plan.

52. D. Mandatory vacation programs require that employees take continuous periods of time off each year and have their system privileges revoked during that time. The purpose of these required vacation periods is to disrupt any attempt to engage in the cover-up actions necessary to hide fraud and result in exposing the threat. Separation of duties, least privilege, and defense in depth all may help prevent the fraud in the first place but are unlikely to speed the detection of fraud that has already occurred.

53. C. The Risk Maturity Model (RMM) is specifically designed for the purpose of assessing enterprise risk management programs. Jeff could conceivably use the more generic capability maturity model (CMM), but this would not be as good of a fit. The software capability maturity model (SW-CMM) is designed for assessing development projects, not risk management efforts. The Control Objectives for Information Technology (COBIT) are a set of security control objectives and not a maturity model.

54. C. Denial-of-service (DoS) attacks and distributed denial-of-service (DDoS) attacks try to disrupt the availability of information systems and networks by flooding a victim with traffic or otherwise disrupting service.

55. B. Baselines provide the minimum level of security that every system throughout the organization must meet. This type of information would not appear in a policy, guideline, or procedure.

56. C. Everyone in the organization should receive basic training on the nature and scope of the business continuity program. Those with specific roles, such as first responders and senior executives, should also receive detailed, role-specific training.

57. C. If the organization's primary concern is the cost of rebuilding the data center, James should use the replacement cost method to determine the current market price for equivalent servers.

58. C. PCI DSS is a standard promulgated by the Payment Card Industry Security Standards Council (PCI SSC) but is enforced through contractual relationships between merchants and their banks. Therefore, the bank would be the appropriate entity to initiate an investigation under PCI DSS. Local and federal law enforcement agencies (such as the FBI) could decide to pursue a criminal investigation if the circumstances warrant it, but they do not have the authority to enforce PCI DSS requirements.

59. A. This is an example of a security champion program that uses individuals employed in other roles in a business unit to share security messaging. The individuals in these roles are not necessarily security experts and do not have a peer review role.

60. A. Keyloggers monitor the keystrokes of an individual and report them back to an attacker. They are designed to steal sensitive information, a disruption of the goal of confidentiality.

61. B. The most appropriate standard to use as a baseline when evaluating vendors is to determine whether the vendor's security controls meet the organization's own standards. Compliance with laws and regulations should be included in that requirement and are a necessary, but not sufficient, condition for working with the vendor. Vendor compliance with their own policies also fits into the category of necessary, but not sufficient, controls, as the vendor's policy may be weaker than the organization's own requirements. The elimination of all identified security risks is an impossible requirement for a potential vendor to meet.

62. A. The missing step of the NIST risk management framework is assessing security controls. This is an important component of the process. The organization has already prepared, categorized the system, selected appropriate controls, and implemented those controls. Before authorizing the use of the system, they must assess the effectiveness of those controls to ensure that they meet security requirements.

63. D. HAL Systems decided to stop offering the service because of the risk. This is an example of a risk avoidance strategy. The company altered its operations in a manner that eliminates the risk of NTP misuse. Risk acceptance involves making a conscious decision to accept a risk as is with no further action.

Risk mitigation takes measures to reduce the likelihood and/or impact of a risk.

Risk transfer shifts the costs of a risk to another organization, such as an insurance company.

64. C. Confidentiality controls prevent the disclosure of sensitive information to unauthorized individuals. Limiting the likelihood of a data breach is an attempt to prevent unauthorized disclosure.

65. A. The emergency response guidelines should include the immediate steps an organization should follow in response to an emergency situation. These include immediate response procedures, a list of individuals who should be notified of the emergency, and secondary response procedures for first responders. They do not include long-term actions such as activating business continuity protocols, ordering equipment, or activating DR sites.

66. B. Although the CEO will not normally serve on a BCP team, it is best to obtain top-level management approval for your plan to increase the likelihood of successful adoption.

67. D. The project scope and planning phase includes four actions: a structured analysis of the organization, the creation of a BCP team, an assessment of available resources, and an analysis of the legal and regulatory landscape.

68. D. Keeping a service up and running is an example of an availability control because it increases the likelihood that a service will remain available to answer user requests.

69. A. A cold site includes the basic capabilities required for data center operations such as space, power, HVAC, and communications, but it does not include any of the hardware required to restore operations. Warm sites, hot sites, and mobile sites would all include hardware.

70. B. In general, companies should be aware of the breach laws in any location where they do business. U.S. states have a diverse collection of breach laws and requirements, meaning that in this case, Greg's company may need to review many different breach laws to determine which they may need to comply with if they conduct business in the state or with the state's residents.

71. B. ISO 27002 is an international standard focused on information security and titled "Information security, cybersecurity and privacy protection: Information security controls." ITIL does contain security management practices, but it is not the sole focus of the document, and the ITIL security section is derived from ISO 27002. The Capability Maturity Model (CMM) is focused on software development, and the Project Management Body of Knowledge (PMBOK) Guide focuses on project management.

72. B. The Communications Assistance for Law Enforcement Act (CALEA) requires that all communications carriers make wiretaps possible for law enforcement officials who have an appropriate court order.

73. B. The Gramm-Leach-Bliley Act (GLBA) places strict privacy regulations on financial institutions, including providing written notice of privacy practices to customers.

74. C. Nondisclosure agreements (NDAs) typically require either mutual or one-way confidentiality in a business relationship. Service-level agreements specify service uptime and other performance measures. Noncompete agreements (NCAs) limit the future employment possibilities of employees. Recovery time objectives (RTOs) are used in business continuity planning.

75. B. The ISC2 Code of Ethics also includes "Act honorably, honestly, justly, responsibly, and legally" but does not specifically require credential holders to disclose all breaches of privacy, trust, or ethics.

76. C. While senior management should be represented on the BCP team, it would be highly unusual for the CEO to fill this role personally.

77. D. Nonrepudiation allows a recipient to prove to a third party that a message came from a purported source. Authentication would provide proof to Ben that the sender was authentic, but Ben would not be able to prove this to a third party.

78. C. Defense in depth states that organizations should have overlapping security controls designed to meet the same security objectives whenever possible. This approach provides security in the event of a single control failure. Least privilege ensures that an individual has only the minimum set of permissions necessary to carry out their assigned job functions and does not require overlapping controls.

Separation of duties requires that one person not have permission to perform two separate actions that, when combined, carry out a sensitive function.

Security through obscurity attempts to hide the details of security controls to add security to them.

Neither separation of duties nor security through obscurity involves overlapping controls.

79. A, B. All ISC2 certified professionals are required to comply with the ISC2 Code of Ethics. All employees of an organization are required to comply with the organization's code of ethics. The federal code of ethics (or, more formally, the Code of Ethics for Government Service) would not apply to a nonprofit organization, as it applies only to federal employees. RFC 1087 does provide a code of ethics for the Internet, but it is not binding on any individual.

80. B. Ben should encrypt the data to provide an additional layer of protection as a compensating control. The organization has already made a policy exception, so he should not react by objecting to the exception or removing the data without authorization. Purchasing insurance may transfer some of the risk but is not a mitigating control.

81. A. The risk assessment team should pay the most immediate attention to those risks that appear in quadrant I. These are the risks with a high probability of occurring and a high impact on the organization if they do occur.

82. D. Electronic access to company resources must be carefully coordinated. An employee who retains access after being terminated may use that access to take retaliatory action. On the other hand, if access is terminated too early, the employee may figure out that they are about to be terminated.

83. D. In a risk acceptance strategy, the organization decides that taking no action is the most beneficial route to managing a risk.

84. A. COPPA requires that websites obtain advance parental consent for the collection of personal information from children under the age of 13.

85. D. The annualized rate of occurrence (ARO) is the frequency at which you should expect a risk to materialize each year. In a 100-year flood plain, risk analysts expect a flood to occur once every 100 years, or 0.01 times per year.

86. D. Wireshark is a protocol analyzer and may be used to eavesdrop on network connections. Eavesdropping is an attack against confidentiality.

87. C. In reduction analysis, the security professional breaks the system down into five core elements: trust boundaries, data flow paths, input points, privileged operations, and details about security controls.

88. D. South Africa's Protection of Personal Information Act (POPIA) governs the processing of personal data and would affect any new enterprise operating within its jurisdiction that handles personal information. PIPL refers to China's Personal Information Protection Law, which would not apply in South Africa. PCI DSS is a set of security standards for entities that handle credit cards and does not relate to privacy law but rather to the security of cardholder data. PIPEDA, the Personal Information Protection and Electronic Documents Act, is Canada's data privacy law and would not be applicable to operations in South Africa.

89. B. Qualitative tools are often used in business impact assessment to capture the impact on intangible factors such as customer confidence, employee morale, and reputation.

90. C. Risks are the combination of a threat and a vulnerability. Threats are the external forces seeking to undermine security, such as the malicious hacker in this case. Vulnerabilities are the internal weaknesses that might allow a threat to succeed. In this scenario the missing patch is the vulnerability, and the malicious hacker is the threat. If the hacker (threat) attempts a SQL injection attack against the unpatched server (vulnerability), the result is website defacement.

91. C. The exposure factor is the percentage of the facility that risk managers expect will be damaged if a risk materializes. It is calculated by dividing the amount of damage by the asset value. In this case, that is $5 million in damage divided by the $10 million facility value, or 50%.

92. B. The annualized rate of occurrence is the number of times that risk analysts expect a risk to happen in any given year. In this case, the analysts expect tornados once every 200 years, or 0.005 times per year.

93. A. The annualized loss expectancy is calculated by multiplying the single loss expectancy (SLE) by the annualized rate of occurrence (ARO). In this case, the SLE is $5,000,000, and the ARO is 0.005. Multiplying these numbers together gives you the ALE of $25,000.

94. C. Information disclosure attacks rely upon the revelation of private, confidential, or controlled information. When the attacker examined the HTML code and discovered sensitive information, this was an example of an information disclosure attack, as the attacker gained information they should not have been privy to.

95. A. Supply chain management can help ensure the security of hardware, software, and services that an organization acquires. Chris should focus on each step that his laptops take from the original equipment manufacturer to delivery.

96. C. Change management is a critical control process that involves systematically managing change. Without it, Lisa might simply deploy her code to production without oversight, documentation, or testing. Regression testing focuses on testing to ensure that new code doesn't bring back old flaws, while fuzz testing feeds unexpected input to code. In a code review the source code itself is reviewed, and this may be done as part of the change management process but isn't what is described here.

97. A. Charles is tracking a key performance indicator (KPI). A KPI is used to measure performance (and success). Without a definition of success, this would simply be a metric, but Charles is working toward a known goal and can measure against it. There is not a return investment calculation in this problem, and the measure is not a control.

98. D. A fitness evaluation is not a typical part of a hiring process. Drug tests, background checks, and social media checks are all common parts of current hiring practices.

99. A, C. Supply chain risks occur when the adversary is interfering with the delivery of goods or services from a supplier to the customer. This might involve tampering with hardware before the customer receives it or using social engineering to compromise a vendor employee. Hacking into a web server run in an infrastructure-as-a-service (IaaS) environment is not a supply chain risk because the web server is already under the control of the customer. Using a botnet to conduct a denial-of-service attack does not involve any supply chain elements.

100. The laws or industry standards match to the descriptions as follows:

1. GLBA: A. A U.S. law that requires covered financial institutions to provide their customers with a privacy notice on a yearly basis

2. PCI DSS: C. An industry standard that covers organizations that handle payment cards

3. HIPAA: D. A U.S. law that provides data privacy and security requirements for medical information

4. SOX: B. A U.S. law that requires internal controls' assessments including IT transaction flows for publicly traded companies

Chapter 2: Asset Security (Domain 2)

1. A. Scoping is the process of determining which controls are appropriate to an organization, environment, or implementation. Bounds checking is the process of making sure that data does not overflow a variable. Data stewards provide oversight and data governance. Tailoring modifies controls to fit a specific situation or need.

2. A. Business owners have to balance the need to provide value with regulatory, security, and other requirements. This makes the adoption of a common framework like COBIT attractive. Data owners are more likely to ask that those responsible for control selection identify a standard to use. Data processors are required to perform specific actions under regulations like the EU GDPR. Finally, in many organizations, data stewards are internal roles that oversee how data is used.

3. B. The best option for Nadia is a cloud access security broker (CASB). A CASB is designed to sit between a cloud environment and the users who use it, and it provides monitoring and policy enforcement capabilities. A next-generation firewall (NGFW), an intrusion detection system (IDS), and a security orchestration, automation, and response (SOAR) tool could each provide some insight into what is going on, but they are not purpose built and designed for this like the CASB is. The NGFW and IDS are most likely to provide insight into traffic patterns and behaviors, while the SOAR is primarily intended to monitor other systems and centralize data for response, making it potentially the least useful in this specific scenario.

4. B. Media is typically labeled with the highest classification level of data it contains. This prevents the data from being handled or accessed at a lower classification level. Data integrity requirements may be part of a classification process but don't independently drive labeling in a classification scheme.

5. A. The need to protect sensitive data drives data classification. Classifying data allows organizations to focus on data that needs to be protected rather than spending effort on less important data. Remanence describes data left on media after an attempt is made to remove the data. Transmitting data isn't a driver for an administrative process to protect sensitive data, and clearing is a technical process for removing data from media.

6. A. A data retention policy can help to ensure that outdated data is purged, removing potential additional costs for discovery. Many organizations have aggressive retention policies to both reduce the cost of storage and limit the amount of data that is kept on hand and discoverable. Data retention policies are not designed to destroy incriminating data, and legal requirements for data retention must still be met.

7. D. Custodians are delegated the role of handling day-to-day tasks by managing and overseeing how data is handled, stored, and protected. Data processors are systems used to process data. Business owners are typically project or system owners who are tasked with making sure systems provide value to their users or customers.

8. C. In a typical data life cycle, collection is the first stage, although some may replace collection with creation. Once collected, data can be analyzed, used, stored, and disposed of at the end of its useful life. Policies may be created at any time, and organizations often have data before they have policies. Labels are added to data during the analysis, usage, or retention cycle.

9. C. Security baselines provide a starting point to scope and tailor security controls to your organization's needs. They aren't always appropriate to specific organizational needs, they cannot ensure that systems are always in a secure state, and they do not prevent liability.

10. A. Clearing describes preparing media for reuse. When media is cleared, unclassified data is written over all addressable locations on the media. Once that's completed, the media can be reused, although it may be possible to retrieve some of the original data using retrieval tools. Erasing is the deletion of files or media and may not include all of the data on the device or media, making it the worst choice here. Purging is a more intensive form of clearing for reuse in lower-security areas, and sanitization is a series of processes that removes data from a system or media while ensuring that the data is unrecoverable by any means.

11. B. Sensitive data scanning tools are designed to scan for and flag sensitive data types using known formatting and structure. Social Security numbers, credit card numbers, and other regularly structured data that follows known rules can be identified and then addressed as needed. Manual searching is a massive undertaking for an organization with even a relatively small amount of data; asset metadata needs to be set first and would have already been identified; and a SOAR is used to automate incident response and orchestrate security actions.

12. D. Spare sectors, bad sectors, and space provided for wear leveling on SSDs (overprovisioned space) may all contain data that was written to the space that will not be cleared when the drive is wiped. This is a form of data remanence and is a concern for organizations that do not want data to potentially be accessible. Many wiping utilities deal only with currently addressable space on the drive. SSDs cannot be degaussed, and wear leveling space cannot be reliably used to hide data. These spaces are still addressable by the drive, although they may not be seen by the operating system.

13. C. Commercial data classification often takes into account the value of the data, any regulatory or legal requirements that may apply to the data, and how long the data is useful—its life span. The impact to national security is more typically associated with government classification schemes.

14. C. Data is often considered based on the data state that it is in. Data can be at rest (on a drive or other storage medium), in use and thus in memory or a buffer and often decrypted for use, or in transit over a network. Data that is resident in system memory is considered data in use.

15. C. A watermark is used to digitally label data and can be used to indicate ownership, as well as to assist a digital rights management (DRM) system in identifying data that should be protected. Encryption would have prevented the data from being accessed if it was lost, while classification is part of the set of security practices that can help make sure the right controls are in place. Finally, metadata is used to label data and might help a data loss prevention system flag it before it leaves your organization.

16. B. AES is a strong modern symmetric encryption algorithm that is appropriate for encrypting data at rest. TLS is frequently used to secure data when it is in transit. A virtual private network is not necessarily an encrypted connection and would be used for data in motion, while DES is an outdated algorithm and should not be used for data that needs strong security.

17. A. Data loss prevention (DLP) systems can use labels on data to determine the appropriate controls to apply to the data. Most DLP systems won't modify labels in real time and typically don't work directly with firewalls to stop traffic. Deleting unlabeled data would cause big problems for organizations that haven't labeled every piece of data!

18. B. The value of the data contained on media often exceeds the cost of the media, making more expensive media that may have a longer life span or additional capabilities like encryption support a good choice. While expensive media may be less likely to fail, the reason it makes sense is the value of the data, not just that it is less likely to fail. In general, the cost of the media doesn't have anything to do with the ease of encryption, and data integrity isn't ensured by better media.

19. D. Destruction is the most complete method of ensuring that data cannot be exposed, and organizations often opt to destroy either the drive or the entire workstation or device to ensure that data cannot be recovered or exposed. Sanitization is a combination of processes that ensure that data from a system cannot be recovered by any means. Erasing and clearing are both prone to mistakes and technical problems that can result in remnant data and don't make sense for systems that handle proprietary information.

20. D. Common practice makes proprietary or confidential data the most sensitive data. Private data is internal business data that shouldn't be exposed but that doesn't meet the threshold for confidential or proprietary data. Sensitive data may help attackers or otherwise create risk and typically refers to any information that isn't public or unclassified, and public data is just that—data that is or can be made public.

21. C. Data at rest is inactive data that is physically stored. Data in an IPsec tunnel or part of an e-commerce transaction is data in motion. Data in RAM is ephemeral and is not inactive.

22. C. The Payment Card Industry Data Security Standard (PCI DSS) provides the set of requirements for credit card processing systems. The Microsoft, NSA, and CIS baseline are all useful for building a Windows 11 security standard, but the PCI DSS standard is a better answer.

23. D. The CIS benchmarks are an example of a security baseline. A risk assessment would help identify which controls were needed, and proper system ownership is an important part of making sure baselines are implemented and maintained. Data labeling can help ensure that controls are applied to the right systems and data.

24. B. Scoping involves selecting only the controls that are appropriate for your IT systems, while tailoring matches your organization's mission and the controls from a selected baseline. Baselining is the process of configuring a system or software to match a baseline or building a baseline itself. Selection isn't a technical term used for any of these processes.

25. B. The controls implemented from a security baseline should match the data classification of the data used or stored on the system. Custodians are trusted to ensure the day-to-day security of the data and should do so by ensuring that the baseline is met and maintained. Business owners often have a conflict of interest between functionality and data security, and of course, applying the same controls everywhere is expensive and may not meet business needs or be a responsible use of resources.

26. D. The third-party company is a data processor—they process data on behalf of Henry's company, which is a data controller. The data is collected about data subjects. Data owners are tasked with making decisions about data, such as who receives access to it and how it is used.

27. B. Many organizations require the destruction of media that contains data at higher levels of classification. Often the cost of the media is lower than the potential costs of data exposure, and it is difficult to guarantee that reused media doesn't contain remnant data. Tapes can be erased by degaussing, but degaussing is not always fully effective. Bitrot describes the slow loss of data on aging media, while data permanence is a term sometimes used to describe the life span of data and media.

28. A. NIST Special Publication 800-122 defines PII as any information that can be used to distinguish or trace an individual's identity, such as name, Social Security number, date and place of birth, mother's maiden name, biometric records, and other information that is linked or linkable to an individual such as medical, educational, financial, and employment information. PHI is health-related information about a specific person, Social Security numbers are issued to individuals in the United States, and SII is a made-up term.

29. B. Typically, data breaches cause the greatest reputational damage as a result of threats to data at rest. Data at rest with a high level of sensitivity is often encrypted to help prevent this. Decryption is not as significant of a threat if strong encryption is used and encryption keys are well secured. Insider threats are a risk, but the majority of insider threat issues are unintentional rather than intentional, making this risk less likely in most organizations.

30. B. Full disk encryption only protects data at rest. Since it encrypts the full disk, it does not distinguish between labeled and unlabeled data.

31. C. This is an example of an end-of-support (EOS) scenario. The company is intentionally ending support and needs to address what happens to the devices next—secure disposal, destruction, or re-sale—depending on data security requirements and policies set by the company. EOL is when a device or software is no longer made or supported, in contrast to end of support, which may be when it is no longer serviced, including via patches, upgrades, or organizational maintenance. Planned obsolescence and device risk management are not terms that are used on the exam.

32. D. Classification identifies the value of data to an organization. This can often help drive IT expenditure prioritization and could help with rough cost estimates if a breach occurred, but that's not the primary purpose. Finally, most breach laws call out specific data types for notification rather than requiring organizations to classify data themselves.

33. B. Downgrading systems and media is rare due to the difficulty of ensuring that sanitization is complete. The need to completely wipe (or destroy) the media that systems use means that the cost of reuse is often significant and may exceed the cost of purchasing a new system or media. The goal of purging is to ensure that no data remains, so commingling data should not be a concern, nor should the exposure of the data; only staff with the proper clearance should handle the systems! Finally, a DLP system should flag data based on labels, not on the system it comes from.

34. A. Classification should be conducted based on the value of the data to the organization, its sensitivity, and the amount of harm that could result from exposure of the data. Cost should be considered when implementing controls and is weighed against the damage that exposure would create.

35. C. Erasing, which describes a typical deletion process in many operating systems, typically removes only the link to the file and leaves the data that makes up the file itself. The data will remain in place but not indexed until the space is needed and it is overwritten. Degaussing works only on magnetic media, but it can be quite effective on it. Purging and clearing both describe more elaborate removal processes.

36. C. TLS is a modern encryption method used to encrypt and protect data in transit. BitLocker is a full-disk encryption technology used for data at rest. DES and SSL are both outdated encryption methods and should not be used for data that requires high levels of security.

37. C. We know that the data classification will not be the top-level classification of Confidential because the loss of the data would not cause severe damage and is not medical data covered by HIPAA. This means we have to choose between private (PHI) and sensitive (confidential). Calling this private due to the patient's personally identifiable information fits the classification scheme, giving us the correct answer.

38. A. A data loss prevention (DLP) system or software is designed to identify labeled data or data that fits specific patterns and descriptions to help prevent it from leaving the organization. An IDS is designed to identify intrusions. Although some IDS systems can detect specific types of sensitive data using pattern matching, they have no ability to stop traffic. A firewall uses rules to control traffic routing, while UDP is a network protocol.

39. A. When data is stored in a mixed classification environment, it is typically classified based on the highest classification of data included. In this case, the U.S. government's highest classification is Top Secret. Mixed classification is not a valid classification in this scheme.

40. B. The end of support of a device or product typically occurs after the end of life and end of sales. Support may continue for a period of months or even years, but eventually support stops too. General availability is found during the main part of a life cycle, rather than at the end, and helps note when the product is out of testing and can be acquired or used by customers or others instead of specific groups like beta testers or early release partners.

41. D. Tailoring ensures that assessment methods are appropriate to the systems, services, and other assets that are being validated and is the best answer here. Scoping is a related term and involves setting the boundaries of security control implementations. Asset management involves how assets are overseen throughout their life cycle, and compliance is a broad term that describes ensuring that regulations, contractual terms, or other requirements are met.

42. B. Group Policy provides the ability to monitor and apply settings in a security baseline. Manual checks by users and using start-up scripts provide fewer reviews and may be prone to failure, while periodic review of the baseline won't result in compliance being checked.

43. B. Providing consent, or agreeing to data collection and use, is important in many data collection scenarios and may be required by law. Remanence occurs when data remains in place, sometimes inadvertently, after it should have been removed or disposed of. Retention is the intentional process of keeping and managing data. Certification is not a data life-cycle process element.

44. A. Amy is a data custodian and is responsible for the technical environment, including things like database structures and the technical implementations of data policies. Some organizations may overlap other data roles, including data controllers or data stewards, but the best answer here is a data custodian. Amy is not a data user and is not a data processor who uses the data on behalf of a data controller.

45. B. A data loss prevention (DLP) system can tag, monitor, and limit where files are transferred to. Jim's company may also elect to use digital rights management tools in combination with a data loss prevention system, but DRM controls how data can be used, not where files are transferred to or where they exist at any point in time in most cases. An intrusion prevention system (IPS) may be able to detect files that are being sent across a network but won't stop files from being copied on workstations or thumb drives. Antivirus is not designed for this purpose.

46. D. Using strong encryption, like AES-256, can help ensure that loss of removable media like tapes doesn't result in a data breach. Security labels may help with handling processes, but they won't help once the media is stolen or lost. Having multiple copies will ensure that you can still access the data but won't increase the security of the media. Finally, using hard drives instead of tape only changes the media type and not the risk from theft or loss.

47. D. Electronic signatures, as used in this rule, prove that the signature was provided by the intended signer. Electronic signatures as part of the FDA code are intended to ensure that electronic records are "trustworthy, reliable, and generally equivalent to paper records and handwritten signatures executed on paper." Signatures cannot provide confidentiality or integrity and don't ensure that someone has reviewed the data.

48. D. Tags that include information about the life span of the data and when it has expired can help with life-cycle management processes, part of data maintenance for organizations. Tags can be as simple as timestamps, or they can include additional metadata like the data type, creator, or purpose that can help inform the retention and disposal process. Rotation of files like logs is commonly done to limit how much space they take up, but rotation itself does not address disposal requirements and information that would guide the disposal process. DRM, or digital rights management, and DLP, or data loss prevention, both address data security and use but not disposal.

49. B. During the data maintenance phase of a typical data life cycle, activities like data scrubbing occur to remove unneeded, incorrect, or out-of-date data. Data retention is not a phase; instead, it is a decision that organizations make based on requirements, laws, or their own needs. Data remanence is also not a phase. Data remanence describes the problem of data that remains after data is removed. Finally, in the data collection phase, data is acquired and may be scrubbed, but the question describes a process occurring after data is no longer needed, not during acquisition.

50. B. Asset tagging is used to make sure that individuals working with assets can determine the security level or practices they require. Tailoring adjusts security requirements to organizational needs. Other controls, such as sanitization and encryption, may be required by a specific asset classification but are not sufficient to meet a full range of security requirements.

51. C. Data labels are crucial to identify the classification level of information contained on the media, and labeling data at creation helps to ensure that it is properly handled throughout its life cycle. Digital rights management (DRM) tools provide ways to control how data is used, while encrypting it can help maintain the confidentiality and integrity of the data. Classifying the data is necessary to label it, but it doesn't automatically place a label on the data.

52. D. The NIST SP 800-88 process for sanitization and disposition shows that media that will be reused and was classified at a moderate level should be purged and then that purge should be validated. Finally, it should be documented.

53. D. Data in transit is data that is traversing a network or is otherwise in motion. TLS, VPNs, and IPsec tunnels are all techniques used to protect data in transit. AES, Serpent, and IDEA are all symmetric algorithms, while Telnet, ISDN, and UDP are all protocols. BitLocker and FileVault are both used to encrypt data, but they protect only stored data, not data in transit.

54. C. The data owner has ultimate responsibility for data belonging to an organization and is typically the CEO, president, or another senior employee. Business and mission owners typically own processes or programs. System owners own a system that processes sensitive data.

55. C. The most difficult location to secure for encryption keys and similar highly sensitive information is in active memory because the data needs to be decrypted to be used. When data is at rest on a drive or in transit via either a local or public network, it can be encrypted until it reaches its destination, and you can use strong encryption in each of those circumstances.

56. A. Chris is most likely to be responsible for classifying the data that he owns as well as assisting with or advising the system owners on security requirements and control selection. In an organization with multiple data owners, Chris is unlikely to set criteria for classifying data on his own. As a data owner, Chris will also not typically have direct responsibility for scoping, tailoring, applying, or enforcing those controls.

57. B. The system administrators are acting in the roles of data administrators who grant access and will also act as custodians who are tasked with the day-to-day application of security controls. They are not acting as data owners who own the data itself. Typically, system administrators are delegated authority by system owners, such as a department head, and of course they are tasked with providing access to users.

58. C. Third-party organizations that process personal data on behalf of a data controller are known as data processors. The organization that they are contracting with would act in the role of the business or mission owners, and others within Chris's organization would have the role of data administrators, granting access as needed to the data based on their operational procedures and data classification.

59. D. While it can be a lot of work, the most complete inventory of active systems and devices can be created by determining what is connected to the network and then finding those assets. Port scans can help to find some systems, but firewalls and other security solutions can prevent systems from being discovered. Staff may not know about all of the systems and devices on the network or may presume that someone else will provide information about shared resources such as printers, security cameras, or other devices. Active Directory is unlikely to contain all devices, particularly if an inventory is needed!

60. B. In most organizations, changing processes so that new systems and devices are added to inventory before they are deployed is the first step in making sure asset inventories are current. Yearly or quarterly updates are too infrequent for most organizations and will lead to gaps as devices are forgotten.

61. C. Eric should use metadata tagging to allow him to use technical tools like DLP and DRM to handle and track data based on its type and content. File extensions do not reveal data security or type, and relying on network share locations to secure data or inventory will lead to gaps in security as files are moved, copied, or stored locally.

62. D. Patents, databases, and formulas are all examples of intangible assets. Tangible assets include things like hardware, cables, and buildings. Personnel assets include employees, and most organizations would be quite concerned if their employees were intangible!

63. D. There is no requirement that data collection be equal or equivalent. Instead, data collection statutes and other requirements often require that only required data is collected, that individuals are made aware of the data collection, and that they consent to the collection. Similarly, data should be collected only lawfully and via fair methods.

64. B. Requiring all media to have a label means that when unlabeled media is found, it should immediately be considered suspicious. This helps to prevent mistakes that might leave sensitive data unlabeled. Prelabeled media is not necessarily cheaper (nor may it make sense to buy!), while reusing public media simply means that it must be classified based on the data it now contains. HIPAA does not have specific media labeling requirements.

65. B. Data in use is data that is in a temporary storage location while an application or process is using it. Thus, data in memory is best described as data in use or ephemeral data. Data at rest is in storage, while data in transit is traveling over a network or other channel. Data at large is a made-up term.

66. C. Validation processes are conducted to ensure that the sanitization process was completed, avoiding data remanence. A form like this one helps to ensure that each device has been checked and that it was properly wiped, purged, or sanitized. This can allow reuse, does not prevent destruction, and does not help with attribution, which is a concept used with encryption to prove who created or sent a file.

67. C. Ensuring that data cannot be recovered is difficult, and the time and effort required to securely and completely wipe media as part of declassification can exceed the cost of new media. Sanitization, purging, and clearing may be part of declassification, but they are not reasons that it is not frequently chosen as an option for organizations with data security concerns.

68. D. Destruction is the final stage in the life cycle of media and can be done via disintegration, incineration, or a variety of other methods that result in the media and data being nonrecoverable. Sanitization is a combination of processes used when data is being removed from a system or media. Purging is an intense form of clearing, and degaussing uses strong magnetic fields to wipe data from magnetic media.

69. A. PHI is protected health information. Personally identifiable information (PII) is any information that can identify an individual. Proprietary data is information that helps organizations maintain a competitive edge or that they want to keep to their own organization or a controlled set of individuals. PID is not a term used for data classification.

70. D. Handling requirements and tools include visual indicators like a distinctive screen background and can help employees remember what level of classification they are dealing with and thus the handling requirements that they are expected to follow.

71. C. If an organization allows media to be downgraded, the purging process should be followed, and then the media should be relabeled. Degaussing may be used for magnetic media but won't handle all types of media. Pulverizing would destroy the media, preventing reuse, while relabeling first could lead to mistakes that result in media that hasn't been purged entering use.

72. B. The data owner sets the rules for use and protection of data. The remaining options all describe tasks for the system owner, including implementation of security controls.

73. B. In the NIST SP 800-60 diagram, the process determines appropriate categorization levels resulting in security categorization and then uses that as an input to determine controls. Standard selection would occur at an organizational level, while baselining occurs when systems are configured to meet a baseline. Sanitization would require the intentional removal of data from machines or media.

74. C. A and E can both be expected to have data at rest. C, the Internet, is an unknown, and the data can't be guaranteed to be at rest. B, D, and F are all data in transit across network links.

75. C. B, D, and F all show network links. Of the answers provided, Transport Layer Security (TLS) provides the best security for data in motion. AES-256 and 3DES are both symmetric ciphers and are more likely to be used for data at rest. SSL has been replaced with TLS and should not be a preferred solution.

76. B. Sending a file that is encrypted before it leaves means that exposure of the file in transit will not result in a confidentiality breach, and the file will remain secure until decrypted at location E. Since options A, C, and D do not provide any information about what happens at point C, they should be considered insecure, as the file may be at rest at point C in an unencrypted form.

77. C. Encrypting and labeling sensitive email will ensure that it remains confidential and can be identified. Performing these actions only on sensitive email will reduce the cost and effort of encrypting all email, allowing only sensitive email to be the focus of the organization's efforts. Only encrypting highly sensitive email not only skips labeling but might expose other classifications of email that shouldn't be exposed.

78. C. Data retention policies can reduce the number of old logs and other files that may need to be produced during a legal case. That can reduce organizational risk, but retention policies need to be in place well before a legal hold is filed. Reducing storage in use does not reduce liability, but it can reduce financial costs, and data retention policies don't tend to limit the number of classifications in use. Legal penalties are not impacted by a retention policy.

79. C. Systems used to process data are data processors. Data owners are typically CEOs or other very senior staff, custodians are granted rights to perform day-to-day tasks when handling data, and mission owners are typically program or information system owners.

80. D. Personally identifiable information includes any information that can uniquely identify an individual. This would include name, Social Security number, and any other unique identifier (including a student ID number). ZIP code, by itself, does not uniquely identify an individual.

81. B. Protected health information, or PHI, includes a variety of data in multiple formats, including oral and recorded data, such as that created or received by healthcare providers, employers, and life insurance providers. PHI must be protected by HIPAA. PII is personally identifiable information. SHI and HPHI are both made-up acronyms.

82. B. Tokenization replaces other data with a random string of characters. These tokens are then matched to the actual values for secure lookups as needed. Anonymization removes all personally identifiable data to ensure that the original subject cannot be identified. Data masking obscures some, but not all, data. Pseudonymization uses a pseudonym or alias to replace other information.

83. B. The Payment Card Industry Data Security Standard, or PCI-DSS, is a credit card industry data security standard that defines how businesses must handle information related to credit cards. CC-Comply was made up for this question. GLBA, or Gramm-Leach-Bliley, modernized financial institution standards, and GDPR is an EU data privacy regulation.

84. C. Due to problems with remnant data, the U.S. National Security Agency requires physical destruction of SSDs. This process, known as disintegration, results in very small fragments via a shredding process. Zero fill wipes a drive by replacing data with zeros, degaussing uses magnets to wipe magnetic media, and clearing is the process of preparing media for reuse.

85. A. The data owner bears responsibility for categorizing information systems and delegates selection of controls to system owners, while custodians implement the controls. Users don't perform any of these actions, while business owners are tasked with ensuring that systems are fulfilling their business purpose.

86. B. PCI DSS provides a set of required security controls and standards. Step 2 would be guided by the requirements of PCI DSS. PCI DSS will not greatly influence step 1 because all of the systems handle credit card information, making PCI DSS apply to all systems covered. Steps 3 and 4 will be conducted after PCI DSS has guided the decisions in step 2.

87. C. Custodians are tasked with the day-to-day monitoring of the integrity and security of data. Step 5 requires monitoring, which is a custodial task. A data owner may grant rights to custodians but will not be responsible for conducting monitoring. Data processors process data on behalf of the data controller, and a user simply uses the data via a computing system.

88. B. Susan's organization is limiting its risk by sending drives that have been sanitized before they are destroyed. This limits the possibility of a data breach if drives are mishandled by the third party, allowing them to be stolen, resold, or simply copied. The destruction of the drives will handle any issues with data remanence, while classification mistakes are not important if the drives have been destroyed. Wiping the data before destruction does not make a meaningful difference for data retention policy concerns. Data permanence and the life span of the data are not important on a destroyed drive.

89. C. RFID tags are a common solution for tracking hardware assets and equipment. They can be queried wirelessly at varying ranges depending on the tags and may be built-in to handheld readers or even included in doorways or arches to track items as they enter or leave a facility. Visual inventory relies on staff checking items, MAC addresses are hardware addresses for networked devices, and not every asset in inventory is likely to have a wireless network capability—or to be on! Steganography is hiding messages in images and doesn't help at all with inventory.

90. D. Record retention is the process of retaining and maintaining information for as long as it is needed. A data storage policy describes how and why data is stored, while data storage is the process of actually keeping the data. Asset maintenance is a noninformation-security-related process for maintaining physical assets.

91. C. The cost of the data is not directly included in the classification process. Instead, the impact on the organization if the data were exposed or breached is considered. Who can access the data and what regulatory or compliance requirements cover the data are also important considerations.

92. B. Symmetric encryption like AES is typically used for data at rest. Asymmetric encryption is often used during transactions or communications when the ability to have public and private keys is necessary. DES is an outdated encryption standard, and OTP is the acronym for onetime password.

93. D. Administrators have the rights to apply the permissions to access and handle data. Custodians are trusted with day-to-day data handling tasks. Business owners are typically system or project owners, and data processors are systems used to process data.

94. A. Knowing the asset's owner also tells you who is responsible for protecting the asset or for delegating that task. While asset owners may be law enforcement contacts, this is not a critical item for asset security. It does not directly help you to establish the value of the asset or to set security classification levels for an asset.

95. A. Tapes may be vulnerable to theft or loss in transit. That means tapes that are leaving their normal storage facility should be handled according to the organization's classification schemes and handling requirements. Purging the tapes would cause the loss of data, while increasing the classification level of the tapes does not align with the standard practices for data classification and handling. The tapes should be encrypted rather than decrypted.

96. A. The correct answer is the tape that is being shipped to a storage facility. You might think that the tape in shipment is "in motion," but the concept is that the data is not being accessed and is instead in storage rather than being sent across a network. Data in a TCP packet, in an e-commerce transaction, or in local RAM is in motion and is actively being used.

97. D. When the value of data changes due to legal, compliance, or business reasons, reviewing classifications and reclassifying the data is an appropriate response. Once the review is complete, data can be reclassified and handled according to its classification level. Simply relabeling the data avoids the classification process and may not result in the data being handled appropriately. Similarly, selecting a new baseline or simply encrypting the data may not handle all of the needs that the changes affecting the data create.

98. A, B, C. Data owners, controllers, and custodians are typically found inside of a company, while data processors are typically third parties.

99. C. Public data is just that—information that can be made public without any harm to the organization, and in fact, it is often information that the organization wants to make available. Private information should stay private inside of an organization, sensitive data may cause damage to the mission of the organization if exposed, and proprietary or confidential information is the most sensitive data that an organization wants to protect.

100. The data elements match with the categories as follows:

Data elements

1. Medical records: B. PHI

2. Trade secrets A. Proprietary data

3. Social Security numbers: C. PII

4. Driver's license numbers: C. PII

Medical records are an example of protected health information (PHI). Trade secrets are an example of proprietary data. Social Security numbers and driver's license numbers are examples of PII; if they were used in a medical context, they may also be PHI, but this question does not ask you to consider them in that context.

101. C. Cloud access security brokers (CASBs) can be on-site or cloud-based and are security policy enforcement points that operate between users and cloud services. A CASB can provide insight into what users are doing, enforce policies, provide threat protection, and even provide data loss prevention capabilities. An SIEM collects logs and event information as part of security monitoring and event management. A DLP system focuses on data loss prevention and data security but won't address an organization's full set of security policies and practices in the cloud, and NGFWs, or next-generation firewalls, provide a variety of security services but are not specifically designed to implement cloud policy.

102. A. The devices have reached end of support (EOS), and the vendor will no longer provide updates or support for it. End of development occurs when no new software updates or patches are being released. End of life and end of sales often occur at the same time when the vendor no longer sells the device. Support will typically continue even after end of life (EOL).

103. D. Asset owners are responsible for assets in an organization, including their procurement, management, and life cycle. Unlike data roles, there are typically fewer asset roles in play, and asset custodian is not a commonly recognized role. Since these are hardware devices, Gary's role is not as a data custodian or owner in the scope of this question.

104. A. Modifying baselines to better suit an organization is known as tailoring. Scoping occurs when baselines are reviewed to ensure that only controls suited to the environment or system are used. Editing and defining are not terms used on the exam for these activities.

105. B. Data location, particularly at rest, may drive compliance requirements based on local or national laws. This concern drives the majority of data location concerns. Ensuring data is not lost is a data handling and management practice topic, geographic location may be related to cost but storage media and services drive cost far more than physical location, and data custodians are likely to work with data regardless of location.

Chapter 3: Security Architecture and Engineering (Domain 3)

1. D. The Brewer-Nash model allows access controls to change dynamically based upon a user's actions. It is often used in environments like Matthew's to implement a "Chinese wall" between data belonging to different clients.

2. A. Fires may be detected as early as the incipient stage. During this stage, air ionization takes place, and specialized incipient fire detection systems can identify these changes to provide early warning of a fire.

3. A. Closed-circuit television (CCTV) systems act as a secondary verification mechanism for physical presence because they allow security officials to view the interior of the facility when a motion alarm sounds to determine the current occupants and their activities.

4. B. In an m of n control system, at least m of n possible escrow agents must collaborate to retrieve an encryption key from the escrow database.

5. A. This is an example of a vendor offering a fully functional application as a web-based service. Therefore, it fits under the definition of software as a service (SaaS). In infrastructure as a service (IaaS), compute as a service (CaaS), and platform as a service (PaaS), the customer provides their own software. In this example, the vendor is providing the email software, so none of those choices is appropriate.

6. B. The Digital Signature Standard approves three encryption algorithms for use in digital signatures: the Rivest, Shamir, Adleman (RSA) algorithm; the Elliptic Curve DSA (ECDSA) algorithm, and the Edwards Curve Digital Signature Algorithm (EdDSA). HAVAL is a hash function, not an encryption algorithm. While hash functions are used as part of the digital signature process, they do not provide encryption.

7. A. In the subject/object model of access control, the user or process making the request for a resource is the subject of that request. In this example, Harry is requesting resource access and is, therefore, the subject.

8. C. Michael should conduct his investigation, but there is a pressing business need to bring the website back online. The most reasonable course of action would be to take a snapshot of the compromised system and use the snapshot for the investigation, restoring the website to operation as quickly as possible while using the results of the investigation to improve the security of the site.

9. C. Using a sandbox is an example of confinement, where the system restricts the access of a particular process to limit its ability to affect other processes running on the same system.

10. D. Assurance is the degree of confidence that an organization has that its security controls are correctly implemented. It must be continually monitored and reverified.

11. A. Maintenance hooks, otherwise known as backdoors, provide developers with easy access to a system, bypassing normal security controls. If not removed prior to finalizing code, they pose a significant security vulnerability if an attacker discovers the maintenance hook.

12. B. The Simple Integrity Property states that an individual may not read a file classified at a lower security level than the individual's security clearance.

13. B. Supervisory control and data acquisition (SCADA) systems are used to control and gather data from industrial processes. They are commonly found in power plants and other industrial environments.

14. B. The Trusted Platform Module (TPM) is a hardware security technique that stores an encryption key on a chip on the motherboard and prevents someone from accessing an encrypted drive by installing it in another computer.

15. D. Intentional collisions have been created with MD5, and a real-world collision attack against SHA 1was announced in early 2017. 3DES is not a hashing tool, leaving SHA 256 (sometimes called SHA 2) as the only real choice that Chris has in this list.

16. C. In an asymmetric cryptosystem, the sender of a message encrypts the message using the recipient's public key. The recipient may then decrypt that message using their own private key, which only they should possess.

17. D. When Bob receives the message, he uses his own private key to decrypt it. Since he is the only one with his private key, he is the only one who should be able to decrypt it, thus preserving confidentiality.

18. B. Each user retains their own private key as secret information. In this scenario, Bob would only have access to his own private key and would not have access to the private key of Alice or any other user.

19. B. Alice creates the digital signature using her own private key. Then Bob, or any other user, can verify the digital signature using Alice's public key.

20. B. The salt is a random value added to a password before it is hashed by the operating system. The salt is then stored in a password file with the hashed password. This increases the complexity of cryptanalytic attacks by negating the usefulness of attacks that use precomputed hash values, such as rainbow tables.

21. A. Hash functions do not include any element of secrecy and, therefore, do not require a cryptographic key.

22. D. A preaction fire suppression system activates in two steps. The pipes fill with water once the early signs of a fire are detected. The system does not dispense water until heat sensors on the sprinkler heads trigger the second phase.

23. B. The Encapsulating Security Payload (ESP) protocol provides confidentiality and integrity for packet contents. It encrypts packet payloads and provides limited authentication and protection against replay attacks.

24. D. The greatest risk when a device is lost or stolen is that sensitive data contained on the device will fall into the wrong hands. Confidentiality processes protect against this risk. Nonrepudiation is when the recipient of a message can prove the originator's identity to a third party. Authentication is a means of proving one's identity. Integrity demonstrates that information has not been modified since transmission.

25. A. Supervisory Control and Data Acquisition systems, or SCADA systems, provide a graphical interface to monitor industrial control systems (ICS). Joanna should ask about access to her organization's SCADA systems.

26. C. The *-Security Property states that an individual may not write to a file at a lower classification level than that of the individual. This is also known as the confinement property.

27. B. The Diffie-Hellman algorithm allows for the secure exchange of symmetric encryption keys over a public network. IDEA and RSA are encryption algorithms. MD5 is a hashing function.

28. D. The principle of least privilege says that an employee should have only the minimum necessary privileges required to perform their jobs. Privilege creep indicates that an employee has accumulated permissions that they no longer require, indicating a violation of the least privilege principle. The trust but verify principle says that organizations should use auditing to ensure that control objectives are met. The fail securely principle says that security controls should default to a secure state in the event of a control failure. The keep it simple and secure principle says that security controls and other technologies should remain as simple as possible while still completing their objectives.

29. C. In a zero trust network architecture, access control decisions should never be made based upon a system's location on the network. Therefore, an IP address should never be used and would be the least appropriate of these options. While the other options have differing levels of security (two-factor authentication is clearly stronger than a password or biometrics alone), they do not violate the principles of a zero trust network architecture.

30. D. While defense in depth is a strong security principle, it is not a component of Privacy by Design. The following are the seven principles of the Privacy by Design model:

 1. Proactive, not reactive; preventative not remedial

 2. Privacy as the default

 3. Privacy embedded into design

 4. Full functionality—positive-sum, not zero-sum

 5. End-to-end life-cycle protection

 6. Visibility and transparency

 7. Respect for user privacy

31. B. Kerckhoffs' principle says that a cryptographic system should be secure even if everything about the system, except the key, is public knowledge.

32. A. Access control vestibules use two sets of doors to control access to a facility. This may be used to prevent piggybacking by monitoring use of the vestibule to allow only a single individual to enter a facility at a time. They may also be used to allow manual inspection of individuals or perform other security screening. Access control vestibules are also commonly known as mantraps.

33. A. While it would be ideal to have wiring closets in a location where they are monitored by security staff, this is not feasible in most environments. Wiring closets must be distributed geographically in multiple locations across each building used by an organization.

34. D. The *-Integrity Property states that a subject cannot modify an object at a higher integrity level than that possessed by the subject.

35. D. The segregation of duties principle says that no employee should have permission to perform two tasks that, when combined, would pose a security risk. In this situation, an employee auditing their own work would create a conflict of interest, so Lana has implemented a segregation of duties. Two-person control is closely related, but it requires that two different employees approve an action. If she required that two managers approve new accounts, that would be an example of two-person control.

36. A, B, C, D. All of these statements are correct. The idea that systems should be designed to operate in a secure manner if the user performs no other configuration is the secure defaults principle. The idea that systems should be designed to fall back to a secure state if they experience an error is the fail securely principle. The idea that systems should be designed to incorporate security as a design feature is the security by design principle. The idea that systems should be designed in a manner that keeps their functionality as simple as possible is the keep it simple principle.

37. A. EAL1 assurance applies when the system in question has been functionally tested. It is the lowest level of assurance under the Common Criteria.

38. B. The system can be designed in a manner that protects the confidentiality, integrity, and availability of data. The research workstations included in the grid are from internal users, minimizing the risk of distributing the data. However, an isolation breach in the distributed computing client could be catastrophic, allowing someone who compromises the controller to assume control of every device in the organization.

39. A. This is an example of a microservices architecture. Each of the component microservices performs a discrete task and then communicates with other microservices using APIs. This might be accomplished using function-as-a-service (FaaS) cloud computing, containerization, and/or virtualization, but there is no indication whether those services are being used in the scenario.

40. A. Adam created a list of individual users who may access the file. This is an access control list, which consists of multiple access control entries. It includes the names of users, so it is not role-based, and Adam was able to modify the list, so it is not mandatory access control.

41. C. Parameter checking, or input validation, is used to ensure that input provided by users to an application matches the expected parameters for the application. Developers may use parameter checking to ensure that input does not exceed the expected length, preventing a buffer overflow attack.

42. D. The defense-in-depth principle suggests using multiple overlapping security controls to achieve the same control objective. Network and host firewalls are both designed to limit network traffic and therefore are an example of defense in depth. The encryption of email and network intrusion detection are unrelated controls and do not satisfy the same objective. The same is true for the combination of CASB and security awareness training and the combination of DLP and multifactor authentication.

43. D. Multistate systems are certified to handle data from different security classifications simultaneously by implementing protection mechanisms that segregate data appropriately.

44. C. For systems running in System High mode, the user must have a valid security clearance for all information processed by the system, access approval for all information processed by the system, and a valid need to know for some, but not necessarily all, information processed by the system.

45. B. Steganography is the art of using cryptographic techniques to embed secret messages within other content. Some steganographic algorithms work by making alterations to the least significant bits of the many bits that make up image files.

46. D. All of these terms accurately describe this use of technology. However, the use of Docker is best described as a containerization technology, so this is the best possible answer choice.

47. A. The kernel lies within the central ring, Ring 0. Conceptually, Ring 1 contains other operating system components. Ring 2 is used for drivers and protocols. User-level programs and applications run at Ring 3. Rings 0 through 2 run in privileged mode, while Ring 3 runs in user mode. It is important to note that many modern operating systems do not fully implement this model.

48. D. In an infrastructure-as-a-service environment, security duties follow a shared responsibility model. Since the vendor is responsible for managing the storage hardware, the vendor would retain responsibility for destroying or wiping drives as they are taken out of service. However, it is still the customer's responsibility to validate that the vendor's sanitization procedures meet their requirements prior to utilizing the vendor's storage services.

49. C. The first thing Casey should do is notify her management, but after that, replacing the certificate and using proper key management practices with the new certificate's key should be at the top of her list.

50. C. The verification process is similar to the certification process in that it validates security controls. Verification may go a step further by involving a third-party testing service and compiling results that may be trusted by many different organizations. Accreditation is the act of management formally accepting a system, not evaluating the system itself.

51. D. In a serverless computing model, the vendor does not expose details of the operating system to its customers. Therefore, the vendor retains full responsibility for configuring it securely under the shared responsibility model of cloud computing.

52. B. The mean time to failure (MTTF) provides the average amount of time before a device of that particular specification fails.

53. C. Asymmetric cryptosystems use a pair of keys for each user. In this case, with 1,000 users, the system will require 2,000 keys. 499,500 would be the correct answer for a symmetric system.

54. A. Mobile Device Management (MDM) products provide a consistent, centralized interface for applying security configuration settings to mobile devices.

55. C. Nonrepudiation occurs when the recipient of a message is able to demonstrate to a third party that the message came from the purported sender.

56. A. The card shown in the image has a smart chip underneath the American flag. Therefore, it is an example of a smart card. This is the most secure type of identification card technology.

57. D. The TEMPEST program creates technology that is not susceptible to Van Eck phreaking attacks because it reduces or suppresses natural electromagnetic emanations.

58. A. Golden ticket attacks use the hash of the Kerberos service account to create tickets in an Active Directory environment. Kerberoasting attacks rely on collected TGS tickets. Pass the ticket attacks rely on tickets harvested from the LSASS process. Brute-force attacks depend on random guessing without any additional information.

59. A. The MD5 hashing algorithm has known collisions and, as of 2005, is no longer considered secure for use in modern environments. The AES, PGP, and WPA3 algorithms are all still considered secure.

60. B. The use of the Mimikatz tool is indicative of an attempt to capture user password hashes for use in a pass-the-hash attack against Microsoft Active Directory accounts.

61. C. In a known plaintext attack, the attacker has a copy of the encrypted message along with the plaintext message used to generate that ciphertext. In a chosen plaintext attack, the attacker has the ability to choose the plaintext to be encrypted. In a chosen ciphertext attack, the attacker can choose the ciphertext output. In a brute-force attack, the attacker simply tries all possible key combinations.

62. B. In a time of check to time of use (TOCTOU) attack, the attacker exploits the difference in time between when a security control is verified and the data protected by the control is actually used.

63. B. In this case, most cloud service models (including IaaS, SaaS, and serverless/FaaS) would require transmitting most information back to the cloud. The edge computing service model would be far more appropriate, as it places computing power at the sensor, minimizing the data that must be sent back to the cloud over limited connectivity network links.

64. B. Wear leveling is about writing to the disk evenly. Encrypting the data would protect against the disclosure of data on portions of the disk that have remnants due to too much wear and having been set aside as no longer usable. Disk formatting does not effectively remove data from any device. Degaussing is effective only for magnetic media. Physically destroying the drive would not permit reuse.

65. C. In an aggregation attack, individual(s) use their access to specific pieces of information to piece together a larger picture that they are not authorized to access.

66. D. While all of the controls mentioned protect against unwanted electromagnetic emanations, only white noise is an active control. White noise generates false emanations that effectively "jam" the true emanations from electronic equipment.

67. B. In a software-as-a-service environment, the customer has no access to any underlying infrastructure, so firewall management is a vendor responsibility under the cloud computing shared responsibility model.

68. C. The grant rule allows a subject to grant rights that it possesses on an object to another subject.

69. B. The system Charles is remediating may have a firmware or BIOS infection, with malware resident on the system board. While uncommon, this type of malware can be difficult to find and remove. Since he used original media, it is unlikely that the malware came from the software vendor. Charles wiped the system partition, and the system would have been rebooted before being rebuilt, thus clearing system memory.

70. C. Lauren has implemented address space layout randomization, a memory protection methodology that randomizes memory locations, which prevents attackers from using known address spaces and contiguous memory regions to execute code via overflow or stack smashing attacks.

71. C. This message was most likely encrypted with a transposition cipher. The use of a substitution cipher, a category that includes AES and 3DES, would change the frequency distribution so that it did not mirror that of the English language. This type of attack, where the attacker only has access to an encrypted message, is also known as a ciphertext-only attack.

72. A. In a zero trust network architecture, the policy engine is responsible for making policy decisions based upon rules and external data sources. It uses a trust algorithm to decide whether to grant, deny, or revoke access, considering factors like identity management, threat intelligence, and security information and event management (SIEM) data. The policy administrator, on the other hand, acts based on the decisions made by the policy engine, establishing or removing communication paths and managing session-specific credentials. The policy enforcement point enforces these decisions by controlling access to resources based on instructions from the policy administrator. Lastly, the subject refers to users, services, or systems that request access or attempt to use rights and is not involved in decision-making.

73. A. The blacklisting approach to application control allows users to install any software they want except for packages specifically identified by the administrator as prohibited. This would be an appropriate approach in a scenario where users should be able to install any nonmalicious software they want to use.

74. A. Heartbeat sensors send periodic status messages from the alarm system to the monitoring center. The monitoring center triggers an alarm if it does not receive a status message for a prolonged period of time, indicating that communications were disrupted.

75. B. In a zero-knowledge proof, one individual demonstrates to another that they can achieve a result that requires sensitive information without actually disclosing the sensitive information.

76. A. When operating system patches are no longer available for mobile devices, the best option is typically to retire or replace the device. Building isolated networks will not stop the device from being used for browsing or other purposes, which means it is likely to continue to be exposed to threats. Installing a firewall will not remediate the security flaws in the OS, although it may help somewhat. Finally, reinstalling the OS will not allow new updates or fix the root issue.

77. A. In a man-in-the-middle attack, the attacker tricks the user into establishing a connection with the attacker. The attacker then establishes a connection to the legitimate server and relays communications between the two, eavesdropping on the contents. A meet-in-the-middle attack is an attack against cryptographic algorithms that use multiple rounds of encryption. There is no indication in the scenario that the attacker used an exhaustive brute-force attack or a specialized timing attack to achieve their goals.

78. A. Digital signatures are possible only when using an asymmetric encryption algorithm. Of the algorithms listed, only RSA is asymmetric and supports digital signature capabilities.

79. C. The Open Worldwide Application Security Project (OWASP) produces an annual list of the top 10 web application security issues that developers and security professionals around the world rely upon for education and training purposes. The OWASP vulnerabilities form the basis for many web application security testing products.

80. A. The information flow model applies state machines to the flow of information. The Bell-LaPadula model applies the information flow model to confidentiality, while the Biba model applies it to integrity.

81. C. The most reasonable choice presented is to move the devices to a secure and isolated network segment. This will allow the devices to continue to serve their intended function while preventing them from being compromised. All of the other scenarios either create major new costs or deprive her organization of the functionality that the devices were purchased to provide.

82. C. Capacitance motion detectors monitor the electromagnetic field in a monitored area, sensing disturbances that correspond to motion.

83. D. Mirai targeted "Internet of Things" devices, including routers, cameras, and DVRs. As organizations bring an increasing number of devices like these into their corporate networks, protecting both internal and external targets from insecure, infrequently updated, and often vulnerable IoT devices is increasingly important.

84. D. The Biba model focuses only on protecting integrity and does not provide protection against confidentiality or availability threats. It also does not provide protection against covert channel attacks. The Biba model focuses on external threats and assumes that internal threats are addressed programmatically.

85. A. In TLS, both the server and the client communicate using an ephemeral symmetric session key. They generate this key using the Diffie-Hellman key exchange algorithm and then communicate using it throughout the rest of the session.

86. B. A Faraday cage is a metal skin that prevents electromagnetic emanations from exiting. It is a rarely used technology because it is unwieldy and expensive, but it is quite effective at blocking unwanted electromagnetic radiation.

87. B. The hypervisor is responsible for coordinating access to physical hardware and enforcing isolation between different virtual machines running on the same physical platform.

88. B. Cloud computing systems where the customer only provides application code for execution on a vendor-supplied computing platform are examples of platform-as-a-service (PaaS) computing.

89. B. A well-designed data center should have redundant systems and capabilities for each critical part of its infrastructure. That means that power, cooling, and network connectivity should all be redundant. Kim should determine how to ensure that a single system failure cannot take her data center offline.

90. B. UPSs are designed to protect against short-term power losses, such as power faults. When they conduct power conditioning, they are also able to protect against sags and noise. UPSs have limited-life batteries and are not able to maintain continuous operating during a sustained blackout.

91. D. Data center humidity should be maintained between 20% and 80%. Values below this range increase the risk of static electricity, while values above this range may generate moisture that damages equipment.

92. A, B. Payment of a ransom often results in the release of a decryption key, but this is not guaranteed by any means. There is also no link between the payment of a ransom and a future data breach, as an attacker may choose to release confidential information regardless of whether the ransom was paid. Depending upon applicable jurisdictions, payment of a ransom may be illegal under corrupt practices laws or embargoes against terrorist organizations. For example, the U.S. Office of Foreign Assets Control (OFAC) issued an advisory in 2020 stating that ransom payments may violate sanctions. Payment of a ransom may also cause attackers to consider the victim a "mark" and demand future payments in exchange for continued access to their data.

93.   D. Alex can use digital rights management technology to limit use of the PDFs to paying customers. While DRM is rarely a perfect solution, in this case, it may fit his organization's needs. EDM is electronic dance music, which his customers may appreciate but which won't solve the problem. Encryption and digital signatures can help to keep the files secure and to prove who they came from but won't solve the rights management issue Alex is tackling.

94.   B. Matt is helping to maintain the chain of custody documentation for his electronic evidence. This can be important if his organization needs to prove that the digital evidence they handled has not been tampered with. A better process would involve more than one person to ensure that no tampering was possible.

95.   A. The certificate revocation list contains the serial numbers of digital certificates issued by a certificate authority that have later been revoked.

96.   A. The point of the digital certificate is to prove to Alison that the server belongs to the bank, so she does not need to have this trust in advance. To trust the certificate, she must verify the CA's digital signature on the certificate, trust the CA, verify that the certificate is not listed on a CRL, and verify that the certificate contains the name of the bank.

97.   C. Covert channels use surreptitious communications' paths. Covert timing channels alter the use of a resource in a measurable fashion to exfiltrate information. If a user types using a specific rhythm of Morse code, this is an example of a covert timing channel. Someone watching or listening to the keystrokes could receive a secret message with no trace of the message left in logs.

98.   C. Self-signed digital certificates should be used only for internal-facing applications, where the user base trusts the internally generated digital certificate.

99.   D. In a fault injection attack, the attacker attempts to compromise the integrity of a cryptographic device by causing some type of external fault. For example, they might use high-voltage electricity, high or low temperature, or other factors to cause a malfunction that undermines the security of the device. Side-channel attacks seek to use information about system activity and retrieve information that is actively being encrypted. Brute-force attacks attempt every possible valid combination for a key or password. In a timing attack, the attacker measures precisely how long cryptographic operations take to complete, gaining information about the cryptographic process that may be used to undermine its security.

100.   The security models match with the descriptions as follows:

   1.   Clark-Wilson: C. This model uses security labels to grant access to objects via transformation procedures and a restricted interface model.

   2.   Bell-LaPadula: A. This model blocks lower-classified objects from accessing higher-classified objects, thus ensuring confidentiality.

   3.   Biba: B. The * property of this model can be summarized as "no write-up."

101. The architecture security concepts match with the descriptions as follows:

1. Time of check: C. The time at which the subject checks whether an object is available

2. Covert channel: A. A method used to pass information over a path not normally used for communication

3. Time of use: D. The time at which a subject can access an object

4. Maintenance hooks: E. An access method known only to the developer of the system

5. Parameter checking: F. A method that can help prevent buffer overflow attacks

6. Race condition: B. The exploitation of the reliance of a system's behavior on the sequence of events that occur externally

Chapter 4: Communication and Network Security (Domain 4)

1. B. BitTorrent is an example of a peer-to-peer (P2P) content delivery network. It is commonly used for legitimate purposes to distribute large files like Linux ISOs and other freely distributed software packages and files in addition to its less legitimate uses. CloudFlare, CloudFront, and Akamai's Edge are all hosted CDNs.

2. B. VDOMs are instances of firewalls, each with their own interfaces and rulesets allowing granular configurations based on security requirements. VDOMs are commonly used to accommodate different purposes, customers, or other needs where separately managed firewall instances are desirable. They don't combine instances; instead, they create separate instances, they aren't domain controllers, and hosting multiple domain names does not require a VDOM.

3. C. Ben is using ad hoc mode, which directly connects two clients. It can be easy to confuse this with stand-alone mode, which connects clients using a wireless access point but not to wired resources like a central network. Infrastructure mode connects endpoints to a central network, not directly to each other. Finally, wired extension mode uses a wireless access point to link wireless clients to a wired network.

4. C. A collision domain is the set of systems that could cause a collision if they transmitted at the same time. Systems outside a collision domain cannot cause a collision if they send at the same time. This is important, as the number of systems in a collision domain increases the likelihood of network congestion due to an increase in collisions. A broadcast domain is the set of systems that can receive a broadcast from each other. A subnet is a logical division of a network, while a supernet is made up of two or more networks.

5. D. The RST flag is used to reset or disconnect a session. It can be resumed by restarting the connection via a new three-way handshake.

6. D. He should choose 802.11ax, which supports theoretical speeds up to 9.6 Gbps. 802.11ac supports up to 5.9 Gbps, 802.11n supports up to 600 Mbps, and 802.11g is only capable up to 54 Mbps.

7. D. Both FTP/S and SFTP are commonly used as replacement insecure FTP services. SFTP offers the advantage of using SSH for transfers, making it easy to use existing firewall rules. TFTP is trivial FTP, an insecure quick transfer method often used to transfer files for network devices, among other uses. HFTPS and SecFTP were made up for this question.

8. A. The Network layer, or layer 3, uses IP addresses for logical addressing. TCP and UDP protocols are used at the Transport layer, which is layer 4. Hardware addresses are used at layer 2, the Data Link layer, and sending and receiving bits via hardware is done at the Physical layer (layer 1).

9. D. Most networks include many edge devices like wireless access points and edge switches. These devices often have a single power supply to balance cost against reliability and will simply be replaced if they fail. More critical devices like routers and core switches are typically equipped with redundant power supplies to ensure that larger segments of the network do not fail if a component fails. Of course, making sure devices are supported so they get updates and that they are under warranty are both common practices for supportable networks.

10. B. Brian is analyzing the jitter, which is the variance in delay between packets. This can indicate issues along the path the packets take. Latency is the time it takes a packet to reach its destination, throughput is a measure of the volume of traffic that can be sent, and signal to noise ratios compare the amount of desired information that is received versus the level of background noise or unwanted data.

11. B. The Remote Access Dial In User Service (RADIUS) protocol was originally designed to support dial-up modem connections but is still commonly used for VPN-based authentication. HTTPS is not an authentication protocol. ESP and AH are IPsec protocols but do not provide authentication services for other systems.

12. C. SIPS, the secure version of the Session Initialization Protocol for VoIP, adds TLS encryption to keep the session initialization process secure. SVOIP and PBSX are not real protocols, but SRTP is the secure version of RTP, the Real time Transport Protocol.

13. B. The firewall in the diagram has two protected zones behind it, making it a two-tier firewall design.

14. D. Segmentation is a critical concept for network designers. Remote PCs that connect to a protected network need to comply with security settings and standards that match those required for the internal network. The VPN concentrator logically places remote users in the protected zone behind the firewall, but that means user workstations (and users) must be trusted in the same way that local workstations are.

15. D. Micro-segmentation is used to logically separate systems and services by defining boundaries between them. This is often part of a zero trust architecture including the use of on-demand access to services. Converged protocols implement other protocols over another protocol like iSCSI or InfiniBand over Ethernet. Physical segmentation uses separate physical devices and infrastructure to provide segmentation. Edge networks place computation and storage closer to the end user.

16. B. Virtual routing and forwarding (VRF) is used to allow multiple routing tables to exist in a virtual router, all working simultaneously as defined by network traffic rules. A VPC may include VRF capabilities, but VRF would still be required to complete this requirement. VLANs are used to separate network segments, not to provide routing, and a content distribution network is used to provide high-performance, denial-of-service-resistant content replication and access from a large-scale network of replicas.

17. B. Disabling SSID broadcast can help prevent unauthorized personnel from attempting to connect to the network. Since the SSID is still active, it can be discovered by using a wireless sniffer. Encryption keys are not related to SSID broadcast, beacon frames are used to broadcast the SSID, and it is possible to have multiple networks with the same SSID.

18. A. Software-defined networking (SDN) uses code to configure and control the network. This allows for agile, programmatic control and configuration as needed from a central control point. SD-WAN provides the same sort of control for wide area network links, which aren't mentioned in this question. Proxy routing occurs when a proxy server routes traffic between clients and other systems, and agile networking is not a commonly used term.

19. C. iSCSI is a converged protocol that supports SCSI storage access via Ethernet. CXL is Compute Express Link, often used to interconnect memory, CPUs, and accelerators. SD-WAN is a software-defined wide area network, and Zigbee is a low-power wireless protocol.

20. B. Peering allows you to connect directly to a provider's network at a peering location where they provide edge facilities. This can reduce ingress/egress costs as well as provide direct paths to their networks and services. Replication of data is not an artifact of or a result of peering. Controlling traffic flows via software-defined routes is done using SD-WAN, and hosting copies of sites at multiple locations is a typical result of using a CDN.

21. C. Traffic sent between systems in the same data center is called east/west traffic since it does not flow across network boundaries. East/west traffic requires additional design work in many organizations if monitoring and other security is desired. Traffic that is external to the data center, either inbound or outbound, is called north/south traffic. Privileged/unprivileged and store/forward are not typically used to describe the traffic flows in the question.

22. A. Multilayer protocols like Distributed Network Protocol (DNP3) allow SCADA and other systems to use TCP/IP-based networks to communicate. Many SCADA devices were never designed to be exposed to a network, and adding them to a potentially insecure network can create significant risks. TLS or other encryption can be used on TCP packets, meaning that even serial data can be protected. Serial data can be carried via TCP packets because TCP packets don't care about their content; it is simply another payload. Finally, TCP/IP does not have a specific throughput as designed, so issues with throughput are device-level issues.

23. B. WPA3's simultaneous authentication of equals (SAE) mode improves on WPA2's pre-shared key (PSK) mode by allowing for secure authentication between clients and the wireless network without enterprise user accounts. If Ben needed to worry about support for WPA3, which may not be available to all systems that may want to connect, he might have to choose WPA2. A captive portal is often used with open guest networks but requires additional work to maintain, and Enterprise mode requires user accounts.

24. A. SMS messages are not encrypted, meaning that they could be sniffed and captured. While using two factors is more secure than a single factor, SMS is one of the less secure ways to implement two-factor authentication because of this. SMS messages can be spoofed, can be received by more than one phone, and are typically stored on the recipient's phone. The primary threat here, however, is the unencrypted message itself.

25. A. 802.11ac operates in the 5 GHz range. The 900 MHz range has frequently been used for phones and non-Wi-Fi wireless networks as well as other amateur radio uses, and 2.4 GHz is used by 802.11n and other protocols. Knowing that multiple ranges are available and that

they may behave differently based on how many access points are in use and whether other devices that may cause interference on that band are in the area can be important for wireless network deployments.

26. B. ARP and RARP operate at the Data Link layer, the second layer of the OSI model. Both protocols deal with physical hardware addresses, which are used above the Physical layer (layer 1) and below the Network layer (layer 3), thus falling at the Data Link layer.

27. D. Internet Small Computer Systems Interface (iSCSI) is a converged protocol that allows location-independent file services over traditional network technologies. It costs less than traditional Fibre Channel. VoIP is Voice over IP, SDN is software-defined networking, and MPLS is Multiprotocol Label Switching, a technology that uses path labels instead of network addresses.

28. A. A repeater, switch, or concentrator will amplify the signal, ensuring that the 100-meter distance limitation of 1000BaseT is not an issue. A gateway would be useful if network protocols were changing, while Cat7 cable is appropriate for a 10 Gbps network at much shorter distances. STP cable is limited to 155 Mbps and 100 meters, which would leave Chris with network problems.

29. B. The use of TCP port 80 indicates that the messaging service is using the HTTP protocol. Slack is a messaging service that runs over HTTPS, which uses port 443. SMTP is an email protocol that uses port 25.

30. C. HTTP traffic is typically sent via TCP80. Unencrypted HTTP traffic can be easily captured at any point between A and B, meaning that the messaging solution chosen does not provide confidentiality for the organization's corporate communications.

31. B. If a business need requires messaging, using a local messaging server is the best option. This prevents traffic from traveling to a third-party server and can offer additional benefits such as logging, archiving, and control of security options like the use of encryption.

32. B. Multilayer protocols create three primary concerns for security practitioners: they can conceal covert channels (and thus covert channels are allowed), filters can be bypassed by traffic concealed in layered protocols, and the logical boundaries put in place by network segments can be bypassed under some circumstances. Multilayer protocols allow encryption at various layers and support a range of protocols at higher layers.

33. A. Fibre Channel over Ethernet (FCoE), Internet Small Computer Systems Interface (iSCSI), and Voice over Internet Protocol (VoIP) are all examples of converged protocols that combine specialized protocols with standard protocols like TCP/IP. Multipurpose Internet Mail Extensions (MIIME) is not a converged protocol.

34. B. When a workstation or other device is connected simultaneously to both a secure network and a nonsecure network like the Internet, it may act as a bridge, bypassing the security protections located at the edge of a corporate network. It is unlikely that traffic will be routed improperly, leading to the exposure of sensitive data, as traffic headed to internal systems and networks is unlikely to be routed to the external network. Reflected DDoS attacks are used to hide identities rather than to connect through to an internal network, and security administrators of managed systems should be able to determine both the local and wireless IP addresses his system uses.

35. D. Observability focuses on the ability to see how an entire system, service, or environment is performing and behaving based on its external outputs. That means that telemetry data—information about what components are doing—is critical and will be gathered using logs, metrics, and real-time analysis. This means that centralizing and aggregating data, enabling alerts for critical errors, and implementing logging using standardized formats are all common practices. Feedback loops are also important, allowing administrators and others to take action when problems or issues are detected.

36. A. IPsec can provide encryption, access control, nonrepudiation, and message authentication using public key cryptography. It does not provide authorization, protocol convergence, content distribution, or the other items listed.

37. B. Zigbee uses AES to protect network traffic, providing integrity and confidentiality controls. It does not use 3DES, and ROT13 is a simple rotational cipher you might find in a cereal box or secret decoder ring.

38. C. The process of using a fake Media Access Control (MAC) address is called spoofing, and spoofing a MAC address already in use on the network can lead to an address collision, preventing traffic from reaching one or both systems. Tokens are used in token ring networks, which are outdated, and EUI refers to an Extended Unique Identifier, another term for MAC address, but token loss is still not the issue. Broadcast domains refer to the set of machines a host can send traffic to via a broadcast message.

39. C. While security features vary from provider to provider, encryption, device-based authentication (for example, using certificates), and SIM-based authentication are all common options for 4G connectivity solutions. Joanna should work with her provider to determine what capabilities are available and assess whether they meet her needs.

40. D. Application-specific protocols are handled at layer 7, the Application layer of the OSI model.

41. B. AVPC, or virtual private cloud, is the environment many organizations operate inside of public clouds. They provide on-demand access to configurable, shared resources operated by the cloud provider inside of their isolated boundaries. VLANs are used to logically separate networks; SDN is software-defined networking, which is typically part of how a VPC is implemented; and CXL, or Compute Express Link, is a converged protocol used to connect CPUs, GPUs, accelerators, and other components at high speeds.

42. D. 802.1x provides port-based authentication and can be used with technologies like the Extensible Authentication Protocol (EAP). 802.11a is a wireless standard, 802.3 is the standard for Ethernet, and 802.15.1 was the original Bluetooth IEEE standard.

43. D. 1000BaseT is capable of a 100-meter run according to its specifications. For longer distances and exterior runs, a fiber-optic cable is typically used in modern networks.

44. A. Port security prevents unrecognized or unpermitted systems from connecting to a network port based on their MAC address. Cloning a permitted or legitimate MAC address attempts to bypass this. VLAN hopping and 802.1q trunking attacks attempt to access other subnets by encapsulating packets so they will be unwrapped and directed to the other subnet. Etherkiller prevention is not a security setting or control.

45. C. Most modern applications support TLS throughout their communications allowing clients to securely connect to the service and to encrypt communications. VPN, either in software or hardware form, will be more complex and unwieldy. Software-based VPN would be more flexible, and hardware-based VPN would be more expensive and more complex. SIPS and SRTP are appropriate for a VoIP environment but are not generally a complete solution for a modern multimedia collaboration platform like Microsoft Teams, Zoom, or WebEx.

46. B. Zigbee is designed for this type of low-power, Internet of Things network, and would be the best option for Chris. Some versions of Bluetooth are designed to operate in low-power mode as well, but Bluetooth isn't in this list of answers. Wi-Fi requires more power, NFC is very short range and would not work across a building or room, and infrared requires line of sight and is rarely used for that reason.

47. C. Separate, physically isolated Ethernet networks that require strong authentication are a commonly used out-of-band (OOB) option. While direct physical access is also an acceptable out-of-band option, it does not work well in a complex, production-oriented environment where devices may not be safe or easy to access. Web clients and nonstandard ports are not out-of-band options as described.

48. A. A content delivery network run by a major provider can handle large-scale DDoS attacks more easily than any of the other solutions. Using DDoS mitigation techniques via an ISP is the next most useful capability, followed by both increases in bandwidth and increases in the number of servers in the web application cluster.

49. C. PPTP, L2F, L2TP, and IPsec are the most common VPN protocols. TLS is also used for an increasingly large percentage of VPN connections and may appear at some point in the CISSP exam. PPP is a dial-up protocol, LTP is not a protocol, and SPAP is the Shiva Password Authentication Protocol sometimes used with PPTP.

50. A, B. Wayne should consider the use of a dedicated VLAN for VoIP devices to help separate them from other networked devices, and he should also require the use of SIPS and SRTP, both secure protocols that will keep his VoIP traffic encrypted. Requiring the use of VPN for all remote VoIP devices is not necessary if SIPS and SRTP are in use, and a specific IPS for VoIP is not a typical deployment in most organizations.

51. C. The Physical layer includes electrical specifications, protocols, and standards that allow control of throughput, handling line noise, and a variety of other electrical interface and signaling requirements. The OSI layer doesn't have a Device layer. The Transport layer connects the Network and Session layers, and the Data Link layer packages packets from the network layer for transmission and receipt by devices operating on the Physical layer.

52. D. WPA3, the replacement for WPA2, adds security features including a new mode called simultaneous authentication of equals that replaces the pre-shared key mode from WPA2 with a more secure option. Overall, it provides security improvements but may not be immediately implemented due to time for hardware and software to fully support it. WPA2 has been the most commonly deployed wireless security standard having replaced WPA and WEP.

53. D. Cut-through switching forwards packets as soon as the destination address is known without waiting for the rest of the frame to arrive. This means that packets are not checked for integrity before being forwarded, optimizing throughput and reducing latency at the expense of error checking. Store-and-forward waits for the entire frame to allow it to be checked using a cyclic redundancy check (CRC) before forwarding it. Blind and forward switching were made up for this question.

54. A. The Transport layer provides logical connections between devices, including end-to-end transport services to ensure that data is delivered. Transport layer protocols include TCP, UDP, SSL, and TLS.

55. B. Machine Access Control (MAC) addresses are the hardware address the machine uses for layer 2 communications. The MAC addresses include an organizationally unique identifier (OUI), which identifies the manufacturer. MAC addresses can be changed, so this is not a guarantee of accuracy, but under normal circumstances you can tell what manufacturer made the device by using the MAC address.

56. C. For long-term connections like backhaul networks, a point-to-point VPN that is connected at all times is the most common choice to ensure all traffic is secured. TLS and SSH are commonly used to tunnel data but require additional attention to ensure that all traffic is tunneled. On-demand VPNs are more commonly used by users than for a connection like a backhaul network link.

57. C. Double NATing isn't possible with the same IP range; the same IP addresses cannot appear inside and outside a NAT router. RFC 1918 addresses are reserved, but only so they are not used and routable on the Internet, and changing to PAT would not fix the issue.

58. B. A Class B network holds 2^16 systems, and its default network mask is 255.255.0.0.

59. B. Enabling waiting rooms allows hosts to allow only intended attendees for events and meetings. Unfortunately, passcodes are easily shared, resulting in Zoom bombing despite the security they appear to offer. Meeting links are automatically generated and randomized, preventing brute forcing, and HTTPS is enabled by default for meetings.

60. A. Real-time fault monitoring for network devices and connections often relies on SNMP and ICMP-based monitoring capabilities. Netflow and syslog are more commonly used for diagnostic and analysis tasks.

61. A. VLAN hopping between the voice and computer VLANs can be accomplished when devices share the same switch infrastructure. Using physically separate switches can prevent this attack. Encryption won't help with VLAN hopping because it relies on header data that the switch needs to read (and this is unencrypted), while Caller ID spoofing is an inherent problem with VoIP systems. A denial of service is always a possibility, but it isn't specifically a VoIP issue, and a firewall may not stop the problem if it's on a port that must be allowed through.

62. A, B, D. RFC 1918 defines three address ranges as private (nonroutable) IP address ranges: 10.0.0.0/8, 172.16.0.0/12, and 192.168.0.0/16. Any of these would work, but many organizations use the 192.168.0.0/16 range for smaller sites or opt to carve out sections of the 10.0.0.0/8 range for multiple remote sites.

63. B. A captive portal is a popular solution that you may be familiar with from hotels and coffee shops. They combine the ability to gather data from customers with an open network, so customer data will not be encrypted. This avoids the need to distribute network passwords but means that customers must ensure their own traffic is encrypted if they are worried about security.

64. C. A UPS system, or uninterruptible power supply, is designed to provide backup power during brief power disruptions ranging from power sags and brownouts to temporary power failures. For a longer outage, Susan will still want a generator or even a secondary power feed from another power grid or provider if possible, but for this specific scenario, a UPS will meet her needs. Dual power supplies help when the concern is losing power from one power supply and would be a great idea for her most critical network devices, but it is rare to have dual power supplies for edge devices like access points or edge switches.

65. B. Fiber-optic cable is best suited to running 100 gigabit speeds. Cat5e, Cat6, and coaxial cable are not rated to those speeds.

66. A. Data streams are associated with the Application, Presentation, and Session layers. Once they reach the Transport layer, they become segments (TCP) or datagrams (UDP). From there, they are converted to packets at the Network layer, frames at the Data Link layer, and bits at the Physical layer.

67. C. If the devices still need to be in production but cannot be patched, Lucca's best option is to use a separate security device to protect them. It may be tempting to simply install a firewall on the device or to disable all the services it exposes to the network, but some devices may not have firewall software available, and even if they do, the underlying operating system may have vulnerabilities in its implementation of its network stack or other software that even a firewall could not protect. Unplugging devices that are needed for protection does not resolve the need to keep them online.

68. C. Software-defined networking provides a network architecture that can be defined and configured as code or software and separates routing processes from packet switching while centralizing control. The 5-4-3 rule is an old design rule for networks that relied on repeaters or hubs. A converged network carries multiple types of traffic like voice, video, and data. A hypervisor-based network may be software defined, but it could also use traditional network devices running as virtual machines.

69. A. Encapsulation adds to the header (and sometimes to the footer) of the data provided by the previous layer. The main body of the data is not modified, and encryption may happen but does not always happen.

70. D. A broken network cable is a layer 1 problem. If you encounter a problem like this and aren't sure, look for the answer that has a different situation or set of assumptions. Here you have three questions that occur at the network (layer 3), all of which have software or protocol implications. A broken network cable is a completely different type of issue and should stand out. Be careful, though! The exam is likely to give you two potentially valid answers to choose from, so work to get rid of the two least likely answers and spend your time on the remaining options.

71. D. Network segmentation can reduce issues with performance as well as diminish the chance of broadcast storms by limiting the number of systems in a segment. This decreases broadcast traffic visible to each system and can reduce congestion. Segmentation can also help provide security by separating functional groups that don't need to be able to access each other's systems. Installing a firewall at the border would only help with inbound and outbound traffic, not cross-network traffic. Spanning tree loop prevention helps prevent loops in Ethernet networks (for example, when you plug a switch into a switch via two ports on each), but it won't solve broadcast storms that aren't caused by a loop or security issues. Encryption might help prevent some problems between functional groups, but it won't stop them from scanning other systems, and it definitely won't stop a broadcast storm!

72. B. Bandwidth describes the maximum amount of data that can be sent via a connection or network in a given period of time, and throughput describes the actual amount of traffic that is sent via the network or connection in a given period of time. The terms are not interchangeable but are closely related.

73. D. In an IaaS environment, the company that provides the cloud environment has final control of all the virtual machines and networks. Thus, to protect data, the best option is to encrypt the data. Unfortunately, Ben cannot fully ensure that traffic in his environment is not being captured and must rely on the cloud hosting provider for that assurance. While preventing the installation of packet sniffers and taps and ensuring that promiscuous mode cannot be enabled are useful habits in an environment that you control, this will not provide the same control in a cloud environment.

74. A. Using the same IP range for an on-site and cloud-hosted data center can be helpful when designing a flat network, but addresses must be carefully managed and allocated even in a space as big as the 10.0.0.0/24 range. If addresses are not properly managed, conflicts may arise that could disrupt production services. MAC address conflicts should not arise unless addresses are manually changed or virtual machines are replicated without changing their MAC addresses. There is nothing in the problem to suggest routing issues.

75. C. A software-defined wide area network, or SD-WAN, is commonly used to manage multiple ISPs and other connectivity options to ensure speed, reliability, and bandwidth design goals are all met. Ben can use SD-WAN capabilities to accomplish his goals to make his hybrid cloud environment successful. Fibre Channel over Ethernet (FCoE) is a storage protocol; VXLAN is used for extensible virtual LANs, not WANs; and LiFi uses visible and infrared light to transfer data.

76. B. Traffic entering and leaving a network is often called north/south traffic. East/west traffic is traffic between systems inside of a network. Foreign/domestic is not a commonly used term, and trusted/untrusted cannot be determined without additional information.

77. A. CXL, or Compute Express Link, is a converged protocol that is an open standard for high-speed communications with accelerators, GPUs, CPUs, and similar devices. VoIP is a telephony protocol, CDNs are content distribution networks, and iSCSI is a converged storage protocol.

78. D. Fiber-optic cable is the most difficult of the listed types of network to capture data from without specialized equipment. Given access to a fiber-optic cable and specialized equipment to tap it, or with access to the endpoints of a fiber-optic cable and an optical tap, access can still be obtained. In either case, disruption may be observed when the cable is cut, spliced, or disconnected, and many attackers will not have access, skills, or the tools needed to do so. Wi-Fi and Bluetooth traffic can be captured using standard wireless cards and tools, and data carried by twisted-pair Ethernet cables is easily captured using commodity tools.

79. C. Buried fiber-optic cable is best suited to long distances, particularly when there are trees or other obstacles blocking line of sight that may interfere with Wi-Fi or LiFi deployments. Ethernet's distance limitations mean that repeaters would need to be powered, and there is no description of other structures or power along the path.

80. B. Endpoint security solutions face challenges due to the sheer volume of data that they can create. When each workstation is generating data about events, this can be a massive amount of data. Endpoint security solutions should reduce the number of compromises when properly implemented, and they can also help by monitoring traffic after it is decrypted on the local host. Finally, non-TCP protocols are relatively uncommon on modern networks, making this a relatively rare concern for endpoint security system implementations.

81. D. The IP address 127.0.0.1 is a loopback address and will resolve to the local machine. Public addresses are non–RFC 1918, nonreserved addresses. RFC 1918 addresses are reserved and include ranges like 10.x.x.x. An APIPA address is a self-assigned address used when a DHCP server cannot be found.

82. B. Since Bluetooth doesn't provide strong encryption, it should only be used for activities that are not confidential. Bluetooth PINs are four-digit codes that often default to 0000. Turning it off and ensuring that your devices are not in discovery mode can help prevent Bluetooth attacks.

83. C. The assignment of endpoint systems to VLANs is normally performed by a network switch.

84. C. Infiniband over Ethernet is commonly used for purposes like this, allowing direct memory access over Ethernet while providing high bandwidth and low latency. iSCSI is used for storage, VoIP is used for telephony, and Compute Express Link (CXL) is used for CPU to device and CPU to memory connections.

85. A, B, C. SD-WAN implementations typically perform all of these functions, combining active data collection via monitoring and response via self-learning and machine intelligence techniques and then applying predefined rules to take action to make the network perform as desired. SD-WAN does not imply or require that all connections are managed by the organization's primary Internet service provider. In fact, SD-WANs are often used to handle multiple ISPs to allow for failover and redundancy.

86. B. The OSI layers in order from layer 1 to layer 7 are as follows:

1. Physical

2. Data Link

3. Network

4. Transport

5. Session

6. Presentation

7. Application

87. C. Valerie is most likely trying to prevent content addressable memory (CAM) table or MAC address table flooding by preventing large numbers of MAC addresses from being used on a single port. If CAM table flooding is successful, switches will not know where to send traffic and resort to sending all traffic to every port, potentially exposing traffic to attackers. IP spoofing and VLAN hopping are not prevented by port security, which focuses on hardware (MAC) addresses. MAC aggregation was made up for this question.

88. C. A pre-admit, client-based NAC system will test systems before they are allowed on the network using a client that can determine more about a system than a clientless model can. Postadmission tests after clients are already on the network and clientless versions are useful when installing clients isn't possible for systems.

89. A. An active/active pair can use the full throughput capability of both devices, but normal deployment models will design to the maximum throughput of a single device to avoid disruption in the event that one of the pair fails. Active/passive designs can only handle the throughput of a single device and allow the secondary device to remain ready to operate but not passing traffic until it is needed. Line interactive is a term often used to describe UPS systems that filter power instead of passing it through, and near-line is a term used to describe backups that are not online but can be retrieved relatively quickly.

90. A. A VPN that allows access to secured VLANs is the most common security design for this type of infrastructure. This allows secured remote access while protecting IoT devices that are often unable to be properly secured and thus cannot be trusted on a more exposed network. IPS does not provide remote access, and private IP addresses alone do not provide a protected network. DLP is used to prevent data exfiltration and won't stop other attacks or provide remote management access. iSCSI is a storage protocol, not a security solution. A VPN and jump boxes are useful, but the devices would not be provided with additional security by iSCSi.

91. D. Most existing satellite internet systems have relatively high latency. Newer low Earth orbit satellites like Starlink appear to provide better latency than higher orbits, but latency and susceptibility to interference from weather are both common concerns for satellite-based systems.

92. C. The application plane of a software-defined network (SDN) is where applications run that use application programming interfaces (APIs) to communicate with the SDN about needed resources. The control plane receives instructions and sends them to the network. The last common plane is the data plane, which forwards devices handling data and takes inputs from the control plane. The monitoring plane is not a common layer in an SDN environment.

93. B. Common drawbacks of multilayer protocols are that they can bypass filters, allow or create covert channels, and allow network segment boundaries to be bypassed. The ability to operate at higher OSI layer levels is normally considered a benefit.

94. C. In order, the layers are Application layer, Transport layer, Internet layer, and Network Access layer.

95. B. Content distribution networks are used to both improve performance and reduce the impacts of denial-of-service attacks. Load-balanced server clusters may be part of the underlying design, but a CDN will more completely address Aadita's needs at the scale described. Micro-segmentation is used to isolate systems and services, not to address multiregion content accessibility and denial-of-service issues. A VPC may be part of a solution, but nothing about a VPC makes it a sufficient solution on its own.

96. B, C. 5G technology includes both a new mutual authentication capability and additional protections for subscriber identities. It does not have specific anti-jamming security features and does not specifically use multifactor authentication.

97. C. Virtual eXtensible LAN (VXLAN) tunnels layer 2 connections over a layer 3 network, in essence extending a LAN over distances or networks that it might not otherwise function over. It does not remove the distance limitations of Ethernet cables, nor does it allow multiple subnets to use the same IP space—that requires NAT or other technologies that remap addresses to avoid conflicts.

98. B. VLANs can be used to logically separate groups of network ports while still providing access to an uplink. Per-room VPNs would create significant overhead for support as well as create additional expenses. Port security is used to limit what systems can connect to ports, but it doesn't provide network security between systems. Finally, while firewalls might work, they would add expense and complexity without adding any benefits over a VLAN solution.

99. D. MAC addresses and their organizationally unique identifiers are used at the Data Link layer to identify systems on a network. The Application and Session layers don't care about physical addresses, while the Physical layer involves electrical connectivity and handling physical interfaces rather than addressing.

100. C. This diagram shows the use of the Session Initialization Protocol (SIP) instead of SIP Secure (SIPS), meaning that SIP is not encrypted. Fortunately, the voice data via the Secure Real-time Transport Protocol (SRTP) is encrypted. Mikayla should look into using SIPS in addition to SRTP.

101. D. Air-gaps are physical separations between systems or devices that prevent communications or connections between them. This prevents network-based attacks and limits the ways that attackers could access the devices. Store-and-forward stores communications and send them after checking for errors. In-band administration occurs over existing interfaces or connections; out-of-band administration uses a separate network or management interface.

Chapter 5: Identity and Access Management (Domain 5)

1. B. Single sign-on provides a single authentication process to allow authorization to multiple services. An access control list, or ACL, is a ruleset used to determine if a subject can gain access to a service or system. Multifactor requires multiple factors, and the specifics of how Henry logged in were not discussed in the question. Finally, role-based access control uses a subject's role(s) to determine if they can access a service or system, and no mention of roles was made.

2. B. Since Jim's organization is using a cloud-based identity as a service solution, a third-party, on-premises identity service can provide the ability to integrate with the IDaaS solution, and the company's use of Active Directory is widely supported by third-party vendors. OAuth is used to log in to third-party websites using existing credentials and would not meet the needs described. SAML is a markup language and would not meet the full set of AAA needs. Since the organization is using Active Directory, a custom in-house solution is unlikely to be as effective as a preexisting third-party solution and may take far more time and expense to implement.

3. D. A policy enforcement point in a zero trust environment receives authorization requests and then sends them to the policy decision point. They are used anywhere that authorization controls are needed. They do not make decisions for the policy engine, can exist beyond workstations and mobile devices, and use policies set at the zero trust control layer rather than just at the endpoint device.

4. C. Voice pattern recognition is "something you are," a biometric authentication factor, because it measures a physical characteristic of the individual authenticating.

5. B. Susan has used two distinct types of factors: the PIN and password are both Type 1 factors, and the retina scan is a Type 3 factor. Her username is not a factor.

6. C. Hardware Security Modules, or HSMs, are the most secure way to store keys associated with a CMS. They provide enhanced key management capabilities and are often required to be FIPS certified. In addition to these advantages, an HSM can improve cryptographic performance for the organization due to dedicated hardware designed for just that purpose. Long keys and using AES-256 are good practices, but an HSM provides greater security and will require appropriate cryptographic controls already. Changing passphrases can be challenging across an organization; instead, securing the passphrases and keys is more important and reasonable for most organizations.

7. B. Brian's organization is using a federated identity management approach where multiple organizations allow identities to be used across the organizations. Each organization needs to conduct identity proofing of their own staff members' identities and provide them with rights and role information that will allow them to use resources within the federated identity environment.

8. A. Authentication that takes attributes such as location, device, and time of day into account is context-aware authentication. This allows organizations to make choices about whether the authentication is appropriate and allowed in addition to the use of credentials. The decision is based on contextual information, not user knowledge or identity factors, which are used only to authenticate. Zero trust may leverage context information, but context-aware authentication alone does not indicate zero trust.

9. B. Decentralized access control can result in less consistency because the individuals tasked with control may interpret policies and requirements differently and may perform their roles in different ways. Access outages, overly granular control, and training costs may occur, depending on specific implementations, but they are not commonly identified issues with decentralized access control.

10. B. A callback to a landline phone number is an example of a "somewhere you are" factor because of the fixed physical location of a wired phone. A callback to a mobile phone would be a "something you have" factor.

11. B. The NIST recommendation to not expire passwords recognizes that users often make minimal changes to their passwords when they are required to change them. In addition, password changes drive significant support overhead as users forget their passwords or otherwise face challenges with them. Longer password lives do create the potential for attackers to have longer to compromise them, but modern password recommendations look for multifactor authentication, which means a compromised password is less of a threat. Hashing new passwords does require computation, but not a significant amount using modern hardware.

12. C. AAA refers to a set of security protocols that are used to identify and authorize users and record their activities. The acronym stands for authentication, authorization, and accounting.

13. A. Active Directory relies on the Lightweight Directory Access Protocol (LDAP) as part of its single sign-on (SSO) implementation. Zero trust is not a SSO implementation, and Shibboleth is an open-source identity management system. RADIUS is not a single sign-on implementation, although some vendors use it behind the scenes to provide authentication for proprietary SSO.

14. B. Knowledge-based authentication relies on information that only the individual who wants to prove their identity is likely to know. This might include a mortgage payment amount, vehicle information, or driver's license number among many options. Cognitive passwords, or security questions, are created by users, which means they aren't suited to this type of identity proofing. Palm scans and USB tokens both require prior engagement with the user as well and thus aren't suited for identity proofing with users who are new customers.

15. D. When the owner of a file makes the decisions about who has rights or access privileges to it, they are using discretionary access control. Role-based access controls would grant access based on a subject's role, while rule-based controls would base the decision on a set of rules or requirements. Nondiscretionary access controls apply a fixed set of rules to an environment to manage access. Nondiscretionary access controls include rule-, role-, and lattice-based access controls.

16. D. Need to know is applied when subjects like Alex have access to only the data they need to accomplish their job. Separation of duties is used to limit fraud and abuse by having multiple employees perform parts of a task. Constrained interfaces restrict what a user can see or do and would be a reasonable answer if need to know did not describe his access more completely in this scenario. Context-dependent control relies on the activity being performed to apply controls, and this question does not specify a workflow or process.

17. D. Password history tracks what passwords have been set previously and will not allow reuse. A specific number of past passwords is typically set, and passwords themselves should not be retained. Instead, properly secured hashes are retained and compared to hashes of the new passwords. Length, maximum age, and MFA do not solve the issue of password reuse.

18. C. Ifeoma knows that a minimum password age of one day will discourage users from resetting their passwords to attempt to return to their original password. Length and complexity do not prevent this if the original password met these requirements, and a maximum age is set in organizations that require password changes on a recurring basis.

19. A. Requiring multifactor authentication (MFA) is a common security measure used to prevent unauthorized access to an account in case of password loss or exposure. SSO allows the use of an account throughout systems or services. Federation connects different organizations together, allowing the use of credentials between trusted partners, and password rotation can help, but lost passwords remain dangerous until the rotation happens allowing days, weeks, or even months of potential vulnerable time.

20. A. Retina scans can reveal additional information, including high blood pressure and pregnancy, causing privacy concerns. Newer retina scans don't require a puff of air, and retina scanners are not the most expensive biometric factor. Their false positive rate can typically be adjusted in software, allowing administrators to adjust their acceptance rate as needed to balance usability and security.

21. C. Mandatory access control systems are based on a lattice-based model. Lattice-based models use a matrix of classification labels to compartmentalize data. Discretionary access models allow object owners to determine access to the objects they control, role-based access controls are often group-based, and rule-based access controls like firewall ACLs apply rules to all subjects they apply to.

22. D. Using an enterprise authentication system like Active Directory that requires individuals to log in with their credentials provides the ability to determine who was logged in if a problem occurs and also allows Greg to quickly and easily remove users who are terminated or switch roles. Using a shared PIN provides no accountability, while unique PINs per user on specifically issued iPads mean that others will not be able to log in. OAuth alone does not provide the services and features Greg needs—it is an authorization service, not an authentication service.

23. A. Logging systems can provide accountability for identity systems by tracking the actions, changes, and other activities a user or account performs. Authorization does not provide accountability because it validates that a person can perform an action, not who is using the identity. Digital signatures can be used to validate an identity, not to provide accountability by proving who is using it, and Type 1 authentication is something you know. Again, logging is the best way to provide accountability for the use of an identity.

24. B. As an employee's role changes, they often experience privilege creep, which is the accumulation of old rights and roles. Account review is the process of reviewing accounts and ensuring that their rights match their owners' role and job requirements. Account revocation removes accounts, while re-provisioning might occur if an employee was terminated and returned or took a leave of absence and returned.

25. A. Biba uses a lattice to control access and is a form of the mandatory access control (MAC) model. It does not use rules, roles, or attributes, nor does it allow user discretion. Users can create content at their level or lower but cannot decide who gets access, levels are not roles, and attributes are not used to make decisions on access control.

26. C. RADIUS is an AAA protocol used to provide authentication and authorization; it's often used for modems, wireless networks, and network devices. It uses network access servers to send access requests to central RADIUS servers. Kerberos is a ticket-based authentication protocol; OAuth is an open standard for authentication allowing the use of credentials from one site on third-party sites; and EAP is the Extensible Authentication Protocol, an authentication framework often used for wireless networks.

27. A. Session identifiers should not be predictable to ensure that attackers can't simply guess or easily brute force session IDS. Web application development best practices currently recommend the use of long session IDs (128 bits or longer) that have sufficient entropy (randomness) to ensure that they will not be easily duplicated or brute-forced. It is also a best practice to make sure the session ID itself is meaningless to prevent information disclosure attacks. Session IDs should expire, however, because a session that never expires could eventually be brute-forced even if all of these recommendations were met.

28. B. Passwordless authentication leverages applications and capabilities such as built-in biometric authentication mechanisms. Extended and alternative authentication are not terms used on the exam. The Fast Identity Online Alliance (FIDO) is an open industry association that provides frameworks for passwordless authentication, but SPOT is not a type of passwordless authentication.

29. B. The posturing capability of network access control (NAC) determines if a system is sufficiently secure and compliant enough to connect to a network. This is a form of risk-based access control, as systems that are not compliant are considered higher risk and either are placed in a quarantine and remediation network or zone or are prohibited from connecting to the network until they are compliant.

30. D. Authorization provides a user with capabilities or rights. Roles and group management are both methods that could be used to match users with rights. Logins are used to validate a user.

31. C. Privilege creep occurs when users retain rights they do not need to accomplish their current job from roles they held previously. Unauthorized access occurs when an unauthorized user accesses files. Excessive provisioning is not a term used to describe permissions issues, and account review would help find issues like this.

32. A. Multifactor authentication is most likely to limit horizontal privilege escalation by making it difficult to access user accounts and to authenticate to a compromised account. Limiting permissions for groups and accounts can also help, but disabling unused ports and services and sanitizing user inputs both address threats that are most frequently associated with vertical privilege escalation attacks.

33. C. Hybrid systems use both on-premises and cloud identity and services to provide resources and tools in both environments. While they can be complex, hybrid systems also provide a migration path to a full cloud deployment or for a fault-tolerant design that can handle on-premises or cloud outages while remaining functional.

34. C. Mandatory access controls (MAC) use a lattice or matrix to describe how classification labels relate to each other. In this image, classification levels are set for each of the labels shown. A discretionary access control (DAC) system would show how the owner of the objects allows access. RBAC could be either rule- or role-based access control and would use either system-wide rules or roles. Task-based access control (TBAC) would list tasks for users.

35. D. Copying existing rights to new groups that have different needs will often result in overly broad privileges. Michelle should create new groups, move all staff into the appropriate groups, and then ensure that they have the access and permissions they need.

36. B. The process of a subject claiming or professing an identity is known as identification. Authorization verifies the identity of a subject by checking a factor like a password. Logins typically include both identification and authorization, and token presentation is a type of authentication.

37. A. Service accounts are commonly set to not have expiring passwords to prevent service outages. Organizations may choose to rotate passwords on a regular basis using automation tools as part of their password management strategy to help avoid issues with exposed or compromised service passwords. Disabling complexity requirements and setting a minimum password age are not commonly done for service accounts.

38. B. Password complexity is driven by length, and a longer password will be more effective against brute-force attacks than a shorter password. Each character of additional length increases the difficulty by the size of the potential character set (for example, a single lowercase character makes the passwords 26 times more difficult to crack). While each of the other settings is useful for a strong password policy, they won't have the same impact on brute-force attacks.

39. A. Interactive login for a service account is a critical warning sign, either of compromise or bad administrative practices. In either case, Alaina should immediately work to determine why the account logged in, what occurred, and if the interactive login was done remotely or locally. A remote interactive login for a service account in any professionally maintained environment is an almost guaranteed sign of compromise. Password changes for service accounts may be done as part of ongoing password expiration processes, limitations should always be placed on service accounts rights to ensure that they are only those required, and a local use of the service account as part of the service is a normal event.

40. A. Organizations that have very strict security requirements that don't have a tolerance for false acceptance want to lower the false acceptance rate, or FAR, to be as near to zero as possible. That often means that the false rejection rate, or FRR, increases. Different biometric technologies or a better registration method can help improve biometric performance, but false rejections due to data quality are not typically a concern with modern biometric systems. In this case, knowing the crossover error rate, or CER, or having a very high CER doesn't help the decision.

41. C. The most efficient use of Derek's time would be to create a group that is populated with all maintenance staff and then to give that group login rights only to the designated PCs. While time-based constraints might help, in this case, it would continue to allow maintenance staff to log in to PCs that are not intended for use during business hours, leaving a gap in the control. Multifactor authentication, as described, does not meet the requirements of the scenario but may be a good idea overall for greater security for authentication across the organization. Geofencing is typically not accurate enough to rely on inside buildings for specific PCs.

42. B, C. Common session management techniques include the use of cookies, hidden form fields, URL rewriting, and built-in frameworks like Java's HTTPS session. IP tracking may be included in session information but is not itself a complete session identifier, and TLS token binding is used to make TLS sessions more secure, not to provide session identification.

43. C. TLS provides message confidentiality and integrity, which can prevent eavesdropping. When paired with digital signatures, which provide integrity and authentication, forged assertions can also be defeated. SAML does not have a security mode and relies on TLS and digital signatures to ensure security if needed. Message hashing without a signature would help prevent modification of the message but won't necessarily provide authentication.

44. B. Integration with cloud-based third parties that rely on local authentication can fail if the local organization's Internet connectivity or servers are offline. Adopting a hybrid cloud and local authentication system can ensure that Internet or server outages are handled, allowing authentication to work regardless of where the user is or if their home organization is online. Using encrypted and signed communication does not address availability, redirects are a configuration issue with the third party, and a local gateway won't handle remote users. Also, host files don't help with availability issues with services other than DNS.

45. A. While many solutions are technical, if a trusted third party redirects to an unexpected authentication site, awareness is often the best defense. Using TLS would keep the transaction confidential but would not prevent the redirect. Handling redirects locally works only for locally hosted sites, and using a third-party service requires off-site redirects. An IPS might detect an attacker's redirect, but tracking the multitude of load-balanced servers most large providers use can be challenging, if not impossible. In addition, an IPS relies on visibility into the traffic, and SAML integrations should be encrypted for security, which would require a man-in-the-middle type of IPS to be configured.

46. B. Discretionary access control (DAC) can provide greater scalability by leveraging many administrators, and those administrators can add flexibility by making decisions about access to their objects without fitting into an inflexible mandatory access control system (MAC).

MAC is more secure due to the strong set of controls it provides, but it does not scale as well as DAC and is relatively inflexible in comparison.

47. C. While signature-based detection is used to detect attacks, review of provisioning processes typically involves checking logs, reviewing the audit trail, or performing a manual review of permissions granted during the provisioning process.

48. A. SAML is an open, XML-based standard used to provide authorization, attribute information, and authentication data. SOAP, or Simple Object Access Protocol, is a messaging protocol and could be used for any XML messaging but is not a markup language itself. OAuth is an authorization framework that exchanges information using APIs, and OpenID Connect is an authentication layer using OAuth that provides both authentication and authorization, but not attribute information.

49. C. Rainbow tables are databases of pre-hashed passwords paired with high-speed lookup functions. Since they can quickly compare known hashes against those in a file, using rainbow tables is the fastest way to quickly determine passwords from hashes. A brute-force attack may eventually succeed but will be very slow against most hashes. Pass-the-hash attacks rely on sniffed or otherwise acquired NTLM or LanMan hashes being sent to a system to avoid the need to know a user's password. Salts are data added to a hash to avoid the use of tools like rainbow tables. A salt added to a password means the hash won't match a rainbow table generated without the same salt.

50. B. Google's federation with other applications and organizations allows single sign-on as well as management of their electronic identity and its related attributes. While this is an example of SSO, it goes beyond simple single sign-on. Provisioning provides accounts and rights, and a public key infrastructure is used for certificate management.

51. D. When users have more rights than they need to accomplish their job, they have excessive privileges. This is a violation of the concept of least privilege. Unlike privilege creep, this is a provisioning or rights management issue rather than a problem of retention of rights the user needed but no longer requires. Rights collision is a made-up term and thus is not an issue here.

52. B. Registration is the process of adding a user to an identity management system. This includes creating their unique identifier and adding any attribute information that is associated with their identity. Proofing occurs when the user provides information to prove who they are. Directories are managed to maintain lists of users, services, and other items. Session management tracks application and user sessions.

53. A, B. Audit logging when combined with user accounts that can reliably be expected to be accessible only to a specific user due to the use of multifactor authentication is frequently used to provide strong accountability for actions taken via systems and applications. A password can be shared, making it less reliable, and time and location requirements are useful security controls but do not impact accountability.

54. D. OAuth is the most widely used open standard for authorization and delegation of rights for cloud services. OpenID is used for authentication, and TACACS+ and RADIUS are primarily used on-site for authentication and authorization for network devices.

55. D. Cameron is using a just-in-time (JIT) system that provides the access needed when it is needed. A zero trust system requires authentication and authorization when actions are performed but does not necessarily require privileges to be granted and removed when they are needed.

56. C. Identity proofing can be done by comparing user information that the organization already has, like account numbers or personal information. Requiring users to create unique questions can help with future support by providing a way for them to do password resets. Using a phone call only verifies that the individual who created the account has the phone that they registered and won't prove their identity. In-person verification would not fit the business needs of most websites.

57. A. In federated systems, a user's access to services is authenticated through their own organization's identity provider (IDP). Service providers query those IDPs when the user attempts to authenticate to the service and, if the request is validated, allow access based on the rules and policies set for the service based on attributes that may be relevant that are provided by the IDP.

58. C. Type 2 errors occur in biometric systems when an invalid subject is incorrectly authenticated as a valid user. In this case, nobody except the actual customer should be validated when fingerprints are scanned. Type 1 errors occur when a valid subject is not authenticated; if the existing customer is rejected, it is a Type 1 error. Registration is the process of adding users, but registration errors and time of use, method of use errors are not specific biometric authentication terms.

59. B. Firewalls use rule-based access control, or Rule-BAC, in their access control lists and apply rules created by administrators to all traffic that passes through them. DAC, or discretionary access control, allows owners to determine who can access objects they control, while task-based access control lists tasks for users. MAC, or mandatory access control, uses classifications to determine access.

60. C. When you input a username and password, you are authenticating yourself by providing a unique identifier and a verification that you are the person who should have that identifier (the password). Authorization is the process of determining what a user is allowed to do. Validation and login both describe elements of what is happening in the process; however, they aren't the most important identity and access management activity.

61. C. Kathleen should implement a biometric factor. The cards and keys are an example of a Type 2 factor, or "something you have." Using a smart card replaces this with another Type 2 factor, but the cards could still be loaned out or stolen. Adding a PIN would address the problem by adding a second authentication factor, but PINs may be written down and are prone to theft or even guessing for shorter PINs, so a biometric factor is preferable if it is available. Adding cameras doesn't prevent access to the facility and thus doesn't solve the immediate problem (but it is a good idea!).

62. C. Enterprise credential management tools, often called password vaults, allow passwords to be securely generated, stored, and managed. They can provide logs of who uses passwords, when they were updated, and if they meet complexity and other requirements. Of course, this means the keys to your environment are all in one place, so securing and managing the enterprise password manager is very important!

63. B. The sudoers file can list the specific users who can use sudo as well as the commands or directories that are allowed for them.

64. C. In a mandatory access control system, all subjects and objects have a label. Compartments may or may not be used, but there is not a specific requirement for either subjects or objects to be compartmentalized. The specific labels of Confidential, Secret, and Top Secret are not required by MAC.

65. D. Passwords are never stored for web applications in a well-designed environment. Instead, salted hashes are stored and compared to passwords after they are salted and hashed. If the hashes match, the user is authenticated.

66. C. When a third-party site integrates via OAuth 2.0, authentication is handled by the service provider's servers. In this case, Google is acting as the service provider for user authentication. Authentication for local users who create their own accounts would occur in the e-commerce application (or a related server), but that is not the question that is asked here.

67. B. The anti-forgery state token exchanged during OAuth sessions is intended to prevent cross-site request forgery (CSRF). This makes sure that the unique session token with the authentication response from Google's OAuth service is available to verify that the user, not an attacker, is making a request. XSS attacks focus on scripting and would have script tags involved, SQL injection would have SQL code included, and XACML is the eXtensible Access Control Markup Language, not a type of attack.

68. A. Knowledge-based authentication relies on preset questions such as "What is your pet's name?" and the answers. It can be susceptible to attacks because of the availability of the answers on social media or other sites. Dynamic knowledge-based authentication relies on facts or data that the user already knows that can be used to create questions they can answer on an as-needed basis (for example, a previous address or a school they attended). Out-of-band identity proofing relies on an alternate channel like a phone call or text message. Finally, Type 3 authentication factors are biometric, or "something you are," rather than knowledge-based.

69. C. An access control matrix is a table that lists objects, subjects, and their privileges. Access control lists focus on objects and which subjects can access them. Capability tables list subjects and what objects they can access. Subject/object rights management systems are not based on an access control model.

70. C. Self-service password reset tools typically have a significant impact on the number of password reset contacts that a help desk has. Two-factor and biometric authentication both add complexity and may actually increase the number of contacts. Passphrases can be easier to remember than traditional complex passwords and may decrease calls, but they don't have the same impact that a self-service system does.

71. C. RADIUS supports TLS over TCP. RADIUS does not have a supported TLS mode over UDP. AES pre-shared symmetric ciphers are not a supported solution and would be difficult to both implement and maintain in a large environment, and the built-in encryption in RADIUS only protects passwords.

72. B. OAuth provides the ability to access resources from another service and would meet Jim's needs. OpenID would allow him to use an account from another service with his application, and Kerberos and LDAP are used more frequently for in-house services.

73. B. Since physical access to the workstations is part of the problem, setting application timeouts and password-protected screensavers with relatively short inactivity timeouts can help prevent unauthorized access. Using session IDs for all applications and verifying system IP addresses would be helpful for online attacks against applications.

74. A. This diagram shows an example of hybrid federation where authentication occurs on-premises and services are provided through a federated identity service in the cloud.

75. B, C. The best answers in the scenario that Chris faces are either RFID or magstripe readers and PIN pads. Guards create ongoing expenses, and any solution without a PIN will allow a stolen or cloned badge to be used without validating that the person accessing the building is a legitimate user. While a guard can prevent a stolen badge and PIN combination, this is only used in environments where the cost is justifiable.

76. A. Yubikeys, Titan Security Keys, and similar devices are examples of tokens. PIV stands for personal identity verification and is a full multifactor authentication solution, not a device. Biometric identifiers are something you are, and a smart card is a card with an embedded chip.

77. C. OpenID Connect is a RESTful, JSON-based authentication protocol that, when paired with OAuth, can provide identity verification and basic profile information. SAML is the Security Assertion Markup Language, Shibboleth is a federated identity solution designed to allow web-based SSO, and Higgins is an open-source project designed to provide users with control over the release of their identity information.

78. C. In a mandatory access control system, the operating system enforces access control, and users cannot delegate rights. Discretionary access control allows users to delegate rights, and neither attribute nor role-based access control specifically meets these requirements.

79. D. In a zero trust reference model-based design, subjects connect through a policy enforcement point. The policy engine makes policy decisions based on rules that are then acted on by the policy administrator, granting or denying access to enterprise resources. Constrained interfaces limit user actions but are not the component connected through to conduct transactions.

80. C. Synchronous soft tokens, such as Google Authenticator, use a time-based algorithm that generates a constantly changing series of codes. Asynchronous tokens typically require a challenge to be entered on the token to allow it to calculate a response, which the server compares to the response it expects. Smartcards typically present a certificate but may have other token capabilities built-in. Static tokens are physical devices that can contain credentials and include smart cards and memory cards.

81. B. Kerberos, RADIUS, and TACACS+ are all commonly used for internal networks. SENTRY was made up for this question.

82. B. Knowledge-based authentication is used by some financial institutions to validate the identity of new users. It uses information from tax and financial records that is unlikely to be available to others, allowing new users to provide details like their last credit card payment, mortgage payment, or other information to validate their identity. A Social Security number is somewhat trivial to acquire via paid services or other means, and manually validating identities is neither quick nor automatic. A biometric factor would require a previous enrollment, making this unsuitable for new customers.

83. B, C. Google accounts, like many cloud identity providers, rely on OpenID and OAuth. Kerberos is used for on-premises environments, and RADIUS is frequently used for authentication and authorization for network devices and services like VPN.

84. C. Best practices for session management involve a long session ID (often 128 bits or longer) and enough randomness or entropy to make it hard to guess session IDs. This makes brute-force or algorithmic guessing attacks unlikely unless there is a flaw in the implementation. These do not prevent denial-of-service or man-in-the-middle attacks, and cookie attacks are focused on acquiring and reading or reusing cookies in most scenarios.

85. D. Risk-based access control models risk using information that is available when the access request is created. Information about the request and the risk it may create is calculated based on risk values and compared to access policies. If the risk value is acceptable, access is granted. One of the most common examples of this in organizations is NAC, or network access control, where a system is profiled to determine security risk and compliance before admission to a network. This can be seen as a more specific example of rule-based access control. Role-based access control bases its decisions on the roles of the individuals, whereas mandatory access control is enforced by the operating system.

86. A. The most important step in securing service accounts is to ensure that they have only the rights that are absolutely needed to accomplish the task they are designed for. Disabling interactive logins is important as well and would be the next best answer. Limiting when accounts can log in and using randomized or meaningless account names can both be helpful in some circumstances but are far less important.

87. B. The NIST zero trust reference design includes both the Policy Engine and the Policy Administrator as part of the policy decision point. The terms *control plane module*, *enterprise management console*, and *zero trust engine* are not used in this context.

88. C. Federation does not necessarily guarantee that services will be shared or made accessible. Member organizations can choose which services they provide and can use more granular controls like role- or organization-based permissions to grant access to services. Payment may be part of a federation agreement or service access, but simply federating does not create or prevent a financial requirement.

89. A. Attributes used for ABAC often fall into one of four categories: subject attributes such as department or title; action attributes such as the ability to view, edit, or delete; object attributes that describe the object that can be impacted; and contextual attributes such as location, time, or elements. Discretionary access control would place these decisions in the hands of trusted subjects, MAC would enforce it at the operating system level, and role BAC would use only roles instead of the full set of criteria Kristen wants to apply.

90. D. The Linux filesystem allows the owners of objects to determine the access rights that subjects have to them. This means that it is a discretionary access control. If the system enforced a role-based access control, Alex wouldn't set the controls; they would be set based on the roles assigned to each subject. A rule-based access control system would apply rules throughout the system, and a mandatory access control system uses classification labels.

91. B. Privilege creep is a constant concern when staff change roles over time. Privileges from previous roles may be easy to forget or to retain during transition because staff may continue to help cover the tasks or processes the individual previously performed. Over time, these forgotten rights and privileges can stack, leaving the staff member with rights that their current role should not have. Registration is a concern for new staff, while de-provisioning is a concern for departing staff. Accountability is typically provided by IAM systems by authenticating and logging access and privilege usage.

92. A. This is a role-based access control (RBAC) chart noting that each group has specific rights by roles. Attribute-based access control (ABAC) would use other attributes including things like location, mandatory access control (MAC) would be enforced by the operating system, and discretionary access control (DAC) allows subjects like users to set rights on objects they control.

93. A. Ensure that users cannot bypass logging by switching to the root user using `sudo su -`. Instead, users who need the ability to perform privileged actions should be added to the `sudoers` list and then logged as themselves performing the actions. Adding all users is likely an overly broad action, whereas removing all users would not allow individual logging under their accounts, nor would they have rights to take administrative actions. Disabling `sudo` doesn't allow administrative tasks except as root, which defeats this requirement as well.

94. C. Single sign-on (SSO) is part of identity federation. It also means that account management is simpler since multiple accounts don't have to be maintained for users who need to access systems and resources across the federation. Productivity can increase because staff don't have to remember multiple logins and can use SSO to log in once instead of multiple times. It does not, however, do anything to prevent brute-force attacks, and in fact, a single account with broad access can make it easier for an attacker to gain that broader access unless solutions like multifactor authentication are put in place.

95. A. A JIT, or just-in-time, provisioning mechanism creates accounts when they are needed rather than creating them in advance. This is an effective method to limit the number of accounts being maintained and can be useful if the number of accounts are part of a licensing agreement that may drive costs higher if users who don't need accounts or are not using them have them. OAuth, OpenID, and Kerberos are not mentioned in the question.

96. B. Windows uses Kerberos for authentication. RADIUS is typically used for wireless networks, modems, and network devices, while OAuth is primarily used for web applications. TACACS+ is used for network devices.

97. D. When very high levels of control are needed or when endpoint devices cannot be trusted, using a centralized environment with remote connectivity and enterprise authentication can provide appropriate security.

98.

1. E

2. B

3. D

4. C

5. A

99. The security controls match with the categories as follows:

1. Password: B. Something you know

2. ID card: A. Something you have

3. Retinal scan: C. Something you are

4. Smartphone token: A. Something you have

5. Fingerprint analysis: C. Something you are

100.

1. A

2. E

3. D

4. B

5. C

Chapter 6: Security Assessment and Testing (Domain 6)

1. B. TCP and UDP ports 137–139 are used for NetBIOS services, whereas 445 is used for Active Directory. TCP 1433 is the default port for Microsoft SQL, indicating that this is probably a Windows server providing SQL services.

2. D. Mutation testing modifies a program in small ways and then tests that mutant to determine if it behaves as it should or if it fails. This technique is used to design and test software tests through mutation. Static code analysis and regression testing are both means of testing code, whereas code auditing is an analysis of source code rather than a means of designing and testing software tests.

3. B. TCP port 443 normally indicates an HTTPS server. Nikto is useful for vulnerability scanning web servers and applications and is the best choice listed for a web server. Metasploit includes some scanning functionality but is not a purpose-built tool for vulnerability scanning. zzuf is a fuzzing tool and isn't relevant for vulnerability scans, whereas sqlmap is a SQL injection testing tool.

4. A. Syslog is a widely used protocol for event and message logging. Eventlog, netlog, and Remote Log Protocol are all made-up terms.

5. C. Fuzzers are tools designed to provide invalid or unexpected input to applications, testing for vulnerabilities like format string vulnerabilities, buffer overflow issues, and other problems. A static analysis relies on examining code without running the application or code and thus would not fill forms as part of a web application. Brute-force tools attempt to bypass security by trying every possible combination for passwords or other values. A black box is a type of penetration test where the testers do not know anything about the environment.

6. B. OpenVAS is an open-source vulnerability scanning tool that will provide Susan with a report of the vulnerabilities that it can identify from a remote, network-based scan. Nmap is an open-source port scanner. Both the Microsoft Baseline Security Analyzer (MBSA) and Nessus are closed-source tools, although Nessus was originally open source.

7. B. CVSS, the Common Vulnerability Scoring System, is used to describe the severity of security vulnerabilities. CCE is Common Configuration Enumeration, a naming system for configuration issues. CPE is Common Platform Enumeration, which names operating systems, applications, and devices. OVAL is a language for describing security testing procedures.

8. C. Jim has agreed to a black-box penetration test, which provides no information about the organization, its systems, or its defenses. A crystal- or white-box penetration test provides all of the information an attacker needs, whereas a gray-box penetration test provides some, but not all, information.

9. A. The key to answering this question correctly is understanding the difference between SOC 1 and SOC 2 reports, and Type I and Type II audits. SOC 1 reports cover financial reporting, and SOC 2 reports look at security. Type I audits cover only a single point in time and are based on management descriptions of controls. They do not include an assessment of operating effectiveness. Type II audits cover a period of time and include an assessment of operating effectiveness.

10. B. WPA3 uses SAE, or simultaneous authentication of equals, and does not send the password over the air. Traditional cracking methods used against previous versions of WPA and WPA2 no longer work. This is not because of complex passwords or MFA, but because of how the handshake's elements are created to avoid sending the password.

11. D. In many cases when an exploit is initially reported, there are no prebuilt signatures or detections for vulnerability scanners, and the CVE database may not immediately have information about the attack. Jacob's best option is to quickly gather information and review potentially vulnerable servers based on their current configuration. As more information becomes available, signatures and CVE information are likely to be published. Unfortunately for Jacob, IDS and IPS signatures will detect only attacks and won't detect whether systems are vulnerable unless he sees the systems being exploited.

12. C. Interface testing is used to ensure that software modules properly meet interface specifications and thus will properly exchange data. Dynamic testing tests software in a running environment, whereas fuzzing is a type of dynamic testing that feeds invalid input to running software to test error and input handling. API checksums are not a testing technique.

13. B. Using a third-party auditor from a well-known and well-regarded firm is often the best option when providing audit and compliance information to third parties. Selah could engage an appropriate vendor for a SOC 2 Type II engagement as one example of a reasonable option to provide detail to her customers. Internal staff assessing against a common standard like COBIT would be the next most acceptable option on this list, with an internal standard less useful than that. Finally, relying on internal personnel not specialized in audits proves to be the least effective strategy in this context.

14. C. Breach and attack simulation (BAS) systems combine red team (attack) and blue team (defense) techniques together with automation to simulate advanced persistent threats and other advanced threat actors when run against your environment. This allows a variety of threats to be replicated and assessed in an environment without as much overhead as a fully staffed purple team would.

15. D. Most organizations use surveys to assess security awareness. Phishing simulators are also frequently used, but only test awareness of phishing issues and techniques, not general security awareness. Gamified applications are continuing to grow in popularity, but the ease of use and availability of surveys make them the most popular. Finally, assessment tests may be used when compliance knowledge assessments are required to meet a specific standard, but testing is not as common as surveying.

16. D. The IP addresses that his clients have provided are RFC 1918 nonroutable IP addresses, and Jim will not be able to scan them from off-site. To succeed in his penetration test, he will have to either first penetrate their network border or place a machine inside their network

to scan from the inside. IP addresses overlapping is not a real concern for scanning, and the ranges can easily be handled by current scanning systems.

17. B. Ethical (or responsible) disclosure practices will provide companies and organizations with a reasonable period of time to fix a flaw and to get that fix into the hands of their customers. Two weeks is unlikely to be a reasonable amount of time for this. Unfortunately, Mark may not be able to persuade the individual to make a different decision, and Mark's company will need to determine what to do about the issue.

18. B. Group Policy enforced by Active Directory can ensure consistent logging settings and can provide regular enforcement of policy on systems. Periodic configuration audits won't catch changes made between audits, and local policies can drift due to local changes or differences in deployments. A Windows syslog client will enable the Windows systems to send syslog to the SIEM appliance but won't ensure consistent logging of events.

19. B. Windows systems generate logs in the Windows native logging format. To send syslog events, Windows systems require a helper application or tool. Enterprise wireless access points, firewalls, and Linux systems all typically support syslog.

20. B. Network Time Protocol (NTP) can ensure that systems are using the same time, allowing time sequencing for logs throughout a centralized logging infrastructure. Syslog is a way for systems to send logs to a logging server and won't address time sequencing. Neither logsync nor SNAP is an industry term.

21. A. When a tester does not have raw packet creation privileges, such as when they have not escalated privileges on a compromised host, a TCP connect scan can be used. TCP SYN scans require elevated privileges on most Linux systems due to the need to write raw packets. A UDP scan will miss most services that are provided via TCP, and an ICMP is merely a ping sweep of systems that respond to pings and won't identify services at all.

22. B. Joseph may be surprised to discover FTP (TCP port 21) and Telnet (TCP port 23) open on his network since both services are unencrypted and have been largely replaced by SSH, and SCP or SFTP. SSH uses port 22, SMTP uses port 25, and POP3 uses port 110.

23. D. Large organizations hire QSAs, or qualified security assessors, to conduct compliance checks. Third-party certification is required for large organizations by PCI-DSS, although smaller organizations can self-certify.

24. A. A test coverage analysis is often used to provide insight into how well testing covered the set of use cases that an application is being tested for. Source code reviews look at the code of a program for bugs, not necessarily at a use case analysis, whereas fuzzing tests invalid inputs. A code review report might be generated as part of a source code review.

25. C. Testing how a system could be misused, or misuse testing, focuses on behaviors that are not what the organization desires or that are counter to the proper function of a system or application. Use case testing is used to verify whether a desired functionality works. Dynamic testing is used to determine how code handles variables that change over time, whereas manual testing is just what it implies: testing code by hand.

26. B. Synthetic transaction monitoring uses emulated or recorded transactions to monitor for performance changes in response time, functionality, or other performance monitors. Passive monitoring uses a span port or other method to copy traffic and monitor it in real time. Log analysis is typically performed against actual log data but can be performed on simulated traffic to identify issues. Simulated transaction analysis is not an industry term.

27. B. Identity and access management (IAM) systems combine life-cycle management and monitoring tools to ensure that identity and authorization are properly handled throughout an organization. Derek should invest in a capable IAM system and ensure that it is configured to use appropriate workflows and to generate the logs and reports that he needs. EDR systems are endpoint detection and response tools and are used to protect against compromise by advanced attackers.

28. C. Vulnerability scanners that do not have administrative rights to access a machine or that are not using an agent to scan remote machines to gather information, including fingerprints from responses to queries and connections, banner information from services, and related data. CVE information is Common Vulnerability and Exposure information, or vulnerability information. A port scanner gathers information about what service ports are open, although some port scanners blur the line between port and vulnerability scanners. Patch management tools typically run as an agent on a system to allow them to both monitor patch levels and update the system as needed. Service validation typically involves testing the functionality of a service, not its banner and response patterns.

29. B. Emily is using synthetic transactions, which can use recorded or generated transactions, and is conducting use-case testing to verify that the application responds properly to actual use cases. Neither actual data nor dynamic monitoring is an industry term. Fuzzing involves sending unexpected inputs to a program to see how it responds. Passive monitoring uses a network tap or other capture technology to allow monitoring of actual traffic to a system or application.

30. B. Real user monitoring (RUM) is a passive monitoring technique that records user interaction with an application or system to ensure performance and proper application behavior. RUM is often used as part of a predeployment process using the actual user interface. The other answers are all made up—synthetic monitoring uses simulated behavior, but synthetic user monitoring is not a testing method. Similarly, passive monitoring monitors actual traffic, but passive user recording is not an industry term or technique. Client-server testing merely describes one possible architecture.

31. B. Jim should ask the information security team to flag the issue as resolved if he is sure the patch was installed. Many vulnerability scanners rely on version information or banner information and may flag patched versions if the software provider does not update the information they see. Uninstalling and reinstalling the patch will not change this. Changing the version information may not change all of the details that are being flagged by the scanner and may cause issues at a later date. Reviewing the vulnerability information for a workaround may be a good idea but should not be necessary if the proper patch is installed; it can create maintenance issues later.

32. B. zzuf is the only fuzzer on the list, and zzuf is specifically designed to work with tools like web browsers, image viewers, and similar software by modifying network and file input to applications. Nmap is a port scanner, Nessus is a vulnerability scanner, and Nikto is a web server scanner.

33. D. Most IaaS vendors will not allow customers to conduct an audit of their systems and infrastructure. Kara is likely to be able to obtain third-party audit reports from her vendor, and the major IaaS vendors typically either make these available publicly or to paying or prospective customers. An internal audit will not assess the underlying infrastructure and services, only those that the organization uses.

34. A. Passive scanning can help identify rogue devices by capturing MAC address vendor IDs that do not match deployed devices, by verifying that systems match inventories of organizationally owned hardware by hardware address and by monitoring for rogue SSIDs or connections.

Scripted attacks are part of active scanning rather than passive scanning, and active scanning is useful for testing IDS or IPS systems, whereas passive scanning will not be detected by detection systems. Finally, a shorter dwell time can actually miss troublesome traffic, so balancing dwell time versus coverage is necessary for passive wireless scanning efforts.

35. B. In most organizations, senior management needs to approve penetration tests because of the risk to the organization and the potential impact of the test. In a small number of organizations, the service owner may be able to make this decision, but penetration tests often have broader impacts than a single service, meaning that senior management is the proper path. Change advisory boards approve changes, not penetration tests, and system administrators may be advised of the test but do not have the authority in most organizations to sign off on a penetration test.

36. D. Regression testing, which is a type of functional or unit testing, tests to ensure that changes have not introduced new issues. Nonregression testing checks to see whether a change has had the effect it was supposed to, smoke testing focuses on simple problems with impact on critical functionality, and evolution testing is not a software testing technique.

37. D. Nmap, Nessus, and Nikto all have OS fingerprinting or other operating system identification capabilities. Sqlmap is designed to perform automated detection and testing of SQL injection flaws and does not provide OS detection.

38. C. Key risk indicators are used to tell those in charge of risk management how risky an activity is and how much impact changes are having on that risk profile. Identifying and monitoring key risk indicators can help track high-risk areas earlier in their life cycle. Yearly risk assessments may be a good idea but provide only a point-in-time view, whereas penetration tests may miss out on risks that are not directly security-related. Monitoring logs and events using a SIEM device can help detect issues as they occur but won't necessarily show trends in risk.

39. C. Passive monitoring works only after issues have occurred because it requires actual traffic. Synthetic monitoring uses simulated or recorded traffic and thus can be used to proactively identify problems. Both synthetic and passive monitoring can be used to detect functionality issues.

40. B. Getting authorization is the most critical element in the planning phase. Permission, and the "get-out-of-jail-free card" that demonstrates that organizational leadership is aware of the issues that a penetration test could cause, is the first step in any penetration test. Gathering tools and building a lab, as well as determining what type of test will be conducted, are all important, but nothing should happen without permission.

41. C. Discovery can include both active and passive discovery. Port scanning is commonly done during discovery to assess what services the target provides, and nmap is one of the most popular tools used for this purpose. Nessus and Nikto might be used during the vulnerability scanning phase, and john, a password cracker, can be used to recover passwords during the exploitation phase.

42. B. Penetration test reports often include information that could result in additional exposure if they were accidentally released or stolen. Therefore, determining how vulnerability data should be stored and sent is critical. Problems with off-limits targets are more likely to result in issues during the vulnerability assessment and exploitation phase, and reports should not be limited in length but should be as long as they need to be to accomplish the goals of the test.

43. B. Code coverage testing most frequently requires that every function has been called, that each statement has been executed, that all branches have been fully explored, and that each condition has been evaluated for all possibilities. API, input, and loop testing are not common types of code coverage testing measures.

44. B. Time to remediate a vulnerability is a commonly used key performance indicator for security teams. Time to live measures how long a packet can exist in hops, business criticality is a measure used to determine how important a service or system is to an organization, and coverage rates are used to measure how effective code testing is.

45. D. Unique user IDs provide accountability when paired with auditable logs to provide that a specific user took any given action. Confidentiality, availability, and integrity can be provided through other means like encryption, systems design, and digital signatures.

46. B. Application programming interfaces (APIs), user interfaces (UIs), and physical interfaces are all important to test when performing software testing. Network interfaces are not part of the typical list of interfaces tested in software testing.

47. C. The Common Vulnerabilities and Exposures (CVE) database provides a consistent reference for identifying security vulnerabilities. The Open Vulnerability and Assessment Language (OVAL) is used to describe the security condition of a system. The Extensible Configuration Checklist Description Format (XCCDF) is used to create security checklists in a standardized fashion. The Script Check Engine (SCE) is designed to make scripts interoperable with security policy definitions.

48. B, C. Test 2's total failure is likely due to a failed test run, but the tests overall show continued improvement with full success in test 4. At this point, most testing processes would consider the testing complete. This does not show coverage, and there is no reason to run a fifth run if the fourth test was successful.

49. C. Simply updating the version that an application provides may stop the vulnerability scanner from flagging it, but it won't fix the underlying issue. Patching, using workarounds, or installing an application layer firewall or IPS can all help to remediate or limit the impact of the vulnerability.

50. C. Selah's social engineering attack succeeded in persuading a staff member at the help desk to change a password for someone who they not only couldn't see but who they couldn't verify actually needed their password reset. Black box and zero knowledge are both terms describing penetration tests without information about the organization or system, and help-desk spoofing is not an industry term.

51. D. The menu shown will archive logs when they reach the maximum size allowed (20 MB). These archives will be retained, which could fill the disk. Log data will not be overwritten, and log data should not be lost when the data is archived. The question does not include enough information to determine if needed information may not be logged.

52. C. Penetration tests typically do not involve blackouts. Application crashes, denial of service due to system, network, or application failures, and even data corruption can all be hazards of penetration tests.

53. B. NIST SP 800-53A is titled "Assessing Security and Privacy Controls in Federal Information Systems and Organizations: Building Effective Assessment Plans" and covers methods for assessing and measuring controls. NIST 800-12 is an introduction to computer security, 800-34 covers contingency planning, and 800-86 is the "Guide to Integrating Forensic Techniques into Incident Response."

54. C. Simulations are the most complete test that can be conducted without the risk that a full failover test creates. Michelle should conduct a simulation to validate as much of her organization's plan as possible. Tabletop exercises and plan reviews provide less complete coverage.

55. C. Hybrid environment audits involve the complexity of both cloud and on-premises audits. That means that the underlying cloud infrastructure may not be auditable, although Lucca's organization's use and configuration of the cloud will be. On-premises audits are not any more challenging to complete than other audits, hybrid audits can be conducted by third parties, and hybrid audits include both on-premises and cloud auditing challenges and requirements as they are not the same as a cloud-only audit.

56. A. Port 22 is used by the Secure Shell (SSH) protocol for administrative connections. If Kara wants to restrict administrative connections, she should block access on this port. Port 80 is used for HTTP, 443 for HTTPS, and 1433 for Microsoft SQL.

57. C. The audit finding indicates that the backup administrator may not be monitoring backup logs and taking appropriate action based on what they report, thus resulting in potentially unusable backups. Issues with review, logging, or being aware of the success or failure of backups are less important than not having usable backups.

58. C. ITIL, which originally stood for IT Infrastructure Library, is a set of practices for IT service management and is not typically used for auditing. The Control Objectives for Information and Related Technology (COBIT), ISO 27001, and the Statement on Standards for Attestation Engagements number 18 (SSAE-18) are all used for auditing.

59. B. COBIT, the Control Objectives for Information and Related Technologies, is commonly used as an audit framework for evaluating the governance and management of enterprise IT in an organization. The DMCA is the Digital Millennium Copyright Act, IEC is the International Electrotechnical Commission that defines standards for electrotechnology, and FISA is the Federal Intelligence Surveillance Act, not an audit standard.

60. B. Kelly's team is using regression testing, which is intended to prevent the recurrence of issues. This means measuring the rate of defect recurrence is appropriate for their work. Time to remediate vulnerabilities is associated with activities such as patching, rather than preparing the patch, whereas a weighted risk trend is used to measure risk over time to an organization. Finally, specific coverage may be useful to determine if they are fully testing their effort, but regression testing is more specifically covered by defect recurrence rates.

61. C. Static program reviews are typically performed by an automated tool. Program understanding, program comprehension, pair programming, software inspections, and software walk-throughs are all human-centric methods for reviewing code.

62. A. To fully test code, a white-box test is required. Without full visibility of the code, error conditions or other code could be missed, making a gray-box or black-box test an inappropriate solution. Using dynamic testing that runs against live code could also result in some conditions being missed due to sections of code not being exposed to typical usage.

63. A. A test coverage report measures how many of the test cases have been completed and is used as a way to provide test metrics when using test cases. A penetration test report is provided when a penetration test is conducted—this is not a penetration test. A code coverage report covers how much of the code has been tested, and a line coverage report is a type of code coverage report, both of which cannot be created in a black-box test since the code is not accessible to testers.

64. C. The changes from a testing environment with instrumentation inserted into the code and the production environment for the code can mask timing-related issues like race conditions. Bounds checking, input validation, and pointer manipulation are all related to coding issues rather than environmental issues and are more likely to be discoverable in a test environment.

65. D. Once a vulnerability scanner identifies a potential problem, validation is necessary to verify that the issue exists. Reporting, patching, or other remediation actions can be conducted once the vulnerability has been confirmed.

66. B. While handling errors and exceptions can be something of an art, the first thing to do in circumstances like these is to review error logs and notifications to try to find out what went wrong. From there, Andrea can make a decision to remediate a problem, send the code back for a fix, or take another action. She might even opt to send the code forward if the error occurred after testing was completed and was with the process flow or another noncritical element, but would do so only if she was absolutely certain that was the case.

67. D. The Common Vulnerability Scoring System (CVSS) includes metrics and calculation tools for exploitability, impact, how mature exploit code is, and how vulnerabilities can be remediated, as well as a means to score vulnerabilities against users' unique requirements. NVD is the National Vulnerability Database, CSV is short for comma-separated values, and Visual SourceSafe (VSS) is an irrelevant term related to software development rather than vulnerability management.

68. D. Network-enabled printers often provided services via TCP 515 and 9100 and have both nonsecure and secure web-enabled management interfaces on TCP 80 and 443. Web servers, access points, and file servers would not typically provide service on the LPR and LPD ports (515 and 9100).

69. A. Nikto, Burp Suite, and Wapiti are all web application vulnerability scanners, tools designed specifically to scan web servers and applications. While they share some functionality with broader vulnerability scanners and port scanning tools, they have a narrower focus and typically have deeper capabilities than vulnerability scanners.

70. A. APIs typically transfer data for web applications via HTTPS, meaning that the API itself is not responsible for encryption. If Frank's team discovers that TLS is not enabled, they will need to work with the infrastructure or systems administration team to ensure that TLS is enabled and in use rather than making API changes. Authorization for object access, authentication weaknesses, and rate limiting are all common API issues. If you're not familiar with the types of issues you might encounter in APIs, you can read more about them in the OWASP API security top 10 at `https://owasp.org/API-Security/editions/2023/en/0x11-t10`.

71. B. Metasploit is an exploitation package that is designed to assist penetration testers. A tester using Metasploit can exploit known vulnerabilities for which an exploit has been created or can create their own exploits using the tool. While Metasploit provides built-in access to some vulnerability scanning functionality, a tester using Metasploit should primarily be expected to perform actual tests of exploitable vulnerabilities. Similarly, Metasploit supports creating buffer overflow attacks, but it is not a purpose-built buffer overflow testing tool, and of course, testing systems for zero-day exploits doesn't work unless they have been released.

72. D. Susan is conducting interface testing. Interface testing involves testing system or application components to ensure that they work properly together. Misuse case testing focuses on how an attacker might misuse the application and would not test normal cases. Fuzzing attempts to send unexpected input and might be involved in interface testing, but it won't cover the full set of concerns. Regression testing is conducted when testing changes and is used to ensure that the application or system functions as it did before the update or change.

73. B. Not having enough log sources is not a common consideration in log management system design, although it may be a worry for security managers who can't capture the data they need. Log management system designs must take into account the volume of log data and the network bandwidth it consumes, the security of the data, and the amount of effort required to analyze the data.

74. D. Random sampling of accounts is the recommended best practice if all accounts cannot be validated. Selecting only recently changed accounts will not identify long-term issues or historic issues, and checking only high-value accounts will not show if there are issues or bad practices with other account types.

75. C. Rebooting a Windows machine results in an information log entry. Windows defines five types of events: errors, which indicate a significant problem; warnings, which may indicate future problems; information, which describes successful operation; success audits, which record successful security accesses; and failure audits, which record failed security access attempts.

76. C. Inconsistent timestamps are a common problem, often caused by improperly set time zones or due to differences in how system clocks are set. In this case, a consistent time difference often indicates that one system uses local time, and the other is using Greenwich mean time (GMT). Logs from multiple sources tend to cause problems with centralization and collection, whereas different log formats can create challenges in parsing log data. Finally, modified logs are often a sign of intrusion or malicious intent.

77. A. Authenticated scans use a read-only account to access configuration files, allowing more accurate testing of vulnerabilities. Web application scans, unauthenticated scans, and port scans don't have access to configuration files unless they are inadvertently exposed.

78. B. Notifying third parties of security issues and vulnerabilities in a confidential manner to allow them to address the issues is considered ethical disclosure. There is not enough information in the question to determine how it was found, and disclosure is not necessarily part of either penetration tests or application tests. How the information as found is not listed, so OSINT is not a useful answer either.

79. D. Since a shared symmetric key could be used by any of the servers, transaction identification problems caused by a shared key are likely to involve a repudiation issue. If encrypted transactions cannot be uniquely identified by a server, they cannot be proved to have come from a specific server.

80. C. Ben should engage a company that can perform a load or stress test to validate how the application performs under both expected and extreme loads so that he knows what a denial-of-service attack based on load will look like. Social engineering does not test the ability of sites to handle load, and penetration testers may conduct denial-of-service attacks but typically do not. Fuzzers send random input to test how applications handle unexpected input rather than relying on extreme load. They might help test for flaws that could result in a denial-of-service condition, but the question specifically asks about load-based conditions, not software flaws.

81. D. The Network Time Protocol (NTP) allows the synchronization of system clocks with a standardized time source. The Secure Shell (SSH) protocol provides encrypted administrative connections to servers. The File Transfer Protocol (FTP) is used for data exchange. Transport Layer Security (TLS) is an encryption process used to protect information in transit over a network.

82. C. Fuzz testers are capable of automatically generating input sequences to test an application. Therefore, testers do not need to manually generate input, although they may do so if they want. Fuzzers can reproduce errors (and thus, "fuzzers can't reproduce errors" is not an issue) but typically don't fully cover the code—code coverage tools are usually paired with fuzzers to validate how much coverage was possible. Fuzzers are often limited to simple errors because they won't handle business logic or attacks that require knowledge from the application user.

83. D. Statement coverage tests verify that every line of code was executed during the test. Branch coverage verifies that every `if` statement was executed under all `if` and `else` conditions. Condition coverage verifies that every logical test in the code was executed under all sets of inputs. Function coverage verifies that every function in the code was called and returns results.

84. C. After scanning for open ports using a port scanning tool like nmap, penetration testers will identify interesting ports and then conduct vulnerability scans to determine what services may be vulnerable. This will perform many of the same activities that connecting via a web server will and will typically be more useful than trying to manually test for vulnerable accounts via Telnet. Sqlmap would typically be used after a vulnerability scanner identifies additional information about services, and the vulnerability scanner will normally provide a wider range of useful information.

85. B. The system is likely a Linux system. The system shows X11, as well as login, shell, and nfs ports, all of which are more commonly found on Linux systems than Windows systems or network devices. This system is also very poorly secured; many of the services running on it should not be exposed in a modern secure network.

86. D. Nmap scans only 1000 TCP and UDP ports by default, including ports outside the 0–1024 range of "well-known" ports. By using the defaults for nmap, Ben missed 64,535 ports. OS fingerprinting won't cover more ports but would have provided a best guess of the OS running on the scanned system.

87. A. When Lucca reviews the recovery time objective (RTO) data, he needs to ensure that the organization can recover from an outage in less than two hours based on the maximum tolerable downtime (MTD) of two hours.

88. C. Diana should request a SOC 3 report, which is intended for distribution to third parties. They include the auditor's opinions and management assertions, along with information about the service organization. SOC 3 reports are specifically intended for external release, unlike SOC 1 (financial reporting) and SOC 2 (confidentiality, security, and privacy) engagements. SOC 4 was made up for the question.

89. A. Showing end users error information about the code, particularly with directory and file information included, means that the application does not perform proper exception handling. Errors should be logged or noted in a way that the administrator can handle, but end users (and attackers!) should not see that information. The software may be handling misuse properly, as the problem does not note if this was due to normal testing or misuse testing. There is no information about debugging code causing the output, and test coverage was not noted in the question.

90. B. Port scanning is the first step toward identifying potentially exploitable services. Data gathering is used to acquire information to prepare for port scanning and other activities. Permission and planning are not used to identify exploitable services but are critical to the overall process.

91. C. Validating that the organization has secure and usable backups is Josh's best answer. In case a system is affected by cryptographic malware, it's important to have reliable backups that are not encrypted by the malware. This requires keeping your backup systems separate from your main systems and potentially implementing version control so that your unencrypted backups are not overwritten by encrypted ones that become inaccessible. Encrypting sensitive data won't stop attackers from re-encrypting it, making it inaccessible. Hashing to detect the attack won't stop it or make it possible to recover, and anti-encryption technology does not exist.

92. D. IT service management, or ITSM, tools include change management and thus the type of approvals and review processes that Joanna is looking for. A SIEM helps with security logs and events, an IPS looks for intrusions and unwanted traffic, and a CMS is a content management tool.

93. D. All of these are useful parts of a backup strategy, but performing full restores from backups on a regular basis is the best option listed. If regular restores work, then individual files will be recoverable, but individual files may not show larger issues with backups. Configuration and setting reviews are important but will not validate the backups themselves, and error messages can indicate problems but won't demonstrate intact logs either.

94. C. Vulnerability scanners cannot detect vulnerabilities for which they do not have a test, plug-in, or signature. Signatures often include version numbers, service fingerprints, or configuration data. They can detect local vulnerabilities as well as those that require authentication if they are provided with credentials, and of course, they can detect service vulnerabilities.

95. A, B. The number of staff who took a given training and the average change in their awareness from before the training to after the training can provide insight into how many trained staff you have and how impactful the training was. Over time, this will allow you to determine if your training is helping and if awareness is increasing. The length of the training does not assess its impact; in addition, the number of events each individual attended does not mean that staff are becoming more aware.

96. C. Ethical (or responsible) disclosure norms include notifying the vendor and providing them with a reasonable amount of time to remediate the issue. Public disclosures before notifying the vendor or in a short period of time are considered unethical in most circumstances. While this time frame varies, 90 to 120 days is not uncommon across the industry due to the complexity of software and other technologies.

97. D. Privilege escalation occurs during the attack phase of a penetration test. Host and service information gathering, as well as activities like dumpster diving that can provide information about the organization, its systems, and security, are all part of the discovery phase.

98. B. Once additional tools have been installed, penetration testers will typically use them to gain additional access. From there they can further escalate privileges, search for new targets or data, and, once again, install more tools to allow them to pivot further into infrastructure or systems.

99. B. Penetration testing reports often do not include the specific data captured during the assessment, as the readers of the report may not be authorized to access all of the data, and exposure of the report could result in additional problems for the organization. A listing of the issues discovered, risk ratings, and remediation guidance are all common parts of a penetration test report.

100. The status messages match with the descriptions as follows:

1. Open: C. The port is accessible on the remote system, and an application is accepting connections on that port.

2. Closed: B. The port is not accessible on the remote system.

3. Filtered: A. The port is accessible on the remote system, but no application is accepting connections on that port.

Chapter 7: Security Operations (Domain 7)

1.   A. The illustration shows an example of a failover cluster, where DB1 and DB2 are both configured as database servers. At any given time, only one will function as the active database server, while the other remains ready to assume responsibility if the first one fails. While the environment may use UPS, tape backup, and cold sites as disaster recovery and business continuity controls, they are not shown in the diagram.

2.   D. The principle of least privilege should guide Joe in this case. He should apply no access permissions by default and then give each user the necessary permissions to perform their job responsibilities. Read only, editor, and administrator permissions may be necessary for one or more of these users, but those permissions should be assigned based upon business need and not by default.

3.   C. While most organizations would want to log attempts to log in to a workstation, this is not considered a privileged administrative activity and would go through normal logging processes.

4.   B. Duress, or being under threat of violence or other constraints, is a concern for organizations such as banks, jewelry stores, or other organizations where an attacker may attempt to force an employee to perform actions. Organizations that expect that a scenario like this may occur will often use duress code words that let others know that they are performing actions under threat.

5.   D. Real evidence consists of things that may actually be brought into a courtroom as evidence. For example, real evidence includes hard disks, weapons, and items containing fingerprints. Documentary evidence consists of written items that may or may not be in tangible form. Testimonial evidence is verbal testimony given by witnesses with relevant information. The parol evidence rule says that when an agreement is put into written form, the written document is assumed to contain all the terms of the agreement.

6.   C. A whitelist of allowed applications will ensure that Lauren's users can run only the applications that she preapproves. Blacklists would require her to maintain a list of every application that she doesn't want to allow, which is an almost impossible task. Graylisting is not a technology option. Configuration management can be useful for making sure the right applications are on a PC but typically can't directly prevent users from running undesired applications or programs.

7.   B. A pseudo-flaw is a false vulnerability in a system that may distract an attacker. A honeynet is a network of multiple honeypots that creates a more sophisticated environment for intruders to explore, rather than a feature Colin could use on a honeypot. A darknet is a segment of unused network address space that should have no network activity and, therefore, may be easily used to monitor for illicit activity. A warning banner is a legal tool used to notify intruders that they are not authorized to access a system.

8. B. Social media is commonly used as a command-and-control system for botnet activity. The most likely scenario here is that the user's computer was infected with malware and joined to a botnet. This accounts for both the unusual social media traffic and the slow system activity.

9. A. John's design provides multiple processing sites, distributing load to multiple regions. Not only does this provide business continuity and disaster recovery functionality, but it also means that his design will be more resilient to denial-of-service attacks.

10. A. NetFlow records contain an entry for every network communication session that took place on a network and can be compared to a list of known malicious hosts. IDS logs may contain a relevant record, but it is less likely because they would create log entries only if the traffic triggers the IDS, as opposed to NetFlow records, which encompass all communications. Authentication logs and RFC logs would not have records of any network traffic.

11. B. Gary should follow the least privilege principle and assign users only the permissions they need to perform their job responsibilities. Privilege creep is a term used to describe the unintentional accumulation of privileges over time. Segregation of duties and separation of privileges are principles used to secure sensitive processes.

12. A. The matrix shown in the figure is known as a segregation of duties matrix. It is used to ensure that one person does not obtain two privileges that would create a potential conflict. Privilege creep is a term used to describe the unintentional accumulation of privileges over time. Two-person control is used when two people must work together to perform a sensitive action. Defense in depth is a general security principle used to describe a philosophy of overlapping security controls.

13. B. Before granting access, Gary should verify that the user has a valid security clearance and a business need to know the information. Gary is performing an authorization task, so he does not need to verify the user's credentials, such as a password or biometric scan.

14. D. Gary should follow the principle of two-person control by requiring simultaneous action by two separate authorized individuals to gain access to the encryption keys. He should also apply the principles of least privilege and defense in depth, but these principles apply to all operations and are not specific to sensitive operations. Gary should avoid the security through obscurity principle, the reliance upon the secrecy of security mechanisms to provide security for a system or process.

15. A, B, C. Privileged access reviews are one of the most critical components of an organization's security program because they ensure that only authorized users have access to perform the most sensitive operations. They should take place whenever a user with privileged access leaves the organization or changes roles as well as on a regular, recurring basis. However, it is not reasonable to expect that these time-consuming reviews would take place on a daily basis.

16. D. Hotfixes, updates, and security fixes are all synonyms for single patches designed to correct a single problem. Service packs are collections of many different updates that serve as a major update to an operating system or application.

17. C. A forensic disk controller performs four functions. One of those, write blocking, intercepts write commands sent to the device and prevents them from modifying data on the device. The other three functions include returning data requested by a read operation, returning access-significant information from the device, and reporting errors from the device back to the forensic host.

18. A. Lydia is following the need to know principle. While the user may have the appropriate security clearance to access this information, there is no business justification provided, so she does not know that the user has an appropriate need to know the information.

19. C. Job rotation and mandatory vacations deter fraud by increasing the likelihood that it will be detected. Two-person control deters fraud by requiring collusion between two employees. Incident response does not normally serve as a deterrent mechanism.

20. B. Quality of service is a feature found on routers and other network devices that can prioritize specific network traffic. QoS policies define which traffic is prioritized, and traffic is then handled based on the policy.

21. A. The change log contains information about approved changes and the change management process. While other logs may contain details about the change's effect, the audit trail for change management would be found in the change log.

22. B. While it may be tempting to tell her staff to simply not connect to any network, Susan knows that they will need connectivity to do their work. Using a VPN to connect their laptops and mobile devices to a trusted network and ensuring that all traffic is tunneled through the VPN is her best bet to secure their Internet usage. Susan may also want to ensure that they take "clean" laptops and devices that do not contain sensitive information or documents and that those systems are fully wiped when they return.

23. D. The Common Vulnerabilities and Exposures (CVE) database contains standardized information on many different security issues. The Open Worldwide Application Security Project (OWASP) contains general guidance on web application security issues but does not track specific vulnerabilities or go beyond web applications. The Center for Internet Security (CIS) maintains benchmarks for securely configuring devices, operating systems, and applications. They do not track vulnerabilities. Microsoft Security Bulletins are also good sources of vulnerability information but are not comprehensive databases of known issues.

24. A, B, C, D. A disaster is any event that can disrupt normal IT operations and can be either natural or human made. Hacking and terrorism are examples of human-made disasters, while flooding and fire are examples of natural disasters.

25. D. The read-through is the least disruptive type of disaster recovery test. During a read-through, team members each review the contents of their disaster recovery checklists on their own and suggest any necessary changes. During a tabletop exercise, team members come together and discuss a specific scenario without making any changes to information systems. During a parallel test, the team actually activates the disaster recovery site for testing, but the primary site remains operational. During a full interruption test, the team takes down the primary site and confirms that the disaster recovery site is capable of handling regular operations. The full interruption test is the most thorough test but also the most disruptive.

26. B. The Grandfather-Father-Son, Tower of Hanoi, and Six Cartridge Weekly schemes are all different approaches to rotating backup media that balance reuse of media with data retention concerns. Meet-in-the-middle is a cryptographic attack against 2DES encryption.

27. B. In this scenario, Helen designed a process that requires the concurrence of two people to perform a sensitive action. This is an example of two-person control. This is different from segregation of duties, where one individual may not have two separate permissions that, when combined, might allow an unwanted action. Segregation of duties applied to a situation like this one might say that the same person may not have both the ability to initiate a request and the ability to approve a request. Least privilege says that an individual should have only the necessary permissions required to carry out their job function. Job rotation is a scheme that has users periodically shift job functions in order to detect malfeasance.

28. C. Evidence provided in court must be relevant to determining a fact in question, material to the case at hand, and competently obtained. Evidence does not need to be tangible. Witness testimony is an example of intangible evidence that may be offered in court.

29. A. A lessons learned document is often created and distributed to involved parties after a postmortem review to ensure that those who were involved in the incident and others who may benefit from the knowledge are aware of what they can do to prevent future issues and to improve response in the event that one occurs.

30. A, C, D. CSIRT representation normally includes at least representatives of senior management, information security professionals, legal representatives, public relations staff, human resources, and engineering/technical staff. Law enforcement personnel would not be included on such a team and would only be consulted as necessary.

31. C. In this scenario, all the files on the server will be backed up on Monday evening during the full backup. The differential backup on Wednesday will then copy all files modified since the last full backup. These include files 1, 2, 3, 5, and 6: a total of five files.

File Modifications
Monday 8 a.m. - File 1 created
Monday 10 a.m. - File 2 created
Monday 11 a.m. - File 3 created
Monday 4 p.m. - File 1 modified
Monday 5 p.m. - File 4 created
Tuesday 8 a.m. - File 1 modified
Tuesday 9 a.m. - File 2 modified
Tuesday 10 a.m. - File 5 created
Wednesday 8 a.m. - File 3 modified
Wednesday 9 a.m. - File 6 created

32. C. Intrusion detection systems (IDSs) provide only passive responses, such as alerting administrators to a suspected attack. Intrusion prevention systems and firewalls, on the other hand, may take action to block an attack attempt. Antivirus software also may engage in active response by quarantining suspect files.

33. C. Physical destruction, an appropriate contract with certification, and secure wiping are all reasonable options. In each case, a careful inventory and check should be done to ensure that each drive is handled appropriately. Reformatting drives can leave remnant data, making this a poor data life-cycle choice for drives that contain sensitive data.

34. D. Secure router configuration guidelines are typically more technical and specific to IT professionals, making them less likely to be included in a general security training and awareness program. These programs usually focus on broader and more universally applicable topics like insider threats, which address risks from employees or contractors; social media impact, which covers the risks of sharing information online; and 2FA fatigue, which relates to the weariness or complacency in using two-factor authentication. These are relevant to a wider audience and are crucial for overall organizational security awareness. In contrast, the specifics of router configuration are usually handled by specialized IT staff.

35. A. The service-level agreement (SLA) is between a service provider and a customer and documents in a formal manner expectations around availability, performance, and other parameters. An MOU may cover the same items but is not as formal a document. An OLA is between internal service organizations and does not involve customers. An SOW is an addendum to a contract describing work to be performed.

36. A. The ITIL framework focuses on IT service management. The Project Management Body of Knowledge (PMBOK) provides a common core of project management expertise. The Payment Card Industry Data Security Standard (PCI DSS) contains regulations for payment card security. The Open Group Architecture Framework (TOGAF) focuses on IT architecture issues.

37. D. Latency is a delay in the delivery of packets from their source to their destination. Jitter is a variation in the latency for different packets. Packet loss is the disappearance of packets in transit that requires retransmission. Interference is electrical noise or other disruptions that corrupt the contents of packets.

38. B. Running the program in a sandbox provides secure isolation that can prevent the malware from impacting other applications or systems. If Joe uses appropriate instrumentation, he can observe what the program does, what changes it makes, and any communications it may attempt. ASLR is a memory location randomization technology. Process isolation keeps processes from impacting each other. A sandbox typically provides greater utility in a scenario like this since it can be instrumented and managed in a way that better supports investigations. Clipping is a term often used in signal processing.

39. D. A transformer explosion is a failure of a human-made electrical component. Flooding, mudslides, and hurricanes are all examples of natural disasters.

40. A. Microsoft Configuration Manager (ConfigMgr) provides this capability and is designed to allow administrators to evaluate the configuration status of Windows workstations and servers, as well as providing asset management data. System Center Operations Manager (SCOM) is primarily used to monitor for health and performance. Group Policy can be used for a variety of tasks including deploying settings and software, and custom PowerShell scripts could do this but should not be required for a configuration check.

41. B. The principle of least privilege says that an individual should only have the privileges necessary to complete their job functions. Removing administrative privileges from nonadministrative users is an example of least privilege.

42. D. There is no need to conduct forensic imaging as a preventative measure. Rather, forensic imaging should be used during the incident response process. Maintaining patch levels, implementing intrusion detection/prevention, and removing unnecessary services and accounts are all basic preventive measures.

43. B. A resource capacity agreement is the most appropriate for Chas's concern, as it specifically addresses the availability of resources in a disaster scenario. This type of agreement ensures that the cloud provider has sufficient resources to meet the needs of their clients, even in the event of multiple simultaneous disasters. It directly tackles the issue of resource allocation and availability, which is Chas's primary concern. In contrast, a nondisclosure agreement is more about confidentiality and doesn't address resource capacity. A mutual assistance agreement typically involves agreements between organizations for support during emergencies but doesn't guarantee specific resource availability. A business partnership agreement is broader and may not specifically cover the detailed aspects of resource availability in disaster scenarios.

44. C. An incident negatively affects the confidentiality, integrity, or availability of information or assets and/or violates a security policy. A computer security incident is an incident that is the result of an attack or the result of malicious or intentional actions on the part of users. The unauthorized vulnerability scan of a server does violate security policy and may negatively affect the security of that system, so it qualifies as a security incident. The failure of a backup to complete properly jeopardizes availability and is, therefore, an incident, but not a computer security incident. The logging of system access and update of antivirus signatures are all routine actions that do not violate policy or jeopardize security, so they are all events rather than incidents.

45. C. Radio Frequency Identification (RFID) technology is a cost-effective way to track items around a facility. While Wi-Fi could be used for the same purpose, it would be much more expensive to implement.

46. C. An attack committed against an organization by an insider, such as an employee, is known as sabotage. Espionage and confidentiality breaches involve the theft of sensitive information, which is not alleged to have occurred in this case. Integrity breaches involve the unauthorized modification of information, which is not described in this scenario.

47. A. In a SYN flood attack, the attacker sends a large number of SYN packets to a system but does not respond to the SYN/ACK packets, attempting to overwhelm the attacked system's connection state table with half-open connections.

48. B. The maximum tolerable downtime (MTD) is the longest amount of time that an IT service or component may be unavailable without causing serious damage to the organization. The recovery time objective (RTO) is the amount of time expected to return an IT service or component to operation after a failure. The recovery point objective (RPO) identifies the maximum amount of data, measured in time, that may be lost during a recovery effort. Service-level agreements (SLAs) are written contracts that document service expectations.

49. C. Zero-day attacks are those that are previously unknown to the security community and, therefore, have no available patch. These are especially dangerous attacks because they may be highly effective until a solution becomes available. The other attacks described here are all known attacks and would not be classified as zero-day events.

50. D. Locard's principle is most relevant to Rob's forensic investigation for trace digital evidence, as it suggests that any contact between two objects results in an exchange of materials. In the context of digital forensics, this principle implies that there is always some form of digital trace or residue left behind when devices interact or when data is transferred.

Kerckhoff's principle states that a system's security should not depend on the secrecy of its algorithm but rather on the secrecy of its keys. The principle of least privilege is a security concept in which a user is given the minimum levels of access—or permissions—needed to perform his job functions. Lastly, the defense-in-depth principle is a layered security approach that establishes multiple levels of defense to protect information. While these other three principles are important in cybersecurity, they do not directly relate to the collection and analysis of digital trace evidence like Locard's principle does.

51. A. Interviews occur when investigators meet with an individual who may have information relevant to their investigation but is not a suspect. If the individual is a suspect, then the meeting is an interrogation.

52. D. The image clearly contains the watermark of the U.S. Geological Survey (USGS), which ensures that anyone seeing the image knows its origin. It is not possible to tell from looking at the image whether steganography was used. Sampling and clipping are data analysis techniques and are not used to protect images.

53. D. The annualized rate of occurrence (ARO) is the expected number of times an incident will occur each year. In the case of a 200-year flood plain, planners should expect a flood once every 200 years. This is equivalent to a 1/200 chance of a flood in any given year, or 0.005 floods per year.

54. B. While all hackers with malicious intent pose a risk to the organization, the malicious insider poses the greatest risk to security because they likely have legitimate access to sensitive systems that may be used as a launching point for an attack. Other attackers do not begin with this advantage.

55. C. In an electronic vaulting approach, automated technology moves database backups from the primary database server to a remote site on a scheduled basis, typically daily. Transaction logging is not a recovery technique alone; it is a process for generating the logs used in remote journaling. Remote journaling transfers transaction logs to a remote site on a more frequent basis than electronic vaulting, typically hourly. Remote mirroring maintains a live database server at the backup site and mirrors all transactions at the primary site on the server at the backup site.

56. B. Hilda's design follows the principle of segregation of duties. Giving one user the ability to both create new accounts and grant administrative privileges combines two actions that would result in a significant security change that should be divided among two users.

57. C. While all of these assumptions are valid premises that Patrick might have going into the exercise, the basic assumption of a threat-hunting exercise is the so-called presumption of compromise. This means that Patrick should assume that attackers have already gained access to his system and then hunt for indicators of their presence.

58. C. The end goal of the disaster recovery process is restoring normal business operations in the primary facility. All of the other actions listed may take place during the disaster recovery process, but the process is not complete until the organization is once again functioning normally in its primary facilities.

59. C. A host-based intrusion detection system (HIDS) may be able to detect unauthorized processes running on a system. The other controls mentioned, network intrusion detection systems (NIDSs), firewalls, and DLP systems, are network-based and may not notice rogue processes.

60. B. The scenario describes a privilege escalation attack where a malicious insider with authorized access to a system misused that access to gain privileged credentials.

61. B. Carla's account has experienced privilege creep, where privileges accumulated over time. This condition is also known as aggregation and likely constitutes a violation of the least privilege principle.

62. C. The mitigation phase of incident response focuses on actions that can contain the damage incurred during an incident. This includes limiting the scope and/or effectiveness of the incident. The detection phase identifies that an incident is taking place. The response phase includes steps taken to assemble a team and triage the incident. At the conclusion of the recovery phase, normal operations are resumed.

63. C. At this point in the process, Ann has no reason to believe that any actual security compromise or policy violation took place, so this situation does not meet the criteria for a security incident or intrusion. Rather, the alert generated by the intrusion detection system is simply a security event requiring further investigation. Security occurrence is not a term commonly used in incident handling.

64. A. DNS traffic commonly uses port 53 for both TCP and UDP communications. SSH and SCP use TCP port 22. SSL and TLS do not have ports assigned to them but are commonly used for HTTPS traffic on port 443. Unencrypted web traffic over HTTP often uses port 80.

65. D. The attack described in this scenario has all the hallmarks of a denial-of-service attack. More specifically, Ann's organization is likely experiencing a DNS amplification attack where an attacker sends false requests to third-party DNS servers with a forged source IP address belonging to the targeted system. Because the attack uses UDP requests, there is no three-way handshake. The attack packets are carefully crafted to elicit a lengthy response from a short query. The purpose of these queries is to generate responses headed to the target system that are sufficiently large and numerous enough to overwhelm the targeted network or system.

66. B. Now that Ann suspects an attack against her organization, she has sufficient evidence to declare a security incident. The attack underway seems to have undermined the availability of her network, meeting one of the criteria for a security incident. This is an escalation beyond a security event but does not reach the level of an intrusion because there is no evidence that the attacker has even attempted to gain access to systems on Ann's network. Security occurrence is not a term commonly used in incident handling.

67. D. To be admissible, evidence must be relevant, material, and competent. The laptop in this case is clearly material because it contains logs related to the crime in question. It is also relevant because it provides evidence that ties the hacker to the crime. It is not competent because the evidence was not legally obtained.

68. C. Gordon may conduct his investigation as he wants and use any information that is legally available to him, including information and systems belonging to his employer. There is no obligation to contact law enforcement. However, Gordon may not perform "hack back" activities because those may constitute violations of the law and/or ISC2 Code of Ethics.

69. B. Software escrow agreements place a copy of the source code for a software package in the hands of an independent third party who will turn the code over to the customer if the vendor ceases business operations. Service-level agreements, mutual assistance agreements, and compliance agreements all lose some or all of their effectiveness if the vendor goes out of business.

70. C. Most security professionals recommend at least one, and preferably two, weeks of vacation to deter fraud. The idea is that fraudulent schemes will be uncovered during the time that the employee is away and does not have the access required to perpetuate a cover-up.

71. A, B, C, E, F. Any attempt to undermine the security of an organization or violation of a security policy is a security incident. All of the events described meet this definition and should be treated as an incident, with one exception. A successful attempt to access a file is certainly a security event, but it is not a security incident unless it is established that the individual accessing the file was not authorized to do so.

72. A, B, C. Egress filtering scans outbound traffic for potential security policy violations. This includes traffic that is likely malicious, such as an outbound SSH scan on port 22. It also includes traffic that appears to be part of an attack or misconfiguration, such as sending traffic to a broadcast destination address. Finally, it includes spoofed traffic generated by internal systems, which may bear a source address from an external network. The normal traffic that the firewall should expect to see is that bearing a destination address on an external network.

73. C. The two main methods of choosing records from a large pool for further analysis are sampling and clipping. Sampling uses statistical techniques to choose a sample that is representative of the entire pool, while clipping uses threshold values to select those records that exceed a predefined threshold because they may be of most interest to analysts. In this case, Allie is only selecting records that exceed an invalid login threshold, making this an example of clipping.

She is not using statistical techniques to select a subset of records, so this is not an example of sampling.

74. B. NetFlow data contains information on the source, destination, and size of all network communications and is routinely saved as a matter of normal activity. Packet capture data would provide relevant information, but it must be captured during the suspicious activity and cannot be re-created after the fact unless the organization is already conducting 100% packet capture, which is rare. Additionally, the use of encryption limits the effectiveness of packet capture. Intrusion detection system logs would not likely contain relevant information because the encrypted traffic would probably not match intrusion signatures. Centralized authentication records would not contain information about network traffic.

75. C. Baseline configurations serve as the starting point for configuring secure systems and applications. They contain the security settings necessary to comply with an organization's security policy and may then be customized to meet the specific needs of an implementation. While security policies and guidelines may contain information needed to secure a system, they do not contain a set of configuration settings that may be applied to a system. The running configuration of a system is the set of currently applied settings, which may or may not be secure.

76. B. During a parallel test, the team actually activates the disaster recovery site for testing, but the primary site remains operational. During a full interruption test, the team takes down the primary site and confirms that the disaster recovery site is capable of handling regular operations. The full interruption test is the most thorough test but also the most disruptive. The read-through is the least disruptive type of disaster recovery test. During a read-through, team members each review the contents of their disaster recovery checklists on their own and suggest any necessary changes. During a tabletop exercise, team members come together and work through a specific scenario without making any changes to information systems.

77. C. Both the receipt of alerts and the verification of their accuracy occur during the Detection phase of the incident response process.

78. C. According to NIST SP 800-137, organizations should use the following factors to determine assessment and monitoring frequency: security control volatility, system categorizations/impact levels, security controls or specific assessment objects providing critical functions, security controls with identified weaknesses, organizational risk tolerance, threat information, vulnerability information, risk assessment results, the output of monitoring strategy reviews, and reporting requirements.

79. D. All of these technologies have the potential to monitor user behavior on endpoint devices. The key to answering this question correctly is realizing the emphasis on the user. Intrusion detection and prevention systems (IDSs/IPSs) focus on network and host behavior. Endpoint detection and response (EDR) systems focus on endpoint devices. User and entity behavior analytics (UEBA) solutions focus on the user and, therefore, would be the best way to meet Hunter's requirement.

80. C. SSH uses TCP port 22, so this attack is likely an attempt to scan for open or weakly secured SSH servers. FTP uses ports 20 and 21. Telnet uses port 23, and HTTP uses port 80.

81. B. Remediation activities seek to address the issue that caused the incident. In this case, that was a web application that was open to SQL injection attack. Adding input validation seeks to remediate this vulnerability. Rebuilding the database is a recovery action, while reviewing logs is done as part of the detection and response effort.

82. C. In an infrastructure-as-a-service environment, the vendor is responsible for hardware- and network-related responsibilities. These include configuring network firewalls, maintaining the hypervisor, and managing physical equipment. The customer retains responsibility for patching operating systems on its virtual machine instances.

83. B. Sandboxing is a technique where application developers (or the recipients of an untrusted application) may test the code in a virtualized environment that is isolated from production systems. White-box testing, black-box testing, and penetration testing are all common software testing techniques but do not require the use of an isolated system.

84. C. While it may not immediately seem like the obvious answer, many firewalls have a built-in anti–SYN flood defense that responds to SYNs on behalf of protected systems. Once the remote system proves to be a legitimate connection by continuing the three-way handshake, the rest of the TCP session is passed through. If the connection proves to be an attack, the firewall handles the additional load using appropriate mitigation techniques. Blocking SYNs from known or unknown IP addresses is likely to cause issues with systems that should be able to connect, and turning off TCP will break most modern network services!

85. A, B, D. EDR platforms do not conduct simulated phishing campaigns. The most common features of EDR systems are analyzing endpoint memory, filesystem, and network activity for signs of malicious activity; isolating possible malicious activity to contain the potential damage; integrating with threat intelligence sources; and integrating with other incident response mechanisms.

86. A. While any cybersecurity activity has the potential to benefit from machine learning and artificial intelligence capabilities, this technology really shines when used for pattern detection and anomaly detection problems. This is the type of activity performed by an intrusion detection system, and, therefore, this system would benefit the most from the use of ML/AI technology.

87. A. Companies have an obligation to preserve evidence whenever they believe that the threat of litigation is imminent. The statement made by this customer that "we will have to take this matter to court" is a clear threat of litigation and should trigger the preservation of any related documents and records.

88. A. Incremental backups provide the option that includes the smallest amount of data. In this case, that would be only the data modified since the most recent incremental backup. A differential backup would back up all data modified since the last full backup, which would be a substantial amount. The full backup would include all information on the server. Transaction log backups are specifically designed to support database servers and would not be effective on a file server.

89. A. Expert opinion evidence allows individuals to offer their opinion based upon the facts in evidence and their personal knowledge. Expert opinion evidence may be offered only if the court accepts the witness as an expert in a particular field. Direct evidence is when witnesses testify about their direct observations. Real evidence consists of tangible items brought into court as evidence. Documentary evidence consists of written records used as evidence in court.

90. D. The standard methods for clearing magnetic tapes, according to the NIST Guidelines for Media Sanitization, are overwriting the tape with nonsensitive data, degaussing, and physical destruction via shredding. Reformatting a tape does not remove remnant data.

91. B. RAID level 1, also known as disk mirroring, uses a minimum of two disks that contain identical information. If one disk fails, the other contains the data needed for the system to continue operation.

92. B. The analysis of application logs is one of the core tasks of software analysis. This is the correct answer because SQL injection attacks are application attacks.

93. C. Quigley may choose to use any or all of these security controls, but data encryption is, by far, the most important control. It protects the confidentiality of data stored on the tapes, which are most vulnerable to theft while in transit between two secure locations.

94. C. Data loss prevention (DLP) systems may identify sensitive information stored on endpoint systems or in transit over a network. This is their primary purpose. DLP systems are commonly available as a third-party managed service offering. Intrusion detection and prevention systems (IDSs/IPSs) may be used to identify some sensitive information using signatures built for that purpose, but this is not the primary role of those tools, and they would not be as effective as DLP systems at this task. TLS is a network encryption protocol that may be used to protect sensitive information, but it does not have any ability to identify sensitive information.

95. C. Disaster recovery teams should always refer media inquiries to the public relations team to ensure a coordinated, consistent response. They should not attempt to answer questions themselves.

96. D. All of these considerations are important when developing an emergency management plan. However, the safety of human life should always be the overwhelming priority, above all other considerations.

97. D. Barry should recruit an independent moderator to facilitate the session. Having a moderator who was not directly involved in the effort encourages honest and open feedback. While it is not necessary to use an external consultant, they may easily fill this role. While it is also possible to find a qualified internal employee to fill this position, it should not be someone who was involved in the incident response effort or has a major stake in the plan, such as Barry, the CISO, or the DR team leader.

98. C. Generators are capable of providing backup power for a sustained period of time in the event of a power loss, but they take time to activate. Uninterruptible power supplies (UPSs) provide immediate, battery-driven power for a short period of time to cover momentary losses of power, which would not cover a sustained period of power loss. RAID and redundant servers are high-availability controls but do not cover power loss scenarios.

99. The terms match with the definitions as follows:

    1. Honeypot: C. A system set up with intentional vulnerabilities

    2. Honeynet: B. A network set up with intentional vulnerabilities

    3. Pseudo-flaw: A. An intentionally designed vulnerability used to lure in an attacker

    4. Darknet: D. A monitored network without any hosts

100. The terms match with the definitions as follows:

    1. Hot site: B. A site with dedicated storage and real-time data replication, often with shared equipment that allows restoration of service in a very short time

    2. Cold site: D. A rented space with power, cooling, and connectivity that can accept equipment as part of a recovery effort

    3. Warm site: C. A site that relies on shared storage and backups for recovery

    4. Service bureau: A. An organization that can provide on-site or off-site IT services in the event of a disaster

Chapter 8: Software Development Security (Domain 8)

1. A. Limiting request rates can prevent abuse of APIs like this one. The other suggestions are all poor recommendations. In general, requests should require HTTPS, tokens are used for security using tools like JSON web tokens (JWT), and HTTP methods may be restricted, but GET, POST, and PUT are some of the most common methods used for API access and are far more typically whitelisted.

2. A, B, C. Botnets are used for a wide variety of malicious purposes, including scanning the network for vulnerable systems, conducting brute-force attacks against other systems, mining cryptocurrency, and sending out spam messages. They are not commonly used to conduct man-in-the-middle attacks, which are normally waged through DNS poisoning or similar mechanisms.

3. C. Code review takes place after code has been developed, which occurs after the design phase of the system's development life cycle (SDLC). Code review may use a combination of manual and automated techniques or rely solely on one or the other. It should be a peer-driven process that includes developers who did not write the code. Developers should expect to complete the review of around 300 lines per hour, on average.

4. A. This code is an example of parameterization, which can help avoid SQL injection. Note that each parameter has a placeholder, which is then passed to the query.

5. C. One of the responsibilities of the release control process is ensuring that acceptance testing is performed, to ensure that any alterations to end-user tasks are understood and functional prior to code release. The request control, change control, and configuration control processes do not include acceptance testing.

6. B. Cross-site request forgery (XSRF or CSRF) attacks exploit the trust that sites have in a user's browser by attempting to force the submission of authenticated requests to third-party sites. Session hijacking attacks attempt to steal previously authenticated sessions but do not force the browser to submit requests. A SQL injection directly attacks a database through a web application. Cross-site scripting uses reflected input to trick a user's browser into executing untrusted code from a trusted site.

7. A. The OpenSSL package is a widely used implementation of TLS encryption that is available as an open-source package. It is not commercial off-the-shelf software (COTS). While it might be developed by third parties, it is more accurate to describe it as open source. The library is available as code for free use, but not as a managed service.

8. D. The error message shown in the figure is the infamous "Blue Screen of Death" that occurs when a Windows system experiences a dangerous failure and enters a fail secure state. If the system had "failed open," it would have continued operation. The error described is a memory fault that is likely recoverable by rebooting the system. There is no indication that the system has run out of usable memory.

9. A, B, C. Software threat modeling is designed to reduce the number of security-related design and coding flaws as well as the severity of other flaws. The developer or evaluator of software has no control over the threat environment, because it is external to the organization.

10. C. In the diagram, `Account` is the name of the class. `Owner` and `Balance` are attributes of that class. `AddFunds` and `RemoveFunds` are methods of the class.

11. D. Rapid Application Development, or RAD, focuses on fast development and the ability to quickly adjust to changing requirements. RAD uses four phases: requirements planning, user design, construction, and cutover.

12. A. Dynamic testing of software typically occurs in a black-box environment where the tester does not have access to the source code. Static testing, white-box testing, and code review approaches all require access to the source code of the application.

13. C. Given the list of options here, the root cause is most likely an issue with an authorization check that does not properly limit users to the authorization that they should have. Data validation issues are more likely to allow injection attacks or to allow bad data to be input, while session management issues would allow session hijacking or might actually cause them to be logged in as another user. Finally, error handling would show up as a problem when errors occurred, which this problem does not indicate.

14. C. Aggregate functions summarize large amounts of data and provide only summary information as a result. When carefully crafted, aggregate functions may unintentionally reveal sensitive information.

15. B. The best protection against buffer overflow attacks is server-side input validation. This technique limits user input to approved ranges of values that fit within allocated buffers. While firewalls and intrusion prevention systems may contain controls that limit buffer overflows, it would be more effective to perform filtering on the application server. Encryption cannot protect against buffer overflow attacks.

16. C. Each of these problems is caused by improper or missing input validation and can be resolved by handling inputs properly. In many cases, this can be done using libraries or methods already built into the language or framework that the developer is using.

17. C. Acme Widgets is clearly in the initial stage of the SW-CMM. This stage is characterized by the absence of formal process. The company may still produce working code, but it does so in a disorganized fashion.

18. B. The Repeatable stage is the second stage in the SW-CMM, following the Initial stage. It should be the next milestone goal for Acme Widgets. The Repeatable stage is characterized by basic life cycle management processes.

19. A. The Defined stage of the SW-CMM is marked by the presence of basic life cycle management processes and reuse of code. It includes the use of requirements management, software project planning, quality assurance, and configuration management practices.

20. D. The Managed stage is the fourth stage in the SW-CMM, following the Defined stage. It should be the next milestone goal for Beta Particles. The Managed stage is characterized by the use of quantitative software development measures.

21. C. Referential integrity ensures that records exist in a secondary table when they are referenced with a foreign key from another table. Foreign keys are the mechanism used to enforce referential integrity.

22. A. Macro viruses are most commonly found in office productivity documents, such as Microsoft Word documents that end in the .doc or .docx extension. They are not commonly found in executable files with the .com or .exe extension.

23. C. The degree of a database table is the number of attributes in the table. Victor's table has six attributes: the employee's user ID, home telephone, office telephone, mobile telephone, office location, and job title.

24. C. The string shown in the logs is characteristic of a directory traversal attack where the attacker attempts to force the web application to navigate up the file hierarchy and retrieve a file that should not normally be provided to a web user, such as the password file. The series of "double dots" is indicative of a directory traversal attack because it is the character string used to reference the directory one level up in a hierarchy.

25. C. Design reviews should take place after the development of functional and control specifications but before the creation of code. The code review, unit testing, and functional testing all take place after the creation of code and, therefore, after the design review.

26. C. Regression testing is software testing that runs a set of known inputs against an application and then compares the results to those produced by an earlier version of the software. It is designed to capture unanticipated consequences of deploying new code versions prior to introducing them into a production environment.

27. D. Assurance, when it comes to software, is the level of confidence that software is free from vulnerabilities, either intentionally designed into the software or accidentally inserted at any time during its life cycle, and that the software functions in the intended manner. It is a term typically used in military and defense environments.

28. C. The change control process is responsible for providing an organized framework within which multiple developers can create and test a solution prior to rolling it out in a production environment. Request control provides a framework for user requests. Release control manages the deployment of code into production. Configuration control ensures that changes to software versions are made in accordance with the change and configuration management policies.

29. D. Aggregation is a security issue that arises when a collection of facts has a higher classification than the classification of any of those facts standing alone. An inference problem occurs when an attacker can pull together pieces of less sensitive information and use them to derive information of greater sensitivity. SQL injection is a web application exploit. Multilevel security is a system control that allows the simultaneous processing of information at different classification levels.

30. B. Code libraries are packages of reusable functions that may be incorporated into individual development projects. Ron could use libraries to easily share code among his team. Code repositories may be used to manage the distribution and updating of these libraries, but that is a second-order use case, making code libraries the best answer. Integrated development environments (IDEs) are tools used by developers to create software, while dynamic application security testing (DAST) is used to verify the correct implementation of code.

31. A. Black-box testing begins with no prior knowledge of the system implementation, simulating a user's perspective. White-box and gray-box testing provide full and partial knowledge of the system, respectively, in advance of the test. Blue boxes are a phone hacking tool and are not used in software testing.

32. B. In this example, the two SQL commands are indeed bundled in a transaction, but it is not an error to issue an update command that does not match any rows. Therefore, the first command would "succeed" in updating zero rows and not generate an error or cause the transaction to roll back. The second command would then execute, reducing the balance of the second account by $250.

33. A. Software development kits (SDKs) are code libraries and other tools made available to assist developers in creating code. An integrated development environment (IDE) may be a component of an SDK, but it is not necessarily part of every SDK. An application programming interface (API) is a set of functions made available to external developers, but the code does not execute on the users' machine, as would a code library or other SDK tools. Data loss prevention (DLP) capabilities are not a component of software development toolsets.

34. C. A fail open configuration may be appropriate in this case. In this configuration, the firewall would continue to pass traffic without inspection while it is restarting. This would minimize downtime, and the traffic would still be protected by the other security controls described in the scenario. Failover devices and high availability clusters would indeed increase availability, but at potentially significant expense. Redundant disks would not help in this scenario because no disk failure is described.

35. D. An inference problem occurs when an attacker can pull together pieces of less sensitive information and use them to derive information of greater sensitivity. SQL injection is a web application exploit. Multilevel security is a system control that allows the simultaneous processing of information at different classification levels. Parameterization is a security control used to reduce the likelihood of attacks that rely upon improper user input.

36. B. Polymorphic viruses mutate each time they infect a system by making adjustments to their code that assists them in evading signature detection mechanisms. Encrypted viruses also mutate from infection to infection but do so by encrypting themselves with different keys on each device.

37. A. The message forum is clearly susceptible to a cross-site scripting (XSS) attack. The code that Linda discovered in the message is a definitive example of an attempt to conduct cross-site scripting, and the alert box that she received demonstrates that the vulnerability exists. The website may also be vulnerable to cross-site request forgery, SQL injection, improper authentication, and other attacks, but there is no evidence of this provided in the scenario.

38. A. The script that Linda discovered merely pops up a message on a user's screen and does not perform any more malicious action. This type of script, using an `alert()` call, is commonly used to probe websites for cross-site scripting vulnerabilities.

39. B. Web application firewalls (WAFs) sit in front of web applications and watch for potentially malicious web attacks, including cross-site scripting. They then block that traffic from reaching the web application. An intrusion detection system (IDS) may detect the attack but is unable to take action to prevent it. DLP and VPN solutions are unable to detect web application attacks.

40. C. Input validation verifies that user-supplied input does not violate security conditions and is the most effective defense against cross-site scripting attacks. Bounds checking is a form of input validation, but it is typically used to ensure that numeric input falls within an acceptable range and is not applicable against cross-site scripting attacks. Peer review and OS patching are both good security practices but are unlikely to be effective against a cross-site scripting attack.

41. B. RStudio is a tool used to assist in the creation of code, otherwise known as an integrated development environment (IDE). Software development kits (SDKs) are code libraries and other tools made available to assist developers in creating code. An application programming interface (API) is a set of functions made available to external developers, but the code does not execute on the users' machine, as would a code library or other SDK tools. Data loss prevention (DLP) capabilities are not a component of software development toolsets.

42. D. Full SAFe is designed to support enterprises in building and maintaining large integrated solutions with the collaboration of hundreds of practitioners. It provides the most extensive level of guidance, with roles, responsibilities, and activities needed to sustainably deliver complex solutions. Essential SAFe focuses on the basic elements of the framework needed to be agile, Large Solution SAFe is for developing large and complex solutions that do not require the constructs of the portfolio level, and Portfolio SAFe is for aligning enterprise strategy with execution but does not address the complexity of building large solutions that Full SAFe is designed for.

43. C. The JVM is the runtime virtual machine that allows the execution of Java code on a device. The JVM implements the Java sandbox, but that is only one of its many functions. The JVM itself is not a change manager or code repository.

44. C. User acceptance testing (UAT) is typically the last phase of the testing process. It verifies that the solution developed meets user requirements and validates it against use cases. Unit testing, integration testing, and system testing are all conducted earlier in the process leading up to UAT.

45. D. When organizations adopt a continuous integration/continuous delivery (CI/CD) approach to software development, they may deploy code extremely rapidly. In fact, some organizations deploy new code to production hundreds or even thousands of times per day using this approach.

46. C. The Open Worldwide Application Security Project (OWASP) is widely considered as the most authoritative source on web application security issues. They publish the OWASP Top Ten list that publicizes the most critical web application security issues.

47. B. Chris is in an Agile sprint phase and is likely developing code based on user stories. Planning includes stakeholder stories, as well as design and test case preparation. Testing involves ensuring that the code works properly and meets requirements. Deployment includes the actual deployment of the application, as well as additional verification and testing.

48. D. Security information and event management (SIEM) systems do correlate information from multiple sources and perform analysis, but they stop short of providing automated playbook responses. That is the realm of security orchestration, automation, and response (SOAR) platforms. Intrusion prevention platforms have a more limited scope, allowing the blocking of traffic based upon analysis performed by the IPS itself. Log repositories simply collect log information and do not perform analysis.

49. B. This is an example of a specific type of buffer overflow known as an off-by-one error. The first line of the code defines an array of 10 elements, which would be numbered 0 through 9. The second line of code tries to place a value in the 11th element of the array (remember, array counting begins at 0!), which would cause an overflow.

50. C. Lost updates occur when one transaction writes a value to the database that overwrites a value needed by transactions that have earlier precedence, causing those transactions to read an incorrect value. Dirty reads occur when one transaction reads a value from a database that was written by another transaction that did not commit. Incorrect summaries occur when one transaction is using an aggregate function to summarize data stored in a database while a second transaction is making modifications to the database, causing the summary to include incorrect information. SQL injection is a web application security flaw, not a database concurrency problem.

51. A. Transport Layer Security (TLS) provides the most effective defense against session hijacking because it encrypts all traffic between the client and server, preventing the attacker from stealing session credentials. Secure Sockets Layer (SSL) also encrypts traffic, but it is vulnerable to attacks against its encryption technology. Complex and expiring cookies are a good idea, but they are not sufficient protection against session hijacking.

52. C. The purpose of the change advisory board (CAB) is to review and then approve or reject proposed code changes. The CAB is not normally involved in the approval of developer credentials, the conduct of lessons learned sessions, or the prioritization of software development efforts.

53. B. `git` is a version management tool that is very commonly used by developers to interact with code repositories, such as those hosted by GitHub. `grep` is a command-line tool used to search files for specific content. `lsof` is a command used to list the open files on a system. `gcc` is a C language compiler used to transform source code into executable code.

54. C. The single quotation mark in the input field is a telltale sign that this is a SQL injection attack. The single quotation mark is used to escape outside the SQL code's input field, and the text following it is used to directly manipulate the SQL command sent from the web application to the database.

55. B. Client-side input validation is not an effective control against any type of attack because the attacker can easily bypass the validation by altering the code on the client. Escaping restricted characters prevents them from being passed to the database, as does parameterization. Limiting database permissions prevents dangerous code from executing.

56. B. PERT charts use nodes to represent milestones or deliverables and then show the estimated time to move between milestones. Gantt charts use a different format with a row for each task and lines showing the expected duration of the task. Work breakdown structures are an earlier deliverable that divides project work into achievable tasks. Wireframe diagrams are used in application UI design.

57. D. Regression testing is performed after developers make changes to an application. It reruns a number of test cases and compares the results to baseline results. Orthogonal array testing is a method for generating test cases based on statistical analysis. Pattern testing uses records of past software bugs to inform the analysis. Matrix testing develops a matrix of all possible inputs and outputs to inform the test plan.

58. B. Cross-site scripting (XSS) attacks may take advantage of the use of reflected input in a web application where input provided by one user is displayed to another user. Input validation is a control used to prevent XSS attacks. XSS does not require an unpatched server or any firewall rules beyond those permitting access to the web application.

59. A. In a white-box test, the tester has access to full implementation details of the system, including source code, prior to beginning the test. In gray-box testing, the tester has partial knowledge. In black-box testing, the tester has no knowledge of the system and tests it from a user perspective. Blue boxes are a phone hacking tool and are not used in software testing.

60. C. Heuristic-based antimalware software has a higher likelihood of detecting a zero-day exploit than signature-based methods. Heuristic-based software does not require frequent signature updates because it does not rely upon monitoring systems for the presence of known malware. The trade-off with this approach is that it has a higher false positive rate than signature detection methods.

61. D. One possibility for the clean scan results is that the virus is using stealth techniques, such as intercepting read requests from the antivirus software and returning a correct-looking version of the infected file. The system may also be the victim of a zero-day attack, using a virus that is not yet included in the signature definition files provided by the antivirus vendor.

62. A. In URL encoding, the . character is replaced by %252E, and the / character is replaced by %252F. You can see this in the log entry, where the expected pattern of ../../ is replaced by %252E%252E%252F%252E%252E%252F.

63. C. Attacks where the malicious user tricks the victim's web browser into executing a script through the use of a third-party site are known as cross-site scripting (XSS) attacks. This particular attack is a persistent XSS attack because it remains on the discussion forum until an administrator discovers and deletes it, giving it the ability to affect many users.

64. C. The Agile Manifesto includes 12 principles for software development. Three of those are listed as answer choices: maximizing the amount of work not done is essential, build projects around motivated individuals, and welcome changing requirements throughout the development process. Agile does not, however, consider clear documentation the primary measure of progress. Instead, working software is the primary measure of progress.

65. B. Each change should be the result of a reviewed and approved request for change (RFC). These RFCs may be approved by the change advisory board (CAB). The security information and event management (SIEM) and security orchestration, automation, and response (SOAR) platforms used by the organization would not normally contain information about the change management process.

66. D. A key-value store is an example of a NoSQL database that does not follow a relational or hierarchical model like traditional databases. A graph database is another example of a NoSQL database, but it uses nodes and edges to store data rather than keys and values.

67. C. A database failure in the middle of a transaction causes the rollback of the entire transaction. In this scenario, the database would not execute either command because doing so would violate the atomicity property of the transaction.

68. B. When using commercial off-the-shelf (COTS) software, customers do not generally have access to the source code and must depend upon the vendor to release security patches that correct vulnerabilities. Other controls, such as intrusion prevention systems and firewalls, may be able to help mitigate the issue, depending upon the nature of the flaw, but they will not correct it.

69. B. Static testing performs code analysis in an offline fashion, without actually executing the code. Dynamic testing evaluates code in a runtime environment. Both static and dynamic testing may use automated tools, and both are important security testing techniques.

70. D. The chart shown in the figure is a Gantt chart, showing the proposed start and end dates for different activities. It is developed based on the work breakdown structure (WBS), which is developed based on functional requirements. Program Evaluation Review Technique (PERT) charts show the project schedule as a series of numbered nodes.

71. D. In a gray-box test, the tester evaluates the software from a user perspective but has access to the source code as the test is conducted. White-box tests also have access to the source code but perform testing from a developer's perspective. Black-box tests work from a user's perspective but do not have access to source code. Blue boxes are a telephone hacking tool and not a software testing technique.

72. D. The Time of Check to Time of Use (TOC/TOU) attack exploits timing differences between when a system verifies authorization and software uses that authorization to perform an action. It is an example of a race condition attack. The other three attacks mentioned do not depend on precise timing.

73. D. Each of these input parameters makes up part of the attack surface of the application. Attackers may opt to target any of them to attack the code or its supporting infrastructure.

74. B. Threat modeling commonly involves decomposing the application to understand it and how it interacts with other components or users. Next, identifying and ranking threats allows you to focus on the threats that should be prioritized. Finally, identifying how to mitigate those threats finishes the process. Once complete, an organization can take action to handle the threats that were identified with appropriate controls.

75. D. The fail closed approach prevents any activity from taking place during a system security failure and is the most conservative approach to failure management. Fail open takes the opposite philosophy, allowing all activity in the event of a security control failure. Fail clear and fail mitigation are not failure management approaches.

76. D. The illustration shows the spiral model of software development. In this approach, developers use multiple iterations of a waterfall-style software development process. This becomes a "loop" of iterations through similar processes. The original waterfall approach does not iterate through the entire process repeatedly. Some variants do allow iteration, but only by allowing movement backward and forward one stage. The Agile approach to software development focuses on iterative improvement and does not follow a rigorous SDLC model. Lean is a process improvement methodology and not a software development model.

77. D. In a software-as-a-service solution, the vendor manages both the physical infrastructure and the complete application stack, providing the customer with access to a fully managed application.

78. A. The request process begins with a user-initiated request for a feature. Change and release control are initiated by developers seeking to implement changes. Design review is a phase of the change approval process initiated by developers when they have a completed design.

79. C. Polyinstantiation allows the storage of multiple different pieces of information in a database at different classification levels to prevent attackers from inferring anything about the absence of information. Input validation, server-side validation, and parameterization are all techniques used to prevent web application attacks and are not effective against inference attacks.

80. C. While Ursula may certainly use an object model, data dictionary, and primary key in her development effort, external developers cannot directly use them to access her code. An application programming interface (API) allows other developers to call Ursula's code from within their own without knowing the details of Ursula's implementation.

81. C. This is an example of software-defined security (SDS), where security infrastructure may be easily manipulated by code. Answering this question is tricky because several of the other terms are closely related. Software-defined security is an example of infrastructure as code (IaC), but SDS is a more descriptive, and therefore better, answer. SDS is commonly used within an Agile development framework. The DevOps approach links together development and operations but is generally called DevSecOps when it also includes SDS.

82. D. Messages similar to the one shown here are indicative of a ransomware attack. The attacker encrypts files on a user's hard drive and then demands a ransom, normally paid in Bitcoin, for the decryption key required to restore access to the original content. Encrypted viruses, on the other hand, use encryption to hide themselves from antivirus mechanisms and do not alter other contents on the system.

83. D. Despite many organizations moving to Agile, DevOps, or other more responsive development methodologies, waterfall remains a strong contender when clear objectives and stable requirements are combined with a need to prevent flaws and to have a high level of control over the development process and output.

84. D. Neural networks attempt to use complex computational techniques to model the behavior of the human mind. Knowledge banks are a component of expert systems, which are designed to capture and reapply human knowledge. Decision support systems are designed to provide advice to those carrying out standard procedures and are often driven by expert systems.

85. B. In level 2, the Repeatable level of the SW-CMM, an organization introduces basic life cycle management processes. Reuse of code in an organized fashion begins, and repeatable results are expected from similar projects. The key process areas for this level include Requirements Management, Software Project Planning, Software Project Tracking and Oversight, Software Subcontract Management, Software Quality Assurance, and Software Configuration Management.

86. C. The critical fact in this question is that Lucas suspects the tampering took place before the employee departed. This is the signature of a logic bomb: malicious code that lies dormant until certain conditions are met. The other attack types listed here—privilege escalation, SQL injection, and remote code execution—would more likely take place in real time.

87. A. The Agile approach to software development embraces four principles. It values individuals and interactions over processes and tools, working software over comprehensive documentation, customer collaboration over contract negotiation, and responding to change over following a plan.

88. C. API developers commonly use API keys to limit access to authorized users and applications. Encryption provides for confidentiality of information exchanged using an API but does not provide authentication. Input validation is an application security technique used to protect against malicious input. IP filters may be used to limit access to an API, but they are not commonly used because it is difficult to deploy an API with IP filters since the filters require constant modification and maintenance as endpoints change.

89. D. An audit kickoff meeting should clearly describe the scope and purpose of the audit as well as the expected time frame. Auditors should never approach an audit with any expectations about what they will discover because the findings should be developed based only upon the results of audit examinations.

90. B. In the waterfall model, the software development process follows five sequential steps that are, in order, Requirements, Design, Coding, Testing, and Maintenance. Note that these phases may be further subdivided. The Requirements phase often begins with System Requirements and then moves on to Software Requirements. The Design phase often begins with Preliminary Design and then moves on to Detailed Design.

91. C. In a platform-as-a-service solution, the customer supplies application code that the vendor then executes on its own infrastructure.

92. D. Input validation ensures that the data provided to a program as input matches the expected parameters. Limit checks are a special form of input validation that ensure that the value remains within an expected range, but there was no range specified in this scenario. Fail open and fail secure are options when planning for possible system failures.

93. B, D. Dynamic application security tools conduct their testing by actually executing the code. This is the case for both fuzzing and web application vulnerability scanning. Code reviews and static analysis packages analyze the code itself but do not execute it, making them static application security testing (SAST) tools.

94. C. The DevOps approach to technology management seeks to integrate software development, operations, and quality assurance in a seamless approach that builds collaboration between the three disciplines.

95. A. Deploying a web application firewall (WAF) may reduce the likelihood or impact of a web application vulnerability and is, therefore, a good example of risk mitigation. Encryption is also a risk mitigation control, but it is less likely be effective against a web application security flaw. Purchasing an insurance policy is an example of risk transference, not risk mitigation. Discontinuing use of the software is an example of risk avoidance, not risk mitigation.

96. D. Dirty reads occur when one transaction reads a value from a database that was written by another transaction that did not commit. Lost updates occur when one transaction writes a value to the database that overwrites a value needed by transactions that have earlier precedence, causing those transactions to read an incorrect value. Incorrect summaries occur when one transaction is using an aggregate function to summarize data stored in a database, while a second transaction is making modifications to the database, causing the summary to include incorrect information. SQL injection is a web application security flaw, not a database concurrency problem.

97. A. The integrated product team (IPT) approach brought together cross-functional teams and was designed by the U.S. Department of Defense in 1995. It was a predecessor to the Agile methodology, which uses tools like the scrum approach and user stories to conduct software development work.

98. B. Storage is an infrastructure component and, therefore, a block storage service is an example of an infrastructure-as-a-service (IaaS) cloud service. Software-as-a-service (SaaS) models provide full applications managed by the provider. Platform-as-a-service (PaaS) and function-as-a-service (FaaS) approaches allow developers to run their own code on an infrastructure platform managed by the provider.

99. The code testing methods match to their definitions as follows:

1. Regression testing: C. A testing method that is used to verify that previously tested software performs the same way after changes are made

2. Integration testing: D. A testing method used to validate how software modules work together

3. Unit testing: B. A testing method that focuses on modules or smaller sections of code for testing

4. System testing: A. Testing on a complete integrated product

100. The terms match to their definitions as follows:

1. Session hijacking: C. An exploitation method that often involves cookies or keys to gain unauthorized access to a computer or service

2. Cross-site scripting: A. An attack that injects a malicious script into otherwise trusted websites

3. Cross-site request forgery: D. An attack that forces a user to execute unwanted actions in a website or application they are currently logged into

4. SQL injection: B. An attack that is designed to execute commands against a database via an insecure web application

Chapter 9: Practice Test 1

1. A, B, D. Packets with public IP addresses will routinely be allowed to enter the network, so you should not create a rule to block them. Packets with internal source addresses should never originate from outside the network, so they should be blocked from entering the network. Packets with external source addresses should never be found on the internal network, so they should be blocked from leaving the network. Finally, private IP addresses should never be used on the Internet, so packets containing private IP addresses should be blocked from leaving the network.

2. B. A content distribution network (CDN) is designed to provide reliable, low-latency, geographically distributed content distribution. In this scenario, a CDN is an ideal solution. A P2P CDN like BitTorrent isn't a typical choice for a commercial entity, whereas redundant servers or a hot site can provide high availability but won't provide the remaining requirements.

3. A, B, C. A forensic disk controller performs four functions. One of those, write blocking, intercepts write commands sent to the device and prevents them from modifying data on the device. The other three functions include returning data requested by a read operation, returning access-significant information from the device, and reporting errors from the device back to the forensic host. The controller should not prevent read commands from being sent to the device because those commands may return crucial information.

4. B. RAID 1, disk mirroring, requires two physical disks that will contain copies of the same data.

5. D. The TGS, or ticket-granting service (which is usually on the same server as the KDC), receives a TGT from the client. It validates the TGT and the user's rights to access the service they are requesting to use. The TGS then issues a ticket and session keys to the client. The AS serves as the authentication server, which forwards the username to the KDC. It's worth noting that the client doesn't communicate with the KDC directly. Instead, it will communicate with the TGT and the AS, which means KDC isn't an appropriate answer here.

6. C. This is an example of a civil investigation because it relates to a contract dispute and will likely wind up being litigated in civil court. Administrative investigations are for internal purposes and are not applicable when a third party is being investigated. Criminal and regulatory investigations may only be initiated by those with regulatory authority, typically government agencies.

7. C. Wave pattern motion detectors transmit ultrasonic or microwave signals into the monitored area, watching for changes in the returned signals bouncing off objects. Infrared heat-based detectors watch for unusual heat patterns. Capacitance detectors work based upon electromagnetic fields.

8. C. Stateful packet inspection firewalls, also known as dynamic packet filtering firewalls, track the state of a conversation and can allow a response from a remote system based on an internal system being allowed to start the communication. Static packet filtering and circuit-level gateways only filter based on source and destination IP addresses and ports along with the protocol being used, whereas application-level gateway firewalls proxy traffic for specific applications.

9. B. A captive portal can require those who want to connect to and use Wi-Fi to provide an email address to connect. This allows Ben to provide easy-to-use wireless while meeting his business purposes. WPA2-PSK is the preshared key mode of WPA and won't provide information about users who are given a key. WPA3's SAE mode would be preferable to WPA2-PSK, but it still does not allow for the data gathering Ben desires. Sharing a password doesn't allow for data gathering either.

10. B. Many modern wireless routers can provide multiple SSIDs. Ben can create a private, secure network for his business operations, but he will need to make sure that the customer and business networks are firewalled or otherwise logically separated from each other. Running WPA3 on the same SSID isn't possible without creating another wireless network and would cause confusion for customers (SSIDs aren't required to be unique). Running a network in Enterprise mode isn't used for open networks, and WEP is outdated and incredibly vulnerable.

11. D. Unencrypted open networks broadcast traffic in the clear. This means that unencrypted sessions to websites can be easily captured with a packet sniffer. Some tools like FireSheep have been specifically designed to capture sessions from popular websites. Fortunately, many websites now use TLS by default, but other sites still send user session information in the clear. Shared passwords are not the cause of the vulnerability, ARP spoofing isn't an issue with wireless networks, and a Trojan is designed to look like safe software, not to compromise a router.

12. C. It is possible that Kevin could use any one of these documents. We should zero in on the portion of the question where it indicates that these are best practices. This implies that the advice is not mandatory and, therefore, would not go into a policy or standard. The fact that the advice is general in nature means that it is likely not well-suited to the step-by-step nature of a procedure. A guideline would be the perfect place to document these best practices.

13. D. Clipping is an analysis technique that reports alerts only after they exceed a set threshold. It is a specific form of sampling, which is a more general term that describes any attempt to excerpt records for review. Thresholding is not a commonly used term. Administrators may choose to configure automatic or manual account lockout after failed login attempts, but that is not described in the scenario.

14. B. RADIUS is a common AAA technology used to provide services for dial-up, wireless networks, network devices, and a range of other systems. OAuth is an authorization protocol used to allow applications to act on a user's behalf without sharing the password and is used for many web applications. OpenID Connect is an authentication layer on top of OAuth that allows clients to verify the identity of an end user. XTACACS, an earlier protocol for network authentication, has largely been superseded by more secure and robust protocols like RADIUS, and its proprietary nature does not fit Sally's criteria.

15. C. In an inference attack, the attacker uses several pieces of generic nonsensitive information to determine a specific sensitive value. In a salami slicing attack, the attacker siphons off minute quantities of money many times to accumulate a large amount of funds. In a data diddling attack, the attacker alters the contents of a database. Social engineering attacks exploit human psychology to achieve their goals.

16. A. The Take rule in the Take-Grant protection model allows a subject to take rights from another object if the subject has the take right over that object. In this scenario, if Alice has the take right over Bob and Bob has read permissions on an object, Alice can use the Take rule to grant herself the read permissions that Bob possesses. The Grant rule is for granting rights to other subjects, not for taking them for oneself. The Create rule is used to create new objects or rights, not to transfer existing ones. There is no Remote rule in the Take-Grant protection model.

17. B. Brute-force attacks try every possible password. In this attack, the password is changing by one letter at each attempt, which indicates that it is a brute-force attack. A dictionary attack would use dictionary words for the attack, whereas a man-in-the-middle or pass-the-hash attack would most likely not be visible in an authentication log except as a successful login.

18. B. Isolation requires that transactions operate separately from each other. Atomicity ensures that if any part of a database transaction fails, the entire transaction must be rolled back as if it never occurred. Consistency ensures that all transactions are consistent with the logical rules of the database, such as having a primary key. Durability requires that once a transaction is committed to the database it must be preserved. Together, these properties make up the ACID model.

19. B. Worms have built-in propagation mechanisms that do not require user interaction, such as scanning for systems containing known vulnerabilities and then exploiting those vulnerabilities to gain access. Viruses and Trojan horses typically require user interaction to spread. Logic bombs do not spread from system to system but lie in wait until certain conditions are met, triggering the delivery of their payload.

20. B, C. The Health Insurance Portability and Accountability Act (HIPAA) is a U.S. law governing the healthcare sector that does provide for criminal penalties. The Sarbanes–Oxley (SOX) Act governs publicly traded corporations and also provides for criminal penalties. The Family Educational Rights and Privacy Act (FERPA) is a U.S. law governing educational records, but it does not provide for criminal penalties. PCI DSS, the Payment Card Industry Data Security Standard, is an industry standard for payment card operations and handling. Because it is not a law, PCI DSS violations cannot incur criminal sanctions.

21. C. The TCP three-way handshake consists of an initial contact via a SYN, or synchronize flagged packet, which receives a response with a SYN/ACK, or synchronize and acknowledge flagged packet, which is acknowledged by the original sender with an ACK, or acknowledge packet. RST is used in TCP to reset a connection, PSH is used to send data immediately, and FIN is used to end a connection.

22. A, C, D. MDM products do not have the capability of assuming control of a device not currently managed by the organization. This would be equivalent to hacking into a device owned by someone else and might constitute a crime. They do normally provide the ability to manage device backups, enforce the use of encryption, and remotely wipe the contents of mobile devices.

23. A. Identity as a service (IDaaS) provides an identity platform as a third-party service. This can provide benefits, including integration with cloud services and removing overhead for maintenance of traditional on-premises identity systems but can also create risk due to third-party control of identity services and reliance on an off-site identity infrastructure.

24. A. Gina's actions harm the CISSP certification and information security community by undermining the integrity of the examination process. While Gina also is acting dishonestly, the harm to the profession is more of a direct violation of the ISC2 Code of Ethics.

25. A. The annualized loss expectancy (ALE) is the amount of damage that the organization expects to occur each year as the result of a given risk. ALE is calculated by multiplying the single loss expectancy (SLE), which is the expected financial loss from a single flooding event, by the annual rate of occurrence (ARO), which is the expected frequency of flooding events per year. The ALE helps organizations to understand the potential impact of risks and to make informed decisions about risk mitigation strategies and investments in protective measures. The exposure factor (EF) is the percentage of the asset expected to be damaged during an incident.

26. C. The whitelisting approach to application control allows users to install only those software packages specifically approved by administrators. This would be an appropriate approach in a scenario where application installation needs to be tightly controlled. Blacklisting, which blocks known malicious or unauthorized applications, would not be as effective in this scenario because it allows all software to run unless it appears on the blacklist. Graylisting and bluelisting are made-up terms.

27. A. This is a clear example of a denial-of-service attack—denying legitimate users authorized access to the system through the use of overwhelming traffic. It goes beyond a reconnaissance attack because the attacker is affecting the system, but it is not a compromise because the attacker did not attempt to gain access to the system. There is no reason to believe that a malicious insider was involved.

28. A. The Company ID column is likely unique for each row in the table, making it the best choice for a primary key. There may be multiple companies that share the same name or ZIP code. Similarly, a single sales representative likely serves more than one company, making those fields unsuitable for use as a unique identifier.

29. C. Personally identifiable information (PII) includes data that can be used to distinguish or trace that person's identity and also includes their educational, financial, and employment information. PHI is personal health information, EDI is electronic data interchange, and proprietary data is used to maintain an organization's competitive advantage.

30. D. 129.53.44.124 is a valid public IP address and a legitimate destination for traffic leaving Bob's network. 12.8.195.15 is a public address on Bob's network and should not be a destination address on a packet leaving the network. 10.8.15.9 and 192.168.109.55 are both private IP addresses that should not be routed to the Internet.

31. D. Binary keyspaces contain a number of keys equal to 2 raised to the power of the number of bits. Two to the eighth power is 256, so the keyspace will increase by a factor of 256.

32. A, B, C, D. Traditional office shredding machines may be used for the disposal of paper records and, depending upon their grade, may also be able to shred credit cards. Industrial shredders are capable of destroying larger pieces of equipment, including removable media and both traditional and SSD hard drives.

33. A. Encrypting the files reduces the probability that the data will be successfully stolen, so it is an example of risk mitigation. Deleting the files would be risk avoidance. Purchasing insurance would be risk transference. Taking no action would be risk acceptance.

34. C. Sampling should be done randomly to avoid human bias. Sampling is an effective process if it is done on a truly random sample of sufficient size to provide effective coverage of the userbase. It is infeasible for a single person to review every single record. In an organization of 50,000 users with a 24% annual turnover, it is likely that at least 1,000 of those records have changed in the last month. This is still too many records to review. Asking account administrators to select the records to review is a conflict of interest, as they are the group being audited.

35. A. In the case of an involuntary termination under adverse circumstances, the user is being fired and may have a negative and potentially hostile reaction. For this reason, it is important to terminate access immediately upon the user being informed of the termination. Terminating access prior to notification may tip the user off to the termination in advance. Leaving access privileges available after termination poses a risk of malicious insider activity.

36. C. The file clearly shows HTTP requests, as evidenced by the many GET commands. Therefore, this is an example of an application log from an HTTP server.

37. A. The Common Vulnerability Scoring System (CVSS) is a standardized approach to rating the severity of vulnerabilities and would be the most helpful tool for Roger's work. The STRIDE and ATT&CK models are used to classify the nature, not the severity, of threats. The PASTA model is designed to help with countermeasure selection.

38. B. Social engineering exploits humans to allow attacks to succeed. Since help-desk employees are specifically tasked with being helpful, they may be targeted by attackers posing as legitimate employees. Trojans are a type of malware, whereas phishing is a targeted attack via electronic communication methods intended to capture passwords or other sensitive data. Whaling is a type of phishing aimed at high-profile or important targets.

39. B. If the vendor operates with reasonable security procedures, it is unlikely that the devices will be tampered with at the vendor's site. Similarly, if Greg's organization has reasonable security procedures, tampering at his site is also unlikely. Misconfiguration by an administrator is always possible, but this is a post-installation risk and not a supply chain risk. It is possible that devices will be intercepted and tampered with while in transit from the vendor to Greg's organization.

40. C. In a single-level security environment, systems should be assigned the classification level of the highest classification of information they are ever expected to process. Systems may not process information that is above their classification level without reclassifying the system upward.

41. C. A hybrid authentication service can provide authentication services both in the cloud and on-premises, ensuring that service outages due to interrupted links are minimized. An on-site service would continue to work during an Internet outage but would not allow the e-commerce website to authenticate. A cloud service would leave the corporate location offline. Outsourcing authentication does not indicate whether the solution is on- or off-premises and thus isn't a useful answer.

42. C. Federation links identity information between multiple organizations. Federating with a business partner can allow identification and authorization to occur between them, making integration much easier. Single sign-on would reduce the number of times a user has to log in but will not facilitate the sharing of identity information. Multifactor authentication can help secure authentication but again doesn't help integrate with a third party. Finally, an identity as a service provider might provide federation but doesn't guarantee it.

43. B. Security Assertion Markup Language (SAML) is frequently used to integrate cloud services and provides the ability to make authentication and authorization assertions. Active Directory integrations are possible but are less common for cloud service providers, and RADIUS is not typically used for integrations like this. Service Provisioning Markup Language (SPML) is used to provision users, resources, and services, not for authentication and authorization.

44. B. Rainbow tables use precomputed password hashes to conduct cracking attacks against password files. They may be frustrated by the use of salting, which adds a specified value to the password prior to hashing, making it much more difficult to perform precomputation. Password expiration policies, password complexity policies, and user education may all contribute to password security, but they are not direct defenses against the use of rainbow tables.

45. C. A honeypot is a decoy computer system used to bait intruders into attacking. A honeynet is a network of multiple honeypots that creates a more sophisticated environment for intruders to explore. A pseudoflaw is a false vulnerability in a system that may attract an attacker. A darknet is a segment of unused network address space that should have no network activity and, therefore, may be easily used to monitor for illicit activity.

46. C. The false acceptance rate (FAR) is the rate at which the system inadvertently admits an unauthorized user, while the false rejection rate (FRR) is the rate at which the system inadvertently rejects an authorized user. Both the FAR and FRR may be modified by adjusting the sensitivity of the system. The crossover error rate (CER) is the point where both the false acceptance rate and the false rejection rate cross. The CER is less subject to manipulation and is, therefore, the best metric to use for evaluating systems. The FDR is not a metric used to evaluate authentication systems.

47. C. Steganography is the art of using cryptographic techniques to embed secret messages within other content. Steganographic algorithms work by making invisible alterations to files, such as modifying the least significant bits of the many bits that make up image files. VPNs may be used to obscure secret communications, but they provide protection in transit and can't be used to embed information in an image.

Watermarking does embed information in an image but with the intent of protecting intellectual property. A still image would not be used for a covert timing channel because it is a fixed file.

48. A. JavaScript is an interpreted language so the code is not compiled prior to execution, allowing Roger to inspect the contents of the code. C, C++, and Java are all compiled languages—a compiler produces an executable file that is not human-readable.

49. D. When a system is configured to use shadowed passwords, the `/etc/passwd` file contains only the character x in the place of a password. It would not contain any passwords, in either plaintext, encrypted, or hashed form.

50. C. The end-of-life (EOL) date for a product is normally the date that the vendor will stop selling a product. It is reasonable to continue using the product as long as support remains available. Rob should begin making plans to discontinue use of the product, pending the announcement of an end-of-support (EOS) date.

51. D. The due care principle states that an individual should react in a situation using the same level of care that would be expected from any reasonable person. It is a very broad standard. The due diligence principle is a more specific component of due care that states that an individual assigned a responsibility should exercise due care to complete it accurately and in a timely manner. Least privilege says that an individual should have the minimum set of permissions necessary to carry out their work. Separation of duties says that no single person should have the right to perform two distinct tasks, which, when combined, constitute a highly privileged action.

52. A. Information should be classified based upon its sensitivity. This may be due to the value of the information to the organization, the damage caused if lost or compromised, or other factors. The source of the information is one possible contributing factor to the sensitivity level. The likelihood of loss or theft is a component of risk but does not contribute to the classification level.

53. A. All of these controls are good practices for protecting sensitive information. However, Perry is most concerned about the risk of interception while in transit over the Internet. Transport encryption would, therefore, be the most appropriate control, as anyone intercepting the information would be unable to read its contents. Storage encryption would protect against the theft of information at rest, rather than in transit over a network. Classification and labeling would not protect against interception. Data loss prevention technology may block the transfer entirely and would not meet the business requirement if it blocked the transmission and would not meet the security requirement if it did not detect the data transfer.

54. B, D. Tangible asset inventories include physical items owned by the organization. This would include server hardware and mobile devices. Intellectual property and files stored on a server are not tangible property and would instead be included in an intangible asset inventory.

55. D. The Physical layer deals with the electrical impulses or optical pulses that are sent as bits to convey data. This is the layer where cable tapping would occur. Attacks at the Data Link, Network, or Transport layers would involve higher levels of activity in the OSI model, such as compromising a device and using a protocol analyzer to sniff network traffic.

56. A. In an IaaS server environment, the customer retains responsibility for most server security operations under the shared responsibility model. This includes managing OS security settings, maintaining host firewalls, and configuring server access control. The vendor would be responsible for all security mechanisms at the hypervisor layer and below.

57. B. Proactive monitoring, aka synthetic monitoring, uses recorded or generated traffic to test systems and software. Passive monitoring uses a network span, tap, or other device to capture traffic to be analyzed. Reactive and replay are not industry terms for types of monitoring.

58. A. Kailey should consult her organization's record retentions policy to determine the appropriate length of time to preserve the records. The organization may be subject to tax requirements in this regard, and many accountants recommend preserving records for at least seven years, but the organization's own requirements may be stricter than these requirements.

59. B. The use of an electromagnetic coil inside the card indicates that this is a proximity card.

60. C. During a parallel test, the team actually activates the disaster recovery site for testing, but the primary site remains operational. During a full interruption test, the team takes down the primary site and confirms that the disaster recovery site is capable of handling regular operations. The full interruption test is the most thorough test but also the most disruptive. The read-through is the least disruptive type of disaster recovery test. During a read-through, team members each review the contents of their disaster recovery checklists on their own and suggest any necessary changes. During a tabletop exercise, team members come together and walk through a specific scenario without making any changes to information systems.

61. B. The Agile approach to software development embraces 12 core principles, found in the Agile Manifesto. One of these principles is that the best architecture, requirements, and designs emerge from self-organizing teams. Another is that teams should welcome changing requirements at any step in the process. A third is that simplicity is essential. The Agile approach emphasizes delivering software frequently, not infrequently.

62. B. Hand geometry scanners assess the physical dimensions of an individual's hand but do not verify other unique factors about the individual, or even verify if they are alive. This means that hand geometry scanners should not be implemented as the sole authentication factor for secure environments. Hand geometry scanners do not have an abnormally high FRR and do not stand out as a particular issue from an accessibility standpoint compared to other biometric systems.

63. A. The maximum tolerable downtime (MTD) is the amount of time that a business may be without a service before irreparable harm occurs. This measure is sometimes also called maximum tolerable outage (MTO) or maximum allowable downtime (MAD). The Recovery Point Objective (RPO) and Recovery Time Objective (RTO) are related but distinct measures.

The RPO focuses on data loss, indicating the maximum period in which data might be lost due to a disruption, and is used to establish the frequency of backups. The RTO, meanwhile, is the target time set for the recovery of IT and business activities after a disruption, aimed to be within the MTD but is not itself a measure of the direct impact on the business operation. The annual loss expectancy (ALE) is not directly related to service interruption but is a metric used in risk assessment to quantify potential annual financial loss from risks.

64. C. Cloud access security brokers (CASBs) are designed to enforce security policies consistently across cloud services and would best meet Bailey's needs. Data loss prevention (DLP) and digital rights management (DRM) solutions may be able to detect, block, and control some use of information in the cloud, but they would not provide a way to consistently enforce security policies across cloud platforms. Intrusion prevention systems (IPS) are designed to detect and block malicious activity and would not be relevant in this scenario.

65. A, D. Organizations should always label classified information in whatever form, paper or electronic, that it appears. This allows employees to apply proper handling procedures. It is also a common practice to encrypt sensitive information both at rest and in transit. Organizations should grant access to classified information on a need-to-know basis.

Automatically granting access to information, whether it is to a visitor or a senior executive, should not occur.

66. B. Masquerading (or impersonation) attacks use stolen or falsified credentials to bypass authentication mechanisms. That term does describe this attack, but you should keep reading the answer choices even after finding a possible correct answer. In this case, replay attacks are a more specific type of masquerading attack that relies on captured authentication tokens, and this is, therefore, a better answer. Spoofing attacks rely on falsifying an identity like an IP address or hostname without credentials. Modification attacks occur when captured packets are modified and replayed to a system to attempt to perform an action.

67. A. OpenID Connect is an authentication layer that works with OAuth 2.0 as its underlying authorization framework. It has been widely adopted by cloud service providers and is widely supported. SAML, RADIUS, and Kerberos are alternative authentication technologies but do not have the same level of seamless integration with OAuth 2.0.

68. C. This scenario describes separation of duties—not allowing the same person to hold two roles that, when combined, are sensitive. While two-person control is a similar concept, it does not apply in this case because the scenario does not say that either action requires the concurrence of two users. Least privilege says that an individual should have the minimum set of permissions necessary to carry out their work. Job rotation moves people through jobs on a periodic basis to deter fraud.

69. C. The parol evidence rule states that when an agreement between two parties is put into written form, it is assumed to be the entire agreement unless amended in writing. The best evidence rule says that a copy of a document is not admissible if the original document is available. Real evidence and testimonial evidence are evidence types, not rules of evidence.

70. A. Network Address Translation (NAT) translates an internal address to an external address. VLANs are used to logically divide networks, BGP is a routing protocol, and G/NAT is a made-up term.

71. B, C, D. SSAE-18 does not assert specific controls. Instead, it reviews the use and application of controls in an audited organization. It is an attestation standard, used for external audits, and forms part of the underlying framework for SOC 1, 2, and 3 reports.

72. A. When creating a digital signature, the sender of a message always encrypts the message digest with their own private key. The recipient (or any third party) may then verify the digital signature by decrypting it with the sender's public key and then comparing that decrypted signature with a message digest that the recipient computes themselves.

73. B. The recovery time objective (RTO) is the amount of time expected to return an IT service or component to operation after a failure. The maximum tolerable downtime (MTD) is the longest amount of time that an IT service or component may be unavailable without causing serious damage to the organization. The recovery point objective (RPO) identifies the maximum amount of data, measured in time, that may be lost during a recovery effort. Service-level agreements (SLAs) are written contracts that document service expectations.

74. C. Change management typically requires sign-off from a manager or supervisor before changes are made. This helps to ensure proper awareness and communication. SDN stands for software-defined networking, release management is the process that new software releases go through to be accepted, and versioning is used to differentiate versions of software, code, or other objects.

75. B. Wet pipe suppression systems have water present in the pipes at all times, posing an unacceptable level of risk for a data center containing electronics that might be damaged if a pipe leaks. Dry pipe and pre-action systems only contain water when triggered in the event of a possible fire. FM-200 is a chemical suppressant commonly used in place of water in data centers.

76. D. Notifications and procedures like the signs posted at the company Chris works for are examples of directive access controls. Detective controls are designed to operate after the fact. The doors and the locks on them are examples of physical controls. Preventive controls are designed to stop an event and could also include the locks that are present on the doors.

77. B, D. Deterrent controls seek to prevent an intruder from attempting an attack in the first place. Guard dogs have an intimidating presence that serves this purpose well. They do also serve to deny, detect, and delay intrusions depending upon their training. Lighting also deters attacks by making potential intrusions more visible, reducing the likelihood that an intruder will enter a well-lit area. Access control vestibules (also known as mantraps) are intended to deny intruders access, rather than deter attempts. Motion detectors are intended to detect intruders rather than deter them.

78. B. This is an example of function-as-a-service (FaaS) computing. However, FaaS is not listed as an answer choice, so you must also know that FaaS is a subcategory of platform-as-a-service (PaaS) computing to answer this question correctly. This model does not necessarily take advantage of containerization. The cloud provider is managing the infrastructure and only making the platform available to customers, so it is not infrastructure as a service (IaaS). The customers are running their own code, so it is not software as a service (SaaS).

79. C, D. The attacker may attempt to perform frequency analysis or a brute-force attack against the large volume of encrypted ciphertext. As the attacker does not have access to the plaintext information, a known plaintext attack is not possible. The attacker also does not have the ability to encrypt information, so they cannot use a chosen ciphertext attack.

80. B. Provisioning that occurs through an established workflow, such as through an HR process, is workflow-based account provisioning. If Alex had set up accounts for his new hire on the systems he manages, he would have been using discretionary account provisioning. If the provisioning system allowed the new hire to sign up for an account on their own, they would have used self-service account provisioning, and if there was a central, software-driven process, rather than HR forms, it would have been automated account provisioning.

81. C. As Alex has changed roles, he retained access to systems that he no longer administers. The provisioning system has provided rights to workstations and the application servers he manages, but he should not have access to the databases he no longer administers. Privilege levels are not specified, so we can't determine if he has excessive privileges. Logging may or may not be enabled, but it isn't possible to tell from the diagram or problem.

82. C. When a user's role changes, they should be provisioned based on their role and other access entitlements. De-provisioning and re-provisioning are time-consuming and can lead to problems with changed IDs and how existing credentials work. Simply adding new rights leads to privilege creep, and matching another user's rights can lead to excessive privileges due to privilege creep for that other user.

83. B. EAL2 assurance applies when the system has been structurally tested. It is the second-to-lowest level of assurance under the Common Criteria.

84. C. Before granting any user access to information, Adam should verify that the user has an appropriate security clearance as well as a business need to know for the information in question.

85. B. During the preservation phase, the organization ensures that information related to the matter at hand is protected against intentional or unintentional alteration or deletion. The identification phase locates relevant information but does not preserve it. The collection phase occurs after preservation and gathers responsive information. The processing phase performs a rough cut of the collected information for relevance.

86. C. The original version of RIPEMD and the MD5 hash algorithms have known vulnerabilities and should no longer be used. SHA-2 and SHA-3 are both considered secure today and provide the same level of security. SHA-3 is, however, less efficient than SHA-2, making SHA-2 the better choice for Dana's needs.

87. D. In the subject/object model, the object is the resource being requested by a subject. In this example, Harry would like access to the document, making the document the object of the request.

88. C. The process of removing a header (and possibly a footer) from the data received from a previous layer in the OSI model is known as de-encapsulation. Encapsulation occurs when the header or footer is added. Payloads are the data portion of a packet, but payloading is not a technical term. Similarly, packet unwrapping is a made-up term.

89. A. CPTED implements three strategies: natural access control, natural surveillance, and natural territorial reinforcement. Natural access control uses barricades and other physical elements to create a separation between secure and insecure spaces. Natural surveillance designs the environment to expose potential intruders to natural scrutiny by legitimate occupants. Natural territorial reinforcement uses fences, signs, and other elements to clearly define secure spaces. Natural intrusion detection is not an element of CPTED.

90. C. If Shahla's organization expands into Canada and handles personally identifiable information as part of its routine business, the most likely new law to affect the organization would be the Personal Information Protection and Electronic Documents Act (PIPEDA). This Canadian federal privacy law governs the collection, use, and disclosure of personal information in the course of commercial business.

PIPL is China's Personal Information Protection Law, POPIA is South Africa's Protection of Personal Information Act, and the CCPA is the California Consumer Privacy Act. Each of these laws governs the handling of personal information within their respective jurisdictions, but would not be the primary concern for a U.S. organization considering expansion into Canada.

91. D. The use of a probability/impact matrix is the hallmark of a qualitative risk assessment. It uses subjective measures of probability and impact, such as "high," "moderate," and "low," in place of quantitative measures.

92. B. Mandatory access control systems can be hierarchical, where each domain is ordered and related to other domains above and below it; compartmentalized, where there is no relationship between each domain; or hybrid, where both hierarchy and compartments are used. There is no concept of bracketing in mandatory access control design.

93. B. Asymmetric encryption algorithms require two keys per user, regardless of the number of participants. Therefore, this six-member team would require 12 keys. If this team were to use symmetric cryptography, they would require $(n*(n-1))/2$, or $(6*(6-1))/2 = 15$ keys.

94. B. Category 5e and Category 6 UTP cables are both rated to 1000Mbps. Cat 5 (not Cat 5e) is only rated to 100Mbps, whereas Cat 7 is rated to 10Gbps. There is no Cat 4e.

95. C. While Ursula may use a variety of different options to meet her needs, the best approach would be the use of a content delivery network (CDN). CDNs are specifically designed for this role, distributing content to many remote endpoints where it may be quickly loaded by local users.

96. D. Smurf attacks use a distributed attack approach to send ICMP echo replies at a targeted system from many different source addresses. The most effective way to block this attack would be to block inbound ICMP traffic. Blocking the source addresses is not feasible because the attacker would likely simply change the source addresses. Blocking destination addresses would likely disrupt normal activity. The smurf attack does not use UDP, so blocking that traffic would have no effect.

97. C. Static packet filtering firewalls are known as first-generation firewalls and do not track connection state. Stateful inspection, application proxying, and next-generation firewalls all add connection state tracking capability.

98. C. All of these controls serve to increase the reliability of power to a server. However, only dual power supplies address hardware issues that arise within the server, allowing the server to continue operation if one of the power supplies fails. Redundant power sources, backup generators, and uninterruptible power supplies (UPS) are designed to increase the reliability of power flowing to the server.

99. A, C. The Remote Desktop Protocol (RDP) and Secure Shell (SSH) are modern approaches to remote access that include encryption features. Telnet and dial-up are outdated approaches that do not provide encryption and should not be relied upon for secure access.

100. B. Latency is a delay in the delivery of packets from their source to their destination. Jitter is a variation in the latency for different packets. Packet loss is the disappearance of packets in transit that requires retransmission. Interference is electrical noise or other disruptions that corrupt the contents of packets.

101. A, B, D. It is entirely appropriate to distribute internal audit reports to anyone in the organization who has a valid need to know. This may include both management and individual contributors responsible for remediating issues as well as board members charged with oversight. It would not normally be appropriate to distribute internal audit reports to external entities, such as suppliers and customers.

102. B. Web applications communicate with web browsers via an interface, making interface testing the best answer here. Regression testing might be used as part of the interface test but is too specific to be the best answer. Similarly, the test might be a white-box, or full knowledge, test, but interface testing better describes this specific example. Fuzzing is less likely a part of a browser compatibility test, as it tests unexpected inputs, rather than functionality.

103. A. Role-based access control gives each user an array of permissions based on their position in the organization, such as the scheme shown here. Task-based access control is not a standard approach. Rule-based access controls use rules that apply to all subjects, which isn't something we see in the list. Discretionary access control gives object owners rights to choose how the objects they own are accessed, which is not what this list shows.

104. D. Fire suppression systems do not stop a fire from occurring but do reduce the damage that fires cause. This is an example of reducing risk by lowering the impact of an event.

105. D. Patents and trade secrets can both protect intellectual property in the form of a process. Patents require public disclosure and have expiration dates, while trade secrets remain in force for as long as they remain secret. Therefore, trade secret protection most closely aligns with the company's goals.

106. D. The Security Content Automation Protocol (SCAP) is a suite of specifications used to handle vulnerability and security configuration information. The National Vulnerability Database provided by NIST uses SCAP. XACML is the eXtensible Access Control Markup

Language, an OASIS standard used for access control decisions, and neither VSML nor SCML is an industry term.

107. D. Breach and attack simulation (BAS) platforms are intended to automate some aspects of penetration testing. These systems are designed to inject threat indicators onto systems and networks in an effort to trigger other security controls. White-box, gray-box, and black-box testing all involve more significant manual effort.

108. A. The Simple Security Property prevents an individual from reading information at a higher security level than their clearance allows. This is also known as the "no read up" rule. The Simple Integrity Property says that a subject cannot read an object at a lower integrity level (no read down). The *-Security Property says that users can't write data to a lower security level than their own. The Discretionary Security Property allows the use of a matrix to determine access permissions.

109. B. The work breakdown structure (WBS) is an important project management tool that divides the work done for a large project into smaller components. It is not a project plan because it does not describe timing or resources. Test analyses are used during later phases of the development effort to report test results. Functional requirements may be included in a work breakdown structure, but they are not the full WBS.

110. B. Network Access Control (NAC) systems can be used to authenticate users and then validate their system's compliance with a security standard before they are allowed to connect to the network. Enforcing security profiles can help reduce zero-day attacks, making NAC a useful solution. A firewall can't enforce system security policies, whereas an IDS can only monitor for attacks and alarm when they happen. Thus, neither a firewall nor an IDS meets Kolin's needs. Finally, port security is a MAC address-based security feature that can restrict only which systems or devices can connect to a given port.

111. C. This scenario violates the least privilege principle because an application should never require full administrative rights to run. Gwen should update the service account to have only the privileges necessary to support the application.

112. B, C, D. Organizations typically use the time to resolve vulnerabilities, the number of account compromises, and the number of attempts by users to visit malicious sites as indicators. The number of scheduled audits is not normally a measure of the performance of an information security team. A more appropriate indicator in this area is the number of repeat audit findings.

113. A. This is a true positive report because the scan detected the vulnerability, and the vulnerability actually existed. The fact that the team later remediated the vulnerability could be noted in the report, but it does not change the result of the scan or its classification. True negatives occur when scans correctly note the absence of a vulnerability. False positives occur when scans report the presence of a vulnerability that does not actually exist. False negatives occur when scans report that no vulnerability exists when one does, in fact, exist.

114. C. Test directories often include scripts that may have poor protections or may have other data that can be misused. There is not a default test directory that allows administrative access to PHP. Test directories are not commonly used to store sensitive data, nor is the existence of a test directory a common indicator of compromise.

115. A. Directory indexing may not initially seem like an issue during a penetration test, but simply knowing the name and location of files can provide an attacker with quite a bit of information about an organization, as well as a list of potentially accessible files. XDRF is not a type of attack, and indexing is not a denial-of-service attack vector. Directory indexing being turned on is typically either due to design or because the server was misconfigured at setup, rather than being a sign of attack.

116. B. Cross-site tracing (XST) leverages the HTTP TRACE or TRACK methods and could be used to steal a user's cookies via cross-site scripting (XSS). The other options are not industry terms for web application or web server attacks or vulnerabilities.

117. C. The chief audit executive (CAE) should report to the most senior possible leader to avoid conflicts of interest. Of the choices provided, the chief executive officer (CEO) is the most senior position and the best option. It is also possible to provide an added degree of independence by having the CAE report to the board of directors, either as a primary reporting line or as a dotted line relationship.

118. C. Data loss prevention (DLP) systems specialize in the identification of sensitive information. In this case, Ursula would like to identify the presence of this information on endpoint devices, so she should choose an endpoint DLP control. Network-based DLP would not detect stored information unless the user transmits it over the network. Intrusion prevention systems (IPSs) are designed to detect and block attacks in progress, not necessarily the presence of sensitive information.

119. B. In the private cloud computing model, the cloud computing environment is dedicated to a single organization and does not follow the shared tenancy model. The environment may be built by the company in its own data center or built by a vendor at a co-location site.

120. A. Load balancing helps to ensure that a failed server will not take a website or service offline. Dual power supplies only work to prevent failure of a power supply or power source. IPS can help to prevent attacks, and RAID can help prevent a disk failure from taking a system offline.

121. D. Integrity ensures that unauthorized changes are not made to data while stored or in transit.

122. C. A star topology uses a central connection device. Ethernet networks may look like a star, but they are actually a logical bus topology that is sometimes deployed in a physical star.

123. C. Input validation ensures that the data provided to a program as input matches the expected parameters. Limit checks are a special form of input validation that ensure that the value remains within an expected range, as is the case described in this scenario. Fail open and fail secure are options when planning for possible system failures. Buffer bounds are not a type of software control.

124. The testing methodologies match with the level of knowledge as follows:

    1. Black box: C. No prior knowledge of the system

    2. White box: A. Full knowledge of the system

    3. Gray box: B. Partial or incomplete knowledge

125. The factors match to the types as follows:

    A. A PIN: 1. Something you know

    B. A token: 2. Something you have

    C. A fingerprint: 3. Something you are

    D. A password: 1. Something you know

    E. A smartcard: 2. Something you have

    F. A retinal scan: 3. Something you are

    G. A security question/answer: 1. Something you know

Chapter 10: Practice Test 2

1. D. The recovery point objective (RPO) identifies the maximum amount of data, measured in time, that may be lost during a recovery effort. The recovery time objective (RTO) is the amount of time expected to return an IT service or component to operation after a failure. The maximum tolerable downtime (MTD) is the longest amount of time that an IT service or component may be unavailable without causing serious damage to the organization. Service-level agreements (SLAs) are written contracts that document service expectations.

2. C. Due care and due diligence can be a confusing pair of terms to keep straight. Chris is engaging in due diligence when he does the preparation and research. Once that is done, he must use due care while undertaking the actions. This is often described in the context of the prudent person rule: would a prudent person have taken the action given the same knowledge? Compliance efforts work to ensure an organization meets regulatory or other requirements. Organizations typically don't take regulatory action—that's left to the government.

3. D. Blue teams are defenders, red teams are attackers, and purple teams combine both attack and defense activities. Yellow and green teams are not commonly described as part of penetration testing.

4. C. Hardware and software can be subject to import and export controls. In the case of AI computation hardware, there are specific limits on what can be exported to China, including limits on performance. Sharif needs to engage the appropriate experts to determine what can and cannot be exported. AI hardware is legal in China, dollar values are not typically the limiting factor for hardware import/export restrictions, and ethics are not a regulatory issue.

5. B. The most realistic but also most disruptive option for disaster recovery plan testing is a full interruption. The least obtrusive but also least similar to real-world scenarios is a read-through. After that, walk-throughs and simulations are each closer to a true scenario, but parallel operations are often the most popular option because it can be done without disrupting the organization and still reasonably test capabilities.

6. C. Cold sites are facilities large enough to use for recovery operations with appropriate power and environmental capabilities but without any additional readiness work done for computing, connectivity, or other needs. Warm sites have equipment and connectivity in place but are not actively handling live data. Hot sites have live data and could take over operations immediately. Frozen site is not a term used to describe a failover or recovery site.

7. B. The data owner is normally responsible for classifying information at an appropriate level. This role is typically filled by a senior manager or director, who then delegates operational responsibility to a data custodian. Data creators do just that—create data—although data creators is not a commonly used role name in data role lists. CISOs are chief information security officers and are typically the top-level individual responsible for security in organizations.

8. A. Off-site backups are the best option for disaster recovery in a scenario where a disaster directly impacts the data center. None of the other scenarios as described will directly address the issue, although snapshots to a remote storage location can act as a form of off-site backup.

9. C. While all of the listed controls would improve authentication security, most simply strengthen the use of knowledge-based authentication. The best way to improve the authentication process would be to add a factor that is not based on knowledge through the use of multifactor authentication. This may include the use of biometric controls or token-based authentication.

10. C. Software-defined networking (SDN) is a converged protocol that allows virtualization concepts and practices to be applied to networks. MPLS handles a wide range of protocols like asynchronous transfer mode (ATM), digital subscriber line (DSL), and others, but isn't intended to provide the centralization capabilities that SDN does. A content distribution network (CDN) is not a converged protocol, and FCoE is Fibre Channel over Ethernet, a converged protocol for storage.

11. C. The best way to ensure that data on DVDs is fully gone is to destroy them, and pulverizing DVDs is an appropriate means of destruction. DVD-ROMs are write-only media, meaning that secure erase and zero wipes won't work. Degaussing works only on magnetic media and cannot guarantee that there will be zero data remanence.

12. C. Backout plans are required in some change management processes to ensure that the thought process and procedures for what to do if something does not go as planned are needed. Validating backout plan quality can be just as important as the change, and you may find, in many organizations, if nobody is watching, that backout plans may read, "Undo the change we made." Rejecting the change won't fix the problem if the change has been made. A change review is useful to identify problems before the change is made. Failover plans are not a term commonly used in change management processes.

13. A. All packets leaving Angie's network should have a source address from her public IP address block. Packets with a destination address from Angie's network should not be leaving the network. Packets with source addresses from other networks are likely spoofed and should be blocked by egress filters. Packets with private IP addresses as sources or destinations should never be routed onto the Internet.

14. B. Virtual private clouds (VPCs) run on cloud-hosted infrastructure providing a secure, isolated pool of resources to be used by organizations to meet their needs. A VLAN is a virtual local area network. While VLANs are part of how most VPCs work, they alone aren't sufficient to create a VPC. An SDN, or software defined network, is used to manage networks through code, and CDNs are content delivery networks used to provide access to content around the globe that helps offload traffic while protecting against denial-of-service (DoS) attacks and other issues.

15. A. While developers may feel like they have a business need to be able to move code into production, the principle of separation of duties dictates that they should not have the ability to both write code and place it on a production server. The deployment of code is often performed by change management staff. Two-person control requires two individuals to perform an action to ensure appropriate oversight. Least privilege is the concept of only providing privileges required to perform a role, and job rotation moves individuals through job roles to ensure that different people perform tasks preventing an individual from exploiting their job function over time.

16. A. Applying a digital signature to a message allows the sender to achieve the goal of nonrepudiation. This allows the recipient of a message to prove to a third party that the message came from the purported sender. Symmetric encryption does not support nonrepudiation. Firewalls and IDS are network security tools that are not used to provide nonrepudiation.

17. A. System A should send an ACK to end the three-way handshake. The TCP three-way handshake is SYN, SYN/ACK, ACK. FIN is used to end a TCP connection, while RST resets the connection.

18. B. TACACS+ is the most modern version of TACACS, the Terminal Access Controller Access-Control System. It is a Cisco proprietary protocol with added features beyond what RADIUS provides, meaning it is commonly used on Cisco networks. XTACACS is an earlier version, Kerberos is a network authentication protocol rather than a remote user authentication protocol, and RADIUS+ is a made-up term.

19. C. Call managers and VoIP phones can be thought of as servers or appliances and embedded or network devices. That means that the most likely threats that they will face are denial-of-service (DoS) attacks and attacks against the host operating system. Malware and Trojans are less likely to be effective against a server or embedded system that doesn't browse the Internet or exchange data files; buffer overflows are usually aimed at specific applications or services.

20. C. The blacklist approach to application control blocks certain prohibited packages but allows the installation of other software on systems. The whitelist approach uses the reverse philosophy and allows only approved software. It is worth noting that the terms *blacklist* and *whitelist* are increasingly deprecated and that you may encounter terms like *block list* or *deny list* and *allow list* as language and terminology shifts. As you prepare for the exam and your professional work, make sure to consider these equivalents. Antivirus software would only detect the installation of malicious software after the fact. Heuristic detection is a variant of antivirus software.

21. B. The exposure factor (EF) is the percentage of the facility that risk managers expect will be damaged if a risk materializes. It is calculated by dividing the amount of damage by the asset value. In this case, that is $20 million in damage divided by the $100 million facility value, or 20%.

22. B. The annualized rate of occurrence (ARO) is the number of times each year that risk analysts expect a risk to happen in any given year. In this case, the analysts expect floods once every 200 years, or 0.005 times per year.

23. B. The annualized loss expectancy (ALE) is calculated by multiplying the single loss expectancy (SLE) by the annualized rate of occurrence (ARO). In this case, the SLE is $20 million, and the ARO is 0.005. Multiplying these numbers together gives you the ALE of $100,000.

24. B. The most frequent target of account management reviews are highly privileged accounts, as they create the greatest risk. Random samples are the second most likely choice. Accounts that have existed for a longer period of time are more likely to have a problem due to privilege creep than recently created accounts, but neither of these choices is likely unless there is a specific organizational reason to choose them.

25. D. The cloud service offerings in order from the case where the customer bears the least responsibility to where the customer bears the most responsibility are SaaS, PaaS, and IaaS. In an infrastructure-as-a-service (IaaS) cloud computing model, the customer retains responsibility for managing operating system and application security, while the vendor manages security at the hypervisor level and below. In a platform-as-a-service (PaaS) environment, the vendor takes on responsibility for the operating system, but the customer writes and configures any applications. In a software-as-a-service (SaaS) environment, the vendor takes on responsibility for the development and implementation of the application while the customer merely configures security settings within the application.

26. A. Breach-and-attack simulation (BAS) tools typically leverage SaaS platforms as well as software agents and virtual machines to perform simulated attacks, which they leverage to provide detailed reports about security issues and their relative risk levels.

27. D. Duress systems are intended to allow employees to notify security or others when they are in a dangerous situation or when they need help. Duress systems may be as simple as a push button and as complex as a code word or digital system that allows specific entries to trigger alarms while still performing a desired or deceptive but real-appearing action.

28. C. While inode information leakage could represent a security concern, it does not pose the same immediate and direct risk as clickjacking, XSS vulnerabilities, or even the contextual importance of knowing the server's operating system. Clickjacking and cross-site scripting are both important issues, and knowing that the server is a Linux server is also important.

29. D. The hearsay rule says that a witness cannot testify about what someone else told them, except under very specific exceptions. The courts have applied the hearsay rule to include the concept that attorneys may not introduce logs into evidence unless they are authenticated by the system administrator. In this scenario, George might also be able to provide a sworn affidavit, but the question doesn't include that option. The best evidence rule states that copies of documents may not be submitted into evidence if the originals are available. The parol evidence rule states that if two parties enter into a written agreement, that written document is assumed to contain all of the terms of the agreement. Testimonial evidence is a type of evidence, not a rule of evidence.

30. B. Key risk indicators (KRIs) are valuable for organizational risk planning and understanding risk perceptions but are not designed for real-time security incident response. Tools like intrusion prevention systems (IPSs), security information and event management (SIEM) systems, and others are better equipped for immediate threat detection and response.

31. B. Worms have built-in propagation mechanisms that do not require user interaction, such as scanning for systems containing known vulnerabilities and then exploiting those vulnerabilities to gain access. Viruses and Trojan horses typically require user interaction to spread. Logic bombs do not spread from system to system but lie in wait until certain conditions are met, triggering the delivery of their payload.

32. A. As simple as the answer may seem, labeling media or even color coding it with sensitivity levels and ensuring staff are appropriately trained on what the levels mean will normally have the biggest impact. Encrypting media can help, but without the labels, files may be stored on inappropriate media. A clear desk policy can help if casual media theft is an issue but is not likely to be an important control in this scenario. Dual control is used to ensure that a task cannot be performed by a single staff member to avoid malfeasance and is not directly useful here.

33. B. MITRE's ATT&CK framework is broadly adopted by threat modeling and threat intelligence organizations and is used as a default model in many software packages and tools. The Diamond Model specifically addresses how to think about intrusions but does not address broader threats, and the other answers were made up for this question.

34. A. The Agile approach to software development states that working software is the primary measure of progress, that simplicity is essential, and that businesspeople and developers must work together daily. It also states that the most efficient method of conveying information is face to face, not electronic.

35. C. Integrity verification software would protect against this attack by identifying unexpected changes in protected data. Encryption, access controls, and firewalls would not be effective in this example because the accountants have legitimate access to the data.

36. C. CAPEC, or Common Attack Pattern Enumeration and Classification, is a dictionary of known attack patterns. STIX is the Structured Threat Information eXpression language used to describe threats in a standardized way, and TAXII, the Trusted Automated eXchange of Indicator Information, defines how threat information can be shared and exchanged. All of these are examples of threat intelligence feed standards.

37. B. Sole sourcing, or relying on a single vendor, can create additional fragility in supply chains due to reliance on a single supplier. Contractual controls including requirements for supplier insurance and liability limitations, having multiple suppliers, and validating their financial stability are all common ways to help reduce supply chain risk.

38. B. SOC 2 reports are released under NDA to select partners or customers and can provide details on the controls and any issues they may have. A SOC 1 report would provide only financial control information, and a SOC 3 report provides less information since it is publicly available.

39. C. An SOC 2, Type 2 report includes information about a data center's security, availability, processing integrity, confidentiality, and privacy, and includes an auditor's opinion on the operational effectiveness of the controls. SOC 3 does not have types, and a SOC 2 Type 1 is only conducted at a point in time.

40. B. Susan asked for a security controls report (SOC 2) and received a financial internal controls report (SOC 1). This question doesn't specify whether a Type 1 or Type 2 report is desired, but most security practitioners will prefer a Type 2 report if they can get it since it tests the actual controls and their implementation instead of their descriptions.

41. C. External auditors can provide an unbiased and impartial view of an organization's controls to third parties. Internal auditors are useful when reporting to senior management of the organization but are typically not asked to report to third parties. Penetration tests test technical controls but are not as well suited to testing many administrative controls. The employees who build and maintain controls are more likely to bring a bias to the testing of those controls and should not be asked to report on them to third parties.

42. C. Bell–LaPadula uses security labels on objects and clearances for subjects and is therefore a MAC model. It does not use discretionary, rule-based, role-based, or attribute-based access control.

43. D. The Family Educational Rights and Privacy Act (FERPA) protects the privacy of students in any educational institution that accepts any form of federal funding. HIPAA is the Health Insurance Portability and Accountability Act and protects sensitive patient data in the hands of insurance and medical providers. The HITECH focuses on electronic health records and data security for healthcare data. COPPA is the Children's Online Privacy Protection Act.

44. D. The Health Insurance Portability and Accountability Act (HIPAA) mandates the protection of protected health information (PHI). The Secure and Fair Enforcement for Mortgage Licensing (SAFE) Act deals with mortgages, the Graham–Leach–Bliley Act (GLBA) covers financial institutions, and the Family Educational Rights and Privacy Act (FERPA) deals with student data.

45. D. Sandboxing tools allow defenders to execute potentially malicious software in an isolated environment that provides instrumentation to capture all actions and changes performed when it is run. SIEM, or security information and event management, tools and SOAR, or security orchestration, automation, and response, tools are used to monitor environments and to respond to incidents but do not provide the ability to test and observe malicious software. SAST, or Static Application Security Testing, tools analyze source code to identify security issues.

46. D. Implementations of syslog vary, but most provide a setting for severity level, allowing the configuration of a value that determines what messages are sent. Typical severity levels include debug, informational, notice, warning, error, critical, alert, and emergency. The facility code is also supported by syslog but is associated with which services are being logged. Security level and log priority are not typical syslog settings.

47. D. RAID 5 is commonly used because it balances resilience and efficiency of storage space used by relying on distributed parity. RAID 0 uses two disks as a single volume, allowing for an increase in speed but a decrease in reliability. In RAID 1, also known as disk mirroring, systems contain two physical disks. Each disk contains copies of the same data, and either one may be used in the event the other disk fails RAID 3 is rarely used and uses byte-level striping and a dedicated parity disk.

48. A. Most vendors use the term *end of life*, or EOL, to denote when the product will stop being sold. End of support typically comes sometime after end of life, and this problem does not specify when end of support (EOS) will occur. Devices will still function after end of life and likely after end of support, but security professionals should raise concerns about the security of devices or software after the end of support because patches and updates will likely no longer be available.

49. C. Interviews, surveys, and audits are all useful for assessing awareness. Code quality is best judged by code review, service vulnerabilities are tested using vulnerability scanners and related tools, and the attack surface of an organization requires both technical and administrative review.

50. B. Unconstrained API calls can lead to denial-of-service conditions, one of the top 10 API security risks identified by OWASP in 2023. Attributing actions to an account requires proper authentication and logging, which are not tied to resource over-consumption. Malicious file access is typically due to improperly configured security, and request forgery attacks typically occur when user-supplied URIs are not validated.

51. C. Tokens are hardware devices (something you have) that generate a one-time password (OTP) based on time or an algorithm. They are typically combined with another factor like a password to authenticate users. CAC and PIV cards are U.S. government–issued smartcards.

52. B. A nondisclosure agreement (NDA) is a legal agreement between two parties that specifies what data they will not disclose. NDAs are common in industries that have sensitive or trade secret information they do not want employees to take to new jobs. Encryption would only help in transit or at rest, and Fred will likely have access to the data in unencrypted form as part of his job. An AUP is an acceptable use policy, and a stop-loss order is used on the stock market.

53. C. Civil cases typically rely on a preponderance of evidence. Criminal cases must be proven beyond a reasonable doubt. Real evidence is object evidence—tangible things that can be brought into a court of law. Documentary evidence are written items used to prove facts. Neither of these is an evidentiary standard; instead, they describe types of evidence.

54. C. Binary key spaces contain a number of keys equal to 2 raised to the power of the number of bits. Two to the eighth power is 256, so an 8-bit key space contains 256 possible keys.

55. C. Scoping is the process of reviewing and selecting security controls based on the system that they will be applied to. Editing is not a commonly used term in this context. Baselines are used as a base set of security controls, often from a third-party organization that creates them. Standardization isn't a relevant term here.

56. B. Background checks are frequently performed to identify potential issues before hiring a new employee. They can identify a variety of concerns and are commonly used across many industries. Nondisclosure agreements (NDAs) are used during and after employment to protect confidential information. Noncompetes are used to prevent employees from working in a similar industry for a given period of time after departure. COA, or certificate of authenticity, is not used in employment situations.

57. D. Systems and media should be labeled with the highest level of sensitivity that they store or handle. In this case, based on the U.S. government classification scheme, the highest classification level in use on the system is Secret. Mixed classification provides no useful information about the level, whereas Top Secret and Confidential are too high and too low, respectively.

58. C. She has placed compensating controls in place. Compensating controls are used when controls like the locks in this example are not sufficient. While the alarm is a physical control, the signs she posted are not. Similarly, the alarms are not administrative controls. None of these controls helps to recover from an issue, and they are thus not recovery controls.

59. D. Insurance is a form of risk transfer. Organizations pay insurers premiums, transferring the risk to them in exchange for the payment. Insurers may mitigate their risk through the terms of the insurance policy and may also insure themselves. Acceptance simply means acknowledging the risk, avoidance would require means to prevent the risk from occurring, and mitigation attempts to reduce the impact of the risk if it occurs.

60. D. A SOC 2 assessment looks at controls that affect security, and a Type 2 report validates the operating effectiveness of the controls. SOC 1 engagement assesses controls that might impact financial reporting, and a Type 1 report provides the auditors opinions of the descriptions of controls provided by management at a single point in time—not the actual implementations of the controls.

61. C. The ability to inspect open-source software (OSS) means that organizations can inspect it but more importantly that others can and often have also inspected it. This results in software that has had far more review than some closed-source or commercial packages (although large organizations may perform more review). The ability to change the code can sometimes be important as well, but changing open-source code in-house can create maintenance issues in the future. Open-source software may be compiled, but the source will still be available. The code being free is not a security advantage or disadvantage.

62. B. Provisioning includes the creation, maintenance, and removal of user objects from applications, systems, and directories. Registration occurs when users are enrolled in a biometric system; population and authenticator loading are not common industry terms.

63. C. Release control occurs after changes are finalized. With changes that are ready to be implemented in hand, release managers can follow their process with steps that typically include removing debugging code and conducting acceptance testing. Request control is the start of a process that allows users to submit change requests, while change control handles the process of ensuring quality assurance happens, that documentation is done, and that security testing is handled. Finally, configuration control is part of software configuration management, not the change process.

64. C. The formula for determining the number of encryption keys required by a symmetric algorithm is $((n*(n-1))/2)$. With six users, you will need $((6*5)/2)$, or 15 keys.

65. B. Patents have the shortest duration of the techniques listed: at most, 20 years. Copyrights last for 70 years beyond the death of the author if owned by an individual, or 95 years from publication or 120 years from creation if owned by a corporation. Trademarks are renewable indefinitely, and trade secrets are protected as long as they remain secret.

66. C. In a risk acceptance strategy, the organization chooses to take no action other than documenting the risk. Purchasing insurance would be an example of risk transference.

Relocating the data center would be risk avoidance. Reengineering the facility is an example of a risk mitigation strategy.

67. C. Uninterruptible power supplies (UPSs) provide immediate, battery-driven power for a short period of time to cover momentary losses of power. Generators are capable of providing backup power for a sustained period of time in the event of a power loss, but they take time to activate. RAID and redundant servers are high-availability controls but do not cover power loss scenarios.

68. C. Password histories retain a list of previous passwords, preferably a list of salted hashes for previous passwords, to ensure that users don't reuse their previous passwords. Longer minimum age can help prevent users from changing their passwords and then changing them back but won't prevent a determined user from eventually getting their old password back. Length requirements and complexity requirements tend to drive users to reuse passwords if they're not paired with tools like single sign-on, password storage systems, or other tools that decrease the difficulty of password management.

69. B. The single loss expectancy (SLE) is the amount of damage that a risk is expected to cause each time it occurs. ALE is the annual loss expectancy (probability of loss times reduction in value if a loss occurs), ARO is the annual rate of occurrence or how often in a given year the event is likely to happen, and AV is the asset value.

70. B. Sanitization includes steps such as removing the hard drive and other local storage from PCs before they are sold as surplus. Degaussing uses magnetic fields to wipe media, purging is an intense form of clearing used to ensure that data is removed and unrecoverable from media, and removing does not necessarily imply destruction of the drive.

71. D. During the Reporting phase, incident responders assess their obligations under laws and regulations to report the incident to government agencies and other regulators.

72. B. The bank that Charles works at is using job rotation to ensure that employees are not exploiting the rights and permissions that they have in their roles. The practice is intended to allow the next person in the role to identify irregularities and to prevent individuals from hiding malfeasance. Dual control requires two or more staff members to complete a task to ensure that a single employee cannot abuse their role. Cross-training ensures that multiple staff members have the necessary skills for a task, reducing the impact of losing a staff member.

73. B. Full device encryption, when combined with mandatory passcodes, offers the strongest defense against data loss from stolen devices. Encryption secures data at rest, making it unreadable without the correct decryption key, while passcodes provide an initial barrier against unauthorized access. Although application management, remote wipe, and GPS tracking are valuable for overall device security and recovery, they do not offer the same level of data protection as encryption and passcodes. Specifically, encryption ensures data security independently of the device's network connectivity or physical location.

74. D. SMTP servers that don't authenticate users before relaying their messages are known as open relays. Open relays that are Internet-exposed are typically quickly exploited to send email for spammers.

75. D. Sending logs to a secure log server is the most effective way to ensure that logs survive a breach. Encrypting local logs won't stop an attacker from deleting them, and requiring administrative access won't stop attackers who have breached a machine and acquired escalated privileges. Log rotation archives logs based on time or file size and can also purge logs after a threshold is hit. Rotation won't prevent an attacker from purging logs.

76. C. A security information and event management (SIEM) tool is designed to provide automated analysis and monitoring of logs and security events. A SIEM tool that receives access to logs can help detect and alert on events such as logs being purged or other breach indicators. An IDS can help detect intrusions, but IDSs are not typically designed to handle central logs. A central logging server can receive and store logs but won't help with analysis without taking additional actions. Syslog is simply a log format.

77. B. Requiring authentication can help provide accountability by ensuring that any action taken can be tracked back to a specific user. Storing logs centrally ensures that users can't erase the evidence of actions that they have taken. Log review can be useful when identifying issues, but digital signatures are not a typical part of a logging environment. Logging the use of administrative credentials helps for those users but won't cover all users, and encrypting the logs doesn't help with accountability. Authorization helps, but being able to specifically identify users through authentication is more important.

78. B. Port address translation (PAT) is used to allow a network to use any IP address set inside without causing a conflict with the public Internet. PAT is often confused with network address translation (NAT), which maps one internal address to one external address. IPsec is a security protocol suite, software-defined networking (SDN) is a method of defining networks programmatically, and IPX is a non-IP network protocol.

79. C. Each of the precautions listed helps to prevent social engineering by helping prevent exploitation of trust. Avoiding voice-only communications is particularly important, since establishing identity over the phone is difficult. The other listed attacks would not be prevented by these techniques.

80. A. The CIS benchmarks provide a useful security standard and baseline to assess systems against or to configure them to. Organizations can adapt and modify the baseline to meet their specific needs while speeding up deployment by using an accepted industry standard. They are not a compliance standard and do not provide provisioning or automation, but tools that do may use the benchmark as a standard to do so.

81. D. Remnant data is data that is left after attempts have been made to remove or erase it. Bitrot is a term used to describe aging media that decays over time. MBR is the master boot record, a boot sector found on hard drives and other media. Leftover data is not an industry term.

82. C. During a parallel test, the team activates the disaster recovery site for testing, but the primary site remains operational. A simulation test involves a role-play of a prepared scenario overseen by a moderator. Responses are assessed to help improve the organization's response process. The checklist review is the least disruptive type of disaster recovery test. During a checklist review, team members each review the contents of their disaster recovery checklists on their own and suggest any necessary changes. During a tabletop exercise, team members come together and walk through a scenario without making any changes to information systems.

83. C. Discretionary access control gives owners the right to decide who has access to the objects they own. Role-based access control uses administrators to make that decision for roles or groups of people with a role, task-based access control uses lists of tasks for each user, and rule-based access control applies a set of rules to all subjects.

84. C. Trusted paths that secure network traffic from capture and link encryption are both ways to help prevent man-in-the-middle attacks. Brute-force and dictionary attacks can both be prevented using back-off algorithms that slow down repeated attacks. Log analysis tools can also create dynamic firewall rules, or an IPS can block attacks like these in real time. Spoofed login screens can be difficult to prevent, although user awareness training can help.

85. D. The four canons of the ISC2 Code of Ethics are to protect society, the common good, the necessary public trust and confidence, and the infrastructure; act honorably, honestly, justly, responsibly, and legally; provide diligent and competent service to principals; and advance and protect the profession.

86. A. The emergency response guidelines should include the immediate steps an organization should follow in response to an emergency situation. These include immediate response procedures, a list of individuals who should be notified of the emergency, and secondary response procedures for first responders. They do not include long-term actions such as activating business continuity protocols, ordering equipment, or activating DR sites.

87. C. Security Assertion Markup Language (SAML) is the best choice for providing authentication and authorization information, particularly for browser-based SSO. HTML is primarily used for web pages, SPML is used to exchange user information for SSO, and XACML is used for access control policy markup.

88. D. Individuals with specific business continuity roles should receive training on at least an annual basis.

89. B. Application programming interfaces (APIs), user interfaces (UIs), and physical interfaces are all tested during the software testing process. Network interfaces are not typically tested, and programmatic interfaces are another term for APIs.

90. A. Product tampering, implants of software or hardware, and counterfeits are all common concerns for gray-market hardware. API vulnerabilities are a concern based on vendor software and may exist and require patching whether a device is purchased through an OEM or the gray market.

91. C. Virtual routing and forwarding (VRF) allows multiple routing tables to be used on the same device simultaneously. This is similar to the concept of VLANs on a layer 2 switch but operating at layer 3. Routing instances operate independently, allowing IP addresses to overlap without conflict, supporting segmentation and thus permitting flexibility for zero trust implementations and other security solutions. VRF can be used to support VPCs, but that is not its only use. It is not like a VPN, and while it can be used with multilayer protocols, that isn't a primary purpose.

92. A. RSA is an asymmetric encryption algorithm that requires only two keys for each user. IDEA, 3DES, and Skipjack are all symmetric encryption algorithms and would require a key for every unique pair of users in the system.

93. D. Function-as-a-service deployments are an example of a serverless deployment running on the cloud provider's cloud environment. Serverless computing solutions like AWS Lambda, Microsoft Azure Functions, and Google Cloud functions require less overhead when applications are designed from the ground up to leverage function as a service technology. ICS is an industrial control system used to manage systems and processes such as utilities or factories. VPCs are virtual private clouds where infrastructure is provisioned and used like a virtual data center, and embedded systems are built into other devices.

94. D. The log entries contained in this example show the allow/deny status for inbound and outbound TCP and UDP sessions. This is, therefore, an example of a firewall log.

95. D. Zero-day vulnerabilities remain in the dangerous zero-day category until the release of a patch that corrects the vulnerability. At that time, it becomes the responsibility of IT professionals to protect their systems by applying the patch. Implementation of other security controls, such as encryption or firewalls, does not change the nature of the zero-day vulnerability.

96. C. An HTML5-based VPN will provide Elle's staff with access to the applications they need without requiring the installation of a client that might be challenging or impossible without managed machines. A client-based IPsec VPN provides additional opportunities for control that a broadly deployed base of directly accessed machines via RDP does not, making it the second-best choice here. Deploying fiber for direct connections for end users is not viable for most organizations based on cost and complexity.

97. B. Edge computing is a technology that involves placing infrastructure closer to the point of use. This approach offers several benefits such as reduced latency, improved performance for local processing, and reduced traffic to remote data centers or the cloud. On the other hand, cloud computing is typically provided at a remote facility, is scalable and frequently multitenant. Hybrid cloud is a combination of local and remote clouds. Finally, microservices utilize loosely coupled services that communicate via lightweight protocols to accomplish specific tasks that are then combined to achieve overall goals.

98. C. The sender of a message encrypts the message using the public key of the message recipient.

99. D. The recipient of a message uses their own private key to decrypt messages that were encrypted with the recipient's public key. This ensures that nobody other than the intended recipient can decrypt the message.

100. D. Digital signatures enforce nonrepudiation. They prevent individuals from denying that they were the actual originator of a message.

101. B. An individual creates a digital signature by encrypting the message digest with their own private key.

102. D. The comparison of a factor to validate an identity is known as authentication. Identification would occur when Jim presented his user ID. Tokenization is a process that converts a sensitive data element to a nonsensitive representation of that element. Hashing transforms a string of characters into a fixed-length value or key that represents the original string.

103. C. The most important item in facility design is the safety of personnel. Once designs take that into account, security, operational effectiveness, and other concerns can be addressed.

104. C. An access control vestibule (sometimes called a mantrap), which is composed of two sets of doors with an access mechanism that allows only one door to open at a time, is an example of a preventive access control because it can stop unwanted access by keeping intruders from accessing a facility due to an opened door or following legitimate staff in. It can serve as a deterrent by discouraging intruders who would be trapped in it without proper access, and of course, doors with locks are an example of a physical control. A compensating control attempts to make up for problems with an existing control or to add additional controls to improve a primary control.

105. C. To ensure emails can be definitively attributed to their senders, Sally needs the capability of nonrepudiation. Digital signatures fulfill this need by using cryptographic techniques to bind a sender's identity to a message, making it impossible for the sender to deny having sent the email. Unlike IMAP, which is a protocol for accessing email, and DKIM, which verifies the domain origin of an email, digital signatures provide cryptographic proof of origin and integrity. Encryption, while securing the content of messages, does not inherently provide nonrepudiation.

106. D. In most situations, employers may not access medical information due to healthcare privacy laws. Reference checks, criminal records checks, and credit history reports are all typically found during pre-employment background checks.

107. A. Naomi's organization operates under the concept of least privilege. Individuals only receive the rights that they need to accomplish their tasks. This also means that the organization will need to ensure that those rights do not accrue to users over time and that they are changed or removed when user roles change. Privileged account management is the process of properly managing accounts with higher levels of privilege like administrative accounts. Job rotation moves employees between roles to ensure that they do not take advantage of the role and that a new set of eyes can help identify problems. Privilege escalation is the process of gaining additional rights when attacking systems or services.

108. A. When a data stream is converted into a segment (TCP) or a datagram (UDP), it transitions from the Session layer to the Transport layer. This change from a message sent to an encoded segment allows it to then traverse the Network layer.

109. C. The user has successfully explained a valid "need to know" the data—completing the report requested by the CFO requires this access. However, the user has not yet demonstrated that they have appropriate clearance to access the information. A note from the CFO would meet this requirement.

110. B. Sharif is using gamification, the process of making awareness efforts like a game to motivate users. Security champions are staff members who are selected or volunteer to advocate for and raise security awareness in their teams and divisions. Social engineering efforts leverage human behaviors, and awareness training is training intended to raise awareness of security risks, issues, and attacker techniques.

111. D. A system inventory is most frequently used to associate individuals with systems or devices. This can help when tracking their support history and aids in provisioning the proper tools, permissions, and data to a system. Both barcode and RFID property tags are used to identify systems, which can then be checked against a system inventory. Finally, enterprise content management tools are used to manage files and data as part of workflows and other business processes.

112. C. The create rule allows a subject to create new objects and also creates an edge from the subject to that object, granting rights to the new object.

113. A. Metasploit provides an extensible framework, allowing penetration testers to create their own exploits in addition to those that are built into the tool. Unfortunately, penetration testing can only cover the point in time when it is conducted. When conducting a penetration test, the potential to cause a denial of service due to a fragile service always exists, but it can test processes and policies through social engineering and operational testing that validates how those processes and policies work.

114. A. Data remanence is a concern due to the storage devices often found in multifunction photocopier/printer devices, particularly for devices used in an administrative headquarters. While compliance may be a concern, we don't know enough about Colin's organization to know if compliance concerns would require this. Asset management and asset inventory can both handle either destruction or sale for most organizations.

115. C. X.509 defines standards for public key certificates like those used with many smartcards. X.500 is a series of standards defining directory services. The Service Provisioning Markup Language (SPML) and the Security Assertion Markup Language (SAML) aren't standards that Alex should expect to see when using a smartcard to authenticate.

116. C. The Children's Online Privacy Protection Act (COPPA) regulates websites that cater to children or knowingly collect information from children younger than 13.

117. A. The Health Insurance Portability and Accountability Act (HIPAA) applies to healthcare information and is unlikely to apply in this situation. The Federal Information Security Modernization Act (FISMA) and Government Information Security Reform Act regulate the activities of all government agencies. The Homeland Security Act (HSA) created the U.S. Department of Homeland Security and, more importantly for this question, included the Cyber Security Enhancement Act of 2002 and the Critical Infrastructure Information Act of 2002. The Computer Fraud and Abuse Act (CFAA) provides specific protections for systems operated by government agencies.

118. C. FedRAMP is a U.S. government compliance program that standardizes how cloud services are assessed, monitored, and handle authorization. There is a FedRAMP marketplace for service providers and services that have been authorized by

FedRAMP. COBIT is an IT management and governance framework, SABSA is a risk-based enterprise information security model, and PCI is a security standard created by and used by the payment card industry.

119. C. Access control systems rely on identification and authentication to provide accountability. Effective authorization systems are desirable, but not required, since logs can provide information about who accessed what resources, even if access to those resources is not managed well. Of course, poor authorization management can create many other problems.

120. B. Checksums validate whether a file or other data object has been changed or modified, and thus, they support integrity.

121. C. The 192.168.0.0 to 192.168.255.255 address range is one of the ranges defined by RFC 1918 as private, nonroutable IP ranges. Scott's ISP (and any other organization with a properly configured router) will not route traffic from these addresses over the public Internet.

122. B. Jack's organization is using a continuous integration/continuous delivery (CI/CD) model where the application is updated and deployed on an ongoing basis. This can allow for an agile application but requires strong testing and validation practices to ensure that bad code doesn't make it into production. Waterfall is a development model that is based on a slower, precise process. SCM is software configuration management, and an IDE is an integrated development environment.

123. A. A well-designed set of VLANs based on functional groupings will logically separate segments of the network, making it difficult to have data exposure issues between VLANs. Changing the subnet mask will only modify the broadcast domain and will not fix issues with packet sniffing. Gateways would be appropriate if network protocols were different on different segments. Port security is designed to limit which systems can connect to a given port.

124. B. Any 10.x.x.x address is a private address as defined by RFC 1918. APIPA addresses are self-assigned by Windows when they cannot contact a DHCP server. 127.0.0.1 is a loopback address that systems use to connect with themselves. Public IP addresses compose the majority of IP addresses with the exception of reserved addresses like those described in RFC 1918.

125. D. Nikto is a web application and server scanning tool and is best suited to Jim's needs. Nmap is a port scanner, Hydra is a login cracking tool, and Metasploit is a complete penetration testing framework but isn't designed specifically to test web applications and servers.

Chapter 11: Practice Test 3

1. B. NIST SP 800-18 describes system owner responsibilities that include helping to develop system security plans, maintaining the plan, ensuring training, and identifying, implementing, and assessing security controls. A data owner is more likely to delegate these tasks to the system owner. Custodians may be asked to enforce those controls, whereas a user will be directly affected by them.

2. C. ESP's Transport mode encrypts IP packet data but leaves the packet header unencrypted. Tunnel mode encrypts the entire packet and adds a new header to support transmission through the tunnel.

3. B. In level 2, the Repeatable level of the SW-CMM, the organization introduces basic life cycle management processes. Reuse of code in an organized fashion begins, and repeatable results are expected from similar projects. The crucial process areas for this level include Requirements Management, Software Project Planning, Software Project Tracking and Oversight, Software Subcontract Management, Software Quality Assurance, and Software Configuration Management. Software Quality Management is a process that occurs during level 4, the Managed stage of the SW-CMM.

4. A. Key risk indicators (KRIs) are often used to monitor risk for organizations that establish an ongoing risk management program. Using automated data gathering and tools that allow data to be digested and summarized can provide predictive information about how organizational risks are changing. KPIs are key performance indicators, which are used to assess how an organization is performing. Quantitative risk assessments are good for point-in-time views with detailed valuation and measurement-based risk assessments, whereas a penetration test would provide details of how well an organization's security controls are working.

5. D. The three-way handshake is SYN, SYN/ACK, ACK. System B should respond with "Synchronize and Acknowledge" to System A after it receives a SYN.

6. A. Systems that respond to pings will show the time to live for packets that reach them. Since TTL is decremented at each hop, this can help build a rough network topology map. In addition, some firewalls respond differently to pings than a normal system, which means pinging a network can sometimes reveal the presence of firewalls that would otherwise be invisible. Hostnames are revealed by a DNS lookup, and ICMP types allowed through a firewall are not revealed by only performing a ping. ICMP can be used for router advertisements, but pinging won't show them!

7. C. Authorization defines what a subject can or can't do. Identification occurs when a subject claims an identity, accounting is provided by the logs and audit trail that track what occurs on a system, and authentication occurs when that identity is validated.

8. C. When a system uses shadowed passwords, the hashed password value is stored in /etc/shadow instead of /etc/passwd. The /etc/passwd file would not contain the password in plaintext or hashed form. Instead, it would contain an x to indicate that the password hash is in the shadow file. The * character is normally used to disable interactive logins to an account.

9. B. The log entries show the characteristic pattern of a port scan. The attacking system sends connection attempts to the target system against a series of commonly used ports.

10. A. Testing for desired functionality is use-case testing. Dynamic testing is used to determine how code handles variables that change over time. Misuse testing focuses on how code handles examples of misuse, and fuzzing feeds unexpected data as an input to see how the code responds.

11. B. Privilege creep is a common problem when employees change roles over time and their privileges and permissions are not properly modified to reflect their new roles. Least privilege issues are a design or implementation problem, and switching roles isn't typically what causes them to occur. Account creep is not a common industry term, and account termination would imply that someone has removed her account instead of switching her to new groups or new roles.

12. C. These are examples of private IP addresses. RFC 1918 defines a set of private IP addresses for use in internal networks. These private addresses including 10.0.0.0 to 10.255.255.255, 172.16.0.0 to 172.31.255.255, and 192.168.0.0 to 192.168.255.255 should never be routable on the public Internet.

13. B. A cognitive password authenticates users based on a series of facts or answers to questions that they know. Preset questions for cognitive passwords typically rely on common information about a user like their mother's maiden name or the name of their pet, and that information can frequently be found on the Internet. The best cognitive password systems let users make up their own questions.

14. B. The Linux tool dd creates a bit-by-bit copy of the target drive that is well suited to forensic use, and special forensic versions of dd exist that can provide even more forensic features. Simply copying files using a tool like xcopy does not create a forensically sound copy. DBAN is a drive wiping tool and would cause Megan to lose the data she is seeking to copy. ImageMagick is a graphics manipulation and editing program.

15. C. The blacklist approach to application control blocks certain prohibited packages but allows the installation of other software on systems. The whitelist approach uses the reverse philosophy and allows only approved software. Antivirus software would detect the installation of malicious software only after the fact. Heuristic detection is a variant of antivirus software.

16. C. Protected health information (PHI) is specifically defined by HIPAA to include information about an individual's medical bills. PCI could refer to the payment card industry's security standard but would apply only in relation to payment cards. PII is a broadly defined term for personally identifiable information, and personal billing data isn't a broadly used industry term.

17. D. A social engineering attack may trick a user into revealing their password to the attacker. Other attacks that depend on guessing passwords, such as brute-force attacks, rainbow table attacks, and dictionary attacks, are unlikely to be successful in light of the organization's strong password policy.

18. A. When someone is forced to perform an action under threat, it is known as duress.

19. A. The term that best describes the type of cloud environment used by Kayla's company, which leverages a major IaaS provider for hosting its web services and a SaaS email system operating in multitenant environments, is a public cloud. A public cloud is where the services are delivered over the public Internet and shared across different organizations. A dedicated cloud, also known as a private cloud, is operated solely for one organization, and this is not the case for Kayla's company. A private cloud is infrastructure operated solely for a single organization, whether managed internally or by a third-party, and hosted either internally or externally, which also does not apply here. A hybrid cloud is a composition of two or more cloud delivery models (private, community, or public) that remain distinct entities but are bound together, offering the benefits of multiple deployment models, which again does not match the company's use of exclusively public cloud services.

20. B. In this scenario, all of the files on the server will be backed up on Monday evening during the full backup. Tuesday's incremental backup will include all files changed since Monday's full backup: files 1, 2, and 5. Wednesday's incremental backup will then include all files modified since Tuesday's incremental backup: files 3 and 6. Therefore, only two files are included in Wednesday's incremental backup.

21. A. Susan is performing passive monitoring, which uses a network tap or SPAN port to capture traffic to analyze it without impacting the network or devices that it is used to monitor. Synthetic, or active, monitoring uses recorded or generated traffic to test for performance and other issues. Signature-based technologies include IDS, IPS, and antimalware systems.

22. A. In a man-in-the-middle attack, attackers manage to insert themselves into a connection between a user and a legitimate website, relaying traffic between the two parties while eavesdropping on the connection. Although similarly named, the meet-in-the-middle attack is a cryptographic attack that does not necessarily involve connection tampering. Fraggle is a network-based denial-of-service attack using UDP packets. Wardriving is a reconnaissance technique for discovering open or weakly secured wireless networks.

23. C. One of the core capabilities of infrastructure as a service is providing servers on a vendor-managed virtualization platform. Web-based payroll and email systems are examples of software as a service. An application platform managed by a vendor that runs customer code is an example of platform as a service.

24. D. The exposure factor is the percentage of the facility that risk managers expect will be damaged if a risk materializes. It is calculated by dividing the amount of damage by the asset value. In this case, that is $750,000 in damage divided by the $2 million facility value, or 37.5%.

25. C. The annualized rate of occurrence is the number of times each year that risk analysts expect a risk to happen. In this case, the analysts expect fires will occur once every 50 years, or 0.02 times per year.

26. A. The annualized loss expectancy is calculated by multiplying the single loss expectancy (SLE) by the annualized rate of occurrence (ARO). In this case, the SLE is $750,000, and the ARO is 0.02. Multiplying these numbers together gives you the ALE of $15,000.

27. C. The two main methods of choosing records from a large pool for further analysis are sampling and clipping. Sampling uses statistical techniques to choose a sample that is representative of the entire pool, while clipping uses threshold values to select those records that exceed a predefined threshold because they may be of most interest to analysts.

28. C. API keys, or application programming interface keys, are passed to services and identify the program, developer, or user. With this information, Mike can programmatically control API usage per user. Of course, if the keys are inadvertently exposed, the API keys themselves could be abused. Session IDs are typically used to identify users of an application, not an API. API firewalls and API buffers were made up for this question.

29. A. An application programming interface (API) allows external users to directly call routines within Fran's code. They can embed API calls within scripts and other programs to automate interactions with Fran's company. A web scraper or call center might facilitate the same tasks, but they do not do so in a direct integration. Data dictionaries might provide useful information, but they also do not allow direct integration.

30. A. A fault is a momentary loss of power. Blackouts are sustained complete losses of power. Sags and brownouts are not complete power disruptions but rather periods of low-voltage conditions.

31. A. Lauren's team would benefit from a credential management system. Credential management systems offer features like password management, multifactor authentication to retrieve passwords, logging, audit, and password rotation capabilities. A strong password policy would only make maintenance of passwords for many systems a more difficult task if done manually. Single sign-on would help if all the systems had the same sensitivity levels, but different credentials are normally required for higher-sensitivity systems.

32. C. Windows systems will assign themselves an APIPA address between 169.254.0.1 and 169.254.255.254 if they cannot contact a DHCP server.

33. A. Enrollment, or registration, is the initial creation of a user account in the provisioning process. Clearance verification and background checks are sometimes part of the process that ensures that the identity of the person being enrolled matches who they claim to be. Initialization is not used to describe the provisioning process.

34. B. Criminal forensic investigations typically have the highest standards for evidence, as they must be able to help prove the case beyond a reasonable doubt. Administrative investigations merely need to meet the standards of the organization and to be able to be defended in court, while civil investigations operate on a preponderance of evidence. There is not a category of forensic investigation referred to as "industry" in the CISSP exam's breakdown of forensic types.

35. B. The Fourth Amendment states, in part, that "the right of the people to be secure in their persons, houses, papers and effects, against unreasonable searches and seizures, shall not be violated, and no Warrants shall issue, but upon probable cause, supported by Oath or affirmation, and particularly describing the place to be searched, and the persons or things to be seized." The First Amendment contains protections related to freedom of speech. The Fifth Amendment ensures that no person will be required to serve as a witness against themselves. The Fifteenth Amendment protects the voting rights of citizens.

36. A. The Electronic Communications Privacy Act (ECPA) makes it a crime to invade the electronic privacy of an individual. It prohibits the unauthorized monitoring of email and voicemail communications.

37. D. The kernel lies within the central ring, Ring 0. Ring 1 contains other operating system components. Ring 2 is used for drivers and protocols. User-level programs and applications run at Ring 3. Rings 0–2 run in privileged mode, whereas Ring 3 runs in user mode.

38. D. The hypervisor runs within the virtualization platform and serves as the moderator between virtual resources and physical resources.

39. A. In the public cloud computing model, the vendor builds a single platform that is shared among many different customers. This is also known as the shared tenancy model.

40. D. During a tabletop exercise, team members come together and walk through a scenario without making any changes to information systems. The read-through is the least disruptive type of disaster recovery test. During a read-through, team members each review the contents of their disaster recovery checklists on their own and suggest any necessary changes. During a parallel test, the team actually activates the disaster recovery site for testing, but the primary site remains operational. During a full interruption test, the team takes down the primary site and confirms that the disaster recovery site is capable of handling regular operations. The full interruption test is the most thorough test but also the most disruptive.

41. C. OpenID Connect is a widely supported standard that allows a user to use a single account to log into multiple sites, and Google accounts are frequently used with OpenID Connect.

42. D. Risk acceptance occurs when an organization determines that the costs involved in pursuing other risk management strategies are not justified and they choose not to pursue any action.

43. A, D. Accounting departments are normally required to separate sensitive duties, such as the ability to add a new vendor and issue a check. Allowing the manager to perform both of these actions would, therefore, violate the principle of separation of duties. Also, it is quite likely that the manager does not need all of these privileges to carry out their work, violating the principle of least privilege. There is no indication that the situation does not follow job rotation assignments or that the access was not properly granted and subject to a management review.

44. C. Decentralized access control makes sense because it allows local control over access. When network connectivity to a central control point is a problem or if rules and regulations may vary significantly from location to location, centralized control can be less desirable than decentralized control despite its challenges with consistency. Since the problem does not describe specific control needs, mandatory access control and rule-based access controls could fit the need but aren't the best answer.

45. B. The U.S. government classifies data that could reasonably be expected to cause damage to national security if disclosed, and for which the damage can be identified or described, as Secret. The U.S. government does not use Classified in its formal four levels of classification. Top Secret data could cause exceptionally grave damage, whereas Confidential data could be expected to cause damage.

46. A. The purpose of a digital certificate is to provide the general public with an authenticated copy of the certificate subject's public key.

47. D. The last step of the certificate creation process is the digital signature. During this step, the certificate authority signs the certificate using its own private key.

48. C. When an individual receives a copy of a digital certificate, the person verifies the authenticity of that certificate by using the CA's public key to validate the digital signature contained on the certificate.

49. A. Mike uses the public key that he extracted from Renee's digital certificate to encrypt the message that he would like to send to Renee.

50. C. Wireshark is a network monitoring tool that can capture and replay communications sent over a data network, including Voice over IP (VoIP) communications. Nmap, Nessus, and Nikto are all security tools that may identify security flaws in the network, but they do not directly undermine confidentiality because they do not have the ability to capture communications.

51. C. The ISC2 Code of Ethics applies only to information security professionals who are members of ISC2. Adherence to the code is a condition of certification, and individuals found in violation of the code may have their certifications revoked. ISC2 members who observe a breach of the code are required to report the possible violation by following the ethics complaint procedures.

52. D. Nonrepudiation is possible only with an asymmetric encryption algorithm. RSA is an asymmetric algorithm. AES, DES, and Blowfish are all symmetric encryption algorithms that do not provide nonrepudiation.

53. D. Modification of audit logs will allow repudiation because the data cannot be trusted, and thus actions can be provably denied. The modification of the logs is also a direct example of tampering. It might initially be tempting to answer elevation of privileges and tampering, as the attacker made changes to files that should be protected, but this is an unknown without more information. Similarly, the attacker may have accessed the files, resulting in information disclosure in addition to tampering, but again, this is not specified in the question. Finally, this did not cause a denial of service, and thus that answer can be ignored.

54. B. Content delivery networks (CDNs) place endpoints at geographic locations around the world and then cache customer content at those endpoints. The CDN servers then handle user requests for data, greatly reducing the burden on the organization's own servers and improving load time. Load balancers would distribute the load among Carmen's own servers and would, therefore, not meet her requirements. TLS acceleration may improve load time by reducing the burden of encryption on servers, but they would not place content closer to end users. Web application firewalls would be used to protect the servers against attack, but this does not match Carmen's requirements.

55. D. The scenario describes a mix of public cloud and private cloud services. This is an example of a hybrid cloud environment.

56. B. Each of the attributes linked to Ben's access provides information for an attribute-based information control system. Attribute-based information controls like those described in NIST SP 800-162 can take many details about the user, actions, and objects into consideration before allowing access to occur. A role-based access control would simply consider Ben's role, whereas both administrative and system discretionary access controls are not commonly used terms to describe access controls.

57. B, D. All of these techniques are valid components of a security awareness and training program. However, users generally find policy reviews and classroom training boring. Gamification and phishing simulations are designed to bring interactivity to the effort and make it more interesting and engaging for users.

58. C. Certificates may only be added to a certificate revocation list by the certificate authority that created the digital certificate.

59. D. Remote journaling transfers transaction logs to a remote site on a more frequent basis than electronic vaulting, typically hourly. Transaction logging is not a recovery technique alone; it is a process for generating the logs used in remote journaling. In an electronic vaulting approach, automated technology moves database backups from the primary database server to a remote site on a scheduled basis, typically daily. Remote mirroring maintains a live database server at the backup site and mirrors all transactions at the primary site on the server at the backup site.

60. A, B, D. The specific data elements covered by state data breach notification laws vary from state to state, but most include Social Security numbers, drivers' license numbers, and bank account numbers when paired with a PIN. No state data breach notification laws include marital status as a covered element.

61. B. Operational investigations are performed by internal teams to troubleshoot performance or other technical issues. They are not intended to produce evidence for use in court and, therefore, do not have the rigid collection standards of criminal, civil, or regulatory investigations.

62. A. Nondisclosure agreements (NDAs) are designed to protect the confidentiality of an organization's data, including trade secrets during and after the person's employment. NDAs do not protect against deletion or availability issues, and noncompete agreements would be required to stop competition.

63. C. Adding a second factor can ensure that users who might be incorrectly accepted are not given access due to a higher than desired false acceptance rate (FAR) from accessing a system. The CER is the crossover between the false acceptance and false rejection rate (FRR) and is used as a way to measure the accuracy of biometric systems. Changing the sensitivity to lower the FRR may actually increase the FAR, and replacing a biometric system can be expensive in terms of time and cost.

64. D. Data custodians are typically responsible for the technical environment and procedures related to data management, which include the backup and recovery of systems to ensure data availability. While data owners are accountable for the data and may decide what needs to be backed up, they do not perform the actual backups. Business owners and data users are more focused on the operational and decision-making aspects of the data's business use and are generally not involved in the technical aspects of data maintenance such as system backups.

65. D. Ron's company is a data processor in this instance, as it is receiving records from the European firm. The European firm is the data controller in this case, as they bear responsibility for the data. The individuals described in the records are the data subjects. Data owners are tasked with making decisions about data such as who receives access to it and how it is used.

66. C. This is an example of two-person control, where two people must concur to perform a sensitive action. Separation of duties is a slightly different principle, where one individual is prevented from holding the privileges to perform two separate actions that, when combined, would result in excessive permissions. Least privilege says that an individual should have the minimum necessary set of permissions to carry out their job functions. There is no indication that least privilege is violated in this scenario. Multifactor authentication is an important security control, but the scenario does not mention whether the administrators use multifactor authentication to perform these activities.

67. C. Salting adds random text to the password before hashing in an attempt to defeat automated password cracking attacks that use precomputed values. MD5 and SHA-1 are both common hashing algorithms, so using them does not add any security. Double-hashing would only be a minor inconvenience for an attacker and would not be as effective as the use of salting.

68. A. Guidelines provide advice based on best practices developed throughout industry and organizations, but they are not compulsory. Compliance with guidelines is optional.

69. A. The Bell–LaPadula model includes the simple security property, which says that no user should be able to read information above their security clearance level. It also includes the star property, which says that a subject should not be able to write data to an object below their security clearance level, and the discretionary security property, which uses access matrices to control access. The Biba integrity model says that users should not be able to read data below their security clearance level.

70. C. Regression testing ensures proper functionality of an application or system after it has been changed. Unit testing focuses on testing each module of a program instead of against its previous functional state. White- and black-box testing both describe the amount of knowledge about a system or application, rather than a specific type or intent for testing.

71. C. Risk transference involves shifting the impact of a potential risk from the organization incurring the risk to another organization. Insurance is a common example of risk transference.

72. A. The four canons of the ISC2 Code of Ethics are to protect society, the common good, the necessary public trust and confidence, and the infrastructure; act honorably, honestly, justly, responsibly, and legally; provide diligent and competent service to principals; and advance and protect the profession.

73. C. A trust that allows one forest to access another's resources without the reverse being possible is an example of a one-way trust. Since Jim doesn't want the trust path to flow as the domain tree is formed, this trust has to be nontransitive.

74. B. Susan's team is performing static analysis, which analyzes nonrunning code. Dynamic analysis uses running code, whereas gray-box assessments are a type of assessment done without full knowledge. Fuzzing feeds unexpected inputs to a program as part of dynamic analysis.

75. A, D. Kevin may choose to pay the ransom, and he may regain access to his data by doing so, but there is no guarantee that the attackers will deliver the decryption key after he makes payment. Additionally, the payment of the ransom may be illegal depending upon the circumstances. He cannot be sure that the attackers do not have access to his information, as the ransomware may have copied data for the attackers' use. Restoring from backup is a good method to regain access to information encrypted by ransomware.

76. A. Remote attestation creates a hash value from the system configuration to confirm the integrity of the configuration. Binding and sealing are techniques used by the TPM to encrypt data. The random number generator (RNG) function of the TPM is used to support cryptographic operations.

77. A, C. Situations where humidity is too high may result in the buildup of moisture and corrosion of equipment. If humidity falls too low, it may result in static electricity issues. Humidity issues generally do not contribute to fires or physical access control failures.

78. A. Hot sites contain all of the hardware and data necessary to restore operations and may be activated very quickly. Warm sites contain the necessary hardware but not the data. Cold sites contain neither hardware nor data. Mobile sites are easily transportable, which is not mentioned in this scenario.

79. B. Syslog uses UDP port 514. TCP-based implementations of syslog use TCP port 601 when unencrypted and use TCP port 6514 when encrypted with TLS. The other ports may look familiar because they are commonly used TCP ports: 443 is HTTPS, 515 is the LPD print service, and 445 is used for Windows SMB.

80. B. PSH is a TCP flag used to clear the buffer, resulting in immediately sending data, and URG is the TCP urgent flag. These flags are not present in UDP headers.

81. B. Fagan inspection is a highly formalized review and testing process that uses planning, overview, preparation, inspection, rework, and follow-up steps. Static inspection looks at code without running it, dynamic inspection uses live programs, and interface testing tests where code modules interact.

82. D. The system is set to overwrite the logs and will replace the oldest log entries with new log entries when the file reaches 20 MB. The system is not purging archived logs because it is not archiving logs. Since there can be only 20 MB of logs, this system will not have stored too much log data, and the question does not provide enough information to know if there will be an issue with not having the information needed.

83. D. The image shown is from a network-connected web camera. This is likely an Internet of Things (IoT) botnet, much like the Mirai botnet that had a major impact on world Internet traffic in 2016.

84. A. Alejandro is in the first stage of the incident response process, detection. During this stage, the intrusion detection system provides the initial alert, and Alejandro performs preliminary triaging to determine if an intrusion is actually taking place and whether the scenario fits the criteria for activating further steps of the incident response process (which include response, mitigation, reporting, recovery, remediation, and lessons learned).

85. C. After detection of a security incident, the next step in the process is response, which should follow the organization's formal incident response procedure. The first step of this procedure is activating the appropriate teams, including the organization's computer security incident response team (CSIRT).

86. C. The root-cause analysis examines the incident to determine what allowed it to happen and provides critical information for repairing systems so that the incident does not recur. This is a component of the remediation step of the incident response process because the root-cause analysis output is necessary to fully remediate affected systems and processes.

87. D. When using symmetric cryptography, the sender encrypts a message using a shared secret key, and the recipient then decrypts the message with that same key. Only asymmetric cryptography uses the concept of public and private key pairs.

88. A. Business logic errors are most likely to be missed by automated functional testing. If a complete coverage code test was conducted, runtime, input validation, and error handling issues are likely to have been discovered by automated testing. Any automated system is more likely to miss business logic errors, because humans are typically necessary to understand business logic issues.

89. A. During the lessons learned phase, analysts close out an incident by conducting a review of the entire incident response process. This may include making recommendations for improvements to the process that will streamline the efficiency and effectiveness of future incident response efforts.

90. B. The Digital Millennium Copyright Act (DMCA) prohibits attempts to circumvent copyright protection mechanisms placed on a protected work by the copyright holder. The Health Insurance Portability and Accountability Act (HIPAA) governs the security and privacy of protected health information. The Gramm-Leach-Bliley Act (GLBA) governs the security and privacy of financial information. The Electronic Communications Privacy Act (ECPA) restricts eavesdropping on private communications.

91. B. Linda should choose a warm site. This approach balances cost and recovery time. Cold sites take a very long time to activate, measured in weeks or months. Hot sites activate immediately but are quite expensive. Mutual assistance agreements depend on the support of another organization.

92. A. Purchasing insurance is a way to transfer risk to another entity. Risk avoidance actions change business processes to eliminate a risk. Risk mitigation activities reduce the likelihood or impact of a risk occurring. Risk acceptance takes no action to control the risk other than acknowledging its presence.

93. D. Gray-box testing is a blend of crystal-box (or white-box) testing, which provides full information about a target, and black-box testing, which provides little or no knowledge about the target.

94. A. The combination of an ID card (something you have) and a PIN (something you know) is a reasonable way to control access to a physical facility. The use of a password is not a user-friendly way to control access to a physical facility. The use of an ID card (something you have) in conjunction with an access token (something you have) does not constitute multifactor authentication because both are something you have factors. The same is true for the use of a retinal scan (something you are) and a fingerprint (something you are).

95. A. Ethernet networks in modern organizations use a star topology, where each device is directly connected to the switch and receives only traffic intended for that device. This reduces the possibility of eavesdropping on other devices.

96. A. Proxy servers can act to anonymize web requests by hiding their true source IP addresses and removing identifying information. Content filters restrict the websites that users may access. Malware filters search for and block malicious code. Caching servers store local copies of frequently requested content to reduce loading time.

97. A. U.S. export control laws contain special provisions around the use of encryption technology, and Evelyn should include details about the software used by her firm in the training. These regulations do not affect content filtering controls, firewall rules, or phishing simulations.

98. A. Skip should use Secure Copy (SCP), which is a secure file transfer method. SSH is a secure command-line and login protocol, whereas HTTP is used for unencrypted web traffic. Telnet is an unencrypted command-line and login protocol.

99. C. The California Online Privacy Protection Act requires that commercial websites that collect personal information from users in California conspicuously post a privacy policy. The act does not require compliance with the EU GDPR, nor does it use the GDPR concepts of notice or choice, and it does not require encryption of all personal data.

100. D. Modern recommendations from the National Institute of Standards and Technology (NIST) are that users should not be forced to change their passwords through the use of password expiration policies. More information on these recommendations can be found in NIST Special Publication (SP) 800-63B, "Digital Identity Guidelines."

101. A. This is an example of federation, where user credentials from one organization are accepted as proof of identity by another organization. The users are not creating new accounts, so there is no identity proofing, enrollment, or provisioning activity taking place.

102. B. Iris scans have a longer useful life than many other types of biometric factors because they don't change throughout a person's life span (unless the eye itself is damaged). Iris scanners can be fooled in some cases by high-resolution images of an eye, and iris scanners are not significantly cheaper than other scanners.

103. D. NIST 800-53 is the standard that describes the security controls mandatory for use on U.S. federal government systems. It provides a catalog of security and privacy controls for all U.S. federal information systems except those related to national security. PCI DSS is a proprietary information security standard for organizations that handle payment cards and is not specific to government systems. ISO 27001 is an international standard on how to manage information security and is not specific to U.S. federal systems. SABSA is a framework and methodology for enterprise security architecture and service management, again not specific to the mandatory controls required by U.S. government systems.

104. C. They need a key for every possible pair of users in the cryptosystem. The first key would allow communication between Matthew and Richard. The second key would allow communication between Richard and Christopher. The third key would allow communication between Christopher and Matthew.

105. D. All of these controls involve the use of encryption, but only Transport Layer Security (TLS) provides a strong, effective means for protecting data in transit. Secure Sockets Layer (SSL) is an outdated method for protecting data in transit that should no longer be used. Full disk encryption (FDE) provides encryption for data at rest. The Trusted Platform Module (TPM) manages encryption keys for use in FDE.

106. C. The SMTP protocol does not guarantee confidentiality between servers, making TLS or SSL between the client and server only a partial measure. Encrypting the email content can provide confidentiality; digital signatures can provide nonrepudiation.

107. D. The single quotation mark in the input field is a telltale sign that this is a SQL injection attack. The quotation mark is used to escape outside the SQL code's input field, and the text following is used to directly manipulate the SQL command sent from the web application to the database.

108. C. TLS provides message confidentiality and integrity, which can prevent eavesdropping. When paired with digital signatures, which provide integrity and authentication, forged assertions can also be defeated. SAML does not have a security mode and relies on TLS and digital signatures to ensure security if needed. Message hashing without a signature would help prevent modification of the message but won't necessarily provide authentication.

109. A. The goal of the business continuity planning process is to ensure that your recovery time objectives are all less than your maximum tolerable downtimes.

110. C. The remediation phase of incident handling focuses on conducting a root-cause analysis to identify the factors contributing to an incident and implementing new security controls, as needed.

111. A. The S/MIME secure email format uses the P7S format for encrypted email messages. If the recipient does not have a mail reader that supports S/MIME, the message will appear with an attachment named `smime.p7s`.

112. A. Aggregation is a security issue that arises when a collection of facts has a higher classification than the classification of any of those facts standing alone. An inference problem occurs when an attacker can deduce information of greater sensitivity from a lower security level fact. SQL injection is a web application exploit. Multilevel security is a system control that allows the simultaneous processing of information at different classification levels.

113. B. Polyinstantiation allows the storage of multiple different pieces of information in a database at different classification levels to prevent attackers from conducting aggregation or inference attacks. Kim could store incorrect location information in the database at lower classification levels to prevent the aggregation attack in this scenario. Input validation, server-side validation, and parameterization are all techniques used to prevent web application attacks and are not effective against inference attacks.

114. B. The tail number is a database field because it is stored in the database. It is also a primary key because the question states that the database uniquely identifies aircraft using this field. Any primary key is, by definition, also a candidate key. There is no information provided that the tail number is a foreign key used to reference a different database table.

115. B. Foreign keys are used to create relationships between tables in a database. The database enforces referential integrity by ensuring that the foreign key used in a table has a corresponding record with that value as the primary key in the referenced table.

116. B. The waterfall model uses an approach that develops software sequentially, spending quite a bit of time up front on the development and documentation of requirements and design. The spiral and Agile models focus on iterative development and are appropriate when requirements are not well understood or iterative development is preferred. DevOps is an approach to integrating development and operations activities and is not an SDLC model.

117. A. The data owner is a senior manager who bears ultimate responsibility for data protection tasks. The data owner typically delegates this responsibility to one or more data custodians.

118. D. Fuzz testing tools are designed to provide invalid or unexpected input to applications, testing for vulnerabilities like format string vulnerabilities, buffer overflow issues, and other problems. A static analysis relies on examining code without running the application or code and thus would not fill forms as part of a web application. Brute-force tools attempt to bypass security by trying every possible combination for passwords or other values. A white box is a type of penetration test where the testers have full knowledge of the environment.

119. B. Warren could use a survey or third-party assessment to evaluate the effectiveness of the campaign, but the best evidence would be provided by a phishing simulation where the organization measures user responses to simulated phishing attacks. Code reviews would not be useful in evaluating the effectiveness of antiphishing campaigns.

120. B. Anomaly-based intrusion detection systems may identify a zero-day vulnerability because it deviates from normal patterns of activity. Signature-based detection methods would not be effective because there are no signatures for zero-day vulnerabilities. Strong patch management would not be helpful because, by definition, zero-day vulnerabilities do not have patches available. Full-disk encryption would not detect an attack because it is not a detective control.

121. A. Whether Rob has standing to report this situation to ISC2 depends upon the canon(s) violated by the activity. This behavior violates canon II, "Act honorably, honestly, justly, responsibly, and legally." Any member of the public may file a claim under canons I or II. Only an employer or someone with a contracting relationship with the individual may file a complaint under canon III. Anyone who is certified or licensed as a professional and subscribes to a code of ethics as part of that licensure or certification is eligible to file a canon IV complaint.

122. A. The emergency response guidelines should include the immediate steps an organization should follow in response to an emergency situation. These include immediate response procedures, a list of individuals who should be notified of the emergency, and secondary response procedures for incident responders. They do not include long-term actions such as activating business continuity protocols, ordering equipment, or activating disaster recovery sites.

123. D. An access control vestibule (or mantrap) uses two sets of doors, only one of which can open at a time. An access control vestibule is a type of preventive access control, although its implementation is a physical control.

124. B. RAID level 5 is also known as disk striping with parity. It uses three or more disks, with the equivalent of one disk containing parity information used to restore data to another disk in the event of failure. When used with three disks, RAID 5 is able to withstand the loss of a single disk.

125. The SOC levels match the report descriptions as follows:

  1. SOC 1, Type 1: D. A report that provides the auditor's opinions of financial statements about controls at the service organization and that includes a report on the opinion on the presentation of the service organization's system as well as suitability of the controls

  2. SOC 1, Type 2: C. A report that provides an assessment of the risk of material misstatement of financial statement assertions affected by the service organization's processing and that includes a description of the service auditor's tests of the controls and the results of the tests and their effectiveness

  3. SOC 2: B. A report that provides predefined, standard benchmarks for controls involving confidentiality, availability, integrity, and privacy of a system and the information it contains, generally for restricted use

  4. SOC 3: A. A general use report that reports on the effectiveness of controls related to compliance and/or operations

Chapter 12: Practice Test 4

1. C. Detective access controls operate after the fact and are intended to detect or discover unwanted access or activity. Preventive access controls are designed to prevent the activity from occurring, whereas corrective controls return an environment to its original status after an issue occurs. Directive access controls limit or direct the actions of subjects to ensure compliance with policies.

2. C. A honeypot is a decoy computer system used to bait intruders into attacking. A honeynet is a network of multiple honeypots that creates a more sophisticated environment for intruders to explore. A pseudo-flaw is a false vulnerability in a system that may distract an attacker. Administrators often include pseudo-flaws on honeypots to emulate well-known operating system vulnerabilities. A darknet is a segment of unused network address space that should have no network activity and, therefore, may be easily used to monitor for illicit activity.

3. C. The crossover error rate (CER) is the point where the false acceptance rate (FAR) and the false rejection rate (FRR) cross over, and it is a standard assessment used to compare the accuracy of biometric devices.

4. A. At point B, the false acceptance rate (FAR) is quite high, whereas the false rejection rate (FRR) is relatively low. This may be acceptable in some circumstances, but in organizations where a false acceptance can cause a major problem, it is likely that they should instead choose a point to the right of point A.

5. B. CER is a standard used to assess biometric devices. If the CER for this device does not fit the needs of the organization, Ben should assess other biometric systems to find one with a lower CER. Sensitivity is already accounted for in CER charts, and moving the CER isn't something Ben can do. FRR is not a setting in software, so Ben can't use that as an option either.

6. B. Personally identifiable information (PII) can be used to distinguish a person's identity. Personal health information (PHI) includes data such as medical history, lab results, insurance information, and other details about a patient. Personal protected data is a made-up term, and PID is an acronym for process ID, the number associated with a running program or process.

7. D. The figure shows the waterfall model, developed by Winston Royce. An important characteristic of this model is a series of sequential steps that include a feedback loop that allows the process to return one step prior to the current step when necessary.

8. B. Encapsulation creates both the benefits and potential issues with multilayer protocols. Bridging can use various protocols but does not rely on encapsulation. Hashing and storage protocols typically do not rely on encapsulation as a core part of their functionality.

9. C. OAuth is used to provide secure delegated access in scenarios exactly like this. OpenID is used to sign in using credentials from an identity provider to other services, such as when you log in with Google to other sites. SAML, or Security Assertion Markup Language, is

used to make security assertions allowing authentication and authorizations between identity providers and service providers. Kerberos is mostly used inside of organizations instead of for federation, as this question focuses on. OAuth is specifically designed to provide secure delegated access, allowing Amanda's application to access users' Gmail contacts without requiring users to share their Gmail credentials. It is widely used by cloud services for this purpose. In contrast, OpenID is primarily for authenticating users with an external identity provider, SAML is used for exchanging authentication and authorization data between providers, and Kerberos is typically employed for internal network authentication, not for cloud-based or federated services as described in this scenario.

10. B. The recovery time objective (RTO) is the amount of time that it may take to restore a service after a disaster without unacceptable impact on the business. The RTO for each service is identified during a business impact assessment.

11. A. Each of these answers may be a concern, but the overriding security concern is whether the hardware and firmware can be trusted or may have been modified. Original equipment manufacturers (OEMs) have business reasons to ensure the security of their products, but third parties in the supply chain may not feel the same pressure. Both availability of support and whether the hardware is legitimate are also concerns, but less immediate security concerns. Finally, hardware may be older than expected, or may be used, refurbished, or otherwise not new.

12. C. When done properly, a sanitization process fully ensures that data does not remain on the system before it is reused. Clearing and erasing can both be failure prone, and of course, destruction wouldn't leave a machine or device available for reuse.

13. C. In a gray-box test, the tester evaluates the software from a user perspective but has access to the source code as the test is conducted. White-box tests also have access to the source code but perform testing from a developer's perspective. Black-box tests work from a user's perspective but do not have access to source code. Blue boxes are a telephone hacking tool and not a software testing technique. Note: as language changes, new terms like zero knowledge, partial knowledge, and full knowledge are starting to replace white-, gray-, and black-box testing terms.

14. D. The DevOps approach to technology management seeks to integrate software development, operations, and quality assurance in a cohesive effort. It specifically attempts to eliminate the issue of taking problems and "throwing them over the fence" by building collaborative relationships between members of the IT team.

15. B. A security information and event management (SIEM) tool is designed to centralize logs from many locations in many formats and to ensure that logs are read and analyzed despite differences between different systems and devices. The Simple Network Management Protocol (SNMP) is used for some log messaging but is not a solution that solves all of these problems. Most non-Windows devices, including network devices among others, are not designed to use the Windows event log format, although using NTP for time synchronization is a good idea. Finally, local logging is useful, but setting clocks individually will result in drift over time and won't solve the issue with many log sources.

16. C. Ethical disclosure involves informing organizations of flaws and issues. Unlike bug bounties, this does not rely on organizations providing financial or other rewards. Ethical disclosure may involve timeframes to ensure that companies do not ignore issues, but a focus on collaboration and public safety is common. CVEs are created when flaws are reported to the CVE program. There is no blackmail behavior involved in this description.

17. A. The single quotation mark in the input field is a telltale sign that this is a SQL injection attack. The quotation mark is used to escape outside the SQL code's input field, and the text that follows is used to directly manipulate the SQL command sent from the web application to the database.

18. D. Procedures are formal, mandatory documents that provide detailed, step-by-step actions required from individuals performing a task.

19. C. The CIS benchmarks are configuration baselines that are frequently used to assess the security settings or configuration for devices and software. Baselining is the process of configuring and validating that a system meets security configuration guidelines or standards.

20. B. A typical incident response (IR) process will begin mitigation efforts after response has started and then will move into the recovery, reporting, and lessons learned phases. It is important to remember that while the IR cycle is drawn as a cycle, it often moves back and forth between phases as new issues or details are identified.

21. C. Data centers should be located in the core of a building. Locating it on lower floors makes it susceptible to flooding and physical break-ins. Locating it on the top floor makes it vulnerable to wind and roof damage.

22. A. The due care principle states that an individual should react in a situation using the same level of care that would be expected from any reasonable person. It is a very broad standard. Crime prevention through environmental design is a design concept that focuses on making environments less conducive to illicit or unwanted actions. Separation of duties splits duties to ensure that a malicious actor cannot perform actions on their own like making a purchase and approving it. Informed consent is a term used in the medical industry that requires that a person's permission is required and that they must be aware of what the consequences of their actions could be.

23. B. Criminal investigations have high stakes with severe punishment for the offender that may include incarceration. Therefore, they use the strictest standard of evidence of all investigations: beyond a reasonable doubt. Civil investigations use a preponderance-of-the-evidence standard. Regulatory investigations may use whatever standard is appropriate for the venue where the evidence will be heard. This may include the beyond-a-reasonable-doubt standard, but it is not always used in regulatory investigations in the United States. Operational investigations do not use a standard of evidence.

24. C. A cloud IaaS vendor will allow Kristen to set up infrastructure as quickly as she can deploy and pay for it. A PaaS vendor provides a platform that would require her to migrate her custom application to it, likely taking longer than a hosted data-center provider. A data-center vendor that provides rack, power, and remote hands assistance fails the test based on Kristen's desire to not have to acquire or ship hardware.

25. B. Warm sites contain the hardware necessary to restore operations but do not have a current copy of data.

26. C. A power spike is a momentary period of high voltage. A surge is a prolonged period of high voltage. Sags and brownouts are periods of low voltage.

27. D. Medical insurance claims will contain protected health information, or PHI. Greg should label the drives as containing PHI and then ensure that they are handled according to his organization's handling standards for that type of data.

28. C. While both an intrusion detection system (IDS) and an intrusion prevention system (IPS) can detect attacks, only an IPS can stop attacks. This requires the IPS to be placed inline. A connection via a network tap, span port, or other similar tool for replicating network traffic will not allow defensive actions to be taken directly by the device.

29. B. Bollards are physical security solutions that are short and strong posts or similar solutions intended to stop vehicles from crashing through or passing an area. Bollards can be used to allow pedestrians and mobility devices to pass while stopping vehicles. Fences and walls will prevent individuals from passing through them, while stairs are challenging for most mobility devices.

30. A. Tara first must achieve a system baseline. She does this by applying the most recent full backup to the new system. This is Sunday's full backup. Once Tara establishes this baseline, she may then proceed to apply differential backups to bring the system back to a more recent state.

31. B. To restore the system to as current a state as possible, Tara must first apply Sunday's full backup. She may then apply the most recent differential backup, from Wednesday at noon. Differential backups include all files that have changed since the most recent full backup, so the contents of Wednesday's backup contain all of the data that would be contained in Monday and Tuesday's backups, making the Monday and Tuesday backups irrelevant for this scenario.

32. A. In this scenario, the differential backup was made at noon, and the server failed at 3 p.m. Therefore, any data modified or created between noon and 3 p.m. on Wednesday will not be contained on any backup and will be irretrievably lost.

33. D. By switching from differential to incremental backups, Tara's weekday backups will contain only the information changed since the previous day. Therefore, she must apply all of the available incremental backups. She would begin by restoring the Sunday full backup and then apply the Monday, Tuesday, and Wednesday incremental backups.

34. D. Each incremental backup contains only the information changed since the most recent full or incremental backup. If we assume that the same amount of information changes every day, each of the incremental backups would be roughly the same size.

35. C. A man-in-the-middle (MiTM), often referred to as a person-in-the-middle or on-path attack, allows an attacker to redirect traffic and thus read or modify it. This can be completely transparent to the end user, making it a dangerous attack if the malicious actor is successful. DNS hijacking would change a system's domain name information, and there is no direct indication of that here. Similarly, ARP spoofing is one way to conduct a MiTM attack, but that detail is not here either. SQL injection is normally done via web applications to execute commands against a database server.

36. B. Record retention ensures that data is kept and maintained as long as it is needed and that it is purged when it is no longer necessary. Data remanence occurs when data is left behind after an attempt is made to remove it, whereas data redaction is not a technical term used to describe this effort. Finally, audit logging may be part of the records retained but doesn't describe the life cycle of data.

37. D. The Authentication Header provides authentication, integrity, and nonrepudiation for IPsec connections. The Encapsulating Security Payload provides encryption and thus provides confidentiality. It can also provide limited authentication. L2TP is an independent VPN protocol, and Encryption Security Header is a made-up term.

38. B. The attack described in the scenario is a classic example of TCP scanning, a network reconnaissance technique that may precede other attacks. There is no evidence that the attack disrupted system availability, which would characterize a denial-of-service attack; that it was waged by a malicious insider; or that the attack resulted in the compromise of a system.

39. C. Windows system logs include reboots, shutdowns, and service state changes. Application logs record events generated by programs, security logs track events like logins and uses of rights, and setup logs track application setup.

40. B. Many organizations delay patches for a period of time to ensure that any previously unidentified flaws are found before the patches are installed throughout their organization. Melissa needs to balance business impact against security in her role and may choose to support this or to push for more aggressive installation practices depending on the organization's risk tolerance and security needs.

41. A. RAID level 0 is also known as disk striping. RAID 1 is called disk mirroring. RAID 5 is called disk striping with parity. RAID 10 is known as a stripe of mirrors.

42. A. Resource capacity agreements are used to ensure that appropriate resources will be available in a recovery scenario. Cold sites have only space and utilities and don't provide full recovery resources. Nondisclosure agreements protect information and won't ensure resource availability, and business continuity agreements are not a term used in the CISSP exam.

43. A. Duress codes are pre-arranged codes used to indicate that the staff member is under duress. They are typically designed to be easy to communicate during normal conversation without alarming whomever may be listening in. Panic buttons are physical buttons used to summon emergency services or responders. Kidnap codes and threat codes were made up for this question.

44. B. Fred's company needs to protect integrity, which can be accomplished by digitally signing messages. Any change will cause the signature to be invalid. Encrypting isn't necessary because the company does not want to protect confidentiality. TLS can provide in-transit protection but won't protect integrity of the messages, and of course a hash used without a way to verify that the hash wasn't changed won't ensure integrity either.

45. A. An attribute-based access control (ABAC) system will allow Susan to specify details about subjects, objects, and access, allowing granular control. Although a rule-based access control system (RBAC) might allow this, the attribute-based access control system can be more specific and thus is more flexible. Discretionary access control (DAC) would allow object owners to make decisions, and mandatory access controls (MACs) would use classifications; neither of these capabilities was described in the requirements.

46. B. The most effective control is to remove the drives and shred them, removing any chance for the servers to leave with data remaining on them. A trustworthy company that can provide a certificate of disposal with appropriate contractual controls may be a reasonable and cost-efficient alternative, but the company may also then want to zero wipe drives before the systems leave to reduce the risk if a system makes it out of the recycler's control. The worst answer here is reformatting, which will not remove data.

47. B. The maximum allowed length of a Cat 6 cable is 100 meters, or 328 feet. Long distances are typically handled by a fiber run or by using network devices like switches or repeaters—not only because of the distance but also because outdoor runs can experience lightning strikes, which won't affect fiber. Knowing that copper twisted pair has distance limitations can be important in many network designs and influences where switches and other devices are placed.

48. B. One of the main functions of a forensic drive controller is to prevent any command sent to a device from modifying data stored on the device. For this reason, forensic drive controllers are also often referred to as write blockers.

49. A. Setting the Secure cookie will allow cookies to be sent only via HTTPS TLS or SSL sessions, preventing man-in-the-middle attacks that target cookies. The rest of the settings are problematic. For example, cookies are vulnerable to DNS spoofing. Domain cookies should usually have the narrowest possible scope, which is actually accomplished by not setting the Domain cookie. This allows only the originating server to access the cookie. Cookies without the Expires or Max-age attributes are ephemeral and will only be kept for the session, making them less vulnerable than stored cookies. Normally, the HTTPOnly attribute is a good idea, but it prevents scripting rather than requiring unencrypted HTTP sessions.

50. B. Data remanence describes data that is still on media after an attempt has been made to remove it. Destroying the drive is a way to ensure that no data is recoverable. Data permanence describes how long data lasts and is not used in the context of data remaining on devices.

51. B. Mandatory access control (MAC) applies labels to subjects and objects and allows subjects to access objects when their labels match. Discretionary access control (DAC) is controlled by the owner of objects, rule-based access control (sometimes called Rule-BAC) applies rules throughout a system, and role-based access control (sometimes called Role-BAC) bases rights on roles, which are often handled as groups of users.

52. B. Identity as a service (IDaaS) provides capabilities such as account provisioning, management, authentication, authorization, reporting, and monitoring. Platform as a service (PaaS), infrastructure as a service (IaaS), and software as a service (SaaS) are cloud service models but do not provide the identity and access management functions described in the question.

53. C. Eavesdropping, denial-of-service attacks, and caller ID spoofing are all common VoIP attacks. Cross-site scripting targets web applications, not VoIP systems.

54. D. This broad access may indirectly violate all of the listed security principles, but it is most directly a violation of least privilege because it grants users privileges that they do not need for their job functions.

55. C. The Secure File Transfer Protocol (SFTP) is specifically designed for encrypted file transfer. SSH is used for secure command-line access, whereas TCP is one of the bundles of Internet protocols commonly used to transmit data across a network. IPsec could be used to create a tunnel to transfer the data but is not specifically designed for file transfer.

56. A. OWASP recommends four critical best practices for libraries and frameworks: using libraries and frameworks from trusted sources that are broadly used and well maintained, maintaining an inventory of third-party libraries, updating libraries and components proactively, and reducing attack surface by limiting what functions can be used. Building your own frameworks and libraries is more likely to result in vulnerabilities for most organizations than using well-maintained and supported existing options.

57. C. The client sends its existing valid TGT to the KDC and requests access to the resource.

58. A. The KDC must verify that the TGT is valid and whether the user has the right privileges to access the service it is requesting access to. If it does, it generates a service ticket and sends it to the client (step B).

59. C. When a client connects to a service server (SS), it sends the following two messages:

- The client-to-server ticket, encrypted using the service's secret key
- A new authenticator, including the client ID and timestamp that is encrypted using the client-server session key

The server or service that is being accessed receives all of the data it needs in the service ticket. To do so, the client uses a client-to-server ticket received from the ticket granting service.

60. B. The service ticket in Kerberos authentication provides proof that a subject is authorized to access an object. Ticket granting services are provided by the TGS. Proof that a subject has authenticated and can request tickets to other objects and uses ticket-granting tickets, and authentication host is a made-up term.

61. C. The first step in a business impact analysis is to identify the business's priorities. Judy should ensure that business areas are all represented and that the functions of each department or area are assessed. Once that is done, she can move on to identifying risks, evaluating likelihood and impact, and then prioritizing the resources available to the business to address the identified priorities.

62. A. Organizations are most often concerned about hotspots creating an unsecured network connection into their secure network via laptops or other devices that are connected to them. Bridging a cellular connection to a network connection to the business's network creates a path that bypasses security controls. Hotspots could be used as rogue access points, but this is a less common scenario. They do not specifically allow wireless data to be intercepted and, in most modern implementations, are encrypted, thus limiting the likelihood of sniffing providing useful data.

63. A. Dry pipe, deluge, and preaction systems all use pipes that remain empty until the system detects signs of a fire. Wet pipe systems use pipes filled with water that may damage equipment if there is damage to a pipe.

64. A. Protected health information (PHI) is defined by HIPAA to include health information used by healthcare providers, such as medical treatment, history, and billing. Personally identifiable information (PII) is information that can be used to identify an individual, which may be included in the PHI but isn't specifically this type of data. Protected health insurance and individual protected data are both made-up terms.

65. B. Manual testing uses human understanding of business logic to assess program flow and responses. Mutation or generational fuzzing will help determine how the program responds to expected inputs but does not test the business logic. Interface testing ensures that data exchange between modules works properly but does not focus on the logic of the program or application.

66. A. A Type 1 authentication factor is something you know. A Type 2 authentication factor is something you have, like a smartcard or hardware token. A Type 3 authentication factor is something you are, like a biometric identifier. There is no such thing as a Type 4 authentication factor.

67. B. System owners develop and maintain system security plans with system administrators, and they have to ensure that appropriate security controls are in place on those systems. System owners also share responsibility for data protection with data owners. System administrators grant appropriate access and apply the controls, whereas data owners own the classification process.

68. A. Jack is performing misuse case analysis, a process that tests code based on how it would perform if it were misused instead of used properly. Use-case testing tests valid use cases, whereas static code analysis involves reviewing the code itself for flaws rather than testing the live software. Hacker use case testing isn't an industry term for a type of testing.

69. A, B, C, D. All of these options are useful to help prevent SQL injection. Stored procedures limit what can be done via the database server, and escaping user input makes dangerous characters less likely to be a problem. Parameterized queries limit what can be sent in a query, and input validation adds another layer of protection by limiting what can be successfully input by a user.

70. C. Both TCP and UDP port numbers are a 16-digit binary number, which means there can be 2^{16} ports, or 65,536 ports, numbered from 0 to 65,535.

71. A. MITRE's Common Vulnerabilities and Exploits (CVE) dictionary and NIST's National Vulnerability Database (NVD) both provide information about vulnerabilities.

72. D. Record retention policies are used to establish what data organizations retain and how long they will retain it for. Keeping data longer than necessary can increase risk to the organization, but having data when needed for investigations, legal compliance, or other business purposes is also important. EOL, or end of life, and EOS, or end of support, apply to hardware or software and not to data. Data classification policies are used to help classify data, which may influence how long it is retained, but classification policies themselves typically do not set retention timeframes.

73. B. Software-defined security (SDS) is an increasingly common approach to security that involves using software solutions and policies to secure environments, rather than traditional hardware-based approaches. This strategy allows for flexible and dynamic security configurations, particularly suited to the cloud's scalable nature. While a root of trust provides a foundational security element in cryptographic systems, policy engines contribute to decision-making in SDS and other frameworks by enforcing security policies. Software-defined networks focus on network management through software, showcasing the broader move toward software-defined approaches in IT infrastructure.

74. A. Antenna placement, antenna design, and power levels are the three important factors in determining where a signal can be accessed and how usable it is. A captive portal can be used to control user logins, and antenna design is part of antenna types. The FCC does provide maximum broadcast power guidelines but does not require a minimum power level.

75. C. Physically destroying the drive is the best way to ensure that there is no remnant data on the drive. SSDs are flash media, which means that you can't degauss them, whereas both random pattern writes and the built-in erase commands have been shown to be problematic due to the wear leveling built into SSDs as well as differences in how they handle erase commands.

76. A. Confidentiality ensures that data cannot be read by unauthorized individuals while stored or in transit.

77. D. OWASP's secure coding practices checklist provides a wide variety of input validation recommendations, including conducting data validation on trusted systems, validating data length, range, and types, and validating all client-provided data before it is processed. Converting all data to the same data type isn't possible because multiple data types are needed for most programs and applications.

78. C. PCI-DSS, or the Payment Card Industry Data Security Standard, is the industry standard Gary's company will need to comply with. ISO27001 and 27002 are information security management standards. FIPS 140 is a standard for cryptographic modules.

79. B. A post-admission philosophy allows or denies access based on user activity after connection based on a predefined authorization matrix. Since this doesn't check the status of a machine before it connects, it can't prevent the exploit of the system immediately after connection. This doesn't preclude out-of-band or in-band monitoring, but it does mean that a strictly post-admission policy won't handle system checks before the systems are admitted to the network.

80. B. The implicit deny principle states that any action that is not explicitly allowed is denied. This is an important concept for firewall rules and other access control systems. Implementing least privilege ensures that subjects have only the rights they need to accomplish their job. While explicit deny and final rule fall-through may sound like important access control concepts, neither is.

81. B. Risks are the combination of a threat and a vulnerability. Threats are the external forces seeking to undermine security, such as the hacker in this case. Vulnerabilities are the internal weaknesses that might allow a threat to succeed. In this case, web defacement is the risk. In this scenario, if the hacker attempts a SQL injection attack (threat) against the unpatched server (vulnerability), the result is website defacement (risk).

82. D. The mean time to detect a compromise is a security KPI, or key performance indicator. KPIs are used to determine how effective practices, procedures, and staff are.

83. C. Val is conducting dynamic application security testing, or DAST. DAST simulates an attacker's actions against software to test it. SAST reviews source code to identify vulnerabilities. FAST and LAST are not software testing methodologies or tools.

84. D. Fiber-optic cable is more expensive and can be harder to install than stranded copper cable or coaxial cable in some cases, but it isn't susceptible to electromagnetic interference (EMI). That makes it a great solution for Jen's problem, especially if she is deploying EMI-hardened systems to go with her EMI-resistant network cables.

85. D. The request control process provides an organized framework within which users can request modifications, managers can conduct cost/benefit analyses, and developers can prioritize tasks.

86. B. Change control provides an organized framework within which multiple developers can create and test solutions prior to rolling them out into a production environment.

87. C. Release control includes acceptance testing to ensure that any alterations to end-user work tasks are understood and functional.

88. A. Configuration control ensures that changes to software versions are made in accordance with the change control and configuration management process. Updates can be made only from authorized distributions in accordance with those policies.

89. D. Coverage analysis is performed to ensure that functionality, requirements, or other elements are completely tested. No misuse cases are described in the question, no interfaces are described, and breach attack simulations are intended to act like an attacker, rather than test for all functions.

90. B. Risk transference involves actions that shift risk from one party to another. Purchasing insurance is an example of risk transference because it moves risk from the insured to the insurance company.

91. C. The Online Certificate Status Protocol (OCSP) eliminates the latency inherent in the use of certificate revocation lists by providing a means for real-time certificate verification.

92. B. A cloud access security broker (CASB) is a tool that sits between on-premises and cloud systems, monitoring traffic and enforcing security policies. This scenario exactly matches what a CASB is designed to do. The other answers were made up; none of these is an actual cloud security device or tool (at least as of the writing of this book!).

93. B. TCP's use of a handshake process to establish communications makes it a connection-oriented protocol. TCP does not monitor for dropped connections, nor does the fact that it works via network connections make it connection-oriented.

94. A. Gamification uses common components from games like points, scores, and competition to engage participants in a security awareness program. None of the other answers uses these together unless they use a gamification component.

95. C. The two most important elements of a qualitative risk assessment are determining the probability and impact of each risk upon the organization. Likelihood is another word for probability. Cost should be taken into account but is only one element of impact, which also includes reputational damage, operational disruption, and other ill effects.

96. B. When a message reaches the Data Link layer, it is called a frame. Data streams exist at the Application, Presentation, and Session layers, whereas segments and datagrams exist at the Transport layer (for TCP and UDP, respectively).

97. A. If the ISC2 peer review board finds that a certified individual has violated the ISC2 Code of Ethics, the board may revoke their certification. The board is not able to terminate an individual's employment or assess financial penalties.

98. D. SDLC approaches include steps to provide operational training for support staff as well as end-user training. The SDLC may use one of many development models, including the waterfall and spiral models. The SDLC does not mandate the use of an iterative or sequential approach; it allows for either approach.

99. A. The Bell–LaPadula model includes the Simple Security Property, which prevents an individual from reading information that is classified at a level higher than the individual's security clearance.

100. A. Identity proofing is the process of validating that the entity or individual claiming an identity is the actual person or organization that they claim to be. This commonly relies on additional information like documents or knowledge that others would not have. Registration is the process of creating an account. FIM is federated identity management, and SSO allows a single sign-on to be used across multiple systems or services.

101. D. The files on the drive are at their most secure when the system is off and the drive is encrypted and not in a readable state. BitLocker decrypts files as needed when in use, meaning that any time after the system is booted files may be accessed, particularly if the user is logged in and access to the system can be gained or if malware is running.

102. C. An IPsec VPN will allow Andrea to keep her networks running as layer 2 flattened networks when necessary while providing the security for her traffic that she wants. TLS operates at a higher network layer, although traffic could be tunneled through it. BGP is a routing protocol, and AES is an encryption algorithm.

103. A. Cellular networks have the same issues that any public network does. Encryption requirements should match those that the organization selects for other public networks like hotels, conference Wi-Fi, and similar scenarios. Encrypting all data is difficult and adds overhead, so it should not be the default answer unless the company specifically requires it. WAP is a dated wireless application protocol and is not in broad use; requiring it would be difficult. WAP does provide TLS, which would help when in use.

104. D. Fred's best option is to use an encrypted, trusted VPN service to tunnel all of his data usage. Trusted Wi-Fi networks are unlikely to exist at a hacker conference, normal usage is dangerous due to the proliferation of technology that allows fake towers to be set up, and discontinuing all usage won't support Fred's business needs.

105. B. Remote wipe tools are a useful solution, but they work only if the phone can access either a cellular or Wi-Fi network. Remote wipe solutions are designed to wipe data from the phone regardless of whether it is in use or has a passcode. Providers unlock phones for use on other cellular networks rather than for wiping or other feature support.

106. C. The goal of business continuity planning exercises is to reduce the amount of time required to restore operations. This is done by minimizing the recovery time objective (RTO).

107. C. The COBIT, or Control Objectives for Information and related Technologies, framework describes common requirements that organizations should have in place for their information systems. It is the only audit or compliance framework on the list. ITSM is the acronym for Information Technology Service Management; CIS is the Center for Information Security, which provides guidelines for system security that can be used to assess systems but is not itself an audit framework; and ATT&CK is a framework for describing threats and attack methodologies.

108. B. The disaster recovery test types, listed in order of their potential impact on the business from the least impactful to the most impactful, are as follows:

1. Checklist review

2. Tabletop exercise

3. Parallel test

4. Full interruption test

Checklist reviews are the least impactful type of exercise because they do not even require a meeting. Each team member reviews the checklist on their own. Tabletop exercises are slightly more impactful because they require bringing together the DR team in the same room. Parallel tests require the activation of alternate processing sites and require significant resources. Full interruption tests are the most impactful type of exercise because they involve shifting operations to the alternate site and could disrupt production activity.

109. C. Redundancy is part of many availability designs. Dual power supplies allow multiple levels of availability support; they allow you to connect servers to distinct power infrastructures and also provide the ability to run if a single power supply dies. Some servers are even set up to use more than two power supplies. Another approach to this type of availability is to use more systems, rather than more expensive systems with greater support for availability.

110. C. The CISSP CBK uses a six-stage process: Detection, Response, Mitigation, Reporting, Recovery, and Remediation. This diagram is missing Recovery. Other standards differ, using different terms or slightly different processes.

111. B. This is an example of peering. Peering can be either public peering, a connection through an Internet Exchange Point via a network connection, or private peering done directly with another entity in a colocation facility. Ingress is traffic coming into a network, egress is traffic that is leaving a network, and east/west refers to network traffic in the same zone or layer of a network.

112. A. A service level agreement, or SLA, contains details about how the service will be provided, what level of outages or downtime is acceptable, and what remedies may exist in the case of outages or other issues. Megan should ensure that the SLA contains both appropriate performance guarantees and penalties that will be of sufficient magnitude to compensate her company for issues while motivating the service provider to maintain a reliable service. An RPA is robotic process automation, an automation technology. An NDA is a nondisclosure agreement, a legal document used to help control the risk of information or data being exposed or shared. An MOU is a memorandum of understanding and is used when two organizations want to work together to document a shared vision or the goals they share.

113. C. Media storage facilities are frequently used when organizations want to securely store backups like tapes in a secure, temperature-controlled facility. Cloud services are not used for physical backup media; hot sites are used to restore operations, not to store backup media; and BaaS is backup as a service—another description for a cloud backup service.

114. A. During a full interruption test, the team takes down the primary site and confirms that the disaster recovery site is capable of handling regular operations. The full interruption test is the most thorough test but also the most disruptive. During a parallel test, the team actually activates the disaster recovery site for testing, but the primary site remains operational. The checklist review is the least disruptive type of disaster recovery test. During a checklist review, team members each review the contents of their disaster recovery checklists on their own and suggest any necessary changes. During a tabletop exercise, team members come together and walk through a scenario without making any changes to information systems.

115. D. Ed's best option is to install an IPv6 to IPv4 gateway that can translate traffic between the networks. A bridge would be appropriate for different types of networks, whereas a router would make sense if the networks were similar. A modern switch might be able to carry both types of traffic but wouldn't be much help translating between the two protocols.

116. D. Henry's biggest concern should be the long-term security and supportability of the IoT devices. As these devices are increasingly embedded in buildings and infrastructure, the support model and security model are important to understand. Both the lack of separate administrative access and the lack of strong encryption can be addressed by placing the IoT devices on a dedicated subnet or network that prevents other users from accessing the devices directly. This will help limit the risk without undue expense or complexity and is a common practice. Finally, lack of storage space can be a concern but is not the most important when looking at the risks IoT devices can create.

117. C. UDP, the User Datagram Protocol, is a connectionless, best-effort protocol that is often used when sending data quickly without strong requirements for reliability features like error correction and detection or flow control to make sense. TCP is connection-oriented and provides those and other reliability features. ICMP, the Internet Control Message Protocol, is used to check routes and paths as well as availability but is not used for significant data transfer in normal cases. SNMP is a network management monitoring protocol.

118. B. The EU General Data Protection Regulation does not require that organizations provide individuals with employee lists.

119. B. Tammy should choose a warm site. This type of facility meets her requirements for a good balance between cost and recovery time. It is less expensive than a hot site but facilitates faster recovery than a cold site. A red site is not a type of disaster recovery facility.

120. B. When data reaches the Transport layer, it is sent as segments (TCP) or datagrams (UDP). Above the Transport layer, data becomes a data stream, while below the Transport layer, they are converted to packets at the Network layer, frames at the Data Link layer, and bits at the Physical layer.

121. D. The Advanced Encryption Standard supports encryption with 128-bit keys, 192-bit keys, and 256-bit keys.

122. D. An application programming interface (API) allows developers to create a direct method for other users to interact with their systems through an abstraction that does not require knowledge of the implementation details. Access to object models, source code, and data dictionaries also indirectly facilitates interaction but does so in a manner that provides other developers with implementation details.

123. B. Ian's best bet is a SOC report, and a SOC 2 Type II report will assess security controls and their application over time, telling him if the organization is responsibly maintaining their security efforts. A SOC 1 report looks at financial controls, and a Type I report only looks at how controls are described, not their application over time. Ian is unlikely to be allowed to run a vulnerability scan against a major provider's infrastructure either internally or externally.

124. D. Pass-the-hash attacks (PtH) often rely on dumped local account databases (the SAM), capturing credentials from the network while they are in transit or from active memory. Pass-the-hash attacks are not typically conducted by downloading hashes from third-party sites.

125. The protocols match with the descriptions as follows:

1. TCP: C. Transports data over a network in a connection-oriented fashion

2. UDP: D. Transports data over a network in a connectionless fashion

3. DNS: B. Performs translations between FQDNs and IP addresses

4. ARP: A. Performs translations between MAC addresses and IP addresses

The Domain Name System (DNS) translates human-friendly fully qualified domain names (FQDNs) into IP addresses, making it possible to easily remember websites and hostnames. ARP is used to resolve IP addresses into MAC addresses. TCP and UDP are used to control the network traffic that travels between systems. TCP does so in a connection-oriented fashion using the three-way handshake, while UDP uses connectionless "best-effort" delivery.

Index

C

F

J

K

L

M

O

P

Q

Online Test Bank

Register to gain one year of FREE access after activation to the online interactive test bank to help you study for your CISSP Certified Information Systems Security Professional certification exam—included with your purchase of this book! All of the chapter questions and the practice tests in this book are included in the online test bank so you can practice in a timed and graded setting.

Register and Access the Online Test Bank

To register your book and get access to the online test bank, follow these steps:

1. Go to www.wiley.com/go/sybextestprep (this address is case sensitive)! You'll see the "How to Register Your Book for Online Access" instructions.
2. Click "Click here to register" and then select your book from the list.
3. Complete the required registration information, including answering the security verification to prove book ownership. You will be emailed a pin code.
4. Follow the directions in the email or go to www.wiley.com/go/sybextestprep.
5. Find your book on that page and click the "Register or Login" link with it. Then enter the pin code you received and click the "Activate PIN" button.
6. On the Create an Account or Login page, enter your username and password, and click Login or, if you don't have an account already, create a new account.
7. At this point, you should be in the test bank site with your new test bank listed at the top of the page. If you do not see it there, please refresh the page or log out and log back in.